World Politics and Tension Areas

WORLD POLITICS
AND
TENSION AREAS

Feliks Gross

NEW YORK UNIVERSITY PRESS · 1966

To Arnold J. Zurcher

IN APPRECIATION OF TWENTY YEARS

OF FRIENDSHIP AND ASSOCIATION

F. G.

INTRODUCTION

FOR MANY CENTURIES war was a predatory business; "honest" in a sense, since man conquered man in order to use him for his own ends without attempting to convince him that he was acting in the moral interest of the conquered, for his liberation, or for his religious salvation. Once the conqueror ruled by force and coercion, he compelled others to work for him or to pay tribute.

War resulted in related types of armed enterprise. Attack resulted in development of defense. Enslavement of hard-working farmers resulted in the willingness of prospective victims to pay for armed protection. In consequence of wars, a class structure grew with armed conquerors or protectors assuming the "natural" position of ruling elites.

With the growth of the great religions, rationalization of wars in the Western world ceased to be regularly predatory.

The first period of predatory, "naked," and defensive wars ended with the decline of the ancient world. Medieval times marked the beginning of the second period: of religious and dynastic wars which, by the eighteenth century, in turn moved into an era of national, interethnic wars. National wars became ideological wars. World War II and its aftermath belong to this period. Religion, nationality, or ideology was frequently—although not always—a rationalization; what Mosca once called "a political formula" of the real motivation of a war—conquest and exercise of power. The desire to exercise power was, and has remained, a common human urge controlled and restrained by the might of competitors, then by custom, and later by law, which was influenced in turn by searching into political philosophy and religion.

Economic objectives of war and expansion played as prominent a role as other economic determinants of aggression, such as the nature of the social-political system. But these were not the only motives, especially for those who were willing to do battle. The significance of the economic factor as a cause of war must not be underestimated; but it is not the only one. Defense of a "way of life"—of a "political culture" based on free, elective institutions has played a powerful role in current and ancient history. Ideologies and political objectives moved groups and individuals.

In our era of ideological wars, as in religious wars, partisans of political creeds are not neutral onlookers, but frequently soldiers and leaders of political armies. Ideological antagonism has resulted in new forms of conflicts.

However, the purpose of this book is not a study of causes or a general study of war, although I fully appreciate the significance and merit of such studies. The purpose of this study is far more limited.

The two major types of international tensions that interest us in this book are those associated with antagonism between ethnic groups and those associated with antagonism between ideological groups. Once ethnic tensions are incorporated into social-political movements, they become ideological, of course, and may develop into international tensions. Reduction of ethnic and race tension, however, is a different problem from political easement. The two types of tensions may merge, telescope into each other, but the nature of the two conflicts is still different. Although I do not deny the existence or possibility of other tensions, I have limited my discussion solely to those two major types: international race-ethnic tensions and ideological tensions. While domestic, internal tensions normally differ from international tensions, they are today often interrelated, and even interdependent.

In our time of nuclear stalemate, limited international conflict remains the dominant expression of antagonism between the world's superpowers and ideologies, the Western and Soviet blocs. Basic antagonisms between the two major power centers are carefully controlled. However, the emergence of a new antagonistic power center, Communist China on the one hand and an integrated Europe on the other, has contributed to a change. Opposition or antagonism is now expressed by overt action, and especially by "stage" strategy and tactics, although conflicts are limited "functionally" and geographically.

Tension areas, comprising limited geographical areas of intense antagonism and local wars, have become a part of the general pattern. But tension areas are neither a new social phenomenon nor an entirely new form of conflict. They also appeared in the past. However, the study of such limited tensions belongs to a more general study of social conflict. Thus, our subject matter is further limited. Narrowing the field of inquiry—although it is still very large—permits us to discover simpler, less complex, patterns of conflict as well as the ways used for the intensification or reduction of tensions. Further, this also allows us to focus our approach and develop theory of the process at a "medium range" level. Where theory meets empirical data, its frame of reference is tested against facts.

This brings us to the matter of method. At first I attempted to relate theory to empirical material, ideas to facts, generalizations to descriptive and comparative case histories. Some effort was also made to develop a theoretical frame of reference closely related to realities, even to pragmatic considerations; hence, the inclusion of a relatively large section of case histories. Nine case histories form special chapters and a number of cases are discussed in reduced form.

Differentiation has been made between interpolitical and intergroup tensions. The first concerns tension between governments and states; the second, between ethnic or race, economic, or ideological groups in different nation-states. Inter-political tensions are of special significance, since the state has the monopoly of political power. In consequence the state, and only the state, can wage a war. But today, international "interpolitical" conflict is not solely a matter of military action, of a violation of international convention, or of diplomatic negotiation and temporary "mending." Such tensions are also social, ethnic, ideological, and economic. Their comprehension involves an understanding of social-economic systems, history, psychological and personality problems, cultural patterns, ethnic and ideological values—in other words, an integrated approach. This involves an area bordering on many disciplines—sociology, anthropology, political science (international relations), social psychology, history, and economics. Each of these disciplines suggests a different aspect. The problem, the general method of in-quiry, and the frame of reference form the integrating device. However, the application of such a vast area of disciplines would require a staff of specialists. In consequence, the general approach must be narrowed to a sociological approach, with the contribution of other disciplines at best indicated and utilized.

The two major approaches are by "process" or "action." The latter is focussed on goals (ideologies), patterns of action (strategy and tactics), and group structure.

The histories chosen for discussion are not limited to "interpolitical" inter-national cases. Studies of interethnic and race relations which are "internal," not international, were also selected for discussion because they illustrate definite patterns, supply comparative material, and are—in a sociological sense—not so complex as certain international tensions. The comparative approach also offers a wide perspective, and permits generalizations within the area of empirical data, besides indicating techniques of control or reduction of tensions. Further-more, a discussion of both internal and international conflicts allows a wider classification of intergroup tension and the formation of a general theoretical approach. The study of "internal" race and ethnic relations also shows that even in a continuing tension situation, groups are not divided solely into "friends" and "enemies"; that the structure of proximity and distance of various groups is complex and differentiated, and therefore offers several choices for the reduction of such tension.

A comparative study of tension as a dynamic process suggests an antagonistic tendency as a continuum, which can be intensified, reduced, or channelled in various directions. Combined with the process approach, the comparative method permits differentiation of patterns as well as choices open to men in a variety of situations.

The case histories presented are intentionally "spread" in time and area, since the comparative approach favored the selection of studies from various periods, different parts of the globe, and distinctive natures and intensities. The beginnings of ethnic and religious tensions are buried in a distant, frequently unknown, past. In two tension histories—Kossovo and Cracow—we attempted to identify them at least five to seven centuries back. Historical material was used in these cases as a means of understanding contemporary social relations and intergroup patterns.

Thus the major scope of this book is a sociological and interdisciplinary study of certain types of tensions, antagonisms, and conflicts within limited geographical areas. Proceeding from ethnic, religious, and racial tensions to those which are ideological, international, and interpolitical, the inquiry progresses from the less to the more complex, since none of them is simple. Thus we find a variety of intergroup and interpolitical patterns and tensions which may require differing techniques of reduction. Most of this volume is devoted to the discussion of patterns of relations between groups and between states; and ways which men have used to intensify or reduce such patterns or tensions. The scope of this book is by no means limited to current affairs, although some case histories cover recent events. An attempt has been made to develop a general theory of limited (geographically and sociologically) tensions on a workable, pragmatic level.

Our discussion is "problem-oriented." Part V is primarily "applied" (Chapter 17) and "normative" (Chapter 18). It deals with selected methods of reduction and the general orientation toward cultural and political pluralism. The Appendices contain related papers. Here are concepts and theories used but not elaborated in the main text. For a further discussion of these topics, the reader is referred to the Appendices of this volume. Here also he will find a case history of the Somali-Ethiopian tensions, written by Mr. Ted Gurr. I wish to express my thanks for this contribution, first written in draft form for the New York University Tension Areas seminar, which exemplifies so well and interestingly a specific type of African tension area.

The reader may find certain repetitions. They are intentional. First of all, concepts and approaches were developed gradually, and case histories required further adjustment of hypotheses and concepts. The application of certain concepts—for instance, reductionism—depends on levels of abstractions and of generalizations. A variety of levels requires reinterpretation or even revision of concepts. Hence, repetition was necessary to facilitate development or application of concepts. It was also needed for clarity of discussion as well as for the sake of those who may read only selected sections.

Case histories and examples also required repetitions. It seemed essential in a comparative and representative approach to limit the number of examples to avoid the type of comparative approach peculiar to the latter part of the nineteenth century, when short (one-sentence-long) examples were supplied by anthropologists, sociologists, or scholars of comparative jurisprudence. When taken out of their general, sociological context these examples are subject to many interpretations and misunderstandings. To limit the study to a single extensive case would be tantamount to the elimination of the comparative approach, essential in this work because of the variety of patterns discernible. The answer, while not entirely satisfactory, was found in a limitation of the number of cases, in a curtailment of their size, and even in repetition, so that the reader would not be overburdened.

Since an attempt has been made to classify and study social relations, the work includes such patterns as separation and self-segregation and their function or effects. This does not mean that the author favors such patterns or policies. They do represent, however, a certain pattern, and require a detached description and discussion. It is my belief that the best method of easing race tensions is the meeting, cooperation, and working together of individuals and groups of different racial groups for definite goals; a process of getting to know one another. In such a process, interpersonal, direct friendly ties are established, essential in the easing of tensions. This is the way of the future and of human progress. Cultural (ethnic), religious, and political differences offer alternative approaches. One of them is pluralism, a concept which recognizes the right to be different and suggests conditions of mutual respect and cooperation in essentials.

It might be wise to stress here that a reduction of tensions is merely one of the topics of this volume, and supplies only a general orientation. The aim of the work is to relate the story of how men controlled and reduced, or intensified, stalemated tensions and conflicts, not how wars and conflicts were won. We do not supply a single answer or a general solution, for there are areas for which we have no such answers or solutions at this time. Self-determination, combined with integration in some broader collectivity of nations, is a legitimate and just answer in many cases. Not all, however, can be answered that way.

We now know that self-determination is not enough. Nations are not independent; they are interdependent. Man's existence depends on modern medicine, technology, mutual aid, and even such a seemingly simple matter as pure water. Self-determination may not provide better sanitation, food, schools, public service, and employment. The very concept of self-determination of nations today requires reinterpretation, broadening, of a nineteenth-century idea. It calls for inclusion of social and economic answers as well as political rights for all, not only for a privileged racial, ethnic, or political minority. The political process of change may also require several gradual stages.

The problem we face is an ancient one: not the elimination of differences and opposition from international relations, but of violence. Differences and opposition frequently father creative social change. Plans for the elimination of violence have been made for many centuries, as have the promises of a millennium. The history of two world wars, however, taught us again about the extreme potentialities of man: the terrifying potentiality for evil, destruction, and extermination (or whatever more "neutral" terms the scientist may prefer), and also the opposite potentiality for self-denial, sacrifice, and mutual aid. Those who have travelled and conversed with men of various races, creeds, and cultures; with those who work hard and earn little or who gain their livelihood in simple economic pursuits in distant parts of the globe have found a common human discourse, understandable to all, despite cultural differences. Common needs, sorrows, or joys are human, understandable to all races and cultures. There, at the very roots of mankind, one discovers also the roots of universalism and pluralism. And in this lies the hope of the world.

My study of tensions continued at the graduate seminar in international relations and area studies in the Area Studies Program of the Department of Government and International Relations at New York University. The generous assistance of the Public Affairs Research Fund of New York University, under a Ford Foundation Grant, made it possible for me to continue my work. Thanks to a generous grant from the Alfred P. Sloan Foundation, awarded in 1964, I was able to concentrate on the manuscript and on further study of limited conflicts during the summer months, and to end my research in time to prepare the manuscript for press. A reduction of my teaching load at Brooklyn College of the City of New York by Dean Walter H. Mais, with additional help for typing, permitted me also to finish some urgent work, such as the preparation of papers and reviews from previous commitments, which delayed work on this book.

For friendly support of my project on tension areas and foreign policy forecasting, I wish to express my gratitude to Professor Arnold J. Zurcher, a prominent scholar in the field of international cooperation, and a friend and colleague for twenty years, who pioneered in area studies and founded the area project at New York University in 1945; and to Professor Alfred de Grazia, with his wide interest and skills in the application of behavioralist approach to political processes and institutions, who deserve thanks for his continuous interest and support. Mr. Ivo Vukcevich, who travelled in Kossovo after his work in my seminar, and Mr. Luan Gashi, who knows and has explored this area for many years besides attending seminars for several terms, were helpful in later research, supplying valuable ethnographic information on Kossovo and on ethnic relations in this area. Professor M. Bernadete of Brooklyn College was generous with his time, giving me an opportunity to discuss with him his native Chanak. Dr. Izak Langnas, not for the first time, assisted me in checking information and data. Mrs. Cynthia Vukcevich carried very ably the technical burden of this project for a long time. Equally able and dedicated in their work were Miss

Claire Stachelak, Mrs. Margaret Dunn Donchi and, for a short period, Miss Carole Moy. The project could not supply a stipend which would reward their work in full. All of them at various times during almost four years worked with dedication. I also want to express my appreciation to those of my colleagues who were generous enough with their time to read parts of the manuscript.

I hope that this work is a beginning, which will be followed by more extensive and rigorous research. My wife and daughter have shown much patience, friendship, and interest in my work during three years when research and writing preempted most of my evenings and weekends, and they deserve my very special thanks.

Certain sections of this book have appeared in a condensed version in journals, or were presented at meetings. A paper on tension area analysis presented at the meeting of the American Sociological Association in Washington in 1962 was later published in Italian in two separate sections in *Il Politico,* a journal of the University of Pavia (1962, Vol. XXVII, No. 4, and 1963, Vol. XXVIII, No. 1). Also, fragments appeared in the *United Asia* anniversary issue (Vol. XV, January, 1963), and the general frame of reference on structure of international relations was published, still in an initial, preliminary presentation, in the *International Social Science Journal* of UNESCO (Vol. XII, No. 2, 1960). The preliminary discussion on the sociology of international cooperation appeared in *Calcutta Review* (Vol. 127, No. 2, May, 1953). An earlier form of Chapter 18, "The Quest of Universal Values," appeared in Italian in *Quaderni di Sociologia* (No. 36, Spring, 1960), and also in the *Journal of Social Research* (India, Vol. I, No. 1, July, 1960). In this work, the text has been revised and above all, extended. The general frame of reference, however, remains. Appendix I "Command and Consensus Structures," in an abridged form, was presented at the Eastern Sociological Meeting in Philadelphia, Spring, 1960. I would like to thank the editors of *Human Relations* for permission to reprint my article, "Human Relations in Central and Western Europe."

Feliks Gross

New York
December 20, 1965

CONTENTS

CONTENTS

LIST OF ILLUSTRATIONS

LIST OF ILLUSTRATIONS

World Politics and Tension Areas

i. The Sociological Pattern
of International Relations

1.

LIMITED TENSIONS

The stalemate

The tendency toward the reduction of power centers, which has been evident in Europe since medieval times, culminated in the mid-twentieth century in a bipolar system of nuclear powers. The power to make the decision for all-out nuclear war or peace has been confined, until recently, to two systems: the Soviet Union and the Atlantic powers. In the former, the centralized form of government during the Stalin era permitted rapid decisions to be made. The Atlantic bloc relied on consultation and consensus, despite the dominant American position in the development and control of nuclear weapons.

As a result of this polarization, the power to make relevant decisions on the maintenance of world peace or the increase of global tensions was confined to these two systems. Recent economic and political developments indicate, however, that a new alternative is possible; that the tendency toward a reduction of power centers is being reversed, and that we are moving toward a "polycentric" scheme of four or five major systems: American, West European, Soviet, Chinese, and neutral. Still, from a pragmatic viewpoint, the problem of what may be termed "nuclear peace" and prevention of World War III can, for the present, be limited to the two major systems. This equilibrium, as other equilibria in international relations at one time, may be temporary, or (let us hope) a step, a stage toward a more constructive and safer answer than the present one.

The development of nuclear weapons and missiles has increased both the chances of lasting peace and the threat of total biological destruction. Since a full-scale world war may lead to a nuclear war and, consequently, to the biological destruction of the initiating and defending parties, it has become unthinkable, or at least highly risky, for the nuclear powers to use such weapons to force a decision.

The distribution of nuclear weapons between the two opposing power centers has reached, for all practical purposes, a point of balance. Both groups have sufficient nuclear explosives and carriers to destroy their opponent. It would seem that, beyond a certain point, an increase in the quantity of carriers and nuclear bombs ceases to increase power or superiority. This may be called a point of nuclear stalemate, since the use of decisive nuclear weapons has been arrested. A qualitative, not a quantitative change—the invention of new types of nuclear weapons—may upset this balance. Another alternative is the proliferation of nuclear powers. Once the new members of the nuclear club decide to act independently, the situation will change, and the danger of the use of such weapons will increase.

Although the present dual system is moving toward a "polycentric" grouping, it can still remain "balanced." While new powers, particularly France, are developing their own nuclear deterrent, a restraint policy is still possible in the West, where a prudent and cautious policy has been followed.

Nuclear weapons in the hands of Communist China represent a different problem. Paradoxically, the association of China and the Soviet Union might have offered an alternative, although an unstable one, to the West. Now, with the two major Communist powers in disagreement, a new bloc, comprising the Soviet Union, India, Western Europe, Great Britain, Japan, the United States, and smaller countries, may have to be formed to make a combination powerful enough to stalemate the Chinese government. Present events suggest the direction of this powerful balance. Plans for world conquest have unfortunately been stated by Chinese communist leaders. Permanent war has been rationalized by them as permanent revolution. Their designs toward continental control are not so difficult to discover. This may change the development of conflict tendencies, increase dangers, escalate global tensions. In spite of all this, however, several alternatives are open; other developments and combinations are possible. They depend largely on changes of political structure and orientations within the countries, as well as the economic problems they may face. However, internal, ideological change within the great powers, especially the Soviet Union and Communist China, are of primary significance; so, likewise, are changes in party and government leadership. Changes in international politics depend largely on directions the internal transformation will take.

The world today is dynamic. To search in what direction the trends move into the future means to evaluate alternatives that are open, since the fate of man as a participant of man-made social processes is not predetermined. A dangerous trend can be channelled, even reversed by those who use reason and humanity instead of emotion and hostility.

As matters now stand, a "zero point" has been reached, and a nuclear stalemate represents a de facto solution; one that is not the best, but still better than total destruction.[1]

New forms of conflict

The Communist camp is not monolithic. Ideological differences have already appeared and will continue. Heresies do not disappear easily, and even if they do fade for a time, they reappear with new vigor under a different name. Western Europe also shows a tendency toward a more independent policy. This differentiation of views offers greater elasticity in international politics and may increase chances of a global détente. Nevertheless, the ideological division into two powerful blocs continues, with a tendency toward an emergence of four, even five, major systems; toward polycentrism.

As a consequence of this impasse, new forms of antagonism and conflict have emerged. These forms existed before, but in the mid-twentieth century they gained in significance and intensity. We may call them "limited" tensions, since as stages of strategy they are controlled and limited *functionally* or *territorially*.

FUNCTIONALLY LIMITED TENSIONS are those contained within certain levels of action. Very limited use is made of the resources which a government has at its disposal. As examples we may list economic tensions, psychological warfare, or the "cold war." Psychological warfare embraces a variety of actions and techniques. Its use varies substantially among states and governments; e. g., that of the British, Soviet, Italian, and German governments during World War II.

The diffusion of selected, but true, information, presented with humor and satire to a territory where the free flow of information is prohibited, may be an effective device. So far, the goal of psychological warfare has been to change attitudes, to reinforce values and ideologies, or to produce action or submission. Mass media are used to influence collective motivation by an appeal to ethnic, religious, or class values; by an intensification of emotion or an appeal to reason and common sense. Frequently, the strategy of psychological warfare has been to produce an intensification of fear, anxieties, and hostilities. In its intensive form it represents a general diffusion of stress and tension. It is a new form of conflict.

So far, mass media in international relations have been utilized chiefly for antagonism or conflict. Nevertheless, psychological strategy for the reduction of tensions is worthy of careful consideration. In theory, its action may be limited to the intensification of tensions on a few levels. However, antagonism or intense tension may develop on economic, psychological, or diplomatic levels.

The United States-Cuban tension during 1962–63 may serve as an example. This tension is territorially limited to Cuba, although its effect spread over Central and South America. It is also limited in a functional sense. The United States government applies pressure on both the economic and diplomatic levels. It also makes a psychological appeal to the Cuban forces opposing Castro's dictatorship. Action toward Cuba was perceived as a part of a policy of stalemating a worldwide expansion.

In this sense the American-Cuban tension is a limited one, both territorially and functionally. Such tension reflects a much broader development—a new strategy and a new form of conflict. The pattern of this strategy has been repeated many times since the end of World War II, and today it may be identified as revolutionary. Such warfare is not an entirely new pattern, but in combination with other elements, the quasi-revolutionary strategy of expansion has become a characteristic international development in our century.

A revolutionary situation in a limited area is usually exploited by an expansionist power, or by the government that represents such a power. An allied political party is formed in the area, and the expansionist government provides it or an associated organization with financial and military support. Meanwhile, the interested government exercises pressure on a diplomatic level and uses its military component as an added element of force. When the revolutionary party assumes power, it becomes closely associated with the expansionist government, and its territory becomes dependent on the latter. The expansionist power then moves by a buildup of *internal revolutionary fronts* and penetration into the tension area. Once a revolutionary party takes over, one stage in the strategy of expansion is accomplished. In that way the government, or power, moves from one tension area to another, expanding its influence as well as its territory.

The pattern of the new strategy comprises a combination of an internal and an external front. The *external front* represents the "formal" military establishment as well as other resources controlled by the supporting government. In that way the combination of an "internal" revolutionary advance with an "external" military support displaces a purely military conflict. The beginnings of such strategy can be traced to the French Revolution, and perhaps even to the religious wars of the Middle Ages. Today, this method is applied as much by the Communist Chinese government as by Egypt's Nasser in the Arab peninsula.

The development and threat of so-called strategic weapons may also lead to the development of new forms of tensions and conflicts and of international controls unknown today in an attempt to avoid major disasters.

Territorially limited tensions appear in extreme form as limited territorial wars. Such conflicts are confined to geographical points which we may call "tension areas." The day-to-day attempts to maintain peace are centered on the stalemating, limiting, or lessening of tensions or conflicts in these areas. *The purpose of this book is to discuss territorially limited tensions—the tension areas.*

At all times social or international unrest has been a part of the condition of life somewhere on this planet. In our time, however, at least some tension areas are symptoms of two major processes: of stages of an ideological war of expansion and a rising process of social discontent, and of a social revolution which appears in scattered points of the globe. Not all tensions are of this nature, and they can also be initiated by armed, well-organized minorities in areas of passive or indifferent population. The social and ideological nature of the appeal, however, requires a long-range view and a long-range strategy. Perhaps more: it involves history and social philosophy.

An aggressor whose goals are frustrated and his action stalemated may substitute his goals, and open a new tension in a different area where he has better chances of success, or where defense is more difficult.

Easing and stalemating of local tensions may not, and usually does not, resolve fundamental and worldwide antagonisms. It may, however, influence a long-range strategy of the aggressor. The strength and determination of the opponent increases greatly the risks of an easy conquest and discourages attack. Early warning signals may consolidate alliances and unions of nations or their governments, which are threatened by the further expansion and infiltration of the aggressive government and parties they control. Time is an important (though uncertain) element of a long-range strategy. It works both ways; trends move in various directions. The time element may work, however, for internal changes within the aggressing states. To repeat, such changes will in turn influence foreign policy, and may weaken, even reverse dangerous trends. The futility of attacks, and expenditures involved, may tire out the aggressor. This did happen in Korea. Time may work also for the aggressor, giving him time to expand his army and war economy. Stalemating combined with strength and firmness is, however, a policy of moderation and hope. Thus a grand strategy of world conquest calls for a long-range strategy of preservation of peace as well as strategy of defense. Such an answer asks for long-range goals and a tentative nondogmatic vision of an organized and peaceful mankind. A vision has its appeal. It integrates groups and nations, points to vital common interests, gives a sense of security and purpose, and supplies the necessary sense of direction.

However, should the strategy of world expansion change, social processes of discontent and unrest may still continue. A general policy-making involves here again a long-range view, understanding of forces at work and directions they may move. Further action involves broad social philosophy, or at least norms and pragmatic, workable approaches and policies in order to transform intentions into reality. Emancipation of nations and national independence is one of the answers. We have learned since that national independence per se, unless rooted in social-economic change and advance, in political institutions based on civil rights and at least a certain amount of freedom, may become only an interlude to new oppressive forms of government.

In the past wild prophecies, auguries of holocausts or of the end of the end of the world, and today, confused ideologies, expressions of subconscious fears and anxieties may foment movements and processes which cannot be arrested by rational appeal. History teaches, however, that a calm view and a vision of a rational and humane society will find support of some peoples. It will contribute a consolidation of forces and permit rational actions by those nations in which reason and humane thinking prevails. Part of mankind—until now—has usually remained sane.

In times when plans for world conquest are proclaimed in the name of a millennium, and messianic ideologies can be manipulated into new crusades called by different names, we must learn to deal patiently, calmly, but firmly with problems which are now a part of our daily life. Weakness, submission, and surrender will encourage aggression. It is not the differences, even the contradictions, which are dangerous but the way contradictions are resolved. Differences and contradictions can be and have been vehicles of change and progress. Without them society may become stagnant. Solving differences by mutual destruction is, however, disastrous.

Primary and secondary tension areas

Not all limited tensions or conflicts are the result of tensions in the bipolar nuclear system. Many differ both in their nature and in their significance in world politics. Tension areas can be divided roughly into two categories: 1] Primary or dependent tension areas and 2] secondary or independent tension areas.

At this point we may indicate only that the primary tension areas are those which depend on the actions of the great powers and which may endanger the peace of large geographical regions—in other words, what we call today world peace. Secondary tension areas are local in nature and depend on minor powers. As long as they remain secondary, the great powers are not yet involved, and the conflict situation develops between the governments controlling the smaller states. Secondary tensions can also be tensions between the great powers that are local in area or nature and may not involve a general conflagration or a general conflict.

2.

CLASSIFICATION OF INTERNATIONAL RELATIONS

Reduction and context

How can international tensions be defined? As in other social processes, international cooperation, tensions, or conflicts form part of a more complex and general social interaction and cannot be separated from their general context as theoretical abstractions. True, a methodological approach to the study of conflict implies a limitation of inquiry or reduction of variables. Nonetheless, the complexity of those processes should not be forgotten, and the interpretation and understanding of international conflicts may require a consideration of the problems *in situ*.

Foreign policy is a key element of the general public attitude of a government. Domestic policies are interrelated with foreign policy. Changes in foreign policy usually require adjustment in domestic policy; similarly, changes of domestic policies affect the conduct of foreign affairs. However, we may separate the two for purposes of method or analysis. The public policy of a government depends in turn on: (1) social-economic conditions, social structure, and economic interests; (2) political systems and institutions; and (3) goals and ideology. These categories are not separate blocs; they are related.

Thus the entire area of international relations forms a wide spectrum of social and political relationships. It is a kind of continuum, with types of relations that can be identified but not sharply separated. They operate on the same continuum and represent various forms of transition. The continuum, in turn, represents a dynamic process of interacting governments and nations. This interaction can be intensified or weakened. When it is intensified, the nature of the relationships changes; the same occurs when the actions grow weaker.

A discussion of general international relations is a necessary preliminary to the identification of the nature of the international tensions which form a part of this continuum.

Process and action approach

We may study international relations as a social process or as separate patterns of action. Both approaches are complementary, not contradictory. Each, however, represents a different vantage point and gives a different "perspective." We may say that they are the result of observation from two different points. The image of international relations that we obtain from one point has a different "perspective" from the picture which we get when our point of observation shifts.

In a social process approach, two or more interacting parties are observed simultaneously. A social process results from the activities of many parties, including conflicting groups. The result of mutual actions is a social process, and the latent and actual mutual influences and actions are called relations. (In this sense, war is a result of the interaction of two or more governments or states.) What we observe in a process approach are the mutual activities of two or more parties (interactions) and their consequences.

In an action approach, our observation is limited to one party and to the effects of its activities on its opposite. For instance, a study of the strategy and tactics of a political party or of a military operation is an action study. Similarly, a study of the strategy and tactics of the Communist Chinese government in its foreign policy is an action study.

In the first case (process approach), we are so located, at least theoretically, that we can observe two or more actors. This is our vantage point. As in a soccer game, we see two parties interacting simultaneously and, provided we have a good seat, we are equidistant from both. In the second (action approach), we are located close to only one actor and we observe him and his actions. If they are rational, his actions are divided into tactical and strategic movements. The tactical movements represent single actions; the strategic, the general direction.

In an analytical study of international relations, both process and action approaches have their applications. For example, in foreign policy forecasts, the action approach may be fruitful. Single actions of a government or of a ruling group are usually parts of a general pattern. We may call such a pattern strategic. This pattern gives us a sense of the general direction in which a given party is moving. It also suggests the direction in which a government, which we may call an actor, may move in the future. The process approach, however, permits us to identify the different types of relationship that emerge from the interaction of two or more parties. The relevance of those differences will be discussed later.

Reductionism is the normal technique of the social sciences in a study of these matters, since it is difficult to discuss the large number of variables that interact simultaneously in most social processes. As a methodological device, therefore, we usually try to reduce our discussion to the major variables involved in a given situation. Other variables are also present, but their presence, and action, are not disregarded or negated in a "reductive" approach.

The very nature of social phenomena in a global, macro-sociological approach imposes the necessity of a theoretical reduction of variables, since there are so many factors involved that no methodological approach would be feasible without such a reduction; hence, a high contingency for error. At present we shall use the process approach in our general classification of international relations and in our identification of international tensions and conflicts.[1]

Our discussion at this point will be limited to interpolitical relations. (Other types will be discussed later.) These are basically relations between governments or states. The government is both decision maker and actor in a given situation, since it controls the state. The state has a monopoly of physical power, and through it the government can mobilize its force and administer the power that wages war. The state also can secure international peace. Therefore, interpolitical relations are, in practice, relations between states. This does not mean that all or most citizens necessarily support the policy of every government in power. The mechanics of decision is more complex.

Citizens may have different views about a given political situation and would perhaps make different decisions than the government that is in power, especially if it is a dictatorship. These differences between the people and the state acting as a coercive association of its citizens have to be kept in mind. I shall therefore use the term "interpolitical relations" to denote relations between the states with the understanding that, in reality, governments make decisions in a variety of ways (either democratically or dictatorially), and that there is a distinction between the government and its citizens or subjects.

Categories

For the average individual the basic international relations are usually reduced to three major categories: cooperation, conflict, and neutrality. We usually note these possibilities in newspaper columns and in conversation, but the sequence should really be: cooperation, neutrality, and conflict. A more detailed discussion of the subject will soon reveal that in each category there is a great deal of variation and we have really to deal with a continuum.

Within the broad category of neutrality we may note many different relationships. For example, neutrality indicates an absence of military-political commitment of a state or government, with a consequent reduction of international commitments to a minimum. But in other fields, such as international trade, cultural exchanges, and international assistance (in times of disasters), there may be substantial cooperation. Thus, within neutrality, various patterns of cooperation are possible.

The limited cooperation which falls under the general category of neutrality may have a variety of intensities. At the end of neutrality is the zero point—one of no relations whatsoever. This is perhaps a theoretical situation.

Under some conditions, the neutrality of the foreign policy between two countries, like certain conflict situations, may more or less approach the zero point, although it may never reach it. A country may reduce its relations in one way or another and limit them to such a point that there is a relative absence of active relationships.

There is a need for defining more general types in our classification of international relations and for separating them into specific categories. For our discussion, international relations will be divided into those which lead to association, neutrality, and dissociation. The models below graphically present the various categories.

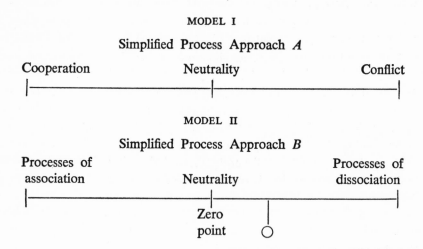

MODEL I

Simplified Process Approach *A*

| Cooperation | Neutrality | Conflict |

MODEL II

Simplified Process Approach *B*

| Processes of association | Neutrality | Processes of dissociation |

Zero
point

The first model represents the two polar relationships of cooperation and conflict, with neutrality in the middle. In the second, we see the processes of dissociation, association, and neutrality and, somewhere below, the zero point.[2] This point is closer to the processes of dissociation, since it represents an absence of any international relations. Moving one step further, we see that the processes of association and dissociation correlate with certain tendencies.

Association corresponds to cooperation. This means that governments or states have a tendency to work or act together, usually because they have common goals or interests. Dissociation, in turn, represents an antagonistic tendency in which states act or work against each other, moving from opposition to antagonistic action and possibly open conflict. The governments work or act against each other because their goals are contradictory or incompatible, and because their interests are conflicting.

Further discussion of these processes and tendencies, as well as further classification, requires substantial modification of Models I and II (see Model III). The differences between models are not contradictory. They represent stages in development. As we shall see, development of the model of a continuum will lead us to the displacement of "neutrality" by cooperation, as well as to the development of parallels (a combination of two lines of continuum, since difference, opposition, even antagonism, appear in cooperative processes; Model III).

What is the difference between a process and a tendency? A process denotes an actual developing interaction between governments, states, or groups; mutually interdependent actions which can be observed as fact. A tendency denotes a general sense of direction and indicates where a policy is moving. We may call it a consistent pattern of policy.

"Social process" is a dynamic concept of continuous change, a "developing" in a certain direction. For example, the Japanese policy in World War II had a consistent pattern of expansion in Southeast Asia—that was the general policy direction of the Japanese government. In such a sense one could speak about the general tendency of its "coprosperity" policy toward China or the Dutch possessions in Southeast Asia. But this tendency appeared in a variety of forms, including aggression in China and Indonesia. Here actual conflict situations reflected the consistent pattern in which the policy was developing.

International cooperation

The discussion of the various types of processes on our continuum should begin with an analysis of the nature of international cooperation. What are the necessary conditions for permanent international cooperation?

In their well-known letter of June 14, 1963, the theoreticians of the Chinese Communist Party argued that lasting international cooperation, as well as peace, is impossible between different political and social systems. When countries live under what they call "socialist" rule (in actuality, the Communist system), permanent peace will be achieved and the danger of future wars eliminated, since war is inherent in the capitalistic system (which breeds imperialism). The determining factors are social and economic. Only a uniform social and economic system—the Communist one—may, in their view, secure peace. The letter is based largely on Mao's theory of contradictions and on his essay *On Theory and Practice*. One has the impression that he authored the letter.

It seems, however, that though this letter may sound logical, it scarcely agrees with reality. First of all, in the United States—allegedly an example of the capitalistic system—the economy is highly mixed. But, whatever the nature of that economy, the fact remains that peace has been maintained in an exemplary manner among the United States, Canada, and Mexico. On the other hand, a true cold war was waged by Stalin against Tito, and today Communist China continues its hostile policy toward Yugoslavia.

Chinese Communists offer a simple answer—Tito's Yugoslavia is not a true "socialist state" according to their theory. But in such a case, war could be waged against any state, any government, which represents a deviation from the orthodox lines of the Chinese Communist Party, and the iron law of heresy indicates that major ideologies produce dissenters.

This is not the first time in history that ideologists have suggested that world peace can be achieved only through ideological uniformity. The devastating and bloody religious wars of history were also experiments in forced uniformity. International cooperation and the elimination of violence do not require the subjection of all mankind to one religious or political creed, or to a single social-economic system. Nor does the maintenance of peace require intensive love and brotherhood. However, there is more to the solution than a simple uniformity of ideas or systems. An attempt in this direction was made by both Christian and Moslem religious leaders and warriors, and was never achieved even after centuries of trying.

A tendency toward the process we called association appears only under certain sociological conditions. First, there must be a common interest or a common goal between the states. Usually, a common interest is reflected in common goals.

The term "interest" cannot be limited to economic interests and motivations. The economic factor is of primary significance in international relations, but it is not the only one. The ideological factor, reflected in goals and values, is also powerful. The emphasis may vary in different historical periods.

The ideological factor is closely related to the maintenance or expansion of political power. While it may be argued that ideology reflects only economic interests, this is true only in certain situations. Under other conditions the ideological and political factors may play dominant roles. The struggle between Stalin and Tito was not primarily economic, although there were economic reasons for their disagreement. Ideological and political issues of power were the primary reasons. The interdependence of those factors can be accepted as a general proposition.

We shall not enter here into the unending discussion of whether value goals are solely a reflection of economic interests or if they can exist as "independent variables." We need only indicate that both goals and interests—the "economic base" and "ideological superstructure"—form important elements in international cooperation. They can be many, and of different significances.

In addition to a common interest, the cooperating parties must also set minimum standards and values as a basis for rules of cooperation. Goals are values which may dominate an action, but there are other values, such as standards of behavior, that are essential in any form of cooperation. Even competitive action, which does not lead to the destruction of the adversary, requires certain commonly accepted rules. We can readily observe this in sports. A set of common rules must be obeyed by both the defeated and the victorious. Negotiation requires a common minimum of standards, an agreement on the "rules of the game," such as respect for an envoy, an ambassador, or the man who comes to negotiate an armistice. But these are not the only requirements. Cooperation even on a small issue implies a certain fairness on both sides and certain mutual services based on common standards which are either accepted or merely imposed by force. A minimum set of rules or norms must be observed in any cooperative effort, even in times of war. This premise was perhaps the great contribution of Grotius's theory.

In addition to common goals and interests and a minimum of accepted values or standards of behavior, skills are also needed for successful cooperation. Cooperation occurs so frequently in human society that it may seem absurd to argue that effective cooperation requires expert knowledge and skills. The fact remains, however, that even in a small village community, effective cooperation requires skills and leadership to coordinate efforts toward common goals.

Of course, international negotiation and international cooperation occur at different levels, but here too, skills are relevant in organizing cooperation. Attitudes have to be created; tensions must be carefully avoided; antagonisms must be put aside; an agenda for negotiations must be carefully and thoughtfully prepared—to mention only a few of the skills required in a cooperative effort.

A successful international organization needs skilled and able architects with a good background in law. The founders of such an organization should try to anticipate future differences, avoid legal formulations which would intensify such differences, and introduce propositions or devices which would permit the weathering of a crisis situation.

Institutions

The instruments of international cooperation, i.e., the institutions, are the next point of consideration. International cooperation, like social cooperation, does not necessarily require an elaborate and formal system of institutions. Sometimes "noninstitutional" cooperation may be even more effective than an institutionalized one.

The history of Swedish and Norwegian relations is a convincing argument for the noninstitutional approach. In 1905, the Norwegian Storting (parliament) dissolved its union with Sweden, and the Swedish Riksdag accepted this dissolution. But the dissolution did not change the peaceful relationship between the states. It was an effective peace policy. Conversely, a historical peace institution like the League of Nations was ineffective in its last stage because it embraced a variety of states with conflicting goals, interests, and ideologies. Some of these states did not desire peace at all, but were set for further expansion. The dominant goals and the interests within the league were incompatible, and its existence did not necessarily foster cooperation. Nor did the Arab League result in an effective cooperation of Arab states, because it was unable to resolve basic conflicts within the Arab nations.

Nevertheless, the techniques of peacemaking and attempts to establish permanent peaceful relations usually lead to the creation of institutions and organizations. Institutions represent an instrumentality of cooperation through which a number of governments with similar goals express the dynamics of their political action.

Techniques of cooperation are clearly related to these instruments. Institutions become viable when proper techniques are used and when the participating governments can reach agreement on particular goals and interests and obey certain rules. One additional element must be added to this complex picture—the will. Cooperation requires a will, a desire, to agree. The formation of institutions of cooperation will not produce results if the member states or the decision makers do not desire such cooperation and fail to implement the goals or interests of cooperation by common action. In a study of international relations this very simple factor should not be overlooked.

In short, international cooperation—by which we understand the cooperation or group action of governments which control the states and can produce action on a variety of levels—requires: (1) common goals and/or interests, (2) acceptance of a minimum set of values or rules of behavior, (3) skills or techniques of cooperation, (4) the will to cooperate, and (5) institutions (organizations) or instrumentalities.[3]

International cooperation is a broad term, embracing a number of possibilities and a variety of social processes of diverse quality and intensity. Accordingly, different types of cooperation may suggest or require a variety of types of institutions. They can be classified into major types:

UNIVERSAL INSTITUTIONS, such as the United Nations or the League of Nations. These political institutions attempt to include all existing states. Their chief objective is collective security and the maintenance of peace.

REGIONAL ORGANIZATIONS, such as the "Nordic Council" of the Scandinavian countries, Finland, and Iceland, or the Benelux Economic Union of Belgium,

Holland, and Luxembourg. These international organizations comprise states within a limited geographical area which have some common interest and goals.

FUNCTIONAL INSTITUTIONS, such as commissions or unions formed for definite but limited purposes. Some of these institutions were remarkably efficient, e.g., the Danubian Commission, established after the Crimean War by the Treaty of Paris in 1856, and later extended to regulate and supervise certain navigation problems of the Danube River. The commission survived wars and revolutions for a hundred years and, as William Miller stated, "as usual the least showy section of this great international document [the Treaty of Paris] has been the most successful." [4] The highly successful International Postal Union belongs in the same category, as does another example of successful, though limited, international pragmatism—the European Coal and Steel Community (signed in Paris in 1951), which led to the establishment of the Common Market.

Functional institutions have been successful within their limited objectives, but they seldom prevented wars or other forms of conflict. The International Postal Union has worked efficiently through two world wars which have shaken the world, but it had no effect on world tensions. The Danubian Commission, efficient as it was, did not prevent the Balkan wars.

Although it might be said that the elimination of war was not the objective of those institutions, some political and social scientists argue that the efficient road to peace is through functional organization. This may have been the case in German-French relations and with the organizations which culminated in the Common Market and will perhaps lead to a closer European union. But there are other examples in the history of international relations which indicate that functional organizations were and are effective within a limited area, usually economic and nonpolitical. We can learn from them about the effective structuring and operating of international institutions. Their major characteristics are limitation of scope and clear presentation of objectives, strong support of the governments concerned, and the will to attain their objectives. The future may, however, indicate that the functional form can be applied successfully in the political and arms-control area. Functional organizations limited solely to the task of international security, arms control, and supervising a gradual disarmament may be the proper effective form of organization.

INTERGOVERNMENTAL INSTITUTIONS such as international conferences or assemblies are formed by official representatives of governments. Unlike functional organizations, they require the agreement of all interested governments on decisions that can be enforced. Their members act as representatives of governments rather than of the institutions. Thus the Council of the European Economic Community, established in 1957, acts by absolute majority; moreover, the members of the commission perform their duties "in the general interest of the Community with full independence." The Balkan Conferences, established by the Balkan states in 1930 with the objective of forming a Balkan union (which was not attained), was an intergovernmental organization since it had a consultative character and never attained the characteristic powers of a functional organization. Like the Balkan Entente (established in 1934), the conferences were regional and intergovernmental.

TRANSIENT AND PERMANENT INTERNATIONAL INSTITUTIONS. Transient institutions are temporary, usually formed *ad hoc* (e.g., an armistice commission) as opposed to permanent institutions, which are intended for long-range policies.

The development of international institutions and organizations is usually indicative of increasing international cooperation among member states. However, this cooperation might not be indicative of a tendency toward peace. *Antagonistic institutions* are formed primarily for the purpose of conflict. They exist because of unrest. The Arab League was, to an extent, an antagonistic institution directed against Israel.

It has already been indicated that there are differences in the practice of cooperation. Some countries have developed international cooperation through a system of institutions; in other cases, peaceful coexistence was achieved without an elaborate system of organizations.

The British and continental doctrines

Attitudes toward international institutions differ between Great Britain and the European continent. This difference is based on dissimilar theoretical approaches to constitutional law and to the philosophy or sociology of law. In the continental theory, law is an instrument—as are the enacted constitutions—and can be used effectively for changes of social and political reality. In such an approach, the law is not only a product of sociological conditions but also an instrument through which society can be shaped and changed. Such a viewpoint is perhaps strongest in French constitutional practice, which has had such an important influence on the European continent.

The dominant British and American theory was different, at least in the nineteenth century. We may take as examples Herbert Spencer and William Sumner. In Spencer's theory, institutions develop spontaneously from existing conditions, and laws are based on well-established customs. It is custom, once formed, which permits the development of successful law. Similarly, in Sumner's theory, folkways, mores, and laws as well as institutions are closely related. Their success depends on their acceptance and on general practice rooted in customs and values. This principle was clearly stated by James Bryce: "Do not give to a people institutions for which it is unripe in the simple faith that the tool will give skill to the workman's hand. Respect facts. Man is in each country not what we may wish him to be, but what Nature and History have made him."

Hippolyte Taine, in his reminiscences of 1849, similarly criticized French political and social institutions: "The house should not be built for the architect alone, nor for itself, but for the owner who has to occupy it." The political structures set up by the French government were demolished thirteen times in twenty years, and never satisfied the French people. Only experience, argued Taine, can determine whether the political structures, or institutions, really fit the character, customs, occupations, even caprices of a nation.[5]

Of course, these are not the only existing views, but they seem to represent the major tendencies which dominated the development of differing theoretical outlooks on the European continent, on one hand, and in Britain and America, on the other. This is the reason why a social scientist or a political practitioner trained in British theories of this period is not very enthusiastic about the proliferation of formal international institutions. He relies instead on a pragmatic, empirical approach, which takes existing interests, values, institutions, and customs into consideration. This difference in outlook appeared in the debates of the European Council. In its initial period, some continental representatives strongly supported proposals for a European federation, while the British delegates hesitated to commit themselves to formal constitutional organizations before a definite need, interest, and will arose.

Integration

The function of an institution can be identified by asking the following questions: (1) what needs and objectives does the institution meet and serve and (2) does it "work" (operate successfully)? From the point of view of function and functioning, the maintenance of peace under beneficent conditions, such as Swedish-Norwegian or Canadian-American relations, does not require elaborate and powerful institutions. Karl Deutsch and his associates called this type of association of states or cooperative systems "a security community." We may also call it "a pluralistic community" and use the established definition for this term, i.e., a group of states which have attained a sense of community; which have practices and institutions strong enough to give an expectation of peaceful change. The members of a pluralistic or security community retain their legal independence and their separate governments. Thus, the institutions are intergovernmental. Intensive forms of the processes of integration represent what Deutsch calls amalgamations or mergers of states.[6]

The process of complete amalgamation, or what we called in a more limited sense "complete integration," represents the final stage of the tendency toward cooperation (as shown on Model III). We may stress here again that such an amalgamation of two or more states may not necessarily ease the tensions or be the only method available. As we have seen, the integration of states may take a variety of forms.

Functional integration is represented today by the European Common Market and the emerging Western European Union. These are new forms of an efficient and workable integration, quite different from the eighteenth- and nineteenth-century patterns of enacted constitutions. Perhaps under British influence, European cooperation has been growing slowly, changing from the consultative system of the Council of Europe to the functional form of cooperation, such as the Schuman Plan and the European Coal and Steel Community. Today this tendency toward integration continues, and the functional mechanism works well and is, perhaps, an innovation in international techniques of cooperation. The emergence of the European Common Market, a result of this complex functional cooperation in many fields through a variety of institutions, has become a major factor of our historical period.[7]

In a logical classification, perhaps on a continuum, the following four forms representing a tendency toward amalgamation should be put in the sequence: (1) functional complex integration; (2) confederal system; (3) federal system; and (4) centralistic integration (or merger of states through a coercive military-administrative action). The fourth form has usually been accomplished through conquest. As a result of the Congress of Vienna in 1815, such a merger was accomplished between Poland and Russia, although the former retained its parliament and, for a time, a certain element of autonomy.

Past experience teaches us that the institutional structure must be chosen carefully and adjusted to the cultural and political patterns of behavior and the values and customs of the cooperating nation-states and governments. Institutions do not in themselves offer a guarantee of international cooperation. Cooperation depends on many factors.

The amalgamation or complete integration of nations has usually appeared in history under conditions of latent conflict, such as the threat of war, or war itself. Tribes have been amalgamated into states as a result of conquest. It would be difficult to find many cases of complete integration resulting solely from economic pressures. I do not underestimate the importance of the economic basis of international development. Neither do I ignore the role of dynamic economic forces in the development of international relations, national expansion, and imperialism. But it would be difficult indeed to find any cases in which a number of states have united through purely rational considerations of economic necessity.

Of course, in any process of international relations we shall find parallel economic phenomena, economic considerations, and economic necessities. Usually, a correlation can be established between economic developments and the processes of integration. But in a long historical experience, it seems to me that these forces were not sufficient to prompt the rapid integration of states. Consequently, states united because of the outside threat of war or became amalgamated through conquest. Of course, there might have been, and usually were, economic considerations at the roots of the conquest. But it was the threat of war or conquest which directly prompted the states to union or amalgamation. In other words, the economic causes of the political action cannot be overlooked, but it is the political action which is significant in such a context. Here the economic element appears in conjunction with the political and the military.

In a sense, Stalin was the great architect of European unity—or at least one of them. His military pressure molded European and Atlantic unity. Later, the dissolution of the colonial European empires contributed an additional factor to European integration. The Coal and Steel Community, which initiated Franco-German collaboration, was influenced by outside threat.

Ideas of European integration can be traced as far back as the thirteenth century. The economic advisability of European integration could be seen in the time of the Industrial Revolution. However, the idea succeeded and took material shape only after the consequences of World War II created an outside threat.

As the governments were united by the outside threat, so the masses, the groups, and the individuals were united by a common ideology and a common power for ideological appeal. Here again, the significance of the economic base cannot be denied.

As a rule, ideas have had a strong appeal when they corresponded to some economic needs. But man's economic needs are not his only ones. An individual has deep-seated psychological needs and possibly ethical needs which are not completely identical with the psychological ones. Some psychological needs are unconscious, and an appeal to them may operate on subconscious levels. Ethical needs, an anthropologist would say, are culturally determined. There exists, perhaps, an even deeper explanation of their nature.

The great ideologies have had a unifying appeal in the West as well as in the Orient, and the great religions have had the potential for uniting and supplying common values to large masses of people. Similarly, social-political systems such as socialism have universalistic tendencies. The universalism of certain religions and ideologies is of significance in international relations, because it indicates that any universal organization will sooner or later require some common denominator and some common values.

The history of great ideals is repetitive. First, small groups produced elaborate and powerful ideological systems. The general appeal of these systems then resulted in extensive social movements which carried the struggles and actions toward the goals outlined in the ideologies. At the moment of victory, the movement of prophets and apostles was institutionalized and the apostles were replaced by secretariats. Once a secretariat was established, the problem of power displaced the problem of ideology, and the maintenance of the power system became paramount. This seems to have happened as frequently with the great religions as with great political ideals.

The "real" and "ideal" institution

We may now return to a general discussion and classification of international institutions and indicate a distinction between the juridical, or formal, approach and the sociological approach. In a juridical approach, the analysis is focussed on the formal, legal structure of an institution and on an interpretation of the legal provisions which govern such an institution. In a sociological approach, it is not the legal but the real which is subjected to inquiry.

In addition to its formal power structure, an institution has its informal organization and power distribution. The real functions of an institution are identified, i.e., the needs it really meets and not the objective it was intended to serve. The workability of the institution, the norms, institutional behavior, organization, and its patterns of action form a vast area of sociological study.

In an analysis of efficiency in international organizations, it is the sociological aspect of institutions and not their legal structure that is relevant. The elimination of war does not always require a fusion of states and a complex system of powerful institutions. As we have already learned, a pluralistic security community may be even more efficient, though less impressive, in its organizational aspect. The workability of institutions depends on many sociological factors. Institutions represent a variety of social tools that man may choose in his efforts to foster cooperation or conflict; (antagonistic) institutions may also serve the latter.

Classification of international cooperation

We shall now proceed with our major task—the classification of the general tendency toward international cooperation: the processes of association. We may proceed in a logical, rather than in an empirical, manner, arranging the processes on a continuum according to their intensity; proceeding from a loose and informal pattern of actions and relations toward an institutional form of cooperation, and eventually to integration. To assist our discussion, we shall follow Model III, which represents an ideal type of a continuum of cooperation.

In a logical, ideal-type classification, we have separated the processes of cooperation from the processes of conflict. It must be remembered, however, that the pattern of international relations is frequently mixed in its nature. Thus, differ-

MODEL III
Processes of Association

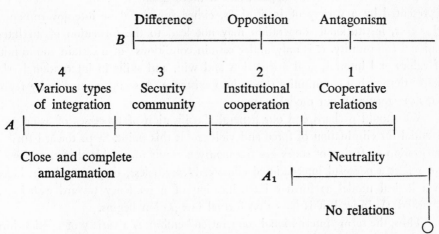

Difference   Opposition   Antagonism

B |————————————|—————————|————

4   3   2   1

Various types   Security   Institutional   Cooperative
of integration   community   cooperation   relations

A |—————————|—————————|—————————|—————————|

Close and complete   Neutrality
amalgamation A_1 |—————————————|

No relations

ences may exist side by side with cooperation in certain fields, and even opposition or antagonism in others. Contrariwise, in times of serious military conflicts between states, limited cooperation may continue in other fields.

Institutions were put on the continuum as evidence of international cooperation and of trends toward the easing of tensions in international relations. This is frequently the case. International institutions of a functional nature, or others limited in scope, may exist even in times of war and conflict. Nevertheless, the development of institutions is often indicative of growing international cooperation.

Model III represents a continuum of processes of association; a general tendency toward cooperation. At the bottom there is a zero point of no relations, and directly above it, a section (marked A_1), running parallel to cooperation, which represents neutrality. (Neutrality, as was indicated, usually involves certain processes of cooperation.)

The mechanism of any cooperative process should provide ways by which differences and oppositions could be expressed and answered without resort to violence. (There is a difference between conformity and cooperation. Absence of difference or opposition is identical with conformity.) In consequence, we shall use three parallel continua. One (marked B) starts with difference and is a part of the continuum of dissociation: of the general tendency toward conflict. The other (marked A) is a continuum of association and cooperation. A third one (marked A_1) indicates neutrality. We shall follow the various types of processes indicated on line A, representing a tendency toward cooperation.

The first type of process is represented by noninstitutional cooperation. Cooperation between states, reduced to elementary relations with no permanent or even transient organization, belongs in this category. Intensification of cooperation is indicative of a greater tendency toward association. At this stage (2) transient and permanent institutions appear, and a more intensive form of association is represented by a variety of institutions, either functional or intergovernmental. However, institutional cooperation may not lead to the formation of an international community. It is only under cetrain conditions—of a certain community of values and interest, goal orientation and will, and skills in international relations—that such a community comes into existence. A security community represents category 3 on our model.

We should perhaps end our general classification of processes of association essential for elimination of force and violence at this point. Steps toward further integration or fusion of states are frequently a result of outside threat, and need not reflect a peaceful international climate. Nevertheless, they must be included in a logical model as further intensification of a tendency toward association (marked 4). Indeed, it is here that formal integration begins.

Thus, the term "international cooperation" embraces a variety of relationships and diverse types of organizations. They differ in their nature and quality, although they represent similar or identical tendencies. Such variety has a practical significance since it offers the possibility of choices and alternatives, while a narrow analysis creates an "either-or" situation in which choice is reduced to extreme forms of conflict or cooperation. From the viewpoint of a decision maker, such a situation may sometimes exist. However, our discussion suggests that a nondogmatic approach, where more than two choices are usually open, may offer a more flexible policy.

MODEL IV

Processes of Dissociation

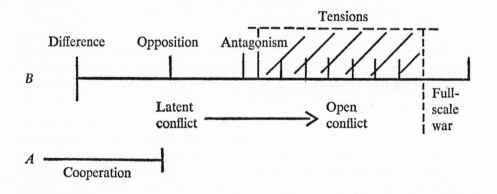

3.

TENSIONS AND CONFLICT

Process approach

The antagonistic tendency in international relations appears in a variety of forms and in processes of different intensities. The polar division into conflict and cooperation, with neutrality lying between, may be logical, but it represents only the extremes of the complex phenomenon we call international relations. Just as tendencies toward the easing of tension or toward cooperation appear in many forms, so do tendencies toward antagonism and conflict. The change of intensity, the change of the "quantity" of the conflict or cooperation, alters the very nature of the process at a certain point.[1]

Returning to our diagrams for the classification of processes of dissociation, we find that Model IV is identical with parallel *B* of Model III. We shall start on the left with Difference, since it is a hypothetical central point.

Differences in views or interest are usually present in processes of cooperation and of tension and antagonism. In a tendency toward cooperation, mechanisms are devised for the adjustment of differences. For example, differences between the American and British governments are resolved by negotiations, discussions, and compromises. In the European community, they can also be adjusted in an additional variety of ways and institutions. The term "adjustment" implies that the solution may not be entirely satisfactory for one of the parties, or even for both parties. Nevertheless, both accept the solution in the interests of maintaining the workability of the institutional system. However, differences may grow into opposition, which represents a more intense process.

23

Opposition is placed second on our scale. When difference appears, it is either in values and views (ideologies) or in definite interests (political or economic). The difference between the Communist Chinese government and the Communist Soviet government might be a difference in views (ideologies) as well as in political (power) interests. For instance, at the meeting of the Soviet-bloc Council for Mutual Economic Assistance (called COMECON), as reported in May, 1963, Rumanian representatives opposed Premier Khrushchev's plans for economic integration in an effort to protect their country's infant industries.

In a regional plan for Eastern Europe, the less efficient industries would have to be closed; the distribution of industrial and economic specialization might also lead to liquidation of certain industrial enterprises. According to reports, the difference was primarily in economic interests, reflected in a difference in economic outlooks and views.

Similarly, in the Western bloc, difference and opposition appeared in 1963 in the NATO system, when General de Gaulle suggested a separate nuclear force for France, independent of the NATO nuclear power system.

A difference of views is not tantamount to political action which interferes with the policies of other parties. "Active opposition" begins when words change to action; when the differing government undertakes steps to block the action of its opponent, or when it interferes with its policies or obstructs such an action. A show of force or the threat of economic action may sometimes be identical with the real act, since it suffices to thwart the activities of the other party. A notable demonstration of this condition was the landing of American troops in Lebanon during the Eisenhower administration. This was an act expressing the opposition of the United States government. As soon as the opposing parties in Lebanon adjusted their policy to the new situation, the American troops were withdrawn.

Opposition is not yet antagonism, but the beginning of it. If the opposition is not eased, it has a tendency to intensify into an antagonism, and eventually into a conflict. Antagonism arises when one party views the ideological, political, or economic goals of the other as incompatible. In 1963 the United States government actively opposed Soviet military penetration in Cuba. Opposition was intensified and became an antagonistic relationship the moment the Soviet missile bases were discovered in Cuba. They represented a direct threat to the security of the United States. The situation was clearly defined by the United States representative in the United Nations, and later by the president of the United States, who expressed opposition to this action. The American representatives indicated unequivocally that unless Soviet policy changed, direct action would have to be taken by the United States government. Preparation for such action began at once. In other words, the process of active opposition was shifting to antagonism and latent conflict. The Soviet Union yielded. Premier Khrushchev promised to remove the missiles from Cuba and, according to official statements, did so. This eased the tension, and moved it from latent conflict to antagonism and active opposition.

In 1956 the press of the United States expressed sympathy with the Hungarian uprising against the Soviet domination. It was felt at the time, however, that any steps beyond "declaratory opposition" (verbal statements with no commitments) would be regarded as open conflict, and the United States government did not take any real action in support of the revolutionaries. Nevertheless, the incompatibility of political goals (antagonism) in this area, as in Cuba, had been stated.

Antagonism, in turn, is related to latent conflict. Thus the process of dissociation and nascent conflict is a "continuum"; a dynamic, changing process of varying intensities. The increase of "quantity" of hostile actions changes, to use a Hegelian dialectical concept, to "quality."

It would be well, at this point, to sum up some of the "marks" of this dynamic, moving process. The difference indicates a disagreement on goals, interests, and even perception, with broad choices for adjustment in the form of open agreements without subordination or surrender of the party. "Declaratory opposition" expresses on a verbal level that views, goals, interests, or decisions of the opposing parties are contradictory or incompatible. In an "active opposition," the actor undertakes such moves as will frustrate actions of the adversary. The goals are contradictory, but not yet incompatible. "Active opposition" is tantamount, however, to the initial stage of antagonism. With it, limited opposition changes to a more intensive and complex pattern. "Opposition" still represents sporadic, disconnected action; "antagonism" is a continuous, consistent policy. At this point, goals or interests are perceived as incompatible. "Conflict" is the "escalation" of antagonism to its most intensive degree, involving a mustering of forces and preparation for, or engagement in, a direct clash of adversaries. The former presents the "latent" form of conflict; the latter, the direct, or "open." The antagonists become enemies and use various forms of force to compel the adversary to surrender, subordination, compromise, or withdrawal.

Action approach

The reader may recall my distinction between action and process approaches. A process in international relations is an interaction, a mutually interdependent relationship, of two or more states. The action approach is reduced to the goals and actions of one of the two parties. One party is, theoretically at least, isolated from this mutual relationship and its goal orientation as well as its actions are analyzed. We shall move now briefly from the process approach to the action-goal approach.

MODEL V

Action Approach (*A*)

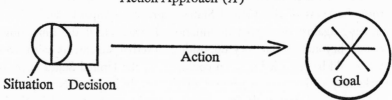

This simple diagram presents the relationship of situation (circle), decision (square), action, and goal (star). A government makes a decision (square), which is transmitted to the administrative executive systems (the apparatus or structure) and thus is transformed into action directed toward the goals identified in the decision of the government.

This analysis leads us to a more complex diagram (Model VI), in which we may observe a decision, closely related to situation, which moves in the form of a message to the bureaucratic apparatus. The actions toward goal attainment are released by the latter. The entire governmental apparatus (also called structure)

MODEL VI

Action Approach (*B*)

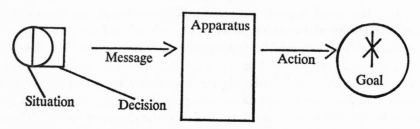

can be and is used by the government for the purpose of goal attainment. A close relationship exists between the nature of the institutions, the type of action, and the goal. All three elements: structure, action, and goal, are closely interrelated. The next diagram (Model VII) shows the structure of the goals and its relationship to tactics and strategy.

Horizontal goal structure

A well-planned, dynamic foreign policy usually has an elaborate goal structure. This structure is either stated and manifest, or is the logical result of a consistent foreign policy of a government with a sense of direction and a certain vision. We shall discuss two types of goal structure: the horizontal and the vertical or alternative.

MODEL VII
Horizontal Goal Structure *A*

Immediate	Intermediate	Distant
✗━━━━━━━━━━━━━━━━━✗━━━━━━━━━━━━━━━━⊗		
Tactical	Stage	General
goals	goals	strategy

Strategic goals

We shall distinguish among immediate, intermediate, and distant goals (Models VII and VIII). Immediate goals are tactical—single actions within the pattern of a given strategic stage. Intermediate goals represent a stage of policy. Distant goals represent the aims of general strategy and indicate the direction of the entire pattern. The concepts of strategy and tactics can be applied in policies oriented toward peace or conflict. Both historically and etymologically, the terms "strategy" and "tactics" originated with the theory of war. Nevertheless, these concepts have a general significance in a theory of social and individual actions.

Rational human actions are frequently structured into immediate, intermediate, and distant goals. Immediate goals represent single actions. Intermediate goals are more elaborate and are a part of strategy. Distant goals correspond to the strategy that sets the general direction and supplies a vision, a general orientation, toward which the foreign policy moves.

Actions or policies are anchored to goals. When a government decides on a policy, it means that it has determined its goal. In a logical sequence it suggests the steps to be taken in achieving this goal. These steps are tactical actions which, put together as a system of actions, are related to the intermediate goal. In other words, the goal releases the action. In a sense, the goal becomes a "quasi cause" and the action, an effect. The relationship between goal and action is very close, and as the goals change, so do patterns of action. Intermediate goals are related both to immediate and distant goals. In a sense, the goal structure determines the structure of the actions or of the policies. Consequently, goals and actions represent different aspects of the same image.

We move now to Model VIII and identify (first on the left) the im-

MODEL VIII
Horizontal Goal Structure *B*

	Immediate goals	(1)	(2)	(3)	Distant goals	
A	✗━━━━━━━━✗━━━━━━━━✗━━━━━━━━✗━━━━━━━━⊗					C
		B	Intermediate B	B		

mediate goals (*A*), followed by the intermediate goals (*B*) [marked (1), (2), (3)], and the distant goals (*C*). If we apply this diagram to a peace policy, the immediate and tactical goal (*A*) may be regarded as an attempt at a conference on nuclear disarmament. Intermediate goal (*B*, 1) is the temporary cessation of nuclear explosion. Intermediate goal (2) is a permanent test ban. Intermediate goal (3) is nuclear disarmament; and the distant goal (*C*) is the elimination of war as an instrument of national policy. The same diagram can be used in an analysis of a conflict policy, with the general strategy of the Communist Chinese government in Southeast Asia serving as an example. (We shall discuss the policy of Mao Tse-tung on a hypothetical level, without any real possibility of verifying the distant goals. The suggested stages have been chosen arbitrarily.)

The first stage, the immediate goal, was the neutralization of Southeast Asia through the creation of a neutralist bloc. Communist China gave strong support to this policy. The second step was the occupation of Tibet, which might be regarded as an intermediate goal. The third step was the total annexation of Tibet; the fourth, penetration into the northern Indian borderland; and the fifth, the occupation of the northern Indian borderland and of territory in the vicinity of Assam, with a simultaneous support of guerrilla warfare in Southeast Asia. This suggests, as a general direction of Chinese policy, expansion into Asia, especially Southeast Asia. The various strategic stages (since strategy is divided into stages) can be related to a variety of intermediate goals, with each goal being a stage of the general strategy. This brings us to Model IX, in which goals are related to stages.

MODEL IX
Horizontal Goal Structure Related to Stages

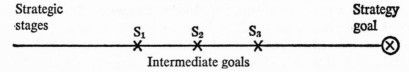

In an "ideal type" approach, policy consists of actions and goals. Once a goal is achieved, the government moves immediately to the next goal. (This is a theoretical approach, but even for analytical purposes it is easier for our purpose to visualize a foreign policy as a number of goals, like milestones, with a government moving from one goal to another.)

Goals are seldom established and followed up as clearly as they are presented on a diagram. Usually they emerge during action. One successful action or policy may suggest the next step. The fact that an opponent yields easily may sharpen the appetite and increase the pressure, with a knowledge of the opponent's weakness contributing to tactics and strategy. In consequence, goals and actions are fused in practical policy.

In an analytical or "ideal type" approach, a policy may be presented in terms of goals which follow one another. However, in practical politics, especially in a policy of conquest, the goals and the strategy are dynamic, changing, elastic. What remains is a general sense of the direction in which a government moves with all its might and all its potentialities, and sense of direction is indicative of its strategy. This brings us to the alternative or vertical goal structure.

MODEL X
Vertical Goal Structure

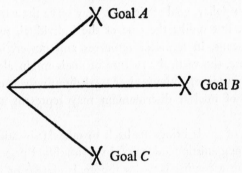

Vertical goal structure

Model X suggests an "ideal type" policy. *A, B,* and *C* are alternate goals. We may start with goal *A*. A government moves in the direction of goal *A,* but its action is frustrated. In conquence, goal *B* is substituted, and the government moves in another direction. But here the action of the government is again frustrated. In consequence, the government moves toward goal *C,* which replaces goal *B* for a time.

Stalin's advance in Europe was frustrated by the formation of the North Atlantic Treaty Organization and by the growing integration of Europe. In consequence, at a certain stage he substituted expansion in Asia (Korea) as a goal for that of European expansion.

The Mainland Chinese government was frustrated in its first advance into India by the support given to India by Great Britain and the United States, and became alarmed by the reaction of nonaligned nations. In consequence, it intensified its action in the South. Goal *A* had been replaced by goal *B.* In both cases, alternate goals may not have represented a change in strategy but in tactics, or in intermediate goals.

Here is the same problem applied to tension areas in specific geographical sectors. Let us imagine that a policy of expansion was frustrated in area *A*. The initiating party, after a short period of quiet, moves into a weaker area (let us say area *B*) or into another area (area *C*). These alternative areas represent certain "substitute-stages" in an elastic strategy. Alternative strategies are more significant than alternative tactics.

The development of nuclear weapons may have changed the strategy of expansion from total war to economic and ideological penetration. The final vision, the final goal, may remain the same, but the pattern of the action changes because of changed conditions. This type of alternative strategy may contribute to the lessening of tensions, or at least to the elimination of full-scale conflict.

Alternative goals are a reflection of a general mechanism of goal substitution. An individual whose wishes or goals are frustrated usually substitutes goals on a variety of levels, since substitution serves a psychological need. In international relations and foreign policy, goal attainment may serve the psychological needs of the decision maker. But unlike the case of the individual, such substitution requires "rational" means, in terms of resources and power, in a general policy analysis. In this sense, the vertical structure of goals might also be viewed as an alternative one; for instance, if the goal of total disarmament cannot be achieved, an alternative goal of nuclear disarmamant may represent a target for a new policy.

The discussion of goals brings us back to our classification of the processes of dissociation, of antagonistic tendencies. In a simplified presentation, conflicting foreign policies mean a conflict between the goals of two or more governments, which represent states. Since a conflict of economic or political interests may be reflected in foreign policy goals, these goals represent ideological as well as economic interests. Opposition begins when the contradiction or incompatibility of goals or interests becomes apparent. A movement toward antagonism begins when this incompatibility sharpens.

Conflict of goals

Returning to our process approach, we shall study the interaction between two governments. The goals of government *A* conflict with the goals and interests of government *B*. In consequence, government *A* acts to interfere with the policies and goals of government *B*.

MODEL XI

Incompatibility of Goals: Antagonism

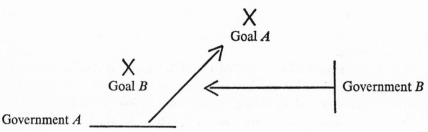

By its actions, government *A* blocks access to goal *B,* and the actions of government *B* are thus frustrated. In practical politics, the situation is much more complex. The strategic goals and the general sense of direction remain, and the frustration usually affects the tactical or intermediate goals. Tensions then appear as a result of the interactions of the governments.

Let us take as an example Hitler's expansionist policy before 1939. After the German occupation of Austria, tensions persisted because the attainment of Hitler's intermediate goals encouraged him to persist in his policy aiming toward his wider strategic goal of expansion over a whole continent.

Again, stalemating of the geographically limited Korean conflict in the 1950's did not remove the danger of Chinese expansion in other areas. The strategic goals of Mao Tse-tung's policy remained, despite the fact that he was unable to reach an intermediate objective because of the blocking action of the United Nations Forces (on our diagram, government *A*).

Such stalemating of tactical movements and easing of limited tensions in definite geographical areas is by no means identical with a reduction of world tensions or of fundamental, strategic tensions. In consequence, tensions begin when antagonism moves to an intensive stage. When antagonism is intensified, the possibility of conflict increases, but remains latent. It is in the nature of conflict that it affects the structure of the organizations of the participants. Both the aggressing and the defending governments must create specialized institutions to deal with conflict, and adjust their structures and reallocate their resources according to a new hierarchy of goals and needs. Thus the aggressing party will expand its military establishment and propaganda apparatus; e.g., the transportation system which would have to supply the aggressing army of the future, etc.

The defending party, in anticipation of conflict, will also adjust its activities and its institutions. A reorganization of military force will probably follow and the military budget will be increased. Mass communications will be expanded. Thus, a conflict situation increases the tendency to centralize the state, and power shifts toward the executive.

In his study of conflict, made sixty years ago, the German sociologist Georg Simmel indicated the relationship between the structure of institutions and conflict behavior. He showed that in a conflict situation the institutions have a tendency to become more centralistic.[2] But his observations were by no means new.

Tensions

We now move to Model XII, which represents a part of the general continuum. (It is a more detailed presentation of a section of continuum *B,* from antagonism to full-scale open conflict.) The area from the beginning of antagonism to open hostilities represents a period of continuous tensions. During such a period actions

MODEL XII
Tensions

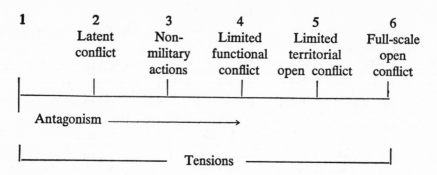

are either manifest or latent. Manifest actions such as aggressive policies in limited tension areas, guerrilla warfare, limited wars, propaganda, or economic blockade involve a counteraction of the defending government. Anticipation of possible hostile action also results in a social and political process which is a consequence of external threat. Thus the tension begins to be a continuous phenomenon, an everyday occurrence, a part of daily life.

We shall start on our diagram with initial antagonism (1), which changes to a latent conflict (2). This antagonism can still be eased, reduced to opposition, and finally solved. For instance, the tensions and antagonisms between Pakistan and India over Kashmir, which changed into open conflict from time to time, entered into a period of partial reduction in May, 1963 and moved in the direction of opposition. From an antagonistic situation (this is perhaps only a hypothetical evaluation), the antagonism was temporarily reduced to opposition. The general tendency at that time was toward mediation, not full-scale conflict. India has since agreed to mediation by the United States and Great Britain in the dispute if Pakistan proposes a third party.[3] In the absence of reduction, however, the antagonism will first move to single nonmilitary actions (3), such as diplomatic action or propaganda intensification, which then lead to limited functional conflicts (4). These conflicts appear in the fields of economics, political nonmilitary activities, intensified propaganda, and mass communication. But this is still not a conflict on all major levels. Not all the resources of the state are involved.

The limited functional conflict might be combined with a limited territorial open conflict (5), in which military forces are brought into action. This intensification of the antagonism leads to the use of violence. The next stage, full-scale open conflict (6), involves the use of substantial resources, including the military potential, for conquest or defense or for frustrating the goals of the conquering or opposing party.

In limited geographical areas, tensions may persist on a reduced scale. Thus, for instance, Berlin is as much an example of a tension area as is Laos. In Berlin, despite whatever negotiations and compromises take place, the incompatibility of goals between East and West Germany and between the United States and the Soviet Union has not yet disappeared. On a tactical or a developmental level, a compromise may be reached or goals may be frustrated, but the general tendency persists and so do the tensions. The latter will disappear if the goals are modified and a compromise is reached adjusting the strategic objectives of both powers.

To recapitulate, tension areas are limited geographical areas in which the latency of conflict results in continuous actions and counteractions directed toward the blocking of aggressive or defensive policies of the contending governments; the aggressor and the defender.

Overt and covert goals

In a theoretical approach the terms "goals" and "actions" are simplified. By "goals" we may visualize the terminal or intermediate aims that a government is trying to achieve through its actions. By "actions," or policies, we understand negotiations and the use of the resources at the disposal of a government in arriving at this terminal point. In practice, however, goals are not always "open" and readily identifiable.

Generally, we may divide goals into open, or overt, and masked, or covert. In a statement of an open goal, the government really means what it says; the stated goal is the condition that the government represents in its demands. When U.S. President John F. Kennedy presented his demand to the Soviet Union for the removal of Russian missiles and men from Cuba, the stated goal was an open goal. This was in reality what the United States government demanded from the Soviet government.

A masked goal is different. Here the stated goal differs from the real goal which a government seeks to achieve. When Adolf Hitler pressed the Czechoslovak government of President Eduard Beneš to grant autonomy and self-government to the German population in the Sudetenland, the stated goal was different from the real one. The real goal was the conquest and dismemberment of the Czechoslovak Republic and incorporation of the Czech territories in the German Reich.

History offers us many other examples. The former Russian foreign minister Sergei Sazonov wrote in his memoirs about Russian demands and plans during the years 1900–1916. Of special interest are the Russian propositions to the Allied governments reflecting the strategy of the Czarist government, its modus operandi, and its stated and covert goals and actions. Sazonov tells us of the Russian imperial government's special interest and long-range plans for Palestine. He states that Russia claimed no special rights or privileges there, but sought only to maintain the influence it had gained under Turkish rule, and asked that Russian pilgrims have free access to the Holy Land. These were the stated goals.

Sazonov tells us that for centuries an endless stream of "pilgrims" travelled to Palestine. A special organization, the Orthodox Palestine Society, was formed; a network of religious institutions was established; and extensive money was invested. But, Sazonov writes: "According to the general rule that in the East everything is in one way or another connected with politics, these institutions, essentially nonpolitical, acquire a certain political significance as indicative of Russian influence."[4]

Goals are not always rational. Too, foreign policy may be conceived by a deviant absolute ruler who might even be insane. Implementation of such foreign policy, however, requires pragmatic action leading to goal attainment—otherwise the policy cannot succeed. History teaches us that irrational goals such as mass conversion to an ideology or religious creed or extermination of dissidents or of people of a different ethnic stock were pragmatically, practically, and rationally implemented. This was achieved because the man who set the direction of foreign policy was frequently not the one who implemented the policy.

What remains usually is a general sense of direction. Human intentions and goal attainments are two different things. What a man conceives and decides, and where history moves and how his action develops, are so frequently divergent that the conceived goal might be entirely contradictory to its attainment. It is enough to look to such parts of the world as South America, and compare the intentions of missionaries in the fifteenth and sixteenth centuries with the result of their missions, in order to visualize the discrepancy between intention and achievement. Goal attainment is the result of the actions of many and of an interaction of contending forces that is usually not anticipated. Still, in foreign policy, the general sense of direction remains.

When they are designed simply, goals such as the conquest of a foreign country are achieved by pragmatic action if enough power is behind the decision. Such goals as the building of a new peaceful organization are more difficult. Yet, very rational goals, such as the Common Market, were achieved when the forces behind them were strong enough, the political skills sufficient, the goals set, and the direction maintained.

In the general conduct of foreign policy, when international relations move from latent to manifest, and action appears in the form of negotiation, goals are usually indicated through the use of a "demand" or an "offer." Between the offer and the demand there is a substantial difference. In an "offer" suggestion, the consent of the recipient is necessary, while "demand" requires subordination, withdrawal, or surrender.[5] A government "offers" alternatives: a status quo or change, usually to mutual advantage. This may lead to a compromise. In a demand, the initiating party gives two alternatives, and a third—compromise—is possible. The "demanding government" insists on (1) subordination without direct use of force; or (2) uses force or pressure leading to subordination (surrender); or (3) suggests or accepts a compromise.

Conflict—resolution

We may now return to our discussion of the possible resolution of a conflict situation, one in which force is used; open or full-scale conflict. History teaches us that when a conflict arrives at an open stage, there are usually two alternatives of resolution. One is an agreement based on compromise; the other, subordination to the will of the stronger party (Model XIII).

MODEL XIII

Conflict—Resolution *A*

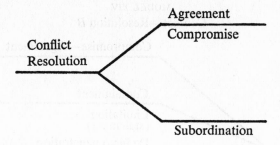

But a scrutiny of more modern cases indicates that today, tensions offer at least five alternatives for the resolution of conflicts: (1) compromise and agreement; (2) containment or limitation of conflict; (3) de facto penetration or sphere of influence; (4) subordination of the conquered nation; and (5) elimination or biological extermination—a "solution" practiced by Hitler and millions of his followers. (See Model XIV.)

Compromise or agreement represents an adjustment of goals; a coordinated effort by both parties to reduce the open conflict and adjust their mutual relations without total subordination of one or the other. The settlement between Great Britain and the thirteen American colonies after the Revolutionary War seems to have had the qualities of a compromise agreement.

Containment or limitation is frequent, especially in our time. In such a situation the contender tacitly admits the superior or equal strength of the opposing forces or its own intention of abandoning the action before a decisive end. This was the case in Korea. The United Nations clearly admitted that it did not intend to pursue its action beyond the borders of South Korea. The evaluation of alternatives and the long-range goal of the United States and its allies—the maintenance of peace—probably favored a policy of limitation or containment of the conflict.

This policy, developed in the United States, became an intermediate strategic objective for some kind of permanent solution; a substitute for a stable peace.

A containment policy represents a policy of unstable peace; it is a "meliorative goal," the best that can be achieved under the circumstances, but not a perfect solution. Containment is not subordination, and it is not an agreement; it is a compromise in which both parties maintain friendly relations and work and live together without further conflict. It is an unstable stop-gap policy of peace. In a containment-limitation solution the latent tension continues.

Subordination indicates that one government, with all the power at its disposal, forces another government to accept its decision. Subordination may also mean that the winning state, through its government, imposes its will and decision on the loser. The defeated nation, through the threat of force and other means, is forced into acceptance.

MODEL XIV
Conflict—Resolution _B_

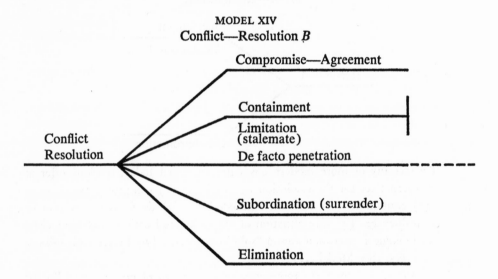

Conflict—subordination

We shall reduce our analysis at this point to two logical "either-or" alternatives. (A possibility of at least five major alternatives has already been indicated.) Model XV presents two polar values: (1) compromise or agreement and (2) subordination. In such a simplified approach, the resolution of a conflict may lead either to a compromise and an agreement or to the subordination of one nation-state by the other.

In considering the process of subordination we find that it suggests two alternative choices: indirect or direct subordination. Indirect subordination does not involve permanent or long-term occupation of territory by the troops of the con-

MODEL XV
Conflict—Subordination

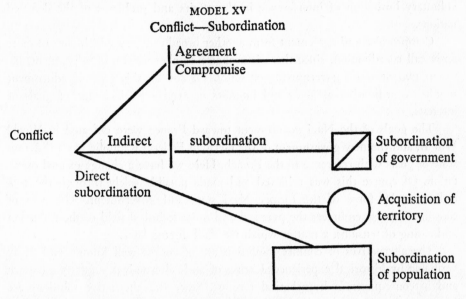

quering government. On the contrary, after a temporary occupation the conquering party exercises influence through a number of indirect means.

After withdrawing most of its army from Japan, the United States government had the means of exercising an influence over the Japanese government for a time. However, American occupation forces rapidly reduced direct controls. Agreement on the principles of self-determination and democracy, free elections, and the establishment of a national administration were encouraged. Such political forces and conditions as could revive expansionist or totalitarian tendencies were reduced by indirect control.

Indirect subordination does not involve every detail of life or even the general functioning of a society. It is usually limited to certain purely political and military, as well as economic, matters. There are a variety of methods for exercising this indirect subordination. Usually the conquering state, represented by the government, has economic and military resources to enforce its conditions in the event of a recalcitrant attitude by the conquered. Indirect subordination is usually limited to specific areas and, as a rule, does not involve continuous direct policing of the territory. In indirect subordination, the native government shares both the power and the responsibilities.

In direct subordination, the population is policed, supervised, and forced into submission by the occupying forces, as in the conquest of Eastern Europe by Germany. Thus, direct subordination is associated with the acquisition of territory. It involves two elements—population and territory. In World War II, Germany used direct subordination. The Western Allies, after a short initial period, applied almost without exception a method of indirect control with a continuous and voluntary limitation of interference in the affairs and problems of the defeated nations.

Compromise and agreement form another broad category which we can more aptly call coordination, since there is a choice of alternatives, of adjustment, between two or more governments or states. Of course, this type of adjustment requires coordination of goals and interests or even a total change of goals or interests.

The goals of the Nazi government toward France were defeated in World War II, and the new government of the German Federal Republic has a different scale of goals with reference to the French. Here we have a change of goal orientation. Of course this was achieved and made possible solely through the subordination by force of the former Nazi state and government. The area of coordination also embraces the practical and more technical field of the reduction and easing of tensions, a matter which we shall discuss later.

The alternatives of conflict resolution are of course well known and easily verifiable by historical experience. Listing of such alternatives suggests a pattern and in consequence a hypothetical forecast. Since the alternative solutions are known, we may suggest a hypothesis that existing antagonisms or conflicts may be resolved within a certain "arc of possibilities." Forecast in foreign policy does not suggest one single alternative answer: "Given a situation A—B will happen." The forecast suggests a hypothesis in form of alternatives which are open: "Given a certain A situation B, C, D, or E may occur." This is a hypothesis, a result of a logical process, not a prediction of certainty. Models XIII, XIV, and XV suggest this type of thinking and forecast.

Competition

One area of relations has not yet been discussed or even indicated: this is competition between the states. Competition differs from both cooperation and conflict as well as from cooperative and antagonistic tendencies, although it is parallel to both. Competition may also appear as one form of a collective effort, supplying channels through which antagonistic tendencies might move, as the German sociologist Georg Simmel suggests.[6]

Each competitor tries to achieve its goal without direct use of the strength of its competitor. Open obstruction or interference with the activities of the competitor would, in reality, change the competition to antagonism. For instance, in spite of numerous and strong tensions between the Soviet Union and the United States, a competitive relationship exists in the field of space. Both are trying to reach the moon first. The competition in space does not impair the strength of the adversary; in a sense it stimulates it. Perhaps in the distant future, pressures of antagonism and conflict between nations will be channelled in a number of competitive activities.

The choice

The discussion of this long continuum of both antagonistic and cooperative tendencies, of the processes of association and dissociation of nations and governments, is not of merely methodological or theoretical interest. It also has a practical consequence. This analysis suggests that international relations offer a large number of choices and alternatives, and that a policy must not necessarily be "either-or." Such an approach supplies a number of solutions to a variety of situations. I have suggested here only a limited number of processes which can be identified on the basis of historical experience.

This suggestion of a variety of choices and alternatives in international relations may seem obvious to the reader. In reality, it is not so. Certain theories in this area indicate that some thought and even some decisions are motivated by the "either-or" approach, in which the ultimate nature of social relations is axiomatic. Mao Tse-tung's theories point to such an approach. His theory of contradiction is based on Hegelian and *sui generis* Marxist dialectics, but it has been developed, with all its logical consequences, to a conclusion that would scarcely be accepted by its originators. In Mao Tse-tung's approach, contradiction is the very nature of things and, within contradiction, antagonism develops. In other words, a contradiction indicates that goals or interests are incompatible, and because of this incompatibility, antagonism develops out of difference.

According to Mao Tse-tung, the differences in modern society lead to contradictions and antagonisms. Mao argues that difference leads to contradiction and, within the contradiction, antagonism develops which must end in an explosion when conditions favor such an explosion. This theory, argues Mao, enables us to understand that "in a class society revolution and revolutionary wars are inevitable, that apart from them the leap in social development cannot be made." [7]

Mao closely follows Karl von Clausewitz, one of the fathers of the theory of total war. In a letter of June 14, 1963, from the Central Committee of the Chinese Party to the Soviet Communist Party, the authors almost repeat Clausewitz's dictum that "war is the continuation of politics by other means. . . ." [8]

This theory no doubt influences direct strategy and practical foreign policy. It seems to me that this "either-or," green or red, policy harbors not only serious dangers but contains empirical errors. Let us put aside for a moment the problems of class war and other social problems within a given society and limit ourselves to external relations.

Within a state, changes may occur that will permit future settlement of relations between states on a coordinated peaceful level, without resort to general conflict. Thus, internal changes within the Yugoslav state under Tito contributed to peaceful relations with neighboring countries during the time of Stalin, and eased tensions. History teaches us that social change is not necessarily violent; that the higher certain civilizations develop, the greater is their tendency to eliminate violence from both domestic and international relations. Stalemating or confining a conflict permits its localization and avoids greater error.

The existence of incompatible interests and goals leading to conflicts cannot, of course, be denied. Human society would become dull without differences and contradictions. Totalitarian states, where differences are suppressed, are indicative of this possibility. The advance or change in a society is frequently the result of difference and contradictions. Therefore, the problem is not to eliminate difference or contradictions but to develop any adjustment of interests and goals or effect changes in societies that would permit the resolution of those contradictions or changes in international relations without the use of violence.

ii. The Nature and Origin
of International Ethnic Tensions

4.

TENSION AREAS

Classification and Structure

The primary tension areas

In world politics today, certain conflicts and tensions in a limited territorial area may be entirely or in part dependent on the policies and decisions of the governments of the major power systems (once called by William T. R. Fox the "superpowers"). These area disturbances are considered as "dependent" tensions, since they are an integral part of what may be called the "big power zone." They are also called "primary" tensions, because of their basic significance in global, political designs concerned with the maintenance of peace or the threat of war.

Moreover, in these struggles for control of continents or even of the entire world that have been characteristic of twentieth-century world politics, the primary tension areas are usually only small segments of larger strategic designs. If we view strategy as a road toward an ultimate goal or set of goals, the primary tension areas may be said to indicate certain paths on such a road, or stages of a plan. In a strategy of expansion or withdrawal, time and space are parallel. A given government or political system (aggregate of governments or states) extends its control over a certain space in a certain time. Both are therefore functionally interrelated. The tension areas form temporary halts in an advance.

The dependent tension areas are *primarily political* in nature. Easing of their tension depends upon decisions by the governments of the big power zone. The Berlin crisis of 1961 and 1962 is a typical example of a primary, dependent tension area. The governing bodies of East and West Berlin may have had some influence on the decision maker, but the decision itself was made neither in Berlin nor in

Bonn. The continuing tension in Berlin could be eased in a matter of days if not hours if an agreement to this effect could be reached between the U.S.S.R. and the United States, the two major decision makers.

The secondary or nondependent tension areas

Secondary or nondependent tension areas do not depend on the "big power zone," but remain local in nature. The big powers may exercise pressure to ease or intensify these tensions, but their conflict and resolution depend on the local populations or neighboring governments. Reduction of such tensions frequently involves big powers, as, for example, in the tension between Turks and Greeks on Cyprus involving the British and American governments in 1964. Today international organizations, primarily the United Nations or North Atlantic Treaty Organization, may interfere and sometimes control or reduce the tensions.

Our political world has always had an abundance of "conflict zones" and tension areas. Such areas were already evident among tribal societies (for instance, hunting grounds). In addition to big power expansionism, there is also the imperialist ambition of the smaller nations. In some of these areas, the tension has a long "endemic" history. Such was the case of Dobrudja, a tension area between Rumania and Bulgaria; or of Kossovo, between Serbia and Turkey (later between the Serbs and Albanians). Today, German-Italian tension in Alto Adige may serve as an example. Another is the Syrian-Turkish tension around Alexandrette.[1]

The secondary or nondependent tensions are "local in their nature," i.e., they are outside the bipolar or polycentric great power system of world politics and develop independently. Such tensions are not an imminent threat to global peace, although the intensification of secondary tension areas may produce local wars. Such wars, in spite of the official theory that "peace is one and indivisible," are possible, and do in fact occur. (The "conquest" of Goa [or "liberation," as some prefer] by the Indian troops in 1961 belongs in this category.) Furthermore, secondary tension areas are not "temporary halts" or stages in the strategic advance of big powers.

However, secondary tensions can be exploited by outside powers to suit their policy objectives. An "outside" government, though not involved directly in a given conflict, may intervene secretly or openly in a secondary situation, in order to deepen or ease the tension.

Intensification of tension can be achieved by: (1) propaganda; (2) diplomatic support of one of the parties; (3) political-moral support of the initiating party (assurance of support); (4) political-active support (such as supplying leadership, party apparatus, press, etc.); (5) economic support (financing a movement); and (6) military support. Such intensification of tensions may "escalate" a secondary tension to a primary one. In consequence, the nondependent tensions may be transformed into strategic objectives of major outside powers and become continental or global in significance.

Structural analysis

The major international tensions of our time are primarily ideological and political. Economic factors are of course closely interrelated; nevertheless, the ideological factors are of paramount significance. A third type of tension is of a psychosocial nature (e.g., race prejudice or ethnic hostility). This type of attitude gains in impetus in combination with a developed ideology (like racism or extreme nationalism) and an "apparatus," such as a political party or even a state. If it is not combined with an organized movement based on ideology, corresponding to certain economic interests or psychological needs, race prejudice per se does not result in international tensions. It becomes a major political-social force when it becomes a movement—organized, led, and directed toward definite goals and integrated by an idea system. In this way, race prejudice is translated into a social and political force that may capture the state or be used by an outside power. Thus, tension of a racial or ethnic type changes to a political or international tension.

A political ideology is social in nature, just as a personal philosophy is without social significance unless it has an influence on groups, such as classes or ethnic units. One may argue, however, that an individual who keeps his personal philosophy to himself is an abstract and hypothetical proposition. An ideology becomes a political force once it integrates a multitude into a group and supplies the goals for social action. The strength of the group depends on the appeal of the ideas and on the interests and needs to which the ideas correspond. The type of structure of the group is also paramount.[2]

In a sociological sense, a political party is an institution. The state is an integral institution, uniting a complex institutional system. In consequence, the study of international relations, in a sociological sense, is focussed primarily on processes between groups or institutions. Even commercial international relations are in a sense "institutionalized," in that they are conducted by corporations or companies rather than by individuals.

The states and other institutions control types of power, essential in either a process of tension or one of effective cooperation. Power is the ability to enforce decisions, and the decisions are enforced by actions of the group. Power, in a sense, is the capacity of a group to move toward a definite goal. However, we may draw a line dividing relations between states from those between all other groups and institutions, and this differentiation seems to be relevant.

"International relations" is a general term, used in a variety of meanings for a complex system of processes and relations. In an outdated sense, it is used to identify relationships between the states conforming to certain usages and norms.

Formal conventional relations between the states are guided by diplomatic customs and ideal norms, while the actual practice deviates strongly from normative standards. Our purpose is to classify the real (empirical facts) rather than the normative —the social processes between states and national groups that can be observed and verified. The subject matter is "what is" rather than "what ought to be."

The empirical reality is very different from the juridical or quasi-juridical norms. Major risks in foreign politics arise when one power tries to act solely according to such norms, while the other one acts outside the accepted, normative pattern of international conduct. For example, Great Britain tried to restrain German expansion under Hitler by diplomatic negotiations, while the Nazi Party extended its power by internal coups (revolutions from above) and seizure of power (from below), as in Austria.

I shall limit my discussion to the structure of international relations. This classification differentiates the types of international processes according to the structure and function of the interacting groups and institutions.

It is suggested that relations between the states differ from relationships between all other types of groups. We shall call them interpolitical relations. The state has a monopoly of "legitimate physical power," that is, it controls the means of violence and physical power, the weapons and the men—in short, the military establishment. In a practical analysis, the government forms the "locus" of power and is a center of decisions. True, an "informal power center" may exercise control over the "formal government." But even in this case, the government is the "locus," controlling the entire complex bureaucratic and military structure. Formal decisions are made by the government. In terms of communications, the decision becomes a "message" fed into the channels of the bureaucratic structure. It then becomes an order, command, or resolution. The decision is executed as communication is moved from one organizational link to another. Once a "message" is enforced, it produces changes in a political environment.

Since the government has a legitimate monopoly of physical power, it can also enforce its decisions by force, within the limits of accepted and observed standards of behavior. Such standards are more or less rigorously observed by governments based on democratic legitimacy. Totalitarian governments, which do not observe such standards, sometimes have a tactical advantage of surprise in a short-range approach.

Governments develop interpolitical relationships on a variety of levels and by a multiplicity of methods. They have a number of instruments at their disposal, such as diplomatic apparatus, military establishments, mass communications, directly or indirectly controlled commercial or industrial corporations, and public or private banks. In a tension situation, a government may limit itself to diplomatic pressures, but it is also capable of using military pressures, economic pressures, and/or propaganda. We shall call these instrumental levels, since they represent a variety of levels of operation.

The field of international relations is not limited to the interpolitical. Groups and individuals of various nations maintain "international relations" within the framework created by the interpolitical system of relations, usually more or less independent of the coercive system of the state. An open society—a democratic state—permits such relations, reserving only certain limited areas of operations for itself. A totalitarian state controls its citizens rigidly; nevertheless, even in such a state some informal relations never disappear.

In any border area, licit or illicit relations usually develop between the inhabitants of neighboring states who live in close proximity to the border, despite limits set up by boundary lines. This is just as true of the United States-Mexican border area as it is of the Canadian-United States or the Swiss-Italian. Borderlines foster the development of specific social and international relations.

Economic development of the border area is frequently influenced by the international frontier. Certain industries and enterprises flourish, thanks to the frontier, and decline when it is changed. In a totalitarian state, however, the borders may be closed and tightly guarded, reducing communications. But even concrete walls have holes. Man's will to communicate is stronger than the inanimate matter of stone and iron.

Such relations are not interpolitical, because they are determined by "private" groups (not a state or government), although some groups of this type may attempt to influence the governments and their policies. We shall call this entire field of relations, for want of a better term, intergroup relations. The state is an integral institution, and has a legitimate monopoly of physical power. These groups are of a different structure from the state, and do not legitimately control the means of violence.

Prewar Silesia, a border area touching on Poland, Czechoslovakia, and Germany, may serve as an example. At the time, the area was inhabited by Germans, Poles, and Czechs. Certain eastern parts had dense concentrations of Poles, others of Germans and, in the southwest, of Czechs. Large sections, however, had what was primarily a mixed population. Similar areas can be found in the Balkans: for instance, Dobrudja, Macedonia, and Northern Epirus. Dobrudja was inhabited by Bulgarians and Rumanians, but there were also other minorities, such as Turks.

In spite of tensions, there was substantial cooperation between the ethnic groups of Silesia. German and Polish labor organizations were closely associated. Czechs and Poles cooperated in the fields of labor, cooperatives, and cultural activities. But there were tensions between nationalistic groups. Stereotyping of nationalities was a general practice, and prejudice was present among many groups. Individual prejudice gained impetus through "institutionalization." Institutes and political parties were dedicated to nationalistic goals.

Such parties did not represent the ideology of peaceful cooperation among nationalities. Ethnic tensions were similarly ideological in nature. The goal was elimination of other minorities or the establishment of the primacy of a dominant nation. Prejudice was intensified through party organizations, with a variety of nationalistic associations and pseudo-scientific institutes supporting the cause of extreme nationalism. In consequence, intergroup ethnic tensions were intensified, and led at times to direct violent action.

Interethnic tensions in a border area can be artificially intensified and organized. Once ethnic or racial hostility is expressed by political parties, ethnic tensions become ideological. Such ideological interethnic tensions can be either intra- or interpolitical. As long as these movements are subject to the policies and actions of the sovereign government of the tension area, the tension is intrapolitical. If two or more neighboring governments are involved, the tension becomes interpolitical. However, intergroup tensions in an area may be primarily ideological. For instance, the present tensions in Southeast Asia are primarily ideological, social-economic, and political, not ethnic, in nature. Ideological tensions as a rule move rapidly into the level of the international-political (interpolitical). For the time being, and for the sake of simplicity, we will limit our discussion to interethnic tensions.

The paramount problem in interethnic tensions is the policy of a government toward such tensions. The government usually controls, directly or indirectly, a number of public and semi-private institutions. In a centrally organized system, such as prewar Germany, Poland, Yugoslavia, or Italy, the government may act through its elaborate bureaucratic apparatus, as well as through the school system. Even in a less centralized system, it may exercise pressure or persuasion on provincial governments, municipalities, or school systems. The government may attempt to win political parties and churches to one or another policy. In other words, it may use the existing network of institutions, the "institutional apparatus," for an ethnic or racial policy.

Every modern society has an elaborate network of public and private institutions, and the actions of those institutions may either reduce the tensions to a stalemate or intensify them. History has given numerous examples of artificial intensification of such tensions. It was practiced before World War I by the Czarist government, and later, between the two world wars, by the German and some South and East European governments. As long as the government remains neutral or makes an effort toward reduction of tensions, the intergroup tensions remain interethnic and sometimes intrapolitical in nature. Such tensions are not international. They can be reduced by techniques such as were developed in the United States or eased by extensive educational programs, mass communication, and psychological and sociological techniques.

Alto Adige on the Austrian border of northern Italy may serve as an example of intergroup ethnic tensions of the fifties. The area is inhabited by Italians and a German-speaking minority with a historical and nationalist tradition remaining from its ties with the old Austrian empire. During the Napoleonic wars, South

Tyrol (today Alto Adige) offered resistance and, led by Andreas Hofer, developed its own unique struggle against Napoleonic rule. Later, as a result of World War I and of secret treaties (1915), South Tyrol became a part of Italy. After World War II, the Statute Act of 1948 created the autonomous region of Trentino Alto Adige.

In the late 1950's, tensions increased between the German-speaking groups, led by the South Tyrolese People's Party, and the Italian population and authorities. These tensions were of an interethnic nature. No doubt the nationalistic tendencies of the German-speaking population played a role in this formerly Austrian area, especially in 1959. Eventually, after strong complaints and manifestations by the South Tyrolese People's Party in 1957, direct negotiations began between the Austrian and Italian governments and the problem was later discussed in the United Nations (1960). In this way an interethnic, intrapolitical tension became interpolitical and eventually was eased. Thus we see that in certain cases, transformation of an interethnic or interracial tension into interpolitical form may reduce tension. This was true to some extent in Alto Adige. Of course, the tension did not wholly disappear.[3] Nevertheless, it is controlled and a continous effort is made to ease. The social-political structure of Alto Adige reinforces ethnic antagonisms. The Austrian Germans control business and generally the economic life of the area. In general terms, economic power is largely controlled by the Austrian-German minority, while political power is controlled by the Italians, who serve in the public administration and police force. There is also a difference in culture, and generally in attitudes and behavior, especially between the "old, native population" and the newcomers from the Italian South. Attempts are, however, made to remedy the situation and create conditions conducive to reduction.

The situation changes, however, when an outside government directly or indirectly supports such tension on various "instrumental levels," and uses it for its own strategic purposes. In such a situation the tension changes to a complex one (intergroup and interpolitical).

The Nazi government supported German nationalist movements in the Sudeten area of Czechoslovakia, where Czechs and Germans had lived together for centuries. Prior to World War I, the Sudetenland had been under Austrian rule. After 1918, the territory became a part of the Czechoslovak Republic. Although there were some latent tensions, the prewar Austrian government neither supported nor instigated them. In consequence, any tensions present were of local significance, and were not very noticeable in this prosperous region.

With Hitler's advent to power, an aggressive party was organized by the local German nationalists. This party grew rapidly in significance, and the German government supported it with all its power. Its tactics were intensification of tension; strategy, capture of the area, and eventual conquest of Czechoslovakia. At the last stage of development, German strategists used two fronts: (1) *external,* pressing on the Czechoslovak borders, and (2) *internal,* using the Sudeten party and intensifying ethnic hostilities and aggression within the Czechoslovak Republic.[4] We call this type of tension within a given area *complex* (interpolitical and intergroup). The intergroup tension was both ideological and ethnic. The Sudeten German Nazis acted against the Czechs, but also against various kinds of democratic groups and orientation in this area, either Czech or German.

There are, however, tensions which are fundamentally interpolitical in nature. Berlin of the present time belongs in this category. It is, in fact, a tension area between the Eastern and Western blocs. The tensions have been "decided" upon and initiated. The fact remains that an ethnic intergroup tension between the East and West Germans does not exist. There has been a real exodus of East Germans to West Germany. There is, however, an interpolitical tension between the German Democratic and German Federal republics, a reflection of the larger East-West tension. Experience teaches that ethnic and racial tensions, especially those which reflect class antagonism and collective psychological hostilities may reach to an explosive point beyond institutional control. The institutional framework breaks down and direct violent action takes over. Not all tensions, however, are of such intense nature.

Structural classes

In consequence, we can divide tension areas into two major *types*—primary and secondary—and three major *structural classes:* a) interpolitical; b) intergroup; and c) complex intergroup and interpolitical.

Ideological intergroup tensions within an area have often been intensified and "escalated" from intergroup to interpolitical and complex. Such tensions can be fostered also by imported, well-organized, ideological "cadre parties." [5] This type of strategy has frequently been used by outside governments, controlled by a totalitarian party. The militant political party and the political, ideological attack are of primary significance in a pattern of seizure of a tension area of a certain type. The army or military units on one hand, and the party on the other, constitute parallel social forces. The outside power acts in turn because of its political, ideological, or economic objectives. Ideology may serve also as a rationalization of military action, the real objectives being power and political expansion or conquest of economic resources, areas of important raw materials or markets.

The division of tensions into interpolitical and intergroup types seems to be relevant. However, both levels are frequently confused by well-meaning experts. Easing of intergroup tensions, especially ethnic tensions, requires different techniques than do the interpolitical. The interethnic tensions can probably be eased in certain cases with the assistance of the government controlling the tension area, or with the support of the neighboring government, through a variety of psychological and sociological techniques similar to those applied in *sui generis* racial and ethnic tension areas in the large cities of the United States. Formal and informal education plays an important role here. Mass communication is used with various degrees of effectiveness. Workshops on intergroup relations are organized, the economic conditions of minorities are explored, and policies are developed to meet economic needs, increase employment, and improve housing.

Ideological, interpolitical, primary tensions were and are usually reduced beyond the local level by direct negotiations and decisions of the governments of the great powers. Such decisions are made on an interpolitical level. However, ideological tensions are difficult to ease when goals and values are incompatible. In such a case, the risk of total defeat, the assessment of superior power, may lead to a reduction of tension on a global level and result in new, limited forms of conflict. Subsequent ideological changes or alterations in distribution of political power within the militant parties may also result in a reduction or intensification of tension.

Economic exploitation is not the full explanation of every tension. The example of the Sudeten German Nazis and their hostile actions against the Czechs was indicative of the ideological tensions based on values (racist ideology) as well as social-psychological needs. The Sudeten nationalists were a prosperous group. They were neither underprivileged nor an object of specific economic or political exploitation. Theirs was an ethnic revolt of the economically prosperous in quest of political power and status and of economic privilege. The tension was not "monocausal," a "sequent" of one, decisive economic "antecedent." [6]

But tension areas are more often reflections of broader and deeper issues, and their reduction depends on the solution of fundamental problems. Political oppression, misery, economic exploitation, and class tensions which breed social unrest and dissatisfaction belong in this area. The uneven distribution of property and income, combined with economic exploitation, produces tensions. Division of property, especially of land, is a result of conquest in many countries. In consequence, it follows ethnic lines. Ruling classes of conquerors control large land holdings. This was true in the Spanish conquest of South America, and was also true in Eastern Europe.

When foreign companies acquire large land holdings, it is usually by purchase. In such cases the labor force is largely native, while control of the property is foreign. Although exploitation by native owners is often more oppressive than that pursued by foreign companies, ethnic differences supply elements of conflict and of additional psychological impetus (they facilitate the process of displacement of aggression). Thus, ethnic tensions may reflect much deeper class tensions, and their easing requires substantial, mostly fundamental, social and economic changes.

It is not my purpose in this chapter to analyze extensively the causes of such tensions. I wish to indicate only that tensions may be caused by conflict of economic interest and of values (ideologies), and that a race or ethnic prejudice is a result of social and psychological factors.[7]

The nature of structural approach; major concepts

The concept of the structure of international relations is an operational device. The suggested structural analysis does not mirror the entire picture of the complex nature of international relations, or the entire sociology of the society of states (which C. A. W. Manning called the jungle of diplomacy) in its institutionalized symbolic manifestations. Why, then, has this frame of reference been suggested?

First of all, any analysis requires a certain order, a system. In such an orderly approach to social-political phenomena, the variables must be reduced. The purpose of this "reductionism" is to single out the essential, relevant variables within a complex matrix of human relations, and is a matter of logical convenience. The indicated variables are only a part of the total picture.

In a sense, a painter reduces elements analogously. A conventional photograph faithfully presents all the details of a given landscape. A painter sketching the same landscape decides what *not to paint*. He selects only certain elements, a few details, and in that way gives us a reflection of reality, frequently more plastic than the conventional photograph.

The concept of a "structure of international relations" is not new. In a somewhat different sense, C. A. W. Manning applies this concept to an "international milieu" as a "complex" of social relations that is reflected in a multiplicity of interacting elements (particularly power, authority, influence, and prestige). This international milieu is then a "network of interlinkages" in "the world of politics, the jungle of diplomacy." [8]

The classification of this paper reduces the concept of the structure of relations. In our case, the study of international relations is problem oriented; accordingly, the approach and method follow this orientation.

The approach is based on two, or respectively, four major concepts: (1) The process or action approach to international relations; (2) The structure of international relations: the nature and classes of groups involved in a process (a) interpolitical, (b) intergroup, (c) complex.

Relationships between complex integral institutions—states—that have a monopoly of physical power are called interpolitical. Relationships between other institutions, groups, or "abstract collectives" (to use Wiese's concepts for unstructured social aggregates united by interest or values, such as a social class or nationality) are called "intergroup." The combination of both is called "complex." The process and structure are closely related. The "escalation" of tensions in tension areas frequently moves from social or ethnic tensions (interethnic) to internal political, with one state involved (intrapolitical); and with further intensification into the third stage, of international political (interpolitical) tensions when at least two governments (states) are involved. We have called this process of intensification "the antagonistic sequence" or "cycle," since it may begin from "below," as a social or race tension, or "on the top," on the interpolitical level. (In Part III of this work I have detailed case studies and examples of such processes.)

The analysis of tensions involves two additional concepts: (3) evaluation of major types of tensions and of the powers involved; primary and secondary tensions. To put this into a Hegelian formula: the quantity of power of governments and the quantity (intensity) of antagonism transform the tension from one of local significance to a general or global tension; (4) ranking of tensions according to their significance as an international problem and their practical pragmatic significance as a matter of peace or antagonism leading to an open conflict as (a) critical, (b) near-critical, (c) consequential, and (d) noncritical.[9]

The sequence is both logical and analytical. Analysis of a concrete case involves all four classifications. The two initial problems and analyses are primarily sociological; the two latter, political.

In 1936 Bronislaw Malinowski pointed to the difference between primitive and modern warfare.[10] It was the emergence of the state that made the difference. In this respect Malinowski's theory can be traced to the evolutionary school, as well as to Gumplovich's theory of state.

Later, in comparative studies of primitive and modern warfare, Malinowski drew a distinction between tribe-nation and tribe-state, which he developed into the concept of nation-culture and nation-state.[11] Tribe-nation represents the tribe as a cultural group (using the word "culture" in the anthropological sense), while tribe-state is the tribe in its "political" sense: an "integral" institution with a monopoly of physical power and a warrior class. He regarded this definition of a tribe as a political or a social unit as essential. In consequence, he argued that the "two principles of statehood and nationality must be kept apart in theory, even as they are different in cultural reality." The two do not coincide. We have instances of a tribe-state as a subdivision of a tribe-nation: the Maori in New Zealand, the Trobriand Islanders, and the Zulu serve as examples.

In other cases, many tribe-nations are united in one tribe-state, and here Malinowski gives examples from East and West Africa. Similar instances can be indicated in advanced societies: Austro-Hungary prior to 1914, a monarchy (nation-state) of fourteen or fifteen nationalities (nation-cultures); or the Germany of many nation-states (nation-cultures) before the Napoleonic wars. Malinowski defines nationhood (nation-culture) as unity of culture: the way of life of a nation, its ideals, traditions, and culture.[12]

There are, of course, two types of relations: between (1) nation-states and (2) nation-cultures. From a theoretical viewpoint, the two should be clearly distinguished, since they are of a different nature. This leads to a further distinction between interpolitical and intercultural relations. The former are relations between nation-states; the latter, between nation-cultures.[13] Such a classification (suggested at first) sharply reduces the variables, but fails to indicate adequately the complex nature of modern international relations. In a practical analysis (intended as a basis for an "opinion" or "decision") it is advisable to classify such relationships which are functionally different into separate subcategories. We shall mention here relations between economic groups (such as banks or corporations) that reflect self-interest, or relationships between social-political movements (such as political parties) that are the result of common values (ideologies) and/or interests.

The term "intergroup" is perhaps more appropriate than the term "intercultural," since it is "operational" and "generic" in nature. It can be used for a variety of relationships, such as interethnic, intereconomic, and so on.

A structural approach introduces some order and sequence in a case study. But relationships are not separate blocs: the interpolitical and intergroup relations are mutually interacting and interwoven. The state influences political and economic relationships, while the economy and social-political movements have their influence on the policy of the state.

The structure of international relations reflects causal relationships, but is not, *per se,* a theory of causation or interaction. It is primarily a classificatory device.

In summary, we may classify tensions under two major categories: primary and secondary. Both primary and secondary tensions may be divided into three major classes: 1] interpolitical, 2] intergroup, and 3] complex.

Intergroup tensions may be divided into a number of subclasses, such as interethnic, interideological, intereconomic. The government which supports conditions causing an international tension may operate on a variety of levels (diplomatic, military, propaganda). In an operational analysis, the political action is the decisive one. We shall define the interpolitical area of actions as one comprising the decisions and actions of the government in power.

Intergroup tensions, especially racial and ethnic tensions of certain types, can often be controlled and eased in an initial stage (prior to the development of antagonistic racist and nationalist, or national-liberation movements, based on definite ideology, using political strategy). Social sciences, such as sociology, psychology, and political science, have advanced to a point where they can give us some understanding of problems, and suggest the line of actions, provided public and private agencies on both sides are willing to work toward such an effect.[14]

The situation changes, however, in tension areas where serious social problems are involved and where an ethnic majority suffers exploitation from an outside colonial power. In such cases, self-determination and emancipation may pave the way for a reduction of tensions. But the emancipation sometimes displaces only the ruling elites or oligarchies.

Elites grow rapidly and frequently move into a military power structure. A top-heavy bureaucratic and military class may grow exploitative. Its program of economic development may be directed toward a "status economy," such as the building of uneconomic steelmills, impressive buildings, and monuments to "redeemers," "benefactors," or whatever name is assumed by those who control power. In such cases the population gets little and continues to be exposed to many hazards, including impure water or poor sanitation. The emancipated elite may also use their newly won power to impose their rule over still weaker nations. In such cases, which occurred frequently in history, emancipation or liberation is only a short interlude in the reduction of tensions in a given area.

The principle of self-determination and emancipation in a tension area was also used as a method of seizure of territory. Therefore, a democratic, national emancipation must be integrated with a program of fundamental social-economic

Political and cultural autonomy still remains the basic concept, as Franklin Frazier in his *Race and Culture Contacts* indicates. It is perhaps only a stage toward a more rational and advanced international system.

The transformation of a tension area into an internal front, whatever the ideological content, may be indicative of a coming change in international balance. A combination of an internal and external front is strategy. It may be used for a variety of ideological objectives—to establish a socially progressive and democratic rule in a given tension area or emancipate a nation from colonial rule—but it may also be used by a neighboring and expanding power to extend territorial claims. Whatever the normative evaluation, an empirical analysis will register a change in distribution of power indicative of forces working toward a change in the temporary equilibrium.

5.

ETHNIC AND RACIAL MINORITIES

The Historical Origin of Tensions

Subclasses of intergroup tensions

In our previous discussion a distinction was made between relations between states, which we called interpolitical relations, and relations between other social groups, called intergroup relations. The state has a monopoly of physical power. In consequence, relationships between governments and states are of a specific nature and significance in international relations. But, interpolitical and intergroup relations are by no means wholly separated compartments. On the contrary, they are interdependent. The government may influence interethnic relations by its intervention and its policies. On the other hand, the relationships between ethnic, ideological, or interest groups influence the policies of a government.

It was also indicated that the term "intergroup tension" includes a variety of relationships and categories. Economic tensions between two different nationalities, as well as other types of tensions, belong to this group.

From the entire class of intergroup relations we shall select two major characteristics for our discussion of intergroup relations and tensions. Using "ethnicity" or "nationality" and political ideology as central characteristics, we shall discuss intergroup tensions and intergroup relations.

Racial tensions are significant, since they are closely related to ethnicity. The difference in physical anthropological characteristics, *per se,* does not interest us here. However, the attitude between social groups with different physical characteristics is of sociological interest; it is a result of culture. Prejudice, according to current theories, is a result of learning, and in this respect is closely related to similar ethnic or religious attitudes toward an out-group or an "anti-group." There is, however, a difference in identification. In a matter of racial tension in Java, in Alabama, or the Transvaal, racial groups can be easily identified. Africa has an abundance of ethnic-racial tensions between various racial groups or subgroups of native stock, to mention only the Watusi and their former subjects, the Bahutu's. Here also, the physical identification of difference simplifies the process of channelling hostility against a definite target and contributes to a specific intensity of hostility. The development of symbolism and prejudice against a "symbolic color" (black as everything negative, white all positive; the devil is black, the angels are white) continuously reinforces the prejudice.

It may be a part of man's psychological apparatus that he reacts to difference with suspicion and hostility rather than with sympathy. And primitive in- and out-groups can readily be identified by headgear, paint, or feathers. Thus group identification by means of bodily "signs" probably arose in the early phase of man's development. Difference in physical characteristics in a primitive society forms both a "natural" symbol of group identification and a barrier, a divide, against the out-group. Strong tribal hostility toward out-groups is an evidence of ancient primitive attitudes, rooted probably in early clashes with the anti-groups.[1]

"Ethnic" hostility and tensions are often far more intensive than "racial" ones. With all the racial tensions in the United States, New York City race and ethnic tensions are far less intensive than those between Greeks and Turks on the island of Cyprus. No one suggests partition of New York City as the only alternative; no major party or social movement advocates limitation of minority rights, although the prejudice is by no means absent.

It is difficult to distinguish "racially" a Greek Cypriot from a Turkish Cypriot. Still, the hostility between them is today far more intensive than "racial" tensions which do exist in New York City among the local Puerto Rican, Negro, and white population of Jewish, Catholic, or Protestant ancestry.

We shall therefore discuss the interethnic and racial tensions, as well as related religious tensions, in the same chapter.

Race divisions do exist on a world scale, and the answer to racial tensions on a global level is a major issue of our century. The political division of the world on racial lines will sooner or later intensify conflicts. Ideologies, rationalization of interests, psychological or psychopathological needs of totalitarian leaders in this area exercise a cumulative effect. It is a matter of democratic political strategy to prevent the formation of racial blocs and to build the future around universal values.

Tensions and antagonisms between various groups exist in a variety of forms in all industrialized and advanced societies. Economic or other forms of antagonism are not characteristics of international relations alone. Two or three companies within a country which compete for the same market may express a quality of antagonism in their competition. This type of antagonism is, of course, outside our interest. The tension becomes relevant for our studies at the point when the antagonism is reinforced or identified as between economic groups of different ethnic or national origin and where the hostilities may become interethnic, racial or, respectively, interideological and interpolitical.

The terms "ethnicity" and "ethnic" correspond roughly to "nationhood," and identify cultural differences ("culture" in an anthropological sense) which can be perceived in values, institutions, language, and even diet or food patterns.

Ideological differences are differences in political values and goal orientations as well as in patterns of political actions (strategy, tactics) and situational analysis (theory). Ideological movements reflect social-economic interests, psychological needs, and/or collective goal orientation.

Tensions are frequently complex in nature. In our discussion of interethnic relations and tensions we select a "vantage point." Our vantage point is at this time nationhood (ethnicity) or ideology. What we first perceive is a tension between two groups which are ethnically or ideologically different. But we do not stop there. On the contrary, we continue by asking the question: What is the origin or the nature of the antagonism between these two groups?

Differences in language, customs, values, and behavior patterns result sometimes in suspicion, even hostility. Values may be incompatible; ideas, antagonistic. In a closer scrutiny, the ethnic differences may have deeper roots than the external ones. Ethnic hostility may reflect economic antagonism of a complex nature, and ethnic differences may coincide with economic differences. Furthermore, frustrations, repressed urges, and hostility may be displaced and move in the direction of a weaker and different group. In such a case, the ethnic nature of tensions reflects deep-seated psychological needs, sometimes, collective psychopathological phenomena. Frustrations and hostilities, when developed in large numbers of individuals, appear in organized forms, in social movements and political parties, and are rationalized in ideologies directed against racial or ethnic groups. Thus an ethnic or ideological tension reflects psychological urges, differences of values, or economic antagonism. But on the surface it appears as a simple struggle between two ethnically different groups. Every tension has dominant causal factors. As a matter of method, those major factors should be selected and identified and their significance indicated.

"Statistical" and "political" minorities

In this study we are concerned with tensions in limited geographical areas. We shall limit the many kinds of intergroup tensions to two major subclasses: ethnic (also racial) and ideological. In a problem study, these are the major subclasses of intergroup tensions which lead to intensive local and general tensions and are reflected or manipulated in international politics. These tensions present specific types of problems. From internal political (intrapolitical) they have frequently been "escalated" into interpolitical (or international political), and have led to major conflicts. In Parts II and III of this volume I shall limit the inquiry on ethnic tensions, since ideological and interpolitical tensions are the subject matter of Part IV.

As was indicated, the variables are related. Interethnic tensions are frequently ideological and social-economic in nature. Thus, reduction is primarily a matter of vantage point. Focussing the inquiry on one major causal factor or variable (we may call this the selection of a vantage point) determines the procedure of inquiry. We start with the selected variable. Initially, this is viewed as an antecedent; the others, as sequent. Later the interaction of variables appears. The accent of the inquiry, however, remains steady.

Interethnic tensions occur on a nationwide scale, but they may also appear with greater intensity in limited areas. Usually tensions occur in "limitrophic" areas, comprising border regions with two or more nationalities or ethnic groups. In such areas as Kossovo, Macedonia, Silesia, Saarland, Sikiang, for example, a number of ethnically or racially different groups live in the same area. Some of these groups are called "minorities." However, a political or ethnic minority is not identical with a statistical minority.[2]

The term "national minority" has been used historically for the identification of a political group which does not exercise full political power or play a dominant role in power distribution. Usually the minority is smaller in number than the dominant ethnic group within the national state. Thus, in all of Cyprus, the Turks form a minority, but in a specific village they may form a majority. In Greece, the Bulgarians in one village may form a majority. In the whole of Greece, however, Slavic-speaking people are in the minority. Accordingly, we may distinguish the "statistical minority" and the "political minority." The former identifies numerical quantity; the latter, ethnicity and distribution of power. For the sake of simplicity we shall use the term "minority" without an identifying adjective to denote ethnic grouping and political position.

In many areas a number of ethnic or racial groups have lived together for centuries. In everyday parlance we speak of "France," "Germany," "Italy," or "Greece." The general reader has the impression that these are monolithic, homogeneous nations composed only of people of the same origin and traditions. Actually, it is difficult to find any state which consists of only one homogeneous ethnic group. Practically every European state, whether in the west, east, or south, has a number of minorities. Italy, for example, has inhabitants of very ancient origin who maintain the traditions of their ancestors. But one also finds Albanian villages in the south; Slovene minorities in the northeast; and Austrian-German minorities in the north.

Ethnic and regional subcultures

Cultural and ethnic differences exist within the same nation-culture. Subcultures, or subnations (as such cultural subgroups are called), are closely related to the dominant ethnic pattern. Similarly, differences in language are called dialects, although they are substantially different languages used by subcultures. Where does the "subculture" end and a new "ethnicity" begin? This depends on whether the differences are considered with a view to discovering self-identification ("subjective nationhood" or "ethnicity") or a distinct culture and language ("objective nationhood"). Sometimes both types (subjective and objective) coincide. The Amish of Pennsylvania use a different language (Pennsylvania Dutch). Their culture values, institutions, and even their material culture are distinct. But the Amish are generally regarded as an American subculture. A Sicilian represents an Italian subculture. His language is distinct, it is more than a slight variation; so is (perhaps to a lesser degree) the "Neapolitan dialect." Those regional differences are strong enough to prompt an American-Italian to identify himself as *"sono Calabrese"* or *"sono Siciliano,"* rather than simply *"sono Italiano."* Such regional identity among Italian immigrants remains strong.

Generally, geographical distribution of a nationality is reflected in cultural differences. In consequence, we may distinguish regional subcultures (an American "Southerner" represents some of those differences) and ethnic subcultures (for instance American-Italian, within the general American cultural pattern). Frequently ethnic and regional subgroups coincide.

Regional, often ethnic, subcultural differences are a result of geographical distribution. Different environment influences culture. A tightly knit community in a given locality has more intense relations within its own group than with an outside world. This contributes to the development of a vernacular and culture corresponding to local needs. Even in an Indian reservation, differences develop between sections of a tribe which live in different neighborhoods. Relative isolation, cultural or geographical, contributes to the maintenance and development of subcultural differences. A self-segregated ethnic group in New York City may be "culturally" more isolated than a fisherman on a Maine island who visits the mainland periodically and whose isolation is "geographical." Ethnic subcultures are frequently viewed as "minorities"; regional parts of the "core-nation."

Historical origins of minorities

In border areas, especially those of commercial or industrial significance, ethnic heterogeneity is frequent. What is the origin of those ethnic groups? How does one explain the variety of racial and ethnic groups in certain areas?

Archeological evidence and historical records indicate that man is essentially a migratory being, and group migration is as ancient as man. Man migrates, but he also tends to develop permanent settlements in areas that he finds favorable for his development or at least adequate for his survival. The origin of those ethnic groups in limited tension areas is of practical significance, and we shall dwell on this issue more extensively. The origin or pattern of arrival of those ethnic groups may have something to do with the beginning of antagonism in a given area. Later, although the original causes of antagonism disappear, prejudice, as an individual and collective psychological attitude, remains and is perpetuated. On the other hand, the ethnic origin is relevant as a symbol or an argument in the reinforcement or manipulation of the antagonism or the prejudice.

Not every ethnic antagonism is the result of "prejudice" alone. The general practice in intergroup relations suggests that most ethnic antagonisms are based on prejudice and falsified stereotypes. However, hostility toward the German conqueror in Poland was not necessarily due to a "stereotype" or to "prejudice," since the German policy of extermination resulted in antagonistic attitudes toward the conquerors as a group. The antagonism was not the result of false "stereotypes" but of a real situation in which the very survival of the conquered group was threatened.

Antagonistic situations of course have led to the development of "stereotypes" and later have propagated "prejudice" against an entire population. But originally, antagonism as a collective phenomenon was the result of a conflict situation connected with conquest and exploitation.

The way a "social image" develops is related, if not integrated, with values and attitudes. A strong "traumatic" experience reinforces certain values and beliefs, which in turn influence perception. Our pattern of perception influences the selection and relating of facts used for our inferences. Those inferences in turn change into a general view or "category." The dominant experience usually sets the direction in development of a "social-image." Only a critical and self-controlled individual builds his inferences on carefully selected "affirmatives" and "negatives."

A distinction should be made between intergroup and interpersonal relations. In certain areas antagonistic attitudes appear in intergroup relations, while interpersonal relations frequently remain friendly. For example, an antagonistic situation had existed between Germans and Poles in Silesia as representatives of the German national groups and the Polish national group. Nonetheless, between individual Poles and individual Germans, as well as between certain Polish and German political groups, the relations were friendly. The same person who could express antagonism against an entire ethnic group could still maintain friendship with a single person or a few individuals in the area. This distinction is relevant, since ethnic antagonism involves collective behavior and group values.[3]

As was mentioned, the origins of antagonism have historical roots. Ethnic antagonism could have originated because of conquest or exploitation. An "anti-group," against which antagonism is directed, might well have been classed as "newcomers." The newcomer to most areas is regarded as having weaker rights to a given territory than the autochthonic population, since primitive concepts of legitimacy are usually rooted in the idea of early occupancy. The present situation, however, might be entirely different. The problem is the development of relationship between various ethnic groups, and this is largely normative. Historical tradition, political ideologies, and values are significant in intergroup relations.

Today, from a rational and humane viewpoint, the problem is how the various ethnic groups, who by a coincidence of history find themselves in the same territory, can live together peacefully as good neighbors, assisting each other in their mutual problems and needs. This would be a rational and reasonable outlook. Someone else may suggest a less humane solution, namely, that minority A, which settled in "Beotia" in 990 B.C., should expel minority B, which arrived 999 A.D., and restore "the historical border"; or that ethnic group B should be transferred forcibly to another territory. A hard-working Albanian laborer in Kossovo, or a Serb farmer in the same area, is not usually familiar with the full history of his origin. He does not know nor care very much who came first and who came second. But this historical information can be transmuted into symbols and used to reinforce existing hostilities or even manipulated to produce hostilities.

There is a difference between the historical origin and the reinforcement and manipulation of antagonistic traditions. Historical origins have to do with the historical veracity and with the sociological nature of the phenomenon, and they are relevant for a number of reasons. First, they help us to understand the origins of the antagonism and, in consequence, of certain values and attitudes.

Prejudice contains a negative value. A negative image of an ethnic group against which the hostility of others is directed contains certain values. In consequence, knowing the historical origin of such antagonism permits us to understand at least the beginnings of those attitudes, values, and social images, or the roots of certain ideologies. However, the process of reinforcement can be developed without a clear objective or intensifying antagonism. If a prejudice or antagonism against a group is already expressed, then the history and nature of its origin, discovered by the younger generation in their school manuals and textbooks, may reinforce the existing hostilities even without the intervention of the government. It depends on the nature of historical facts. But a party or a government may reinforce this antagonism by falsifying or manipulating the information and transforming it into political symbols which can be easily manipulated. Manipulation involves the conscious reinforcement of antagonism. Without a tendency toward manipulation, exposure to an experience or to historical information may still result in the reinforcement of antagonism.

Exposure to information that the British people are ruled by an elective government, without any further manipulation, may result in antagonism against British colonial rule. On the other hand, historical information about a lost battle in Ethiopia was manipulated by Mussolini and the Fascists as a symbol to intensify antagonism against the Ethiopians.

As I have mentioned before, the areas where tensions appear are frequently inhabited by an ethnically mixed population. Sometimes one may distinguish two, three, or even four different ethnic groups in the same village, each speaking a different language, dressing differently, and having different food habits. This variety of ethnic groups may be found in practically any American or European and in most Asiatic urban centers. As in the tension areas, the variety of nationalities in a large city is the result of migration, but here the comparison ends. In tension areas the variety of ethnic groups is the result of specific types of migration.

As we shall see, there are many types of migration. Migration is also an economic phenomenon and results in certain types of social and political patterns. It may produce different class structures and social relations. In consequence, class structure or occupational distribution frequently coincides in such areas with ethnic differences. Thus, competition or class tension coincides with ethnic tensions. The projection of class structure into ethnic divisions has a cumulative effect on the nature of conflict. A class conflict automatically becomes an ethnic conflict, and ethnic conflicts in turn intensify the class antagonism.

Our classification of migrations is not an a priori one, but is based on historical experience and relevance for our subject matter. Here, the migrations are classified according to their effect on ethnic diversification and development of tensions. Accordingly, we may distinguish the following migratory movements: 1] war; 2] colonization; 3] integral mass migration; 4] forced population transfers; 5] optional population transfers; 6] chaotic displacement; 7] free immigration that is: a) assimilative, b) differential (nonassimilative), and c) complementary; 8] penetrating; and 9] nomadic. The variety of ethnic groups in tension areas is frequently a result of one or more of those migratory movements.

6.

MIGRATIONS AND TENSION AREAS

War

War and conquest also represent a specific type of migratory movement. In a lecture delivered before the medical association in Graz in 1875, Ludwik Gumplovich advanced his well-known theory of the origin of the state. In Eastern Europe, he said, the nobility represents the conquerors; the peasants, the native population. In the cities one can see the descendents of the immigrants.[1] Gumplovich's observation was correct to a certain extent, and although his theory of the origin of the state has been heavily criticized, there is a kernel of truth in it. Earlier, Ibn Khaldoun, the Arab historian and geographer of the fourteenth century, observed that everywhere in his "culture-area," one can discover the rule of the nomads. States—argued the Arabian scholar—are a creation of the conquest of the sedentary people by the nomads. In many areas of the world the emergence of a stable state and the disappearance of tribal organization coincides with conquest. The conquering elite frequently become the nobility or upper class. In that way, part of the conquering nationality appears as a ruling class, with the conquered as a subject; the ethnic division coincides to an extent with class division.

Not infrequently, the conquering elite intermarries or merges with the local aristocracies, effecting a social mechanism for the continuation of class rule. The newcomers establish themselves as landowners, governors of the provinces, or mayors of the cities. The local elites assist in the maintenance of the new power structure, and, for a time, retain some remnants of their own past glory, as in the case of the Spanish conquest of America.

Nevertheless, the ruling classes or the privileged in such areas are identified with the conquering group. The experience of Eastern Europe is instructive. Before World War II, in the Polish Ukraine, the large landowner, the nobleman, was, as a rule, of Polish descent, while the "middle" and the small peasant were frequently Ukrainian. In some villages the landlord, of "noble" origin, was a Pole; the "middle-class" farmer was Ukrainian; and the peasant was again a Pole who had settled there after serving in the manor. The class distribution followed the ethnic divisions.

In the eastern German provinces prior to 1918, the large landowner was a German or a Pole. A farmhand, however, was usually Polish. Certain classes or social elements of Germans who conquered this territory also became large landowners, although there were also German workers and craftsmen. The class division followed the ethnic division in the village. Here again the ethnic division, if not identical, coincided with the class division.

In the part of Lithuania that belonged to Poland before 1939, the large landowners were usually of Polish descent, while the peasantry was either Byelorussian, Polish, or (around Suvalki) Lithuanian. In East Prussia prior to 1939, the large landowners were German, while the farmhands were Polish.

Let us survey briefly the origin of this class and ethnic distribution. In the Ukraine, the Poles advanced as a conquering nation and established their dominant position between the fourteenth and seventeenth centuries. In the villages the land-owning classes were Polish or Polonized Ruthenian (Ukrainian) nobility. The peasant population, however, remained Ukrainian or only partially Polish. There were villages where Polish and Ukrainian populations lived together in a slow penetration of two nationalities within the same territory, resulting in areas of mixed population.

In the eastern German provinces prior to 1918 (which were western Polish provinces before the partition), the Germans came as conquerors and occupied the territory in three partitions. At the end of the eighteenth century they assumed a ruling position. They purchased land or took it away from the Poles, appearing as landed gentry coexistent with the Polish landed gentry and as prosperous middle-class farmers competing with the Polish middle-class farmers. The farmhand and the small farmer, however, remained Polish. The mixed population was also the result of the interpenetration of two populations in limitrophic areas.

In Lithuania, the situation was somewhat different. Poland and Lithuania formed a union in the fourteenth and fifteenth centuries. The Lithuanian nobility slowly acquired Polish customs, language, and the general cultural pattern, while the peasantry remained Lithuanian. Thus, the ethnic division coincided with class and cultural differences. In the limitrophic area the peasantry was Byelorussian, but the nobility identified itself as Polish. However, as a result of interpenetration and wars, the population in limitrophic areas was mixed, and at certain times ethnic differences were intensified and used for political purposes.

If we move to any other part of the world, we may discover similar phenomena. In South America the landowning class is largely of Spanish origin. Its members are the descendents of former conquerors and administrators who became the ruling upper class, while the peasantry remained largely Indian or Mestizo.

In Serbia, prior to the insurrection of 1815, the Turk, or a convert Moslem Albanian or Serb identified as a Turk, was the administrator; the Greek was the tax collector; and the Orthodox Serb was a peasant or a small trader. Here again, certain ethnic groups were identified with certain classes. Actually, not every Greek was a tax collector, nor every Turk a soldier, nor every Serb either Orthodox, a peasant, or a trader. In Bosnia and Hercegovina Serbs even became dedicated Moslems. Nonetheless, to a certain extent, the stereotype was the rule. In consequence, ethnic identification and ethnic images coincided with class images and, in a period of intergroup tension, one antagonism invigorated the other; ethnic antagonism reinforced class or social antagonisms.

The Turks appeared in the Balkans as a result of conquest between the fourteenth and seventeenth centuries. It was the Turkish defeat in Vienna at the end of the seventeenth century which marked the decline of Ottoman control of southeastern Europe. Those of the Serb nobility who tried to preserve their status converted to Islam and identified themselves with the ruling Turkish group.

War, conquest, and other forms of foreign domination usually result in changes within three major areas: 1] economics; 2] political power; and 3] military structure. In consequence, the original conquest or establishment of domination sets a direction for the development of the class structure, property distribution, and the distribution of political power. In the border areas where, because of long migrations, the population is more diversified, the three processes are intensified through national or ethnic differentiation.

Institutions have a tendency to perpetuate themselves, and so has power. In consequence, a century after the establishment of domination, certain ethnic groups are identified with definite status positions or classes. High officials and high army officers are usually recruited from the dominant nation. Of course there are exceptions, but the major pattern is usually propagated. Similarly, the pattern is reflected in class structure. In that way, after a long historical development, ethnic differences are identified with different positions in political power, in the military system, and in the social-economic system. Tensions and conflicts within those three areas are reflected in ethnic hostilities.

Colonization

What makes colonization distinct from other forms of migration? Colonization is the migration of a section of a given nation or a group of nationals to a new settlement. They bring their own economic, political, and social institutions and usually establish themselves in the new land as a compact settlement, for instance a city or a village. A colony results from the branching out of a nation to a different territory or to a different continent.

The new colony is geographically but not culturally separated from the mother country. Native institutions, as well as economic systems, religious beliefs, ideologies, and entire cultures, are continuously invigorated by visits to the motherland or by an influx of new colonists. The strength of the colony freqently depends on the motherland; in fact, in most historical cases the significance of the colony consisted in this dependence on the strength of the motherland.

A refugee and a colonist are two different things. When a refugee escapes to another country, he usually has no political or economic support, but must depend on friends or local good-will. In a highly civilized country he may rely on mutual-aid institutions and philanthropic organizations and, of course, on the legal protection granted by the host country. In less favorable conditions he seeks the support of powerful friends or earlier settlers of his own nationality, race, and religion. If his skills are important for the host nation, he may secure his position without difficulty.

It is different with the colonist. He arrives as a member of a compact group with its own institutions and economic system. Usually he brings his tools and skills and, armed with the support of his native country, he settles as an equal or a master. He is neither a servant nor a member of a subordinate group. The earlier inhabitants of the guest country soon learn that any harm done to the colonist will be avenged by the mother country or by the entire colony.

History teaches that in a long period of development, the colonists assume a dominant position. This has been the case from the time of Phoenician and Greek colonies in the Mediterranean to the establishment of English colonies in India and Africa. As a result, two types of antagonism developed: 1] between the mother country and the colony; and 2] between the colony and the earlier inhabitants of the guest country.

The first type of antagonism led to wars for independence and emancipation of the colonies from the control of the motherland. This happened in America and in other parts of the world. Once the colonies developed their own political and intellectual elite and their economic system was strong enough, there was a tendency to separate from the mother country.

The ideological and value differences should not be underestimated. In some colonies, free institutions developed to a higher degree than in the mother country. In others, nationalism germinated with time. Antagonism of the new, colonial elites grew against the old, metropolitan elites and bureaucracies which were imposed by the motherland and were no longer regarded as native; just as antagonism grew against the exploitative policies of the motherland vis-à-vis the colonies. In the struggle against the motherland the colony could sometimes win the support of the native host population. In some cases, however, the native inhabitants supported the armies of the motherland against the colonies. Once independence was achieved, the antagonism between the local population and the colonist often reappeared, frequently coinciding with class antagonism.

Colonization played an important role in the history of medieval Europe. The maritime republics, especially Venice, established colonies in the Levant and on the Mediterranean coast. The Venetian colonies were ruled by their own officials. Twice a year the Venetian fleet, escorted by warships, voyaged to the colonies[2] and contributed to the strength of the colonies vis-à-vis their surrounding populations.

After the Tartar invasion of Eastern Europe, especially of Poland, colonization began in the thirteenth century and continued during the fourteenth century. German colonists were invited to establish themselves in the ancient Polish cities or to build new cities. They came with their skills, traditions, and law. They enjoyed a number of privileges, including those of the Magdeburg Law, which later exercised a significant influence on the development of Polish legal institutions.[3]

Colonization was a result either of war or negotiation. Treaties or contracts were made with the rulers of the host territories, securing the colonizers the right to establish permanent settlement. Other colonies were built as a result of expansion and war.

Because of this development, the colonies formed cohesive and integrated economic units in a territory inhabited by ethnically different populations. They were generally more properous than the native population, representing a different culture and sometimes different skills. The colonies had a tendency to establish their rule over the entire territory. Frequently, they also had at their disposal a military force, either of their own or of the mother country. Antagonistic tendencies developed as a result of: 1] the very fact of difference in culture and the tendency to impose the dominant culture; 2] economic competition or conflict; 3] competition for political power; or 4] competition for military control of a given area.

The descendants of the colonists as a rule tried to maintain the rights secured to their ancestors by a previous government. They controlled or owned the better parts of the land and even important economic resources. In time, the nature of the old colonies changed; the native population moved into the cities of the colonists, developed native sections, and fostered the growth of cities with segregated patterns.

Modern medicine, science, and agricultural technology were frequently brought by colonists. Their public health programs and public schools frequently improved the condition of the native population. As modern economy developed and the native population lacked the skills necessary to maintain and develop a new economic and technological system, the colonists stepped in to fill the gap. It took time for the native population to develop its own skilled manpower. Nevertheless, political ideas appeared before technical skills developed fully and foreign exploitation became apparent. The colonist frequently brought an ideology and a philosophy, as well as institutions of freedom which the natives enjoyed to a certain extent, while the ideas exercised their own dynamic influence. The philosophy of freedom combined with nationalism and reinforced by economic antagonism resulted in an interethnic tension which often became interpolitical in nature.

Again in the case of colonization, the initial pattern frequently determined the development of the relationship between the newcomers and the native population in the areas of economics, politics, and culture. It influenced class structure and social-economic relations.

In certain areas where the mixed population resulted from earlier colonization, the resultant tensions reflected the original sociological pattern. Not every colonization produced tensions, but under certain conditions ethnic differences arising from colonization coincided with economic and political divisions and were intensified to interpolitical tensions.

Integral mass migrations

Integral mass migrations are more "massive" than colonization. This name was chosen arbitrarily to identify those shifts of population which embraced entire nations or tribes. These great and organized migrations usually resulted in the creation of areas of mixed population. The tribes or the nations moved in territories where there was at least some population. If they moved further, part of the tribe or nation was left behind, thus creating an area of two or more ethnic groups.

What is the difference between colonization and integral mass migration? Colonization involves two geographically separated entities: the motherland and the colony. In time, the separation results in cultural and political differences. The motherland remains a "permanent center," the "core-nation"; the colony is a "branch-nation" which has a "permanent base" in the motherland, at least for a time. During population shifts which we have called integral mass migration, the entire nation or tribe changes its territory, thus continuity is not disrupted.

The history of Europe offers an abundance of examples of integral mass migrations extending back to prehistoric times. To start only with the fifth century, a number of major migrations were recorded: the Huns in the fifth century; the great migration of Avars in the sixth century; the mass migration of Bulgars in the seventh century; the migration of Magyars in the ninth century; of Tartars in the thirteenth century; and of Turks in the fourteenth century. The integral mass migrations were frequently but not always connected with war and conquest.[4]

What happened when such large mass migrations took place, especially when combined with conquest? Sometimes the local population was absorbed. Often it was the conquerors who were absorbed by the local population. For example, the present Bulgaria is the result of mass migration and the integration of the local population with the conquerors. Similarly, the Magyars conquered what is today Hungary, and integrated with the local population. In some areas, the Magyars become the ruling class. This could be noticed, for instance, in Slovakia, where the large landowners were Hungarian noblemen, while the local peasantry was chiefly Slovak.

The Slavs are recorded historically under the name of Slavs or Sclaveni by the Byzantine historians of the sixth century when they appear as allies or tributaries of Avars. In the seventh century the Slavic occupation of the Balkan peninsula and part of the islands was completed. Then the Slavs moved down the valleys and mixed with the local population of Hellenic Illyrian, or other origins, and in the border territories where those massive migrations took place, a mixed population emerges and survives to the present day.[5]

As a result of such migration we find small islands of those migrant tribes who moved farther on, leaving some of their members behind. In other cases the main host settled down and the local population formed a minority within the sea of the numerous and powerful migrant group.

Forced and optional population transfers

Forced population transfers are well known from the experiences of World War II. They were extensively applied by Adolf Hitler and by Stalin after 1939. Large sections of the population of Eastern Europe were forcibly transferred to other territories. Usually the reason given was the difference in nationality, class, ideology, race, or religion. In that way the Polish population was transferred from the eastern Polish provinces occupied by the Soviet Union to the Siberian labor camps. Large sections of the Polish population were transferred or expelled from Silesia and the western Polish provinces by the Germans. Similar transfers occurred in many other parts of Eastern Europe after the Nazi and Soviet occupations.

The slave trade was merely a forced population transfer throughout many centuries. In its general appearance it was not too different from Hitler's population transfers. There was, however, a difference in function and objectives. The slave trade was economic and exploitative in its main function. Hitler's and Stalin's population transfers were economic, political, and ideological. Behind the slave trade was a "rational-economic" motivation. Hitler's population shifts and extermination policy had psychopathological elements proving that man had potentialities for "rational" and irrational" oppression, hostility, cruelty, and exploitation of the weak. The slave owner paid a price for his "hands," and a slave was personal property; loss of his life meant loss of money. Hitler's slaves could be replenished by new raids and persecution. The slave as individual property was far better treated, in spite of his tragic fate.

A distinction should be made between optional and compulsory transfer. Optional transfer is usually based on treaties or international agreements, and the population is given an opportunity to choose one or another nationality. Experience teaches, however, that there are grades of coercion in all transfer policies. Some are more humane and respectful of individual choice. At the other extreme we will find transfers which are sometimes related to extermination policies. In modern times, propositions for population transfers appeared long before World War I.

Between the wars, population exchanges and optional transfers were made among Bulgaria, Turkey, and Greece, and in the beginning these transfers were regarded by many as a successful solution of the minority problems. It did not take long to discover that they contributed only to the further uprooting of the population.[6]

After the war, the problem of ethnic minorities and population exchanges again became a subject of discussion and of international treaties. Unfortunately, the representatives of the victorious states did not show originality and skill in solving the problem. While the transfers, at least in the Eastern European countries, were enforced in a more civilized and humane way than by the Germans, they were based on ethnic, or almost racial, premises. For instance, Hungarian populations were transferred from certain parts of Slovakia merely because of their nationality. During the war the Slovak Republic was an ally of Nazi Germany, and from the viewpoint of the official war record of the Hungarian and Slovak authoritarian governments, there was not much difference, or a slight difference, perhaps in favor of Hungary.[7]

Population transfers were regarded by some as one of the best policies for easing conflict in tension areas. A coercive or optional transfer of minorities from the tension area, according to such an approach, would result in an area inhabited by one national group; in that way, by a transfer of the minority, the problem would be solved. The transfer of the Poles from eastern Polish provinces into eastern German provinces, if the territorial integrity of present Poland were maintained, might prove a solution in time. But forced transfer of population did not solve the issue in many other historical cases. It only created new problems and resulted in human suffering.

Transfer is by no means a generally effective way of solving minority or ethnic problems. Man migrates, human societies move. The establishment of areas which seem ethnically homogeneous is usually illusory and temporary. With time, the population in the border areas will begin to mix through such types of migrations as arise through trade, the need for certain skills, or even simple human choice. Transfers of population, whether optional or forced, are by no means ideal solutions of ethnic tensions.

Chaotic displacement

War—especially World War II—is closely identified with the organized mass displacement of population. Chaotic migration is the result of persecution, local famines, the threat of war, and the destruction of cities. From 1939 till perhaps 1947, large sections of the population were continuously on the move. For most people this displacement ended either with migration to a new country or a return to the old. In some cases, however, many displaced persons simply remained where they were. (It might be interesting to note that in the 1940's the number of persons in Europe either displaced or transferred was estimated at about 40 million—about 10 per cent of the entire population.[8]

Displacement or transfer of populations, whether optional or forced, resulted in new areas of mixed populations and often produced tension areas or increased nationalistic and antagonistic tendencies. On the Israeli border, the Gaza strip—comprising a temporary settlement of Arabs—is the result of mass displacement because of war, and it qualifies as a tension area of a specific type, since it is inhabited by only one nationality of the limitrophic area, the Arabs. Nevertheless, relations in the border area are tense, and antagonism persists.

Powerful movements have also created areas of mixed ethnic population by transfer and displacement, although in certain countries they may have resulted in more ethnically homogeneous populations. Whether transfers eliminated tension or transferred it to new and sometimes more explosive levels of political action is a problem which we shall not discuss at this time.

Free immigration

The three major types of free immigration are: a) assimilative; b) differential (nonassimilative); and c) complementary migration. Free immigration of population is a phenomenon which affected the history of the Western Hemisphere during the eighteenth and nineteenth centuries. (Again the term has been chosen for the purpose of distinguishing a separate and different class of migration.) "Free immigration" reflects to a greater or less degree the choice of the immigrant. An English scholar who immigrates to the United States because he finds a greater opportunity for his work exercises his "free choice" in a higher degree than a Jewish scholar who emigrates to Holland to escape the Inquisition. A Sicilian farm worker who decides to change his place of residence has a relatively free choice. He may move to another part of Sicily or emigrate to Brazil or the United States.

The causes of the great migratory movements to North America since the seventeenth century can be divided into religious, political, and economic. Immigrations because of religious and political persecutions are less "free," in sense of choice, than those for economic reasons. A persecuted person has to leave his country and go to one which offers freedom of conviction and tolerance.[9]

Unlike the colonist, the immigrant does not import his own laws and political-economic institutions. He accepts those of the host country.

The assimilative pattern prevails in Western Europe and, more especially, in the United States and some units of the Commonwealth of Nations such as Canada, Australia, and New Zealand. Here the immigrant usually is willing to accept the basic institutions and values, and the economic, social, and political pattern of the host country. He may retain some of the cultural traits of his country of origin for a time, such as his language, his food habits, and most likely his religion, but the condition of his success is acculturation to the new country. Since the immigrant comes to the new country to improve his living standard, he is usually aware that in an economically advanced host country improvement depends on his assimilation of the prevailing work habits and values. As a first generation immigrant he may have certain difficulties in assimilation, but his children, at least in the context of Anglo-American culture, will find few problems.

Free assimilative immigration, it seems to me, seldom results in the intensification of minority-group tensions in the border areas. But there have been cases where free immigration has increased local intergroup tension. For example, the immigration of French-Canadians to Vermont has increased this Catholic ethnic group in sections of northern New England. In certain communities, a "silent" prejudice against the Catholic French-Canadian population may be noticed, but it is relatively weak and has no major political significance, since the state and federal authorities respect the differences and, whenever necessary, make an effort to ease tensions.

Not all free immigrants assimilate easily. Cultural differences between the immigrant and nationalities of the host country are often of such a nature that assimilation, such as is known in the United States or Canada, does not take place. For example, the Greeks as colonists might have borrowed cultural traits and artifacts, but they did not merge with local nations. Greeks did not assimilate in Egypt, and frequently, though not always, a German immigrant did not assimilate in Bohemia.

Students of nationality problems in Europe were long puzzled by the fact that a newcomer to Western Europe or America assimilated more readily than one arriving in Eastern Europe. In the Balkans, a Serb and an Albanian do not assimilate easily, nor do a Greek and a Bulgarian (the very proposition may sound like an anathema for some). The same Serbs, Albanians, Bulgarians, and Greeks assimilate in such matters as clothing, behavior, work patterns, and even language within a generation or two of arriving in the United States. The tendency to maintain the traditional pattern as much as possible, and to absorb as little as possible of a neighbor's cultural elements or those of the host nations, presents a "nonassimilative" or, as it was also called, a "differential" pattern.

This phenomenon is by no means limited to the Balkans. Prior to World War II, the Chinese section of Yokohama represented a separate cultural and linguistic community. One could readily perceive the difference, even in dress. The Chinese simply did not "assimilate." Someone may comment that racial differences might have contributed to this difference. But it can be pointed out that the Japanese absorbed European and American patterns in their culture.

Some ethnic groups assimilate faster and with less resistance than others, while in certain cultural environments the resistance to assimilation never ends. Two general hypotheses are suggested: 1] host countries which are highly advanced economically and have a cultural pattern which the immigrant regards as superior, which offer the immigrant improvement of his own economic conditions without forcing him into denial or rejection of his tradition, heritage, and values, form a favorable environment for a free and assimilative immigration. Where the political and cultural rights of an immigrant are respected, where he is not forced into assimilation—he is willing to accept at least the basic institutions and patterns of the host country. 2] Differential or nonassimilative immigration may lead to patterns of self-segregation or "indifference" which may not necessarily result in tensions. (See Separation, Part III, Chapter 7.)

A differential pattern in an ethnic democracy, with a tendency to accept basic values and institutions of the host country, may also lead to pluralism. On the other hand, the differential pattern, combined with economic and political differences and antagonisms, may be manipulated or used for the intensification of antagonism in tension areas.

In tension areas, assimilative immigration offers less probability of tensions than does "differential" immigration. However, in a democratic approach, there is no argument against a differential pattern. Perhaps an empathic viewpoint may assist us in understanding "differential" attitudes. A Greek in Egypt retains traditions of an old and great culture. His children are taught this tradition and Hellenic values become part of their value structure. No matter how friendly a Greek may be toward his Arabic neighbor, he is yet unwilling to abandon his ancient heritage and religion and dissolve his identity in a cultural ocean which is strange to him.

In Canada or the United States he may retain his heritage and still accept the political system and culture of the host country, whose administration does not question his cultural preferences, and which permits him to publish his papers, speak over the radio, and discuss politics in his vernacular. Interestingly enough, the latter "political climate" fosters assimilation.

Incidentally, by "nonassimilative," we do not understand a pattern that necessarily rejects any cultural borrowing or accommodation. Without some kind of accommodation, the mere fact of existence in a host country is not possible. The problem, however, is what and how much is assimilated, and above all, how it is integrated in one's own culture.

Free migration is sometimes complementary. In medieval times "complementary migration" was frequently nonassimilative in nature. Today, the situation has changed. The economic development of a nation frequently requires the borrowing of skills and arts from other nations that are educationally, technically, or economically better developed. Should a government envisage the economic or cultural development of its own country, it may encourage the immigration of foreigners who are scholars, craftsmen, or technicians. In medieval times this type of immigration occurred frequently, and at that time certain skills were more divided on national ethnic lines than they are today.

Because of their historical development, the Jewish population represented such skills as trading and certain crafts to a high degree. After the Tartar invasions of Poland in the thirteenth and fourteenth centuries, the Polish rulers, especially King Kasimir, welcomed the settlement of Jews in Polish towns.[10] This was a "complementary population," supplementing the trades and skills that were weak or absent in Poland at that time. The Germans had arrived as colonists after the Mongol invasion, but the development of the country needed the presence of trades and crafts which the Jews did best. It is beside the point whether the intention of the ruler in welcoming the Jews was to gain their skills or to assist them in their flight from areas where they were persecuted. Sociologically important and interesting is the function which they performed in societies that welcomed them. They complemented the native population in such areas as trade and finance. This was basically true of Jewish immigration in Europe after the persecutions in Spain, Germany, and England. They settled in their new countries as a complementary population. It is true that early documents also mention Jews as farmers. More significant, however, were their economic specializations which supplemented the needs of the host country.

Complementarity of immigration is a significant factor in the history of tensions. The host country eventually develops its own skills and its own professional classes. Sooner or later they come into competition with the complementary immigrant who retains his differences of religion, language, and even clothing. These differences are perpetuated historically by the laws and customs of the host country, sometimes by persecution but also because of the strength of the values and institutions retained by the migrants.

In the history of Europe the Jews were in a certain sense a complementary nation. Therefore, one factor in the increase of tensions between Jews and non-Jews was the growth of a competitive class in the host country. In such cases the religious or ethnic differences served as a means of rationalizing economic competition and antagonism. As I have said, antagonism between ethnic groups is not solely of an economic nature, although the economic factor cannot be overlooked. Ethnic antagonism is a complex mechanism. Thus, complementarity eventually develops into competition and tensions are intensified, as was frequently the result in many parts of Europe.[11]

In modern times new types of "complementary migration" are apparent. Now, the scholar or highly specialized scientist is a welcome immigrant, even in a country with a large manpower reserve of scientists, scholars, and professors like the United States. Some countries bar foreign scholars, and do not recognize foreign degrees. The new "complementary immigrant" in the United States has little difficulty in adjusting to his new environment. The United States liberal policy toward foreign scholars has contributed to the revolutionary scientific advance of the nation. Opportunities for teaching and research are given to a scholar who was frequently refused such assistance in his native land. The attitude of the university and of the authorities is appreciated by the newcomer and contributes to his rapid assimilation, without resulting in tensions.

Newly emancipated Asian and African nations also invite "complementary immigrants" with sorely needed skills. However, in 1964 the president of the Republic of Ghana followed the medieval policy of expulsion once—as he thought—the job was done and such skills were no longer necessary. This expulsion of foreign professors was indicative of an instability which does not favor the complementary immigrant.

The immigration pattern of the Chinese population in the Far East is frequently complementary in nature. In the Caribbean area, the Chinese immigrant often represents new business. As a complementary immigrant, the Chinese retains his cultural pattern, his language and his connections. Hard working and skillful, he usually succeeds in developing a business enterprise in which he employs his own kinfolk. In that way, the ethnic difference combines with class or with occupational difference. Thus in Southeast Asia, economic antagonism influences and reinforces ethnic prejudices. Both can be used by contending governments or political parties to intensify tension for wider strategies of territorial, ideological, or political expansion.

Penetrating migrations

The slow penetration by single families or small groups into the territory of a host country presents a specific type of migration. Especially in a border area, intensification of the density of a different ethnic group is accomplished by a slow migratory movement, often combined with the economic complementarity of the new groups. This was probably the nature of the German migration to Polish Silesia; of the Poles to Lithuania or the eastern provinces of the Ukraine; of Russians to Chinese lands; and of Chinese to Southeast Asia. The American migration to Mexico and Hawaii had this slow, penetrating quality. Such migrations sometimes leads to the eventual absorption of the border territory by the mother country of the penetrating migrant. The tension which may arise in such areas can be utilized by neighboring or outside governments or political parties for their own objectives.

Nomadic migrations

Nomadism is a way of life based on repeated wanderings of organized groups. The relationship between the culture, especially the organization, of the group and its means and modes of production (technology), on one hand, and the natural environment, on the other, explains the nature of nomadic movements. However, the nomadic way of life is also closely related to the value structures.

The rich variety of nomadic movements can be classified roughly as: 1] typical nomadism; and 2] rhythmical semi-nomadic movements, with typical nomadism being subdivided into short- and long-range nomadic patterns. To the former belong such ethnic groups as the Bushmen of Africa or the Australian aborigines; to the latter, Bedouins and such African desert people as the Tuaregs. In short-range nomadism, the group migrates within the boundaries of a definite area, and changes places when supplies of food and water are exhausted. In long-range nomadism, the boundaries of the area are not so strictly defined. They may extend several hundreds of miles, as did at one time the Tuaregs of the Sahara. In both types of migration movement is continuous but irregular.

The rhythm of the nomadic movement is determined by the seasons. Periodical semi-nomadism or rhythmical semi-nomadism may be divided into: (1) one-settlement and (2) two-settlement. One-settlement semi-nomadism is characteristic of the nomads of the steppes, for example, the Kirgiz who formerly spent the winter in stable settlements and led a nomadic life in the summer. Two-settlement semi-nomadism is based on two stable settlements, with migration limited to changes of seasons; as, for example, the winter and spring migrations of the Yakuts. The essential feature of this movement is the seasonal rhythm of the migration according to sharp climatic changes. The change of place occurs every year at the same time: the beginning of summer and winter.[12] These ancient ways, recorded in the nineteenth century, have probably been strongly affected by modern technological and social changes.

Nomadic migration may result in ethnic tensions, since a variety of tribes may migrate within the same area. Sometimes a symbiosis is established, and no tension emerges. Some hostility and prejudice may exist, but physical clashes are usually avoided, with the nomadic movements adjusted through custom or law. We find such migratory movements in Europe in the form of transhumance.

Political boundary lines do not necessarily respect the established habits of the nomadic people. They are sometimes drawn through customary pastures and migratory areas. The nomadic group may meet with an artificial political border-line guarded by armed soldiers who do not permit them to move in areas where they had been accustomed to migrate for centuries.

With the establishment of national states and the change from tribal to state organization, a government representing a nationalistic state may attempt to oust pastoral visitors from a traditionally mixed territory now recognized by international treaties as "national." In consequence, a once peaceful area may become a tension area. The tension begins by a rather complex conflict between the migrating tribal group—an ethnic group—and the military detachments of the host country. In a short time the tension becomes interethnic and interpolitical, since the migrating tribe usually has the support of its own government. Thus tension moves from antagonism to conflict in three stages:

1]

The first stage involves the migration of different tribes or ethnic groups in the same territory. We assume that the tribes do not fight one another, but follow a pattern of "indifference." They meet on a given territory and possibly exchange or trade a bit, but there is no specific cooperative pattern.

2]

The second stage is the establishment of a borderline, with clashes between the migrating tribe and the host country's military detachments or ethnic groups. The migratory group now becomes an "anti-group."

3]

In the third stage, the area changes to one of complex tension between the two governments (interpolitical tension) as well as the two ethnic groups (interethnic tension).

Of course, other patterns are not only feasible but have occurred in history. Wandering nomads have frequently attacked the local people and enslaved or conquered them. Historically, nomadism was not infrequently connected with brigandage and robbery, with periodic attacks on the host country. Thus nomadism may be associated in certain areas with repetitive raids and attacks which must be blocked by military detachments or by the native tribes. In that way certain areas of nomadic migration became areas of tensions. The Somali-Ethiopian border area represents this type of tension. (Discussed below in Appendix III).

Interethnic patterns and migratory movements

Various types of migratory movements have contributed to the ethnic variety of some areas. As I have mentioned before, ethnic diversification is frequent, especially in border areas. In quest of political domination or more permanent peace, political parties and nations try to establish ethnically homogeneous areas by a variety of devices. One policy is that of population transfer. This tendency to establish monoethnic areas—areas inhabited by one single ethnic group—contradicts the very nature of man and human society. Even plants travel. Man has a tendency to migrate, choosing to settle where conditions are opportune for the development of his own potentialities; where he can function successfully. The transfer of population may establish monoethnic areas for a time; perhaps it may serve to thin out the inhabitants of a so-called minority group. In the long run, however, someone else will arrive in the border areas. The permanent establishment of monoethnic areas with simultaneous economic advancement is almost impossible. Man's economic, scientific, and technological advance depends on continuous exchange and communication. Isolation has usually led to a cultural dearth.

Thus territories of mixed ethnic population are witness to various types of migratory movements combined with the permanent settlement of some of the migrant groups. It has already been mentioned that the pattern of social, economic, and political relationships between the various ethnic groups is to a certain extent dependent upon: (1) the initial social-economic pattern established between the host and guest nations; (2) values and ideologies which guided the policies; and (3) institutions of the host nation.

Even in economically advanced democracies, the original pattern leaves its traces. The Negro arrived in America as a result of forced migration. A Mexican in California belongs to a "conquered" minority. The American-Italian or American-Filipino came by his own choice. The subsequent status of each ethnic group, until recently, reflected the type of migration. Of course there are other important factors involved. Nevertheless, to some extent, the relative social position of a minority reflects the original type of migration.

The long rivalry between new England and new France is over. The British colonist won; his institutions, his British and Protestant values are the stuff of a successful, working democracy in both Canada and the United States. The international relations of the two neighbors today belong to the most civilized in modern history.

Minority groups enjoy full rights in Canada. Still, the separate social status of the French-Canadian is a very distant reflection on this victory. A "very distant," we repeat, since so many factors are involved: preservation of religious freedom, economic patterns, and cultural patterns.

Relations between various ethnic groups influence the relationships between governments. In border areas, however, the relationships between the ethnic groups, at least in East European, Asiatic, and West European history, were more often used by governments for their own broader political objectives. Therefore, the dominant pattern of such relationships is of relevance for our study of tensions.

Theoretically we may distinguish monoethnic and polyethnic, or mixed, areas. Monoethnic areas are those which are inhabited by a single ethnic group without substantial minorities; polyethnic (mixed), by many and different ethnic groups.

Relations between various ethnic groups in mixed areas may vary from close association to antagonism and conflict. (The reader is referred to the classification of international relations discussed in the preceding section.) It has been indicated that the relationships between nations can be viewed as variations on a continuum. With a change in intensity, the relations move from one class to another; from cooperative relations to differences, opposition, and antagonism. As a rule, several types of relationships develop between nations. In times of antagonism some cooperation survives, permitting subsequent adjustment and negotiation.

What is true about nation-states is also true, with certain changes, of relations between ethnic groups. Here too the variation in types of relations can be viewed as changes in intensity on a continuum. It is difficult to draw sharp lines between various types of cooperation. However, distinctions do exist, and the difference between cooperative and antagonistic patterns is clear. Between the two extreme processes of association and dissociation on our model we shall replace "neutrality" with "indifference." Therefore, from the processes of association we move to the central point of indifference, and then to various processes of dissociation, with conflict as the extreme in antagonistic processes.

The concept of indifference is an "ideal type," a medial point on a theoretical model. In an extreme case, indifference means no relations whatsoever between ethnic groups. Under usual conditions it suggests the existence of two ethnic groups in the same territory, having very limited relations of antagonism or association. In practice, the indifferent relationship is close to what we call the pattern of self-segregation. Total indifference seldom occurs; in reality there is a pattern of group separation with limited processes of association. In rare cases, it may operate successfully as a device for the avoidance of antagonism. (See the discussion of the Shoshone and Arapaho Indians and of Chanak in Part III.)

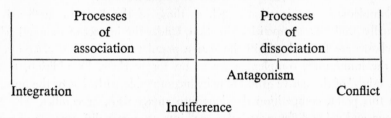

MODEL XVI
Interethnic Relations and Processes

Processes of association	Processes of dissociation
	Antagonism
Integration	Conflict

Indifference

Processes of dissociation between ethnic groups are also of various levels of intensity. Some kinds of difference or competition are not necessarily synonymous with antagonism. Not all members of antagonistic groups engage in antagonism, nor are all relations, even between antagonistic groups, purely antagonistic. Frequently, the pattern of relations lies somewhere in between. Too, the antagonistic relations between ethnic groups in one tension area may not be comparable to the antagonistic relations in another. They may differ in nature and intensity.

Causation of ethnic antagonism

What are the causal factors of ethnic antagonism? Monocausal schools have sought to reduce them to a single variable. However, there are many factors. We shall limit our discussion of causal factors to the major and general types:

1]

Economic factors as conditions of ethnic tensions. Economic tensions reinforce ethnic tensions when ethnic division coincides with class divisions or other forms of economic subordination. Usually only a part of an ethnic group forms a dominant "upper class." Nevertheless, a "social image" is formed and prejudice extends to the entire ethnic group.

In the past, as well as during World War II, conquest led to economic and political division based on ethnic or racial lines. In order to maintain power, an ideology was essential since ideology determines legitimacy of power; the right to control the weaker and the conquered. In an authoritarian state a nationalist and racist ideology is advanced as a "political formula" of the ruling class (to use Gaetano Mosca's terminology).

Racial superiority is claimed by the dominant or conquering elite. It becomes a part of philosophy and is taught and believed, since it corresponds to a definite interest. The conquered are indoctrinated with the idea of their inferiority. However, the ideology is not shared by all members of the ruling ethnic or racial elites, and seeds of opposition usually grow within the "philosophical minority." Ideas and moral motivation, especially moral protest, have often been historically more powerful than weapons and economic power.

An economically competitive position of two different racial or ethnic groups, especially in border areas, may also reinforce ethnic tensions.

Complementary migrations, such as those of the Jews in medieval times, eventually produce a competitive situation. Under the impact of economic change, new classes are formed within the native population. The new classes compete with the immigrant, complementary group for markets. In addition, the "economic ethos" of the native group may be incompatible with that of the immigrant. From this point, competition develops into antagonism, or conflict. The ethnic, religious, and value differences "telescope" into economic differences and reinforce antagonism. Thus, various levels of cultural and economic differences act as a "reinforcement mechanism." Should the "complementary migrant" move into an unattractive occupation, from which the native or the earlier immigrant moved to a higher-paid one, the competitive process may not take place.

2]

Differences in political status. An uneven distribution of political power between different racial, ethnic, or religious groups often results in ethnic, racial, or religious tensions. A minority may enjoy a status that is at once economically favorable and politically unfavorable. This type of status may last for a long time, as in the case of Greek merchant and financial classes in the Turkish empire. Here again, political differentiation coincides with racial, religious, and ethnic differences. Thus, increase of political tensions reinforces ethnic tensions.

3]

Difference in values, institutions, and ideologies. The values of the two or more ethnic or religious groups in a given area are sometimes incompatible. "Incompatibility of values" may also extend to ideologies. However, the most frequent incompatibility is in religious values. At an earlier tribal stage, often ethnic groups share the same religion. Sooner or later the religious beliefs, even if, like Christianity, they are universal in nature, assume ethnic characteristics.

Religious history teaches that, in the past, closely related religious communities emphasized the contradictory values or beliefs rather than the shared one. Protestants and Catholics were irreconcilable, as were Roman Catholics and the Greek Orthodox. Still, the basic tenets remained the same, since Christianity is a universalization of Judaic ethics. However, for many hundreds of years the stress was on difference, not on universality. The changes initiated by Pope John XXIII therefore had unusual significance.

Similar antagonisms can be observed in ethnic differences. The Poles and Russians are neighbors, and at least "linguistic" brothers. Language harbors values; it reflects culture. Yet, the ethnic antagonism between Poles and Russians is strong. Again, the Croats and Serbs belong to the same basic nationality. Their religions are different. Croats are Roman Catholic; Serbs, Orthodox. Croats use the Latin alphabet; Serbs, the Cyrillic. During the interwar period, ethnic antagonism increased between these two groups and led to the formation of extremist nationalistic groups. (During World War II the Croat Fascist Ustashis favored a policy of genocide, and "limited" extermination of Serbs.) Yet the Serbs and Croats speak practically the same language (Serbo-Croat).

Incompatibility of religious beliefs is frequently intensified by the policies of the organized church. Thus, incompatibility of religious values intensifies ethnic difference. Ethnic groups may also embrace certain political ideologies, creating an incompatibility of ideological values that leads to antagonism. But such "incompatibilities" also exist within the ethnic groups. In the Sudetenland, large sections of the German ethnic group embraced National Socialism which was incompatible with the values of the Czechs and those Germans who were Democrats, Social Democrats, or Communists.

4]

Psychological and general sociological incompatibility. Some cultures develop, or favor the development of, certain behavioral patterns and personality types that may differ substantially from those of other cultures. Difficulties in integration or in the adjustment or reconciliation of different behavior may lead to antagonistic feeling, or it may assist the reinforcement of another type of incompatibility, for instance, economic antagonism.

5]

Psychological needs. Ethnic or racial hostility reflects deep psychological problems, sometimes even pathological needs; urges of destruction and aggression. When such urges appear among many within the same group, they mutually reinforce each other and become collective in nature. Frustration of wishes because of political, economic, racial, or ethnic barriers may change to a need for aggression. Such processes are not conscious but they are real. A process of displacement follows, and aggression is directed against an ethnic or racial group that is plainly recognizable because of certain characteristics. Displaced aggression moves in the direction of previously established prejudices.[18] Such needs are sometimes psychopathological in origin. Nevertheless, a deviant personality may appeal precisely to those needs.

To recapitulate, economic difference between ethnic groups is by no means the only factor responsible for ethnic clashes and antagonisms. But it is a mistake to underestimate its significance. However, experience teaches us that values and ideology as well as psychological urges are also strong motivating forces in collective behavior and may result in a reinforced ethnic and religious antagonism.

iii. Interethnic Relations and Tensions: Case Histories

7.

SOCIAL DISTANCE AND DYNAMICS OF ETHNIC RELATIONS

Ranking of ethnic proximity and distance

We have already indicated that the various types of international relations can be presented as a continuum representing two tendencies, one toward association or cooperation and the other toward dissociation or antagonism. We have called the middle point neutrality or indifference. It has been suggested that different classes of association or dissociation present a variety of types of intensity of those relations. The transition from one type to another is frequently of such a nature that it is difficult to establish sharp and definite categories. Nonetheless, an individual, in relating himself to other societies or individuals, identifies social distance or promixity. Also, while acting a social role as a member of an ethnic group, he views other individuals or groups from the vantage point of their ethnicity. He identifies the position of the corresponding individual or group in terms of ethnic (respectively social) proximity or distance.

Ethnic identification varies in significance according to the social situation. We play many roles and, in any given situation, the emphasis of our identification varies. A farmers' association defending the economic interest of wheat farmers identifies itself with a similar occupational group, as does an individual farmer acting within his occupational group. In other situations, when an ethnic or a religious or national identity is essential, an individual or group identifies with a suitable group.

In an antagonistic situation ethnic, racial, or religious identification is strong. If the antagonism grows, the identification becomes more intense. The very survival of an individual may depend on his identification with his in-group; alone, he is weak vis-à-vis an antagonistic group. Both aggression and defense intensify proximity within the in- and pro-group and distance from the out-group and the anti-group.

Generally, we identify ethnically with an *in-group* when we meet different ethnic groups or are in a situation in which we have, or wish to play, a role in which the ethnic identity is essential or dominant. Where a respect for differences prevails and cultural democracy is attempted, the need for continuous identification as a part of a defense mechanism arises only on rare occasions. In a tension area, the ethnic conflict forces groups and individuals to identify the social environment in terms of proximity and distance.

Even in an antagonistic situation, the world is not divided solely into friends and enemies. The social groups which surround an individual in a mixed ethnic or racial area are not only diversified but also represent a definite gradation of proximity, distance and, frequently, antagonism. Usually he finds definite terms in his own language to identify various categories of distance. Classification usually involves terminology, and an artificial and involved terminology makes simple things complex and difficult. Nonetheless, the problem of reducing complex relationships to a limited number of ranks requires clarification and, sometimes, the introduction of new terms.

The person who plays an ethnic role at a given moment, who identifies himself with an ethnic or religious group and views other groups from this vantage point in terms of social distance or proximity, will be called an "ethnic actor." The groups or individuals that belong to other ethnic or racial groups and are viewed by the actor from the point of view of social distance or proximity will be called "ethnic respondents."

Our Model (XVII*A*) of ethnic proximity represents a continuum, parallel to the continuum of two tendencies: association and dissociation. In the middle, the dividing line is drawn through point *O*, and represents neutrality or indifference. I shall put the actor at the extreme point of the line (on the left side), within his own in-group. In a multiethnic area, he may see the following groups according to social proximity or distance: 1] his own in-group; 2] associated groups, or friends; 3] neighbors, on whose limited assistance or help he can count; and 4] friendly out-groups. The last are somewhat distant groups, with no special relationship to our actor's in-group; ones that, although not antagonistic, are not committed to active assistance; friendly, although distant and close to indifference. The first three categories belong to a large class of "pro-groups" that form a more or less actively cooperating, assisting system. The fourth lies between the pro-groups and the dividing line of indifference.

From the indifference line to the right, the social distance increases rapidly, and the antagonistic relationships are represented by various ranks of antagonisms.

MODEL XVII, DIAGRAM A

Models of Ethnic Distance

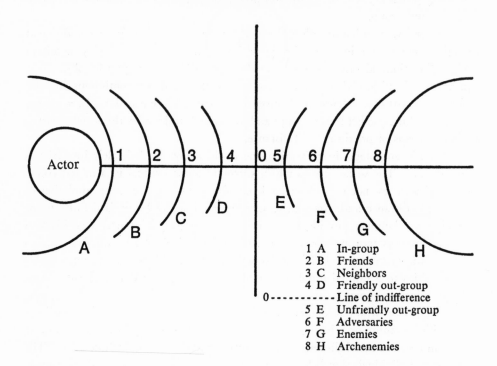

1 A In-group
2 B Friends
3 C Neighbors
4 D Friendly out-group
0 ---------- Line of indifference
5 E Unfriendly out-group
6 F Adversaries
7 G Enemies
8 H Archenemies

Between the line of indifference and the broad class of "anti-group," an actor may identify 5] an "unfriendly out-group"—not yet necessarily an active enemy or an antagonist, but nonetheless passive and unfriendly. Then come the "anti-groups"—antagonists with a variety of ranks. We start with 6] adversaries, antagonists without a tendency toward the destruction or total subordination of our actor's in-group and leaning more toward 7] enemies and 8] archenemies (German, *Eberfeinde*).

The enemy represents a temporary hostility by a group whose antagonistic role changes in history; the "hereditary" or "archenemy" represents a group toward which hostility is transmitted by traditional lore and history books from generation to generation. The younger generation learns about past hostilities with this group, so that a continuation of the quarrel in time and space is regarded as a historical duty; a matter of national honor and obligation.

We may also, by reversing the positions, use a variant of this model for the purpose of ranking (XVII*B*). The antagonistic tendencies will be presented to the left of the indifference line; the tendency toward association on the right. Plus (+) will be used as a symbol of proximity; minus (—) as a symbol of dis-

MODEL XVII, DIAGRAM B

Ranking of Ethnic Distance and Proximity

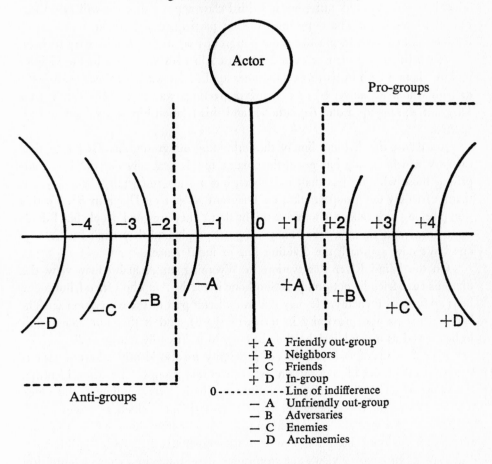

+ A	Friendly out-group
+ B	Neighbors
+ C	Friends
+ D	In-group
0	Line of indifference
− A	Unfriendly out-group
− B	Adversaries
− C	Enemies
− D	Archenemies

sociation or antagonism. The point of indifference will be *0*. In consequence, our ranks will be: (+1) friendly out-groups; (+2) neighbors; (+3) friends; (+4) in-group. On the antagonistic continuum: (−1) represents the unfriendly out-group; (−2) adversaries; (−3) enemies; (−4) archenemies. In such a model, the actor's vantage point is in the middle—at the *0* point. On one side are those "with us"; on the other, those "against us."

This is of course a tentative model, and the categories are tentative. In various cultures and indifferent situations more or fewer ranks may be identified. However, our models are by no means theoretical. In a tension area the relations are not simply green or red. The dividing lines are frequently complex. The groups are ranked in a more complex way than a simple division into friends and enemies.

Of course, in times of conflict, the division into pro- and anti-groups becomes sharp. Between the two groups, however, a new class emerges—the neutrals. Some are friendly neutrals; others, unfriendly. Others, still, are entirely indifferent. Thus between pro- and anti-groups, a third class appears that we will call, theoretically, out-groups. The out-groups do not participate actively in a process of tensions and conflict. In practice some out-groups try to profit, others try to help.

A Christian Albanian or even a Moslem Albanian who lives in the vicinity and to whom a Serb in Kossovo sometimes applied for water in times of drought or with whom he conversed or exchanged greetings was a *neighbor* (rank 3 on Diagram *A,* rank + 2 on Diagram *B*), and this relationship was valued and respected.

Just before the dividing line of the forbidding out-group, there is yet another category which usually has no distinct name but is generally described as comprising those who are less than neighbors, but are not unfriendly. We may call them a friendly out-group (rank 4 on Diagram *A,* + 1 on Diagram *B*). To this group belong those about whom one might say: "They are good people but I don't know them well enough," or: "They are good people and they don't bother anyone." We now approach the dividing line of indifference.

On the Wind River Reservation in Wyoming an Arapaho may view the Shoshone as a friendly out-group. A Shoshone is not the Arapaho's friend, but today he is no longer his enemy. He may live in a distant part of the reservation (neighborhood means also proximity in terms of space), and is therefore too distant to be viewed as a neighbor; he thus belongs to a "friendly out-group."

Identifications of various grades of proximity are also identifications of various patterns and grades of cooperation between ethnic groups. The actor identifies the range of social distance or proximity on a basis corresponding to the range on the continuum of cooperation, i.e., on a continuum which represents tendencies toward cooperation or antagonism. The dividing line—where the continuum of proximity changes to a zone of distance—starts the point of indifference. But even when an actor views out-groups and anti-groups in a concrete empirical situation, their antagonistic status does not necessarily fit in a zone of one color. Even the "pro" and "anti" out-groups do not form a clear division into green, orange, and red; there is a large area of variations between them.

On the scale of distance, we first notice a group, called the *unfriendly out-group* (Diagram *A,* rank 5; Diagram *B,* rank —1). Indeed, it is difficult to find a definite common term for this category. An actor may describe them in a conversation—"You'd better keep away and don't mix with these people"—or use an insulting stereotype.

Beyond the unfriendly out-groups is the class of "anti-groups," comprising a number of categories. (Here we had to coin a term, calling this subclass the anti-groups.) In this large class the social distance varies from "an antagonist" (rank 6 on Diagram *A;* —2 on Diagram *B*) to a "hereditary enemy" (rank 8 or —4). Let us use a concrete example, following the plan of the model.

In Teschen, Silesia, in 1938, a period of intensive tensions existed between the Czechs, on one hand, and Poles and Germans, on the other. In such a conflict situation, the Czechs continued to view the Poles as "adversaries" rather than enemies. At the same time, the German Nazis were seen as enemies, or "arch-enemies." The long tradition of wars, conflicts, German invasions, and subjugation, and the history of a ruthless counterreformation led by Austrian rulers, had created the image and the reality of the Nazis (personifying the traditional German enemy) as brutal conquerors who advocated the extermination or enslavement of the Slavs. The Nazis were part of a pattern in which they were identified with an enemy whom one fears, and who should be opposed and fought in a struggle for survival.

The term *adversary* or *antagonist* (rank 6 on Diagram *A;* —2 on Diagram *B*) can be found in many languages, and is weaker and more "neutral" than the term for enemy. When the antagonism moves into an acute stage of conflict, the adversary may change to an "enemy." For instance, during World War I, the Bulgarian was, for the Serb, an *enemy* (rank 7 on *A;* —3, *B*), but he was an enemy in a direct war situation, on the battlefield. He was not a "hereditary enemy." For the Greek, however, who fought the Turks or the Bulgarians during World War I, both the Turk and the Bulgarian were identified as "hereditary enemies," archenemies, and enemies of a thousand years (rank 8 on Diagram *A;* —4, *B*). After the war ends, the *archenemy* remains an enemy.

In the Balkan wars that ended in a Turkish defeat, the official Greek or Serb image of the Turk was that of an archenemy. Even the peace treaties didn't change the official view.

The conquering and expanding state was frequently, if not as a rule, ruthless and brutal toward the conquered. Only a few democratic and pacifist-oriented teachers tried to emphasize the achievements of both nations and to foster favorable conditions for cooperation and the elimination of conflict. Usually, nationalism intensified hostilities. The civil servants and teachers assigned to the area held views which gave assurance that antagonism and resistance would continue. Those who favored reconciliation seldom were employed in tension areas of Europe prior to 1945.

Thus, three large groups of relationships can be identified: the pro-groups, the out-groups, and the anti-groups. The pro-groups reflect social proximity; groups one can count on in times of conflict. The out-groups contain both friendly and unfriendly "neutrals"; people and groups one cannot depend on for active support. Some may sympathize; others, although unfriendly, may not take any hostile action. Out-groups are neutral on both sides of the continuum, lying to the left and to the right of the point of indifference. The third type, the anti-groups, represents various gradations of distance and hostility. Here are groups which may ally themselves against your group in times of conflict.

Models XVIIA and B suggest a distance and proximity scale.[1] Model B, assigning a minus sign (−) for distance and plus (+) for proximity, suggests four ranks of proximity and four ranks of distance. Model A suggests 8 ranks of distance. The greater the distance, the higher the number. The closer the proximity, the lower the number. In a study of attitudes toward the pro- and anti-groups in a tension area we can construct a scale consisting of eight values. Every rank may be identified by a corresponding term or description.

The identification of the distance and proximity of social groups also reflects the pattern of ethnic relations and those of cooperation and antagonism. In inter-political relations, such identification reflects policies. It is neither simple nor easy to move directly from social distance 8 to category 2; from the position of arch-enemy to one of close friendship. In certain cases, an emotional crisis or manipulation may facilitate such a transformation. However, with some effort at negotiations, it is easier to move the social distance from, say, rank 7—the enemy—to a zone of indifference and the position of an out-group.

The elimination of conflict or of violence does not require universal brotherhood, intensive love, or cordial friendship. It is enough to consider strangers as a friendly out-group, even as an indifferent out-group, in order to control dislikes, prejudices, and hatreds. Above all, it is imperative to avoid hurting people simply because they are different. This is the first step. Such a modest solution may create the first conditions for a tolerable, and later friendly, relationship. Thus the reduction of tensions is achieved by the reduction of ranks in social distance, a process that can be evaluated.

Perception and social distance

Individual perception of the social environment is not determined solely by empirical and verifiable experiences. Two persons may perceive the same environment in a different way. Thus, in a tension area, the perception and ranking of an ethnic group depends on what we may call "the range of perception" of the perceiving person, "the actor." Such perspective and its direction may influence the development of the image of a social environment.

Recently, I advised in research in one of the depressed areas of New York City. On one hand, a student was trying to identify the social problems of this area; on the other, to find out the problems perceived by the residents, and the ranking in urgency that they gave to various needs of the community. This area is inhabited chiefly by lower-income groups that belong to racial and ethnic minorities. Many of the people are on relief. We visited, among others, the apartment of a family from the Caribbean area. The head of the family was at work. We spoke to his wife.

The apartment was clean and well-kept, and it was evident that the tenant could afford such minor luxuries as a television set. Nevertheless, the area was dilapidated, and so was the house, although the rent was relatively high.

Unemployment was a major problem in the area. Others were housing, delinquency, the passive attitude of tenants, social isolation, and a host of other problems. In addition, this was a period of struggle for integration; of the improvement of civil rights for the minorities.

A simple conversation with neighbors on the street could have indicated the problems. However, in a lengthy conversation, our resident was unable to identify any social problems other than her own. It was cold in her apartment; the heat did not work. The house was not only dilapidated, but almost entirely abandoned. She was the only tenant and her rent was high for what she was getting. Her range of perception was short, limited to the problems of her own family.

In interviews with other residents we discovered that the range of perception varied considerably. In some cases, social perception extended to the neighborhood and the street. One woman, the mother of a large family, discussed in detail the problems of safety on her street; the need of clothing for her family. However, in her evaluation of the problems of her social environment, she did not reach beyond her neighborhood and her street.

The third respondent, who worked at the airport and probably belonged to a union, had the widest range. He was the father of a large family and, in addition, supported some abandoned children whom his wife had found in the neighborhood. They both knew the needs of their own community; the problem of deterioration of entire communities; problems of unemployment; and general issues of discrimination, to which they seemed to be sensitive. They also stressed the limitations of the school system and of education in general. Thus, the first tenant represented a narrow range of perception; our third respondent, a broad range.

In a tension area one person may perceive another ethnic group solely through his immediate experience in his own neighborhood. Another observer may form his "social image" of an ethnic group on the basis of a wide experience, acquired through travels in a wider area or through reading.

For instance, one Pole in Silesia may perceive a German as he sees him in his own neighborhood. Another perceives the German ethnic group as a whole, on the basis of his travels in Berlin or in Frankfurt or in Bonn. The ranking of the two observers is different, as is the image of the ethnic group. In still another case, one Pole may perceive Germany through his reading of Goethe, Humboldt, and Kant, and his enjoyment of classical and Romantic German music; another, through the experiences he suffered under Hitler, Himmler, and Heydrich. These are of course extreme and academic examples. Nonetheless, each individual may rank the German ethnic group differently. Thus the distance and the proximity will be different, as will the social image of the nation.

The perception of an ethnic group, however, is far more complex. The value structure of the observer influences the perception, i.e., the way the facts are perceived. The values influence the selection of facts, even the direction of observation.

The ideology of a political man, a person strongly motivated by ideological issues, acts both directively and selectively. During the Hitler period, a German pacifist viewed French and Polish pacifists as members of his own in-groups (so, conversely, did the French and Polish pacifists); while a German Nazi was the enemy, he belonged with the German nationalists to the anti-groups.

The range of perception (and the distance) as well as the direction and the selection of facts—all have an influence on judgment and decisions. In addition, situations influence attitudes. Man plays many roles, each of which may require a different value orientation. A multivalent personality type will show a tendency to change attitudes, or may operate on several value systems.

Differences exist also in what may be called the collective range and direction of perception. For instance, Hadley Cantril, in his research on major social concerns of groups, discovered that fear of nuclear war and of war in general was mentioned on his scale by 21% of American respondents and by only 2% of Brazilian respondents. Among national aspirations, peace was mentioned by 48% of American respondents and by only 4% of Brazilians; a better world with more international understanding, by 12% of the American respondents, but by none of the Brazilians.

The geopolitical situation of Brazil may partially explain this difference in range and direction. There was also considerable difference in opinion on "Leading National Aspirations" between Brazilian legislators and the general public. An improved and decent standard of living was mentioned by 64% of the legislators and by only 35% of the public. This difference in range of perception between leaders and followers is of interest and significance.[2]

Our individual perception is influenced by many factors; not solely by the situation and our values. Our own psychological needs may influence the direction of our perception and the development of our judgment. Our knowledge and experiences, skill and ability to relate facts, affect the way in which inferences are made on the basis of perceived facts. Last, but not least, our training, critical outlook, and ability to think in abstract terms are part of the fiber of broad generalizations, which may in turn affect decisions. The redirection of the perception, the opening of a new dimension in a perception range, may affect our judgment and encourage a reduction of tensions. Antagonistic attitudes may yield and move to the point of indifference. Individual perception and evaluation of ethnic groups may differ with the collective image, the collective representation, of such groups. Within the same ethnic group, several collective representations may correspond to a variety of attitudes. Gordon Allport skillfully applied the concept of a curve J to situations in which two or more group differences or ethnic characteristics exist.[3]

In times of conflict the social image of an "enemy" is manipulated and used to strengthen the in-group feeling, to eliminate differences within the in- and pro-groups; on the other hand, this sharpens the defensive or aggressive attitude toward the anti-group. Differences of concepts and views are controlled in authoritarian societies; they are eliminated or driven underground. The action is determined according to collective representations, and what is claimed as dominant values and group interests.

The network of institutions

The intensification (frequently called "escalation") or reduction of tensions depends to a large extent on the policies of public and private institutions. Government is frequently viewed in terms of a single decision-making agency. However, it controls a large number of institutions and a bureaucracy, and an entire apparatus of institutions which may be considered as an institutional network of private agencies.

The concerted action of public and private institutions affects the intensification or reduction of ethnic tensions, since their influence is substantial. In addition, the institutional apparatus—the government—controls the means of violence, since it has a monopoly of physical power. In certain situations the policies which involve the entire apparatus may be decisive in reducing or at least in restraining ethnic tensions within an area. But there is a limit to institutional effectiveness. Ethnic or race tensions may reach an explosive point, as was mentioned before, a point beyond control of the institutional network. Once the institutions break down, a revolutionary stage may begin. This is not necessarily tantamount to a progressive and democratic change. A revolution may also institute an oppressive majority or minority over the rest of the society (for instance, the disintegration of the Czechoslovak Republic in 1938). The integration of a disorganized multitude into a new community usually requires new ideas, values, and institutions in accord with, or perceived as in accord with, interests and views of the most active groups and often, in not so distant stages, in accord with the political interests and views of the new ruling elites.

The concepts of ranking of ethnic distance and proximity in a tension area, of the range of perception, the antagonistic sequence, and the institutional network were applied in selected examples which follow this discussion. Each example is discussed from a different vantage point, and in every case the variables are reduced in a different way. My purpose was to indicate the variety of ethnic problems and relations as well as the processes of intensification and reduction of tensions. The patterns of interethnic relations vary, and different patterns may require different techniques of reduction.[4]

Not all of these represent international tension areas. They were chosen, however, because the variety of ethnic patterns and relations illuminates the nature of international tension areas rooted in ethnic or racial antagonism.

Examples

The first example represents a pattern based primarily on friendly indifference: that of two tribes of Plains Indians, the Arapahos and the Shoshones, who live on the same reservation. The two groups view each other as friendly outgroups. Interpersonal relations are rare. Intergroup relations are usually of a religious nature, or take the form of intertribal festivities. The Sun Dance and the Peyote cult function as social mechanisms which periodically reinforce the pattern of limited, friendly relations and cooperation. The Arapahos and the Shoshones therefore represent an ethnic pattern of voluntary separation or self-segregation which is neutral and, in its general nature, nonantagonistic.

The second case illustrates interethnic relations in Chanak, a Turkish town, in the first decade of the twentieth century. The institutional apparatus of the Chanak government is indifferent and rarely intervenes in matters of religion or nationality involving the various ethnic groups which live in the town. The Greeks, Turks, Jews, and Armenians follow a pattern of self-segregation. Intergroup relations are exceptional. The interpersonal relations, however limited in scope, are frequent and friendly. The ethnic groups can be mutually ranked as friendly out-groups, and also as neighbors. However, with the increase of interpolitical tensions, the official Turkish antagonism against the Armenians became intensive, and led Turkey to persecutions of the Armenians.

The third case, that of Kossovo in Yugoslavia, demonstrates the social dynamics of tension and antagonism in a strategic multiethnic area of the Balkans. The intensification and reduction of tension between the Serbian, Montenegrin, and Albanian populations follow in general the stages of an "antagonistic cycle." They move from interethnic to interpolitical. The ethnic relations, however, were and are complex. Even in times of hostilities, when the division into pro- and anti-groups was sharp, Albanian and Serb sections of the population, of common tribal traditions or ideologically related and identified with the same political creed, maintained friendly ties. They could be rated as "friends," while other ethnic Albanian groups were viewed by the Serbs of Kossovo as enemies. The case study of Kossovo suggests the impact of migratory patterns on ethnic relations and social structure.

The fourth case concerns ethnic relations in Silesia—an area divided between Czechoslovakia, Germany, and Poland—and suggests a variety of ethnic ranks of proximity and distance. In Upper Silesia, before World War II, the apparatus of public institutions was frequently used to escalate or reduce ethnic tensions. After the Polish-German agreement, extremist German organizations changed their aggressive tactics, while a similar party in Czechoslovakia, controlled from the same power center, intensified its attacks against the Czechs and the Czechoslovak Republic. At the same time the decision makers in Berlin escalated tensions in one area and eased them in another, using the same party structure and a similar mechanism.

The fifth case, a study of the city of Cracow, Poland, describes the historical development of an interethnic and interreligious pattern between Christians and Jews—between a population of Polish and Jewish origin and intermittent influxes of Germans—in a period of almost a thousand years. The ethnic pattern is shaped mainly by policies of two institutional systems: the church and the crown. By the end of the nineteenth century, several types of interethnic relations appear and continue to exist simultaneously.

Certain groups follow a pattern of self-segregation and view the others as an out-group. Others, the extremists, view those of a different religion and ethnicity as adversaries or generally as an anti-group. At the same time, a process of integration takes place, and groups, political parties, and whole sections of the Christian and Jewish population maintain friendly relations, acting toward the establishment of a pluralistic pattern. In this way, Cracow represents a multiple pattern.

In the sixth case, that of New York City, the discussion is focussed on public and private institutions. Here the public and private agencies cooperate to enforce a public policy of pluralism and integration. Prejudice and discrimination exist, and problems are not fully solved, but the agencies represent a consistent policy and philosophy.

8.

FRIENDLY NEUTRALITY AND
ETHNIC SEPARATION

*Separation and Intertribal Relations: The Arapahos and
the Shoshones of the Wind River Reservation*

The interethnic pattern

The Arapaho and Shoshone Indian tribes live on the same Wind River Reservation,[1] but in separate groups. They show no desire or tendency to integrate.
Their settlements are in two separate and somewhat distant areas. Intergroup relations are reduced to ritualistic intertribal festivities such as the Sun Dance, the
rodeos, and joint councils on common economic interests and property on the reservation. The members of the two tribes show neither love nor hostility toward
each other. On the whole, their attitude is one of neutrality and cool correctness.
The pattern is one of separation combined with neighborliness and periodic reinforcement of intergroup relations by common rituals and cooperative economic
activities. The ethnic proximiity is one of "friendly out-groups."

The reservation; relations between the two tribes

The Wind River Reservation of Wyoming measures about 3,600 square miles.
It is located at the entrance to the Shoshone National Forest, which separates the
reservation from Yellowstone National Park, about 50 miles distant. The reservation consists of valleys, rich forest areas, lakes, trout streams, and excellent pastures.
It is also rich in oil. In 1878 the Shoshones, led by their famous Chief Washakie,

settled on this reservation and signed a treaty. They occupied the eastern part of the reservation, around Fort Washakie and east of it. The tents of the Arapahos were pitched around the mission of Ethete, in the western part of the reservation. The Shoshone came first, the Arapahos later.

Even in the 1950's the Shoshones were remembered in local lore as traditional enemies of the Arapahos. The Cheyennes, the Dakotas, and the Arapahos were the historic enemies of the Shoshones, who frequently joined the settlers and the American troops in the wars against the former three.[2]

In the years after World War II, the Shoshones and the Arapahos shared the same reservation. The Indian culture was still vigorous, and tribal solidarity was strong. Between the tents of the Arapahos and the log houses and tents of the Shoshones, there was an uninhabited area of at least 15 miles used by both tribes for hunting and grazing.

In the idiom of intergroup relations, this was a pattern of self-segregation, not imposed by any third authority. However, the concept of self-segregation is not entirely appropriate. Here, after all, were two different tribes organized largely on informal lines but strongly integrated within their own units, especially the Arapahos. Perhaps the term "separation" is more appropriate.

Contacts were rare. Nonetheless, there was no hostility between the tribes; even "anti-locution" (insulting language) could not be noticed—at least not by this writer during several summers spent among them. In the sign language still in general use among the older generation, however, each tribe could, and sometimes did, express condescension toward the other. But beyond these expressions one could not notice any other signs or expressions of anti-tribal prejudice. The Arapahos, however, had no love for the Shoshones.

It was well remembered that they were once mortal enemies, and a distance was carefully kept between the tribes. But still, they were exemplary neighbors and I observed neither fighting nor any hostile action between them during the period from 1947 to 1952 when these observations were made.

The Arapaho children were raised in a cultural climate of neighborhood, social distance, and tradition that the Shoshones were once the archenemies of the Arapahos. Some prejudice, perhaps even antagonism, must have been latent but it was carefully controlled. I found evidence of it only once during the time I was there. It was an announcement before the Sun Dance.

The Sun Dance is a religious ritual combined with fasting and penitence, that can be initiated by either tribe. Once, when the Shoshones organized the dance, they invited the Arapahos. In the Arapaho cooperative, a handwritten announcement was posted: "Arapahos are welcome to dance in the camp at the Shoshone Sun Dance. Don't listen to rumors. You are all welcome. Shoshone Dance Committee. Signed, Chairman."

Ethnic separation

Between these tribes there is no tendency toward integration, nor even the slightest idea of this concept. The subjective and objective nationalities are merged in each tribe. In other words, the culture of both tribes is distinct, and the tribal identification in both units is very strong. Every individual identifies himself by his tribal name and tribal symbols. A tendency toward closer cooperation is not encouraged, although members of the influential Peyote cult form an exception. (The Peyotists, a religious sect, are a separate, small, and secret society, a lodge.)

This pattern of friendly separation is by no means favored by the nature of the economics of the reservation nor enforced by historical traditions. It seems that it grew slowly and that the old chief Washakie, who was a tribal statesman, contributed to this aspect.[3]

The historical traditions were those of continuous war and fighting until about 1876, when the tribes settled on the reservation. The ancient lore was transmitted to the children and repeated at the campfire or at noon at the green circle before the mission. But this was not the only way. In the summer time, an Indian father would take his sons on an automobile trip, or within the reservation in his horse-drawn wagon, and show them the places of battles. He told his sons heroic stories of conflict, war, and destruction.

In 1947 each tribe had about 1,500 members on the reservation. The two owned collectively: (1) oil, (2) timber, (3) hunting grounds, (4) ranges, and (5) pastures. The oil rights were farmed out to large companies. Collective ownership was administered by a business council, elected by all members of the tribe. Everyone over 35 years of age had the right to be elected a member of the council and everyone had voting rights at age 21. Authorization to the business council to take action was given by the general council of the two tribes.

Only once did the Arapaho council request to divide the reservation between themselves and the Shoshones. This request, however, was never put into operation and the Arapaho never repeated it. The reservation remained under joint tribal ownership. There was never a proposal to divide the reservation among the individuals, although there was a tendency toward separation among the younger generation.[4]

Intertribal meetings and rituals

Both Shoshones and Arapahos participated in the meetings of the general council, which were orderly and well conducted. There were no tensions at the meetings which this writer had the opportunity to observe. Without brotherly love, Arapahos and Shoshones met in their economic intertribal councils and discussed and decided upon matters in a peaceful manner. They were fine speakers, and the dignity of the Indian council meeting was reflected in their business councils. Without love—they could administer their bitribal collective property.

The common ownership of land, oil rights, pastures, and forests could have created an opportunity for intertribal rivalry, tensions, and hostilities, but it did not. Neither the economics nor the idea systems, "the base" nor "the superstructure" were used toward the reinforcement of hostilities. And still it was the buffalo and the enemy which were the themes of life and, as an anthropologist said 50 years ago, the most constant ideas in the minds of the western nomads.[5] By the twentieth century there was a will to maintain the pattern of friendly separation.

But both Shoshone and Arapaho met as representatives of the tribes at intertribal functions. To these festive occasions belonged, above all, the Sun Dance. As I mentioned before, the Sun Dance is not a secular activity. It is an extended ritual that usually lasts for five days; a religious service marked by fasting and penitence. During the summer, Sun Dances are organized by both tribes. The Arapahos invite the Shoshones and the Shoshones reciprocate. After World War II, the Sun Dance spread over the plains again, and it was still vigorous on the Wind River Reservation.

At the large Sun Dances, other Indians also participated—the Crows, the Cheyennes, the Utes. The delegates of these tribes arrived in automobiles, pitched their tents, and participated in the dances. In that way, the dance reinforced the Indian identity of all the Plains tribes. Its function was not to integrate them into a single cultural unity. It was a kind of "ritualistic mechanism" based on limited common values, perhaps even institutions, which reinforced the Indian community while simultaneously encouraging tribal diversity. Members of different tribes could be recognized (for instance, Shoshones and Arapahos spoke different tribal languages and had a different ornamentation on their moccasins) and their tribal identity was emphasized.

The intertribal general council and the activities of the business council were other areas that reinforced the friendly relations and certain cooperative patterns between the tribes. Both groups also met at rodeos and celebrated July 4 together, which they had assimilated as a national holiday. In consequence, the separation of the tribes was not identical with their isolation. There were periodic activities which contributed to good neighborly relations and to the strengthening of intertribal ties. The Sun Dance, in particular, which ends with a feast in which visitors from all tribes participate, helped to iron out differences and nascent antagonisms. Thus it functioned as a social mechanism, restoring from time to time the limited intertribal solidarity.

The Shoshones had more social relations with the non-Indian Americans than the Arapahos, perhaps because they were closer to the towns of Lander and Fort Washakie. They also adopted a few white men, some of whom married Shoshone women. There were no white men among the Arapahos. The Arapaho society still has a generational class structure. The older generation holds high status and the authority to enforce the dominant values.

In the religious service and rituals of the Indians and in their prayers, the theme of peace and human brotherhood was stressed, especially during the secret Peyote Lodge meetings. In the general value structure these norms ranked high.

To recapitulate, in tribal lore, in everyday conversation, there is no love between the Arapaho and Shoshone, but there is peace, cooperation and a reserved, moderate attitude, sometimes friendly, sometimes cold, reminiscent of the not so distant past.

Peace without love

The Arapahos and the Shoshones developed a de facto limited pluralistic system. Both groups lived in separate areas, and the cooperation between the tribes was limited to the narrow field of economics and religious activities. The mechanism of religious rituals and celebration continuously reinforced the pattern of limited cooperation and also served as a mechanism for easing the tensions as well as controlling the latent prejudice. As was mentioned before, few "interpersonal" relations were noted between them—no personal friendship, intermarriage, or non-tribal, individual partnerships. But intergroup relations (unlike the case of Chanak, to be discussed) were vigorous, and appeared in rituals, meetings, and celebrations. Of course, common Indian tradition and values may explain this in part. (The Poles and Ukrainians in our later discussion, although both of Slavic background, never developed similar mechanisms.) Arapahos and Shoshones viewed each other as neighbors, as friendly out-groups perhaps, but never as anti-groups.

But the in-group concept is a relative one. The writer was present at so-called "rehearsals" for the Sun Dance, which are performed at night before the fire, and also remained alone one night at a large Sun Dance, when many Indian tribes met. At this time all the Indians were the "in-group," and the three non-Indians present were ignored to a point that the division was apparent. Songs, violent incantations and bodily movements, drums, and fire affected the Indian meeting: emotions built up rapidly. Next morning, however, attitudes changed, and everyone was friendly again.

We may call this pattern limited pluralism, but it is preferable perhaps to identify it as a system of friendly neutralism; of separation associated with limited cooperation.

This description may end with a note from my field book.

AUGUST 29, 1948

An interesting problem still is the question of how the Arapahos, the scourge of the plain, became rather suddenly a peaceful and relatively friendly tribe, and how it happened that sons and grandsons of Arapaho warriors became friendly and prayed for peace and human brotherhood. This deserves a broad discussion and research. When I asked Arapahos about it, they were unable to give an answer. Dr. Roberts, who has been on the reservation for 60 years and was witness to this change told me, "You need law and authority."

Nations sometimes change when they are conquered, and when they are humanely treated, they may perhaps become peaceful as did the Arapahos. Nations change through defeat, revolutions and victory. The disappearance of the buffalo and the final defeat of the Indians must have contributed to the change. Could the change of Arapaho psychology and values bring some enlightenment to our problem—the changing of the attitudes in Europe?

Separation and interpersonal relations: Chanak [6]

The ethnic pattern

In 1910, Chanak, a town in Asia Minor inhabited by Greeks, Armenians, Jews, and Turks, was an example of friendly neutralism in ethnic relations as a result of ethnic self-separation combined with limited interpersonal relations. Each of the ethnic groups belonged to a different religion, and each inhabited a definite section of the town. The ethnic and religious communities seldom met together as groups. However, although the various communities lived separately, they were not isolated from one another. Unlike the Arapaho-Shoshone relations, where the two tribes met only as separate ethnic units during intertribal religious celebrations and economic meetings, and had no interpersonal relations, the Jews, Greeks, Turks, and Armenians of Chanak did not meet together on any particular occasion but communed as individuals.

Interpersonal relations were limited in scope but frequent between Jewish traders and Turkish peasants; between Armenian or Greek craftsmen and their customers of different nationalities. In consequence, a pattern of ethnic separation was combined with limited but friendly interpersonal relations. Generally, there was no open antagonism or hostility between the groups, but neither was there any effort toward integration or broad cooperation. Interethnic or interreligious associations did not exist and were not encouraged.

Between 1905 and 1910, the pattern of ethnic and religious separation was relatively free of hostilities and tensions. The diverse ethnic and religious groups lived together peacefully, regulating mutual relationships through their own communal institutions. Direct discussion and negotiation by the religious representatives supplied the mechanism for the easing of tensions or settling of differences between the groups. Later, however, the persecutions of Armenians in Turkey had echoes also in Chanak.

The urban communities

In Chanak, the Turks were Moslems; the Greeks, Greek Orthodox; the Jews belonged to the Mosaic faith; and the Armenians to the Gregorian and Catholic churches. Each of these ethnic religious groups formed its own community. The Turks lived close to the sea around the citadel. Southwest of it was the Armenian section. South of the Armenians were the Jews, and below them, the Greeks.

Every group kept its identity. The communities were not separated by law or by walls. A Turk or an Armenian, a Jew or a Greek, could live in any section of the town. However, traditionally and by custom, members of the ethnic groups settled only in their own community. Later, Jews of means settled near the seashore. From the center to the sea ran a business street in which crafstmen and merchants from all these communities had their business premises. Here, one could see the stores and workshops of Jewish carpenters, Armenian shoemakers, and Armenian or Greek businessman. This was the busiest section of the city.

Each national community had its own place of worship. The Armenians and the Greeks each had one large church; the Jews had three synagogues; and the Moslems had several mosques. The groups were always identified ethnically, and there was no tendency or policy of integration. Nor did the Turks impose their culture on other ethnic groups. The Turkish government required only that the Turkish language be taught, to a degree, in the schools of the various communities.

Every community had its own schools. There was, however, a Turkish high school, and any qualified student was admitted. The Greeks and the Jews preferred to go to their own high schools, where the French language was required. They neglected to learn Turkish, and spoke it very little. Interestingly enough, the Armenians, who were later persecuted by the Turks, spoke good Turkish and many of them were educated in Turkish schools.

Separation and class structure

The communities were governed by their own people, their own communal institutions, even their own laws. The Turkish government interfered little in their affairs, and if tension arose between two communities, it would be settled between the individual religious leaders. In the Jewish community Hebrew law was applied, especially in business matters between Jews and in matrimonial and family affairs.

The communities were entirely separated from each other by their culture as well as their own tendency toward self-segregation. There was no feeling that one ethnic group had a higher status than another, or was subordinated to another, with the exception of the Turks, who held a special position. The Jew, the Greek, and the Armenian usually belonged to a higher income and social class than the Turkish peasant. Nevertheless, the "minorities" realized that political power was in Turkish hands, and maintained a certain caution in their relations with the Turks. ("We all knew that the power was with the Turks; dealing with the Turks was a cautious business—this meant we had to talk politely.") The political structure was not identical with the social-economic stratification. "The political ruling classes" and the "social base" of political power did not coincide with the social-economic class structure. In fact, these were different stratifications.

In Jewish homes there were Jewish servants. They were decently treated. The Armenians, the Turks, and the Greeks also had servants of their own kind. Sometimes the Greeks served as gardeners in other ethnic and religious groups, and they had a well-earned reputation for their gardening skills. In a sense, ethnic relations were not projected into class relations.

Every ethnic group had its own class stratification. However, the distribution of political power was a different matter. All political power was in the hands of the Turks. The Jews, the Greeks, and the Armenians had no political power whatsoever.

Interpersonal relations

The opportunities for interpersonal relations were many, but limited in scope. "Bread and meat for holidays was baked in a privately owned but 'communal' oven. The same oven was used by Turks, Jews, and Greeks who lived in the vicinity where the neighborhoods met. Men or servant girls from various ethnic religious groups used to bring their food for baking to the stove. There they would meet and talk." Occupational specialization and the division of labor and of trades were, to a large extent, ethnic. But in a sense, the ethnic groups were complementary. Each had specialists in certain trades. Jews were known as tailors, Greeks as gardeners and bricklayers, Armenians and Greeks as traders in cloth and linen.

My father, who was a dry goods merchant, used to send me to Armenian homes to fetch cloth. There I would meet the Armenians.

In times of the harvest my father used to take me to the villages, where we visited the peasants. I remember visiting Ali, who greeted my father, "Good morning Haji Joseph." They called my father Haji since he had been to Palestine. Then my father would trade with the Turkish peasants, who paid for the merchandise in grain, not in money. The price of the grain was given by my father according to the official price which he learned from the tax collector in the town. In the evening, the Turkish farmer would offer us his best room, which I remember as very clean, and the best food he had, and we had pleasant conversation with him. Similarly, when he came to town he would visit us and we would extend hospitality to him. The relations between my father and the farmers were always excellent. We were very friendly and we invited them home.

The only place where friendships of a less sporadic nature were made was the high school, where youths of all ethnic backgrounds met and studied in the same classes. Turkish was the language in which the subjects were taught. I cannot remember any public functions in which all nationalities participated except one—the birthday of the sultan.

A feeling of greater community arose on only one occasion, and an attempt was made to integrate all groups into one nationality. This was during the Young Turk revolution, when enthusiasm for it swept the various nationalities in Chanak. The Turkish officers who rebelled against the sultan advocated a single "Ottoman" nationality for all ethnic and religious groups. According to their program, every inhabitant of the empire was an Ottoman, whatever his religious and ethnic background.

But this interlude was short. Soon afterward came a time of strong political propaganda and unrest, marking the beginnning of ethnic tensions and ethnic hostilities. This was the situation in 1910. Later, with the increase of political action and nationalism, strong anti-Armenian tendencies appeared and, as is commonly known, the Armenians of Turkey suffered persecutions at the hands of the Turks.

Peace without virtue

We will limit our observations to 1905–1910, before the nationalistic political action appeared on the scene and before the Armenians were blamed for their cooperation and sympathies with the Russians. In this limited period, ethnic communities were sharply separated, but interpersonal relations, although limited, were frequent. Economically, the populations depended on each other. The government, while securing the preponderance of the Turks and Moslems, did not interfere in the internal affairs of the other communities.

Tensions were eased through interpersonal relations or direct negotiations between representatives or religious leaders of the communities. But there were no permanent institutions regulating these relations nor any permanent association to which all the groups belonged in a cooperative union. The relationship between the ethnic groups generally ranked between the status of "neighbors" and "friendly out-groups." For example, the Turkish peasant belonged to an out-group, while a Greek probably viewed the Armenians as somewhat distant neighbors. This was a pattern of ethnic separation, combined with frequent interpersonal relations.

When interethnic relations entered the political phase, tension began. It started when the Turkish nationalists and government began their action against the Armenians. At this point, the interethnic relations changed into intrapolitical, complex relations, with the government in power supporting a policy directed against one of the minorities. Chanak was not an exception. Other Turkish towns could provide similar examples.

The pattern of relations in Chanak has its roots in old Turkish institutions and in the very nature of the Turkish state. The millet system of the Turks gave at least some cultural and religious autonomy to the subordinate groups, and contributed to the establishment of a certain ethnic pattern. The "ideology" and practice of Turkish bureaucracy were rooted in indifference and inefficiency. The Turks were not a busy type of people who interfered continuously in the life of the community. However, when political power or taxes were involved, the heavy Turkish hand was visible.

Turkish laziness and indifference contributed more to tolerance and tolerable life than the active ways of obsessive preoccupation with personal and private matters of subjects and the efficiency of an inquisition. Thus, in a historical perspective some sins may turn out to be virtues, while virtues may later appear as bigotry.

9.

ETHNIC TENSIONS IN KOSSOVO

Serbs, Albanians, and Montenegrins

The area; the pattern of ethnic tensions

Kossovo, sometimes called Southern Serbia, is today a part of Yugoslavia. It was awarded to Serbia after the Balkan Wars. After World War I, Serbia became part of the Yugoslav state and in consequence Kossovo became part of Yugoslavia. After World War II, Kossovo, which had been briefly annexed by the Albanians, was returned to Yugoslavia. It now forms an autonomous region within Serbia, combined with Metohiya into an area called Kosmet. In the north, Kosmet borders on Montenegro, an autonomous republic within the Yugoslav state; in the west, on Albania; and in the south, on Macedonia, another autonomous republic within the Yugoslav state. In the east the Serbian territories border on Bulgaria.

Kosmet is inhabited by three major groups: the Serbs, the Albanians, and the Montenegrins, a subcultural or subnational group of the Serbs. Tensions among the three ethnic groups are of a specific nature, though latent at present. In Kossovo the tensions passed several times through the three major stages and, after conflicts, were usually subdued, controlled, or partially eased. They remained, however, as a latent phenomenon, a potential threat.

In modern times the following stages could have been observed: 1) a growth of interethnic tensions; 2) the intensification of interethnic rivalry into an intrapolitical tension, one in which the state takes part, usually supporting one ethnic group against a so-called minority; 3) an interpolitical and interethnic tension (a complex tension) in which at least two states, two governments, are involved. Other states actively sought to expand into the territory or to intensify its tensions to the point of open conflict.

Today the interethnic tensions are controlled and eased to a certain extent. They do exist, but are not encouraged by the present Yugoslav government. On the contrary, the present government seems to have made definite attempts to reduce tensions through a variety of political measures. Nevertheless, some potential ethnic tension does exist. Mutual relations between the ethnic groups are mixed; both cooperative and antagonistic. Between the two governments—Yugoslav and Albanian—there is now open antagonism. However, this antagonism has not been reflected in the policies of the Yugoslav government toward the Albanian minority in Kossovo. The government may favor the Serb element, but there is no open prejudicial action against the Albanian minority. Informed Albanian sources abroad suggest, however, that the situation has deteriorated in the 1950s.

Migrations and ethnic groups

From the fifteenth century until the end of the Balkan Wars, Kossovo was part of the Ottoman Empire. Turkish rule left a cultural imprint on the population and on the social relations among the various ethnic groups. While the origin of these ethnic groups is primarily of historical significance, it also has some political importance.

A century and a quarter ago, the French historian François Guizot stated in his Paris lectures that time is the strongest argument of Western legitimacy. Those who arrive first claim the territory. The latecomer is considered to have weakest claim. So, the historians and statesmen of continental Europe were and are constantly on the lookout for the "autochthonic argument" to prove that the nation they represent was the earliest occupant of a given territory. Once the historical evidence, true or false, is found, it is usually processed into official memoranda, into symbols or rituals, and slowly channelled into textbooks.

Theories of early arrival become arguments in diplomatic negotiations and are used to reinforce nationalism. When the government wishes to escalate tension, it can manipulate the social myths of autochthonism to intensify emotions. But the nature of migration, I have said, is not solely of propagandistic or political significance. It frequently influences the distribution of land, and the military and political control of an area.

In this case, however, it was not the early migration but the Turkish occupation that probably had the greatest influence. In the Balkans, the Slavs were relative newcomers. They arrived between the sixth and seventh centuries. But the Greeks and the Illyrians were already there. As far as Kossovo is concerned, the issue is more controversial. And since historical and archeological research has so often been associated with political objectives, it is not easy to judge the arguments. We can only indicate that many scholars, especially Serbs, support the thesis that the Albanians are the most recent colonizers of this area. Probably they first came between the end of the seventeenth century and the beginning of the eighteenth, immediately following the desertion of the Christian Serbs. Those Albanians who embraced Islam were protected by the Turkish government and assisted as loyal subjects.

On the other hand, some Albanian and Italian scholars argue that the Albanians are autochthonic in the area, and can be traced back to the thirteenth century. Others go even further, and argue that the autochthonic Albanians retreated before the Slavs; returned by the thirteenth and fourteenth centuries and were assimilated by the Serbs or left; and returned again by the seventeenth and eighteenth centuries. It is an involved and confused argument, in which historical documentation and linguistics have been used extensively to support the various theories.[1] I do not intend to estimate its validity.

Generally speaking we can identify three, or even four, major types of migrations in this area:

THE FIRST IS CONQUEST.

THE SECOND IS TRIBAL OR INTEGRAL MIGRATION such as that of the Slavs in the sixth and seventh centuries. Conquest might have been combined with tribal migration; or perhaps certain conquered areas were not inhabited. In any event, migration in the form of conquest or invasion occurred many times in the history of this area.

THE THIRD TYPE IS THE PENETRATING AND SLOW MIGRATION into the territory that must have taken place especially during the Turkish occupation.

THE FOURTH TYPE IS THE INTERNAL COLONIZATION which was recorded historically after World War I when Montenegrins were brought to Kossovo as settlers.

Nationality and religion

As I mentioned before, the Turkish period left a strong impression on social, political, and religious relations in this area as well as on the entire Balkan region. By the end of the fifteenth century the Turks had overrun large sections of the Balkans and firmly established their rule.

After the historic Battle of Kossovo in 1389, the Serbian state was destroyed. Less than a century later, Albanian resistance to the Turkish invasion ceased with the death of the last great Albanian leader, Skanderbeg. The conversion to Islam had a fundamental significance in social, political, and economic relations in this area. Islamic converts were identified with the conquerors and the ruling nation; those who remained Christian belonged to the subordinate group. Hostility developed between them.

Religions and ethnicity merged. The Orthodox Christian was identified as a Serb; a Bosniak Moslem, as a Moslem or a Turk; and a Moslem Albanian, as a Moslem or a Turk. A number of Albanians remained Christians, some were Roman Catholics, but large numbers were converted to Islam. Turkish rule emphasized religion rather than ethnic origin.

In times of national revival and emancipation, the prevailing attitudes confused the ethnic and religious issues. National identity was frequently confused with religious identity, or perhaps both were regarded as complementary and necessary aspects of nationhood. I must, however, add the reservation "to an extent," since Bosniaks were Moslems, yet they remained Serbs. Nevertheless, in popular Serb parlance the Bosniak was identified with the Turk.

The Turkish heritage; the millet system

Relations among the three ethnic groups were shaped during the Turkish administration and later under Serb and Yugoslav rule. The Turkish occupation left a strong imprint on the values, institutions, behavioral patterns, and social-economic conditions of the Balkans.

To state that Turkish rule was despotic is only part of the truth, since it was full of contradictions. There were periods of oppression, but there were also times of milder administration. In one area the government might be mild, in another, oppressive and even ruthless. Also, it varied substantially in different historical periods.

In the seventeenth century the disintegration of the Ottoman Empire began and Ottoman rule declined. Throughout the entire Turkish period, however, the village communities and religious groups were able to preserve a certain amount of autonomy. In certain periods the condition of the peasantry under Turkish rule was perhaps even better than that prevailing in certain parts of Europe, where serfdom became widespread and highly oppressive.

Village autonomy and religious freedom under the Turks resulted from both the "millet" system and the typical Turkish administrative indifference, incompetence, and inefficiency. The latter attributes also had a ruinous effect on the population. While they provided a certain freedom in the village communities, they also facilitated oppression and ethnic and religious feuds.

Mohammed II, the conqueror of Constantinople, invited the Greeks to return. He reinstated the patriarch in Constantinople and gave him both spiritual and temporal power, including a personal bodyguard. The Greek Orthodox Church gained broad autonomy, as did the other religious denominations. Every major religion—Catholic, Jewish, the Protestant, the Gregorian Armenian, Moslem—had its own "millet" (a kind of limited religious autonomy) and administered its own religious affairs. The head of the millet, the "millet Bashy," also had some civil power.[2]

Especially in the earlier period of its rule, the Turkish government was more tolerant than the states which called themselves Christian at that time. Turkey welcomed persecuted Jews from Spain in the fifteenth century and from Russia in the nineteenth. Orthodox Greeks preferred to be subjects of Turks than to come under Roman Catholic control. Nevertheless, the position of the Christian in Turkey was inferior and he suffered from indignities and many burdens. In addition, the Turkish military forces were oppressive and predatory and the tax burden was very heavy.

The Turkish administration, however, did not penetrate inland to any great extent, especially in the period of its decline. In the village communities, in clans and tribes, a share of the power remained with the local population. Native rulers were often oppressive. Brigandage was common. Ethnic and religious feuds between the inhabitants were frequent. Local Turkish administrators had neither the skill nor the efficiency to control the people. Their attitude was one of general indifference as long as taxes were collected, money supplied, and the subjects did not rebel against the ruler. Within the empire, however, the local pashas exercised extensive power and were frequently oppressive.[3]

The ethnic structure

Thus, the basic pattern of religious and ethnic relations was established during the Turkish rule in the Balkans, a rule that extended in some areas until the beginning of World War I. More than Central and Eastern Europe, and even Western Europe, the Balkans preserved an archaic ethnic division, because Turkish control froze the existing ethnic conditions and arrested change.

In the same period, Western Europe passed through a process of integration. States developed and tribes were united into one nation. In Eastern Europe also, various principalities, under powerful central governments, underwent the same processes as Western Europe. In consequence, various ethnic groups were molded into one nationality by the political machinery of the states. Some subcultural differences always remained, however, because differences were never fully obliterated.

National consciousness emerged as large national states grew slowly, from the end of the medieval time to the modern period, culminating in the nationalist movements of the nineteenth century.

The Balkans moved into modern history without either the contemporary Western industrial and agricultural revolutions or the Western development of national states. They also retained a different ethnic structure. Their ethnic divisions were deeper; they were also complicated by the survival of tribal organizations and by a strong religious identification.

The conversion to Islam was strong in certain areas, especially in Bosnia and Albania, and the converts became more conservative than the native Turks. In Bosnia, the Bosnian-Moslem nobles exercised extensive power. Many of them had settled in Serbia as landowners and had become possessors of the soil. The Albanians were, in the main, converted to Islam, although many were Catholic or Orthodox. Albanians comprised the elite of the Turkish troops, and many achieved the highest positions in the Turkish army administration, as did Serbian-Moslem converts.[4] The converts were a privileged group. They were separated from the rest and, as a historian of the Balkans has said: "distinct and apart, the two nations, conquerors and conquered, lived thus nearly 400 years." [5]

Ethnic antagonism and prejudice

For the Serb, the Turk was at best an outsider, a member of an out-group. But when antagonism intensified, and Serbs were killed, the Turk was identified as the "hereditary enemy." In turn, the Orthodox Serb was subdued and exploited by the Turkish authorities. Thus hostilities and antagonism grew out of experience. The social image, or what is frequently called an ethnic stereotype, contained elements from everyday experience. But it was extended from a unique experience with some Turks to the entire Turkish nation and the Moslem religion. Actually, there was some truth mixed with prejudice in this social image.

In the distribution of political power the Turk was superordinate; power rested with him. In the remainder of the class structure, political, religious, and ethnic divisions coincided with nationality.

The military and civilian distinctions coincided with the ethnic. The Turk, the native Moslem, was a soldier and administrator. A Moslem Serb or Albanian was a peasant, a soldier, or a noble. The distinction between conqueror and conquered, ruler and ruled, was emphasized on a number of levels. When, in the nineteenth century, exploitation and oppression increased, the distinction was reflected in ethnic antagonism.

Ethnic and religious differences were intensified with cumulative strength in Macedonia and Kossovo, where the diversity of the population was strong and the antagonism sharp. (Under Turkish rule the Moslems in Kossovo were probably in the majority, as is indicated by a number of sources,[6] but this was a religious, not an ethnic, majority.)

Since the majority of the Albanians in Kossovo were Moslem and champions of Turkish and Islamic causes,[7] they were in continuous and mutual antagonism with the native Orthodox Serb population. These were the two major out-groups, changing in times of antagonism into anti-groups.

However, as we shall see later, the tribal organization of the Albanians and of the Serbs made social relations more complex than a simple division into pro-groups, out-groups and anti-groups; into groups of friends, neutrals and enemies. There was no straight line between the Albanians and the Serbs, and there were still tribal divisions which complicated the picture and made it more interesting.

But hostilities between Albanians and Serbs subsided from time to time and then, the tension eased to a point of "indifference" and the former anti-group became again an out-group. When differences increased, the ranks changed to antagonistic groups, then to enemies. The traditional social image of an archenemy reappeared and was manipulated to intensify hostility and aggression. At this point massacres were not infrequent, and became a tragic part of ethnic relations in the Balkan area, especially in Macedonia and Kossovo.

There is a difference between a war and a massacre, which may be a consequence of war. But the Kossovo and Balkan massacres were generally inflicted not only by hostile armies but also by ethnic groups acting as tribal groups and later as political military organizations or as partisans.

When hostility becomes intense and the out-group is branded as the enemy, moral consideration and restraint toward the out-group breaks down. Mutual solidarity and aid are then limited to the pro-groups which are integrated, and antagonism is directed against the anti-group with no mercy and no consideration. The range of moral judgment and moral restraint is limited to one's own tribal group and to allies. Those who inflict the sufferings frequently do not regard the act as immoral but as an act of justice.

Thus, the massacre became part of the Balkan political picture. The history of the intensification of ethnic tensions is marked by the frequency of those massacres. In Kossovo, they caused the Orthodox Christian population to desert certain areas and seek a haven under the Austro-Hungarian monarchy. Among them, according to Albanian sources, were also Christian Albanians. However, according to family traditions (still alive), thousands of Albanians escaped before the on-rushing Serbian army when certain areas were ceded to Serbia after San Stefano and the Berlin Treaty in 1878.

Massacres were answered by countermassacres. The Albanians descended from the mountains and attacked Serb villages. The Turkish government was too weak to protect the life or property of its subjects, and in a situation of interethnic tribal struggle, it frequently supported the Moslem group, which it regarded as Turkish. So the Serb remained helpless vis-à-vis the combined might of a state and a large ethnic group. But he too responded in terms of collective responsibility. He went to the mountains, formed his "cheta," and attacked Albanian villages and Turks to avenge his injustices. And so it continued through the emergence of the Serbian state and the years of the nineteenth century.

Historians of this period who knew the conditions from their own experience indicate the general insecurity prevailing especially in Albania, Macedonia, and Kossovo.[8] Step by step these struggles, massacres, and raids shaped the social image, values, and attitudes of the Serbs toward the Moslem Albanians.[9]

It appears from contemporary descriptions that until the end of the nineteenth century, the Albanians had the upper hand in Kossovo. Subsequently, the counter-action of the Serbs became stronger. In this area, where the tradition of blood vengeance still survived among the Albanian tribes and the Montenegrins (a sub-cultural nation of the Serbs), the massacres supplied the customary motives for the continuation of a ruthless struggle.

In a massacre, unlike in war, women and children suffer almost as much as men do. Houses are burned; property destroyed. The massacre is an expression of a belief in the principle of collective responsibility; it is directed against the tribe as an entire community and against the property of the tribe or ethnic group.[10]

Joyce Cary, who was a member of the British Red Cross during the Balkan War, gives us a balanced picture despite his pro-Montenegrin sympathies. To judge from his writing and personal observations it would seem that neither side showed mercy for its opponent. Nevertheless, he indicates that the Montenegrins preferred to take prisoners rather than to kill. Cary witnessed many battles and also saw the behavior of the armies after the action.

He witnessed executions of Turks who were taken prisoners by Montenegrins. He also saw Turks killing wounded Montenegrins. His descriptions indicate that the population was directly involved in fighting, and that many civilian Montenegrins, irregular fighters and old men, helped the Montenegrin army and frequently accepted very dangerous assignments.[11]

Cary's account, obviously sympathetic toward the Montenegrins, is interesting. However, Pierre Loti, the well-known French writer, quotes extensively from a report of the Austro-Hungarian counsul in Prizrend concerning the entry of the Serbian army into the city during the Balkan War. The consul reports that the Serbs fired on the inhabitants. Finally, despite the fact that the consulate had international immunity and the Red Cross flag was flying next to the Austrian flag, Serb officers and soldiers entered the consulate and killed Albanian families who had found refuge there.[12] The Austrian government consistently supported Albania, and the information is pro-Albanian.

In World War I, the Albanians generally sided with the Austrians, while the Serbs were on the side of the Allies. This did not help to ease the mutual tensions in Kossovo. On the contrary, tensions were intensified. The interwar period between 1918 and 1940 was a respite in the history of the massacres. With the outbreak of World War II, the massacres were resumed in the Balkan Peninsula with unusual virulence.

The Axis powers awarded the Kossovo area to the Albanians. Immediately, the Albanians burned or destroyed the houses of the Serb-Montenegrin colonists who had been brought there by the Yugoslav government between the two wars and given land which once had belonged to Albanians.

The massacres spread to the whole Balkan Peninsula. A Croat fascist state was created, led by Ante Pavelich. Croat Ustachi detachments, either Moslems from Bosnia or Catholics, started systematic massacres of the Orthodox Serb villages in other parts of Serbia. The Chetniks responded to these massacres by active defense and counter action. The persecuted tried to stop the terror by counterterror, but frequently it was simply an act of unrestrained vengeance. Today it is not easy to reconstruct the tragic past. No doubt, Serb partisan actions during this long guerrilla warfare were also ruthless; Albanians usually accuse the Chetniks of countermassacres. Today, the memories still remain. But Albanian observers, one-time partisans, argue that their countermassacres were not a matter of vengeance, and that it would be incorrect to identify them as actions of revenge, since they were only a means of "getting rid of a problem." The fact is that this type of war developed into a pattern.

Since sections of the Albanian population sided with the Germans, their hostility was channelled against the Serb population. An attempt was made to form special SS divisions of Albanians, with an ideology similar to that of the German units. However, democratic Albanians resisted. Soon a democratic resistance movement was organized, directed against fascists, Nazis, and collaborators. Albanian partisans cooperated with the Yugoslav guerrillas or partisans. Eventually, Communist Albanian guerrilla units emerged, supported by Soviet command.

The Serbs suffered atrocious massacres. Armed Ustachi and Nazi armies were thrown against Serb villages. Between them, they massacred and exterminated the civilian population.[13] News of it spread rapidly through the Serbian territory, producing countermassacres. Some observers argue that if it had not been for such Serb reactions, the destruction of the Serb population would have been even more severe. To survive this mutual process of killing, men and women were hiding their real political, ethnic, and religious identity while displaying such symbols as would please the conquerors of the day.

The Serb counter actions were also directed against the Moslem population in Kossovo. Thus the Nazis exterminated the Serbian population in the occupied territories. The Ustachis killed the Serbs. The Serb-Chetniks countered their action, and the partisans killed those who supported the Chetniks and the Ustachis. The partisans appealed to all the ethnic and religious groups and organized them under the Communist ideology. Thus, the war was a war of all against all and, at the end, it was very difficult to escape the dangers and punishments inflicted by a variety of mutually exterminating groups. Centuries of massacres in this area culminated in a holocaust directed mainly against the Serb population. In consequence, the Serbs turned against the groups whom they rightly or wrongly identified with the attackers. Thus, again, did ethnic neighbors turn into arch-enemies in war.

Violence has been part of political relations between men for centuries, but in the course of history it has been substantially eliminated from Western Europe, America, and, to an extent, Eastern Europe. However, a pattern of violence remained part of the political scene in the Balkans.[14] Interestingly enough, during the interwar period and during the war tensions between Moslem and Catholics in Bosnia, Herzegovina and Kossovo were practically absent. Even today there are no tensions between Moslem and Catholic populations. However, tensions between the Orthodox and the two other denominations were at one time strong for various reasons.

Land and antagonism

There were other factors also that had their share in the development of ethnic images and hostilities in this area. After World War I, Kossovo was given to the new Yugoslavia, which started a broad action of land reform. Settlers were brought from Montenegro and given lands which had belonged to Albanian landlords, villages, and the Turkish state. The reform regulations had provisions which permitted a certain elasticity.[15] However, the Montenegrin, the Serb element, was favored at the expense of the Albanians.

To understand the Yugoslav viewpoint, one has to remember that Kossovo is regarded as a cradle of the Serb state. Here the battles against the Turks were fought, here the Serb population suffered from foreign occupation. In terms of "historical justice," the land should have been restored to those who had fought to retain their national heritage. No doubt, under the Turks, the Orthodox Serb population had suffered more than any other group. Nonetheless, a new economic antagonism set in—that of the Albanian peasant against the newcomer, the Montenegrin.

Cumulative antagonistic tendency

As I mentioned previously, the Balkans did not share the economic and agricultural revolutions of Western Europe. Nor did they have an early and powerful industrial revolution of their own to mold their various ethnic groups into one nation with a unified cultural pattern. Also, the Balkans, including

Kossovo and Albania, did not share the crucial period from the end of the religious wars till the French Revolution, when the religious identification was separated from the ethnic, at least on the European continent.

True, there were religious persecutions in Europe, but by the end of the eighteenth century, the democratic principle that ethnicity and religion are separate areas was established. This principle had been stated earlier by the American political theorists and in the Declaration of Independence, where nationality was proclaimed a matter of common values and common beliefs. But in the Balkans, there has been no revolution, no bill of rights; only a slow deterioration of ethnic and religious amity through a long series of invasions, occupations, and oppressions that set one group against another, in a progression from out-group to anti-group, and, sometimes, to enemy.

Antagonism has a cumulative tendency. One type of antagonism reinforces the other in a continuous interaction. The ethnic antagonism reinforces the economic and, vice versa, religious tensions are projected into ethnic and economic. In consequence, ideological or religious tensions may appear as "rationalization" of economic tensions, which are regarded by some as the only "real," verifiable tensions. In fact, however, there are several interacting causal factors, each reinforcing the antagonistic tendency. Some are stronger; others, weaker. For an "operational" and analytical approach they should be considered as separate though interacting variables, because they cannot be overlooked in a policy formulation.

In the Balkan area an antagonistic cycle appeared many times. The tensions began with hostile action between two ethnic groups. In the second stage, the government supported one ethnic group against the other. In the third stage, the tension changed to interpolitical; to a tension between two or more governments.

During the Balkan War the tension of the third stage included wars between Montenegro, Serbia, and Turkey (in addition to Bulgaria and Greece). These wars were reflected in ethnic antagonisms or hostilities among the Montenegrin, Serb, and Albanian populations. This was a complex, open conflict on both the ethnic and political levels. During World War II the tension was complex, political, and ethnic.

Latent intergroup tensions and hostile attitudes were utilized by the German political and military authorities. Antagonism was manipulated from "above," reinforcing an "endemic" intergroup ethnic tension of a very high intensity. Rumors circulated among the population that Kossovo would become part of Albania and the Serb population would be expelled. This of course also greatly intensified Albanian-Serb tensions. In consequence, the tradition of the ancient feuds on one hand, and the experience of World War II on the other, intensified the attitudes of hostility between the Serb and Moslem Albanian populations.

Ethnic relations on a community level

From this general history of ethnic, interethnic, intraethnic, and interpolitical tensions, the reader may develop a picture of a continuous war in which everyone was against everyone else. But there were often long periods of neighborliness, of correct if not friendly relations between these groups. Without this neither the Serbs nor the Albanians could have survived for so many centuries. It must also be realized that acute hostilities in the form of massacres and war were catastrophic explosions which, because of historical conditions, occurred in this corner of the world more frequently than in Western Europe. Nevertheless, the catastrophe was not the only tradition from the past. As I mentioned before, Turkish rule and the wars contributed to the development of attitudes, and in consequence a social image of ethnic groups grew. The attitudes, however, changed in a variety of ways.

There was a difference in the attitude of the Serb toward the Albanian in his own village, who perhaps belonged to his own tribe, and "Albanians" as (what Leopold Wiese calls) an unfriendly "abstract collective"—Moslem Albanians as a nation, as a category, and as a social image. For the Serbs of Kossovo this antagonistic or out-group image of Albanians as a whole was not identical with their attitude toward their own neighbors in the village. In addition, the abstract social image took milder forms at certain historical periods than in times of crisis. Intergroup relations are not static. The social situation affects perception.

The "range of perception" of a neighbor differs from the perception of "Albanians" or "Serbs" as an abstract collective social image. In fact, those are two different social images, two different concepts of groups. The well-known saying, "Some of my best friends are ——," uttered with a certain pride by nationalists or racists, contains elements of truth. It says, "I relate well on an interpersonal (or community) level, especially with those whose personality appeals to me. I hate them as a 'collective,' or a 'tribe,' as a social image."

There are also individual and group differences. Nonetheless, hostility on a level of "an entire nation" is not identical with concrete relating between individuals, neighborhoods, or communities. The two levels are frequently inconsistent, being positive on the community or personality level and negative on the national or general level, as opposed to a "consistent" pattern of relationship that is positive or negative, simultaneously, on both levels. (See Appendix II, "Human Relations in Central Eastern Europe.")

I shall now narrow the field of interest to social relations on a community level, using the Albanians and the Serbs in Kossovo as an example. Here we may discover that social relations are by no means identical with continuous hostility. They are more complex and much more friendly. Also, they differ from tensions on a broader level in times of critical intensification.

The cultural difference between the Moslem Albanians and Serbs and Montenegrins in Kossovo is very evident. There is also a difference in religion. The Albanians, as already noted, are predominantly Moslem, but a small percentage are Catholic. The Serbs are Greek Orthodox, although the Bosniak Serb may often be a Moslem. Religious identification is strongly integrated with ethnic identification. The Moslem Albanian differs from the Serb in his general culture.[16]

The food habits of the Moslems and the Christians are different, whether they be Moslem Serbs or Christian Serbs; Moslem Albanians or Catholic Albanians. The values of the Albanians, Montenegrins, and Serbs in Kossovo also differ. But neither food habits nor values are incompatible. They simply contribute to the general concept of in-group and out-group.

The tribal organization, which was strong in the latter part of the nineteenth century, weakened through the years. It exists today only as a common bond of "blood." The extended family tie is still strong, however, especially among Albanians. It is interesting to note that both Albanians and Serbs frequently belong to the same tribes. This strengthens their belief in the common origin of Albanians and Serbs in this area.

Today we find three major groups in Kossovo: Serbs, Albanians, and Montenegrins. The Serbs and Albanians call themselves *meshtantsy*. The Montenegrin colonists are called *naselniks*. Between the wars at least, there was a certain feeling of solidarity between the Serbs and Albanians who claimed long domicile in the area; a sort of "in-group" feeling of the *meshtantsy* vis-à-vis the *naselniks*.

Despite the tradition of hostilities in Kossovo, especially on the interpolitical level, we shall find today many behavioral patterns, institutions, and possibly customs, indicative of neighborly relations between the Albanians and the Serbs. Many Serbs and Albanians belong to closely associated kin tribes, and tribal solidarity is stronger than ethnic hostility. Each expresses a greater affinity to his own nation, perhaps, in certain historical moments, but the tribe is fundamentally a closer group than the abstract nation, a typical secondary group. Tribal and clan proximity cuts across the ethnic lines.

However, this tribal kinship grows continuously weaker, and while remembered, it has lost its old vigor. Some traces survived among the Montenegrins and the Albanians. Nonetheless, the past traditional patterns of mutual aid suggest that interethnic tensions can be eased by intensification of other types of loyalties and by emphasizing other social ties and roles.

The custom of blood brotherhood survived into our century. According to this custom an Albanian adopted a Serb from an associated tribe as his brother.

Individual friendships between Serbs and Albanians were frequent, but marriage between Orthodox Serbs and Moslem Albanians was an exception, until recently.[17]

Mutual respect for religious beliefs and hospitality is evident, especially during the holidays. At festive times, Orthodox Serbs visit Moslem Albanians and share their meals and festivities. Similarly, Moslem Albanians visit Orthodox Albanians or Orthodox Serbs.

The exchange of hospitality between people of different faiths or different ethnic origins is of considerable significance in reinforcing cooperation and neighborly patterns. "Interdining" has a symbolic significance. Dietary laws form an indirect barrier of interethnic or interreligious relations. Their function is to separate rather than to unite; since the caste system prohibits interdining. However, hospitality, friendship, and custom overcome the barrier.

Group animosity or hostility is not expressed in daily fights or insults. However, where fist fights are incompatible with custom, values, and general culture, physical aggression between two or more persons might be less frequent, but once aggression appears as a physical fight, then it is much more violent and dangerous, since weapons or other objects are used. In consequence, a simple fight with the use of bare hands is relatively a mild form of channelling aggression into overt behavior, into a physical expression.

Between the wars, there were cases of fighting among the youths of the different ethnic groups. They sometimes started over a scarcity of water or over the demand of priority in the use or renting of a threshing machine.[18]

Reports and information from Kossovo are frequently contradictory. It seems, however, that after autonomy was granted and liberal nationality rights extended to Albanians, and Albanian language introduced to schools, tensions have eased considerably, and physical violence between Serbs and Albanians was not a problem. The feuds within the Albanian community, according to this information, did not disappear.[19] Recent information suggests that the situation has changed and substantially deteriorated.

Internal and external tensions

Blood vengeance still exists among the Albanians even under Communist rule. Stories of traditional feuds were recently reported from certain communities (Pristina). Today, these feuds are usually settled within the antagonistic families. However, they are as a rule between Albanians and not between Albanians and Serbs.[20] They are a reflection of in-group tensions, and indicate that tensions are perhaps more intensive within the Albanian group than with the neighboring Serbian group.

In a discussion of ethnic or even interpolitical tension, internal tensions are usually underestimated or even overlooked, yet they may be stronger than external tensions. Possibly with the lessening of the external tension, the aggression or the aggressive tendencies and hostilities are displaced inward, toward the members of the in-group.

Perhaps there is a relationship between internal and external group tensions. In times of strong external tension and hostility, group solidarity increases and the inner tensions decline. However, when the external tensions are eased, a tendency to channel the hostility and aggression inward may increase.

Control of ethnic tensions

During the interwar period, illiteracy among Albanians in Kossovo was high. Most schools were conducted in the Serb language. Some Albanian schools were organized after the Young Turkish Revolution of 1908 but were later abandoned. The present Yugoslav government has opened schools to Albanians, and Albanian students are well represented in national universities.

The area is an autonomous district and elected Albanian representatives meet with Serbian representatives in common institutions. Of course this is a Communist and de facto one-party system, therefore a basic difference of opinion is not welcomed. However, the present government neither supports nor instigates ethnic or interethnic feuds or hostilities.

The "apparatus" of public institutions is of primary significance in minority politics and interethnic tensions. The pressure of the state—through its political institutions, the administrative network, a variety of agencies, and the educational system—is a powerful instrument in the control and reduction of ethnic tensions. In addition, political parties and private agencies, including the church, acting in concert with public institutions, may help substantially to control and ease antagonisms.

Prejudice is deeply rooted in the human personality and cannot be easily eliminated. But by pressure from public institutions and concerted educational action, discrimination can be curbed and violent expression subdued and restrained. Today, though Yugoslavia is a dictatorship, the administrative and party apparatus in Kossovo discourages ethnic tensions and makes an effort to control and reduce them. If this tendency toward reduction continues, the younger generation may grow up with a different outlook.

Today, new problems are pressing in Kossovo and Yugoslavia, and new educational opportunities are available. The present generation faces new political, economic, and social problems. With a proper educational policy, a new social image may emerge; new attitudes may be formed, built on the positive traditions of neighborliness and friendship. Both hostility and friendship are bricks of the Albanian-Serb history in Kossovo. Emphasis on the "positive" values, customs, and traditions and a weakening of the "negative" heritage of hostilities may lead to the reduction of tensions. However, hopes should not influence the selection of fact, although they always do to some extent at least.

Cultural differences between various ethnic and regional groups in Jugoslavia are substantial. Economic conditions in various provinces or republics vary greatly. Some behavioral patterns, values, and traditions still clash. Ethnic and political hostilities have not been obliterated, and tensions, even if controlled and perhaps subdued, did not disappear. Nor is the problem of Kossovo, although it has an autonomous status, a closed political issue. The Albanians exercise strong influence in this area. Albanian nationalism in this area recently increased, and dreams of an Albanian Kossovo did not disappear. Even between Albanian and Serb communists certain tensions have been noticed, according to recent reports. The Serbs are rather on the defensive. The tension between the Albanian and the Jugoslav governments was not eased by 1965. Among the Albanians abroad, strongly opposed to present rule, the hopes of an Albanian Kossovo are still alive.

Community and ethnic distance

A number of relationships between Albanians and Serbs can be identified, each representing a different rank of ethnic distance. For an Albanian, a Serb from the same tribe in Kossovo is a friend; sometimes a blood brother, a member of an in-group. A Serb in the same village whom he visits and assists is a neighbor, even a good neighbor. Other Serbs are outsiders (out-group); they speak a different language and represent a different tradition. In times of crisis, these outsiders may become enemies or even archenemies. This, of course, is a highly simplified picture. The relationship is by no means static. As the situation changes, so may the social distance between Albanians and Serbs. A friend or a tribal kinsman may bear an even closer relationship in times of persecution. Contrariwise, an outsider may become an enemy. The interethnic relations as well as interpolitical relations must be viewed as gradations on a continuum. The distance diminishes or increases with the changes in the situation; and the situation can be manipulated.

Manipulation of tensions

Now let us return to the question of "antagonistic sequence" which I discussed earlier. Usually the antagonistic sequence moves from ethnic to intrapolitical, and from intrapolitical to interpolitical. In other words, once an ethnic tension appears, a government usually moves in to enforce the dominant policy of a country. If this policy affects a so-called minority, another government may intervene to protect its nationals or coreligionists or simply to expand its territory. Sometimes an external government escalates the tensions, as one stage in a long-range strategy. In that way, the tension moves from interethnic to interpolitical and becomes a major issue of world politics. But the sequence may be reversed and move from interpolitical to interethnic.

The case of Kossovo indicates that with the outbreak of World War II the Nazi government and local extremists instigated interethnic tensions. Many Albanians favored the Germans at first, since Albanian action against the Serbs was supported by the German authorities and by fascists of various hues.

Thus, the antagonistic cycle may begin either from above or from below. If from below, it starts with a revolutionary movement on an ethnic national level that later gains the support of an outside government; if from above, it is instigated and manipulated by the government which supports, intensifies and exploits an initial, perhaps weak, tension for its own objectives. In an Albanian village somewhere in Kossovo, in a folk culture that moves intact into an industrial period, the ethnic identity and tribal roots are still strong. With such a system of values, in-group identification is integrated and strong, but the profile of the out-group is also sharp and distinct.

It is not easy to move from one extreme to another: from extreme hostility to love and close friendship. But with the proper and skillful operation of the machinery of public and private institutions, ethnic relations may move slowly from the level of hostility to one of friendly neutrality.

10.

SOCIAL-POLITICAL MOVEMENTS, GOVERNMENT, AND ETHNIC TENSIONS

Interethnic and Interpolitical Tensions
in Silesia Between the Wars

The area

Silesia, located in a strategic corner of Europe, is inhabited by Germans, Czechs, and Poles. Before World War I, Silesia was divided between Germany (Upper Silesia) and Austria-Hungary (Teschen Silesia).

In medieval times Silesia normally belonged to Poland, but in the twelfth century it was divided into principalities. By the middle of the fourteenth century most of the Silesian principalities came under Bohemian (Czech) rule. The German advance toward Silesia also began early, and by the fourteenth century German political and cultural influence was noticeable.

In its long history, Silesia's borders changed many times. Much of the country was absorbed by Germany as it advanced slowly to the east. The borders also shifted through penetrating migration and conquest and through dynastic succession. With the Industrial Revolution, the importance of Silesia increased greatly because of its excellent coal mines. Its land was also fertile and it had other natural resources.

The end of World War I saw a period of instability in Silesia, marked by Polish uprisings, international agreements, and plebiscites. As a result of these settlements Silesia was partitioned. Upper Silesia was divided between Germany and Poland; Teschen Silesia, between Czechoslovakia and Poland. Lower Silesia remained German.

Culturally the sections were quite different. In Upper Silesia, German rule combined with the coal mines and the heavy iron and steel industry to produce a different social environment, a different pattern of life, and a different type of subculture from that of Teschen Silesia. Under Austrian sovereignty, Teschen Silesia developed high-quality textile and other industries, and retained its agriculture. Both the Austrian and German rule and their cultural influences were different, and they produced different political, economic, and cultural patterns.

It must be remembered also that Silesia had been a typical Central European border area of three major states, where three population groups met and penetrated. In such areas, nationalistic feelings were intensified. Old prejudices were frequently manipulated by bordering governments and their agencies as well as by political parties.

Political and ethnic relations

Ethnic and political relations are closely connected. However, a method of analysis and a problem-solving approach require a separation of the two for proper consideration.

Ethnic tensions are frequently maintained and reinforced by the political actions of governments, private associations and institutions, and political parties. The reinforcement of such tensions may operate in a variety of ways, notably through textbooks and teachers. The example of Silesia shows a close relationship between political actions and ethnic tensions, and the intensification of ethnic antagonisms into international interpolitical tensions. In this chapter, I shall discuss ethnic relations in Silesia between the wars.

Upper Silesia was an area of frequent political and ethnic tensions. A direct armed struggle between the Poles and the Germans took place immediately after the war, as the Poles mounted a number of insurrections against German rule. German military organizations were also active. Plebiscites, although conducted under international control, produced new tensions and conflicts. Everyday life, however, was not necessarily one of continuous struggle. Between the wars—and before the advent of Hitler to power—international treaty provisions supplied the limited protection and restraining influence of international public opinion.

The League of Nations conventions had established a system for the protection of minorities which was in force in Silesia. It was far from perfect, but the German minority in Polish Upper Silesia used its provisions skillfully and effectively. Weak as they were, these provisions formed a worthy beginning and experiment.[1] In the international conventions and agreements extended to Silesia, the league had a number of specific provisions for the protection of national minorities. Although the system was difficult to enforce and not fully effective, Upper Silesia was closely observed by the league, which set a certain public policy for its peoples.

In Czech (Teschen) Silesia, the democratic Czechoslovak Republic respected the political rights of the Polish minority. Polish associations, political parties, and unions were active. Generally speaking, they were permitted to develop freely until the last days of the first Czechoslovak Republic.

In both the German and Polish parts of Upper Silesia, the tendency to secure a dominant position for a single national-ethnic group was the public policy. This led to frequent antagonism. Internal tensions were reinforced by outside governments which, at certain periods, instigated discord.

The orientation of the central government was reflected in Silesian politics, since the public administration was centrally organized and self-government was limited. Democratic and left-of-center governments followed policies aimed at reconciliation and granted more rights to minorities.

Some German minority organizations in Polish Silesia followed a policy of extreme nationalism, but there were also democratic and social-democratic German groups which favored cooperation with Poland. With the establishment of semi-dictatorship in Poland, both German and Polish social-democratic organizations had to fight for their existence, while in the German part of Silesia, they were totally destroyed or brutally persecuted with the advent of Hitler. In Polish Upper Silesia, the democratic parties, in spite of difficulties, survived until the war, when they went underground.

The League of Nations minority treaty was intended to secure the protection of minorities. Conversely, the democratic parties favored cultural autonomy and ethnic as well as religious pluralism. But pluralism is not only the problem of the majority; it is also a problem of minorities. Nationalist parties of ethnic minorities which had the support of powerful states (or states that they believed were powerful) acted sometimes against their own government.

In 1938, the Czechoslovak Republic was destroyed by the pressures, and finally the invasion, of the German, Hungarian, and Polish governments and armies. The three governments were assisted by nationalistic minority organizations within Czechoslovakia—the German pro-Nazi party, the Slovak right-wing nationalist parties, and less important minority organizations. The German and some Polish Social-Democrats sided with the Czechoslovak Republic. In the struggle, Teschen Silesia played a major part in the drama.

Teschen Silesia is an example of interethnic tension intensified by manipulation and reinforced by material, military, and diplomatic support from external governments. The tension area in this case was used as a strategic stage for further expansion.

A pluralistic system, in which the minorities enjoy freedom of political organization, may transform a country into a tension area if extreme and antagonistic movements develop among the minority groups. The policies of such movements may produce tensions, enabling powerful outside governments to step in and utilize the tensions for their own expansion.

Not all the demands of the minorities are necessarily justified. Demands for self-government and autonomy, for civil rights and political rights in the sense of democratic value structure, are. But events preceding World War II taught us that free institutions are often abused and used to destroy a democratic republic, as was done by the Sudeten German party in Czechoslovakia. A nationalistic and extremist minority movement can use a pluralistic system and political liberties for the destruction of political liberty and pluralism.

Ethnic identification

The problem of subjective national (ethnic) identification is by no means as simple in border areas as it is in some isolated areas. Each individual plays a number of roles and has many loyalties. His dominant loyalties may change with historical development. Intermarriage, changes of citizenship, and school and mass media influences have a powerful impact on attitudes and processes of self-identification. Multivalence in this area may be expressed in changes of identity or in the assumption of a variety of national identities in different periods of one's life or in diverse situations. On one hand, national self-identification is perhaps stronger in border areas because of the antagonistic nature of intergroup relations; on the other, because of migration and other factors, certain personality types absorb differing value systems and identifications without having the desire or the capacity to reintegrate their experience around a single core of values or develop their own, well-integrated and independent identification.

Border areas are frequently areas of antagonism. Antagonism strengthens the in-group feeling and the need for identification. Self-identification with an ethnic group is a part of a defense mechanism. Identification with a "reference group" strengthens the security of an individual and his chances of survival. However, in an antagonistic situation not all identify themselves with the stronger group. When attacks are directed against a minority group, danger reinforces the psychological need in some individuals for identification with the weaker minority group. National identification or political and moral values become more dominant on the value scale than even the wish of individual biological survival. Moral imperatives are at such moments an important motivating force. Hence some of those who have open alternatives join rather the weaker and attacked minority as a matter of principles and moral identification.

The "resister's" value scale is different from that of the "multivalent opportunist." In a border area the latter may switch his identification and allegiance to the stronger in a moment of crisis. This was seen following the German occupation of Eastern Europe, when some of the so-called "Aryan" members of conquered nations claimed an earlier German ancestry. They changed their identity to what was called *Volksdeutsche* (Folk Germans), acquiring some privileges of the conqueror at the price of participating in the persecution of their own kinfolk and neighbors.

Between the "resister" of a strong identification and the "opportunist" who changes identity according to situation, is the "positivist," who represents a policy of survival under oppressive conditions. Instead of struggle, he chooses "organic work" and nonviolent action to secure the best possible advantage for his group. It is among the resisters and the positivists that one may find those who attempt to ease tensions and look for such peaceful solutions of race and ethnic problems as pluralism or integration.

Multivalence, however, is not synonymous with opportunism. In a border area—as we shall see—multivalence, resulting from the primary group structure and the general social environment, is frequent. When your father is a Czech, your mother a German, and your father-in-law a Pole, a single ethnic identification is neither simple nor even "objective." A son in such a family might identify himself simultaneously with two national ties. Indeed, with a proper policy and education, such multivalence could build a bridge toward reconciliation.

Persons of such mixed background might understand the problems well enough to foster intergroup cooperation. They could integrate their aims with the dominant values of humanity and cooperation. This of course would require a well-integrated personality type. However, regional identification may in some cases displace the national. A Silesian of Polish-German ancestry might choose to identify himself primarily as a "Silesian" (*Slonzak*) rather than as a Pole or a German.[2]

Ethnic relations in Czech Teschen Silesia

Our discussion will best be illustrated by a study of ethnic relations in the Czech part of Teschen Silesia, especially in the town of Teschen, prior to World War II.

Teschen Silesia was inhabited by Czechs, Germans, and Poles. Some, however, identified themselves solely as "Silesians," dropping their national ethnic identification and replacing it with the regional.

There were three key minorities in Teschen: the Poles, the Czechs, and the Germans. The Polish and Czech sections of the town were divided by the River Olza. Popular tradition had it that this was the place where the three brothers—Czech, Lech, and Rus, the founders of Poland, Bohemia, and Ruthenia or Russia —decided to go off in the three opposite directions of the world and establish three states. Teschen takes a certain pride in this tradition.

The hereditary national enemy (*Erbfeind*) was already identified for Teschen children in the early grades of the elementary school. For the Poles and the

Czechs, this national enemy was the Germans; for the Germans, it was the Poles and the Czechs. Relations between the Czechs and the Poles differed from those between the Poles and the Germans. While the Czechs regarded the Poles as neighbors and fellow members of the Slavic community, their feeling of hostility toward the Germans was quite clear. The Poles in turn regarded the Czechs as "younger brothers" who formed the "weaker part" of the community. In times of tension they ranked the Czechs as outsiders.

Actually, one could identify four ethnic groups in Teschen: the Poles, the Germans, the Czechs, and the Silesians, comprising that part of the population which did not try to join any of the other groups. The Germans also emphasized their separateness. They had their own nationalistic organizations.

The middle-class Poles relied heavily on their history for their behavioral patterns. They affected a courteous language and traditional politeness which the Czechs, who came from a more democratic and pragmatic tradition, did not share. The Poles also had a longer history to fall back upon in times of defeat, while the Czechs, who lost their independence in the seventeenth century, had to rely on the achievements of the present and the expectations of the future. That contributed to a difference in attitudes and perhaps to different value orientations.

The ethnic division of Teschen was more complex than it appeared. In 1938, the Polish government was allied with Nazi Germany against Czechoslovakia, and parts of Teschen Silesia were occupied by the Polish Army. Those Silesian Poles who sided with the Czechoslovak Republic against the invaders were viewed by the Czechs as members of the pro-groups. German and Polish nationalists were considered members of the anti-groups, but divided into two ranks: Poles were merely "adversaries"; Germans were "archenemies," because Austrian Germans had fought the Czechs, and led cruel counterreformations against them, and German Nazis had destroyed the republic both from within and without. Thus, the entire historical and political tradition was brought into the picture. However, the sharp divisions in times of war were chiefly the result of a "conflict" situation. We may therefore return to the problems of "range" and "perspective" of perception.

In times of conflict, the enemy appears as a social image, a stereotype. Identifications based on proximity or distance at a primary or secondary level differ in perception. As was mentioned earlier (Chapter 9: discussion of Kossovo), an enemy may be identified in terms of an "abstract collective," or as a real member of the community. As an abstract collective, Germans in times of tensions and conflict were enemies of the Czechs. But in the villages around Teschen, a German worker and a member of a union was ranked as a friend and an ally by a Czech union member.

Ideological identification also changes the ranking of proximity and distance. Social-Democrat members of a union who voted for Social-Democratic candidates to the Czechoslovak parliament regarded themselves as members of the same "pro-groups," whether they were Germans, Poles, or Czechs.

Sometimes, members of the same family identified themselves with different ethnic groups. In one case, the head of the family was Czech. His daughter, while identifying herself with the Czech nationality, married a Pole. One of her brothers identified himself as a German, another as a Silesian. We see, therefore, that ethnic proximity and distance are not necessarily static. The ranking of groups and individuals changes with a change of situations. In consequence, a powerful government may reduce or escalate ethnic tensions by applying pressures, manipulating them into a political conflict.

The government and intensification of tensions

The policies of the state in an ethnic tension area are of primary significance, since the government controls the instruments of power. Therefore, a tension analysis suggests an inquiry into the relationship of public institutions, primarily the government, toward ethnic groups—especially minority groups—and state minority policies in general.

At a crucial moment of tension in 1938, irredentist action against the Czechs was supported by the Polish government in Czech Silesia. Bombs were planted and sabotage was perpetrated by a small group operating from Polish Teschen. In addition, an influential Polish daily campaigned against the Czechoslovak Republic and supported the Polish government in power. However, the Polish democratic parties, fighting against their own dictatorship, opposed the anti-Czech policy in their meetings and publications. Some of the most prominent Polish leaders of the Peasant, Christian Democratic, and Social-Democratic parties found political asylum in Czechoslovakia.

The Polish government used and manipulated these tensions to further its own political objectives.[3] In certain Polish sections, even among a few old-time Social Democrats and trade unionists, bitter memories remained of the First World War, when during the Polish-Soviet War, the Czechoslovak army moved into a disputed territory. These sentiments were played up in this critical moment of the Czechoslovak Republic, to the detriment of both nations.

Ethnic relations in Upper Silesia

The ethnic pattern in Polish Upper Silesia was different. The two major groups there were the Germans and the Poles. Until World War I Germans represented the conquering population; the Poles, the conquered. The mines and steel mills were owned primarily by German companies, and businessmen, professional men, and government officials were mainly German. The Poles were primarily workers and peasants. To a degree, class division coincided with ethnic division, with the status of the Poles being relatively lower.

Upper Silesia had long been a border area of ethnic struggles. The powerful German state represented a policy of "Germanization," and for many years during Bismarck's chancellorship of Germany, the strong anti-Polish policy of the eastern German provinces was reflected in Silesia. The plebiscites resulting in the division of Upper Silesia into Polish and German areas did not weaken nationalistic tendencies, and discontent grew. A number of right-wing organizations became active and, after Hitler's advent to power, new parties and organizations were formed, with large sections of the German minority coming under the direct or indirect influence of Nazism.

A Polish-German treaty of friendship was signed by Hitler in 1934. Subsequently, on November 7, 1937, the Polish and German governments each issued an identical "Declaration on the subject of the treatment of minorities." Following these two events, the German right-wing nationalistic organizations and their partisans changed their tactics and restrained their activities. They enjoyed special treatment as a "favored minority" in Polish Silesia. Surface tensions subsided, and the area remained outwardly calm until the outbreak of the war.

In the period of Polish-German "friendship"—which was for Hitler a mere tactical move to secure peace on his eastern flank for his annexation of Austria and Czechoslovakia—the right-wing German nationalist organizations "behaved." They made frequent declarations of loyalty, and ceased to be aggressive. In this way, a social-political movement, strongly disciplined and well organized, reduced tensions on the surface on the orders and in accordance with the official policy of the Nazi Party and of the German government. In reality, however, the German right-wing groups fought the anti-Nazi Catholic and social-democratic German organizations. They prepared an underground intelligence network in Polish Silesia and actively supported the German invasion. Some of the political leaders of those organizations were later decorated by Hitler.[4]

In this case a political party of an ethnic group, following a Nazi ideology, was centrally organized and employed a definite strategy and tactics. It formed a social force, controlled by an outside government and party, with the reduction or intensification of tension determined by the policy of that government. This relationship was both interethnic and interpolitical. The tactics of internal tensions were changed in accordance with changes in the external government's strategic design of conquest. When open conflict came in 1939, it was "complex" in its nature. The German ethnic right-wing groups supported the military and political aggression against Poland.

During the interwar period, there were individuals, organizations, and groups on both sides, however small, which sought some kind of understanding. In Breslau (Wrocaw), Catholic pacifists, among them prominent educators, met with Polish pacifists, League of Nations partisans, and university students in search of answers and understanding. Polish and German social-democrats in both German and Polish Upper Silesia organized joint meetings and conferences, viewing their movements as part of the same labor pro-group. Even as late as the 1930's, such meetings were organized by German social-democrats in Beuthen (Bytom), at that time in German Upper Silesia.

In times of intensified propaganda and crisis social attitudes toward the opposed nationality changed. Antagonism was intensified. Ethnic tensions changed from internal political (intrapolitical) to international-political and complex. At certain periods, this cycle of tensions moved from below (for example, in times of Polish insurrections) and was escalated into an interpolitical and complex phase. With the advent of the nationalistic governments it was manipulated from above through right-wing movements.

Social-political movements

The growth of the Nazi movement in Germany had its influence in Poland, where a new German nationalist party was organized along similar lines. It held mass meetings at which existing moderate groups were excoriated. Leaders of the moderate German Catholics and Social-Democrats continued to oppose nationalist tendencies and evinced apprehension of the new fascism. However, with the growth of national socialism in Germany, both the moderate democratic Catholic center and left-of-center movements in Silesia began to decline.[5]

It is interesting to reexamine the use of German nationalist parties in the Sudeten area (in Czechoslovakia) and in Silesia. The German extremist organizations in both areas were similarly organized and their ideologies were identical. Actions of both parties were dependent on decisions of the outside apparatus located in Berlin. In Czechoslovakia, the party was used to escalate intergroup tensions; in Silesia, to reduce them. Both efforts were made during the same period—between 1934 and 1938. Eventually, in Czechoslovakia, outside pressure at the diplomatic and military levels was combined with the internal front, comprising the Sudeten German nationalist movement. The combined pressure finally broke the democratic structure of Czechoslovak policy.

Unusual political acumen was not needed to understand this tactic of aggression and seizure. It was indicative of the Nazi timetable for the absorption of its neighbors: first, Austria; second, Czechoslovakia; third, Poland; then, in turn, the Balkans and the Soviet Union.

At this time another alternative was still open to countries on the Nazi agenda of conquest—the interpolitical. A union of the Polish and Czechoslovak republics would have created an element of strength in Eastern Europe. The governments of such a confederation would have encouraged a strong alliance, if not a union, with the Balkan states and other East European countries. A united East Europe could have influenced the policies of Britain, France, and the Soviet Union, stiffening the attitudes of those countries toward Hitler's Germany. Within such an international bloc a policy toward extremist right-wing German groups could have assumed a different aspect.

Interethnic problems of this type require political action. Reduction of primary or world tensions also demands strength, determination, and action; not weakness. Willingness to compromise on basic issues is usually interpreted by aggressors as a symptom of weakness.

Dictatorship and the reduction of tensions

It is generally true that democratic influence and an increase of voting rights usually lead to greater religious tolerance and the reduction of ethnic antagonism. Nonetheless, paradoxical as it may seem, two governments, both advancing nationalistic policies—one authoritarian, the other semi-dictatorial—were in a position to reduce tensions but moved instead to a point of indifference, or even limited cooperation with one faction. While controlling the entire apparatus of public institutions and enforcement machinery as well as the party apparatus, they were able —in more or less authoritarian conditions—to escalate or reduce tensions on command.[6] This happened in Upper Silesia.

The Polish governor of Silesia pursued his "polonizing" policy, avoiding any tensions with the German right-wing, pro-Nazi minorities. This policy was also pursued in other Polish provinces. In turn, the German nationalistic minority parties in Poland, under direct or indirect command from Hitler's headquarters, ceased their pressure for greater autonomy.

Meanwhile, slowly and securely, the German regime built its network of intelligence within the country, preparing for the future invasion of Poland and fifth-column operations. During the years 1937–1939, tensions were sharply reduced, at least on the streets and in everyday life, between the German right-wing minorities and the Polish apparatus of public institutions. Polish societies and parties controlled by the government followed the public line.

At that time the two democratic German groups that had once had much influence among the German minority groups, and which vigorously opposed racism and Nazism—the Catholic Party (Katholische Volkspartei) and the German Social-Democratic Party (corresponding to the German S.P.D.)—declined in influence and number, while the extreme right grew stronger.

Once Hitler and his ruling group decided upon war, emotions were escalated, and an armed and ruthless conflict was initiated in which the German nationalists participated extensively. This is perhaps an extreme case, but it is indicative of the potentialities of reduction and escalation of ethnic tensions by a government apparatus under nondemocratic, authoritarian conditions.

Hostilities were redirected against the defenseless minorities. The psychological need for aggression, which had been reinforced, was channelled against a less dangerous target. In that way, hostility and aggression, not unlike destructive energy, were controlled by an apparatus, and directed against a desirable target.

The League of Nations provisions of a universal nature were unilaterally revoked by the Polish government while a bilateral Polish-German arrangement settled temporarily the problem of the German minorities in 1937.[7] Of course, this arrangement did not extend to other minority groups.

Some inferences

In the ethnic relations in Silesia, we have a renewed suggestion of the variety of rankings in social distance and proximity. The relative degree of social distance is, to an extent, part of a dynamic social process. With the intensification or easing of tension, identification of social distance or proximity changes. This may be obvious; the diversity of distance is not. Here again, experience shows that in times of tension or of relative ethnic equilibrium, ethnic groups are not simply divided into friends and enemies. Secondly, regional identification is sometimes complementary to ethnic or national. At times it may weaken if not displace national-ethnic identification, as we have seen in the case of Silesia.

Social-political movements on the one hand, and government and its agencies on the other, usually affect ethnic relations and tensions, and the reduction of such tensions. Once an ethnic antagonism is structured by a powerful national-political party, which in turn controls the government, ethnic antagonism moves into a political phase. At this stage, the antagonists control the means of violence: weapons, mass communication, and other instruments of political power.

The German Nazi movement grew by the manipulation and intensifying of ethnic and religious hostilities. The party finally seized control of the German state and used its power to foster and escalate ethnic tensions into interpolitical tensions in practically all border areas including, at strategic times, Upper Silesia.

Paradoxically, the tension and conflict problems of Silesia supply some hopeful experience. Even in the "endemic" tension area of Upper Silesia during the interwar period there were some individuals, movements, and groups, ineffectual though they sometimes were, who were searching for understanding and cooperation in times when hatred was the official policy. True, the appeal of the extreme nationalists was more effective. Hatred and hostility is a powerful political device, since it releases pentup aggression, and works on the emotional level to destroy rational control. Still, there were other tendencies. Simple divisions into "anti" and "pro" groups—"we" and "the enemy"—did not apply to those people whose values and ideological orientation rejected ethnic and religious prejudices.

Upper Silesia was also an area of international experimentation. The agencies of the League of Nations were active here in minority affairs. International agencies supervised plebiscites and acted as moderators or mediators; others operated to moderate and reduce tensions. The League of Nations failed in Silesia and also, eventually, as a world forum. Minority treaties in Upper Silesia failed to supply adequate protection; plebiscites did not solve the problems of a border area.[8] But this was one of the early experiments in world mediation, and through it a principle was introduced; a principle of international legitimacy. The protection of minority groups and the solution of nationality problems is now recognized as the proper domain and legitimate function of an international institution.

11.

A MULTIPLE ETHNIC PATTERN

Ethnic and Religious Relations in Cracow

The general pattern

Ethnic and religious relations in Cracow, ancient capital of Poland, at the end of the nineteenth and the beginning of the twentieth century are of specific interest, because of the presence of several diametrically different patterns. These patterns, the result of long historical development, were not complementary but contradictory, and sometimes the contradictions increased. They corresponded to various levels and degrees of acculturation; to different political and ideological orientations; and, in many cases, to different social and economic relations.

The city of Cracow was inhabited at that time by Roman Catholic and Jewish populations and by a small Protestant community, with the Jewish population forming a complex subculture of many degrees of acculturation. Ethnic and religious divisions in Cracow were complicated by the class structure, and by a variety of political orientations that contributed to their diversity.

Orthodox Jewish groups, which preserved their own specific culture, combined a pattern of strong self-segregation with neutrality toward outsiders. A minor group of Polish-Catholic nationalists joined self-segregation with hostility toward other groups that increased in times of tensions. Between the two extremes there were many Polish-Catholics and Jews who were de facto integrated. Furthermore, there were other Polish and Jewish groups which favored a pluralistic solution (cultural autonomy).

Nonetheless, in a period of intensified hostilities following World War I, the extremists, especially right-wing student organizations, were active in the city and not without influence on those sections of the population which were undecided and ambivalent. On the other side of this complex picture, Polish groups and parties which opposed anti-Semitic actions were also active and vocal, though not fully effective.

The origin of a minority

The Jews of Poland were by no means newcomers. Their presence in this area had been mentioned as early as 965 by an Arabic-Jewish traveller. Documents of the twelfth and thirteenth centuries also provide information about the Jews in Poland who, it seems, enjoyed greater security and tolerance than their Western counterparts.

In the early fourteenth century Cracow already had a Jewish street and a Jewish gate (*Porta Judaeorum*), with its own synagogue, bath, and square (*Vicus Judaicus*). Jews at that time formed a prosperous community.

The Polish King Casimir (Kazimierz) the Great welcomed Jewish immigrants to Poland in the fourteenth century. Historical evidence indicates that he had some personal sympathy for the Jews, but he also understood the economic significance for a predominantly rural country of a people skilled in trade and certain crafts. The Jews in medieval times also represented a strong financial element.

Jewish immigration to Poland increased in times of persecutions in Germany, especially during the Black Death, for which they were blamed. Some may have also moved eastward from Silesia where the German penetration was stronger.

The Jews of Cracow enjoyed substantial autonomy and self-government; they even had their own courts. But with the death of King Casimir, their condition deteriorated. In addition, once "native" (national or religious) traders, merchants, and craftsmen grew in numbers and power, economic antagonism against the competitive and complementary Jewish "foreign group" telescoped into ethnic or religious hostilities. But this was by no means the only cause of anti-Semitism.

In the fifteenth and sixteenth centuries, conditions for the Jews in Poland were favorable, although not entirely free of persecution. This is testified to by the great Jewish scholar and codifier Moses Isserles (known as Remu; 1520–72), who wrote to a friend: "I believe it is better to eat dark bread in our countries . . . because in our lands we do not feel hatred, as you feel in Germany." [1]

The situation of the Jewish minority at that time must be viewed against contemporary European history. In Cracow, they were able to develop their own culture and influence, although tensions sometimes increased and they became the victims of pogroms and persecutions. In the fifteenth century, the Franciscan friar John Capistrano delivered a number of anti-Jewish sermons in Cracow's market square. Interestingly enough, he spoke in a foreign language that had to be translated, but he was able to arouse the population against the Jews, whom he accused of stealing holy vessels and other crimes.[2]

As early as the time of King Casimir a new township was founded, called Kazimierz, which still exists. It was inhabited by Jews and remained a center of Jewish population and culture. During the Inquisition, prominent Jewish scholars such as Dr. Calahora, physician to the Polish kings, found refuge in Cracow. The Jews enjoyed royal favor, and their scholars and physicians were respected; a pattern that was to last for centuries. In 1264 a Polish prince promulgated the Statutes of Kalish, a document of toleration incorporating similar sentiments expressed by Pope Innocent IV in a Papal Bull issued in 1247. The crown thus represented the tendency toward restraint and protection if not toleration.

In 1267 the Church Council of Breslau issued discriminatory rules against the Jews in Silesia and Poland.[3] Thus, the crown on the one hand, the church hierarchy on the other, formed the two extreme poles of a diarchy. Later, while the Jagellonian Dynasty flourished, the church hierarchy often exerted antagonism against the Jews, despite Pope Innocent's proclamation.

The crown and the church were the two most powerful institutions in Poland, although the growth of the nobility and the increasing power of the aristocracy (princes) limited the powers of the crown. In Cracow, however, they remained the centers of decisive power. The church controlled the idea-systems and rituals; the crown controlled the sword, the physical power. Through religion and ritual the church could exercise influence over the crown.

But the general hypothesis that the crown always protected the Jews, and the church was hostile to them must be modified. Actually, the position of both varied. The crown imposed heavy taxes and, at times, repressive measures. During the Hussite Revolution in Bohemia, Hussite Protestant influences penetrated deep into Poland. Their presence must have fostered a more tolerant trend among some Polish theologians, for at the Council of Constance in 1414, the Rector of the University of Cracow decried forced conversion to Catholicism and staunchly defended his views.[4]

The church and the crown were not the only institutional systems, though they were the most powerful. The townspeople controlled the municipality and the burghers of Cracow were frequently competitors of the Jews.

Here we reach the problem of the "masses," of the "social base," where hostility penetrated. The Jews were moneylenders, merchants, scholars, and artisans. The Christian merchants eventually became their competitors and, thus, the religious and ethnic antagonism was telescoped into the "economic base." The hostility was reinforced by economic factors, especially in moneylending. Generally, interest was high and business exploitative and frequently ruthless in medieval times. The antagonism between the lender and borrower arose from the very nature of the business. Here, economic antagonism intensified the religious and ethnic antagonism. Usury was identified with the stereotype of a medieval Jew. However, the moneylenders formed only a fraction, a social "subclass," of a large and active Jewish community.

The pattern established in the fifteenth century continued to modern times. The crown, and later the central administration, restrained the antagonism against the Jews. The church hierarchy continued to be the center of opposition, although individual priests or orders maintained friendly personal relations with them.

The eighteenth-century renaissance of enlightenment and liberalism in Western Europe coincided with the decline of the Polish Republic (the official name of old Poland). As the republic declined so did the Jewish communities in Poland. Although the condition of the Jews in Western Europe improved very rapidly at that time, it was not mirrored in Poland. The ancient Polish capital declined and so did the significance of the ancient Jewish borough. With the partitions of Poland at the end of the eighteenth century, Cracow became part of Austria-Hungary.

The impetus for Polish independence resulted in insurrections and revolutionary struggles; efforts that parts of the Jewish population actively supported. The insurrectionists, reflecting nineteenth-century progressive democratic tendencies, proclaimed full equality of all Poles irrespective of religion and they appealed to "the Israelite brethren" for their cooperation. The national poet Adam Mickiewicz compared the fate of the Poles to the fate of the Israelites. Thus, a tie between Polish patriotic insurrectionists and Polish Jews was established and a foundation laid for future integration and unity.

Now the concept of the separation of religious belief from national or ethnic identity appeared in its initial form. The insurrectionists and revolutionaries were identified as Poles whether they were Christians or Jews. The Jews appear in revolutionary proclamations as "Israelites" or as the "people of the Old Testament" (*Staro-Zakonni*); perhaps distinct, but brethren of the Poles.

After the revolution of 1848, Austria-Hungary rapidly changed to a constitutional monarchy. The parliament in Kremsier made a serious effort to transform the monarchy into a federal, ethnic democracy but this attempt failed as did revolution. However, civil and political rights were extended and, after the granting of the compromise constitution in 1867, conditions were generally stabilized. The Jews now enjoyed equal rights and the conditions for their growth had been created.

Viewed in historical perspective, the Austrian bureacracy was relatively liberal-conservative and efficient—"relatively," when viewed against conditions in Central and Eastern Europe. The nationality policy now became paramount for the very survival of the monarchy, and the ruling bureaucracy supported those who did not directly attack its integrity.

The Poles made full use of the provincial self-government and municipal autonomy granted them by the constitution. Polish institutions, schools, theaters, and culture generally developed; so did their Jewish equivalents. In this part of Poland there were no insurrections after 1846 and the activities of the people were directed to what was called "organic work."

A general pattern of Christian-Jewish relations developed that survived until World War II. It was created by: (1) the new insurrectionist and democratic tradition, which influenced large sections of the Polish educated classes and powerful political parties; (2) the general restraining and moderating policy of the new and modern bureaucratic apparatus, which was well trained in the universities.

Ecology of an ethnic pattern: the Orthodox; self-segregation

At the beginning of World War II, the ecology of the town coincided with the patterns of ethnic religious relations. After the German occupation this scheme ended with the extermination of the Jewish population. Then, however, the various sections of the town represented the respective patterns. The ancient borough of Kazimierz (Casimir) remained for centuries a Jewish city and the center of Jewish life. The heart of the old city was inhabited by the Hassidic Jewish population. They spoke Polish, but among themselves they used Yiddish; most of them also knew German well. And of course they knew Hebrew as a sacred language.

The Hassidic Jews represented a distinct culture rooted in ancient and strong values as well as stable institutions. There was little if any tendency toward change and acculturation with other ethnic groups. The Orthodox had their own class structure. At the top was the prosperous merchant; at the bottom, the pious beggar. There was a large middle class of merchants, and below them small traders and craftsmen. Life was not easy, and few were wealthy. The tailor or the cobbler who worked on the Jewish street earned far less than his Christian counterpart who worked in the well-established shops of the midtown area. However, the Orthodox worker, like the Orthodox merchant, had no desire to move out of the Jewish section. He did not advocate integration with other groups nor any change in his customs or religion.

In the ancient streets, some almost forgotten skills and crafts could still be found. A *sofer* (a religious scribe) worked from dawn to dusk writing the holy scrolls. In the evening the faithful would meet in congregation in the *stybel* and sit around the table with the rabbi, discussing the Scriptures and analyzing theological problems. A Jewish artisan hesitated to move away from his neighborhood. He had to be close to the synagogue and to the place where his congregation met. Here tailors, cobblers, and small merchants achieved status, not by their skills but by their learning and their piety. Wealth was unimportant. The pious man and the wise man were highly regarded, and education, especially in religion, held the highest value.

This was a socially introverted group, little concerned with the doings of the outside world. For them, the Christian town consisted of out-groups; some friendly, some hostile. They had no desire to establish closer ties with those of a different religion. Nonetheless, between individual Orthodox families and those farmers and peasants who brought their products from the country on the market day, friendships were frequent and warm. But between the middle man and the peasant, antagonisms were not uncommon. The peasant's work was hard and his income low. Eventually, the establishment of peasant cooperatives even eliminated the middle man in certain areas.

The Orthodox Jews were not a burden to the city, since they took care of their own poor and sick. Nor were they a demanding minority. Their energies were socially "introverted" toward perfection in religion, knowledge, and personal economics. Discrimination was suffered patiently. The Jewish representatives protested vigorously, but without self-pity. This was a separate community, self-segregated by its own will, culture, and tradition.

The transitional area: the "secular"

The section between Casimir and the center of Cracow developed as a transitional area in the latter part of the nineteenth century. It was inhabited by the Jewish middle class: merchants and small entrepreneurs. Here also lived a part of the secular Jewish population. Similar groups could be found on the other side of the Vistula in Podgórze, a town built at the end of the eighteenth century.

Jewish secular workers varied in their political and ethnic orientations. Some actively supported the Jewish Socialist Party (the Bund). Until the end of World War I, the Jewish middle class and artisans favored the Democratic Party and a Jewish party associated with the Democrats, called the Independents. The latter had a number of members in the provincial diet as well as in the Vienna parliament. There were representatives of the Democrats in parliament, the provincial diet, and the municipal councils, some of whom were Christian, and some, Jewish. A number of Jewish workers and youths later followed the Zionist movement. Until about 1914, the Zionists and the Bundists were comparatively weak, while the influence of the Independent Party was strong among the Jewish community.

Ideologically, the Jewish Socialist Party advocated the development and preservation of the Jewish culture and language. It developed a program of cultural pluralism and autonomy. In this respect its program was close to the ideals later expressed by the Austrian Social-Democrats O. Bauer and Karl Renner.[5]

Bund members formed a cultural subgroup, representing the development of a new culture based on Jewish, Polish, and European socialist and democratic values and institutions. Their "political culture" was primarily Western in ideology and party structure, but it retained general Jewish values. The language was Yiddish. So were the songs and publications. However, Bundists differed from Orthodox Jews in their political and class orientation.

The traditions of the Polish insurrections and revolutions were reflected in the attitudes and values of the Jewish middle class and its workers. Before World War I, the Jewish middle class, and especially the "intelligentsia" which supported the Democratic Party, considered the politically liberal and democratic Christian Poles as both neighbors and friends. The Jewish socialist workers also viewed the Polish Socialist Party and the Polish workers, at least ideologically, as their friends and allies. The Polish trade union, workers' education, and political movements were also part of their ideological pro-group. Differences in culture and ideology were answered by a concept of cultural autonomy which, as has been seen, closely resembles a cultural pluralism.

However, ideological objectives and tendencies are not identical with social realities. Anti-Semitic feelings still appeared and had a tendency to come up in everyday life. Nonetheless there were sections of the Polish population to whom the Jews were ideologically close. Some groups, individuals, and leaders on both sides supported policies of close cooperation and friendship, although the Orthodox Jews still favored cultural isolation. They differed greatly in dress, behavior, customs, values, even language, from the local population. Those differences were of course deepening the isolation, since customs and behavioral patterns sometimes clashed.

Class, political parties, and attitudes prior to World War I

The major parties which controlled the votes before World War I were the Democrats, the Conservatives, and the Polish Democratic Socialists (PPSD). The more powerful Democratic Party and its leading newspaper, the popular *New Reform* (*Nowa Reforma*), represented a policy of close cooperation between the Christian and Jewish populations. It followed the tradition of the "Democratic Society," the original democratic revolutionary organization of Poland, and exerted a strong influence in parliament. This party and the associated Independent Jews favored cultural pluralism. Pointing to the American experience, they argued that a Pole could be Jewish or Christian; that the Jewish population was firmly established in Poland and could preserve its own religion and cultural heritage while maintaining its identity as part of the Polish nationality. Members of these parties did not hesitate to call themselves Polish Jews.

The Polish Social Democratic Party (later Polish Socialist Party) actively opposed anti-Semitism. So did the unions. The daily papers of both groups fought the anti-Semitic tendencies of the Christian-Democratic and National-Democratic parties. The Social Democratic Party cultivated the traditions of the insurrections of 1863 and the revolutions of 1846, 1848, and 1905 and followed their pattern for its intergroup relations. Some of the socialist leaders at the turn of the century were participants in the 1863 insurrections, other were descendants of insurrectionists. They practiced integration in everyday life, although anti-Semitic sentiment survived among the rank and file.

To the right of the Social Democrats were the Conservatives, who generally supported a policy of moderate tolerance. The Conservative Party in Cracow, unlike its counterparts in other sections of Poland, had a liberal wing among the university professors. They were highly critical of the anti-Semitic activities of the local Christian-Democratic and small National-Democratic parties.

The Polish Christian-Democrats were the party of the lower middle class and the craftsmen. They resembled the Christian Socialist Party of Vienna—headed by Lueger—which, at the turn of the century, had an anti-Semitic program. In Cracow, the Christian-Democrats represented the more prosperous craftsmen still organized in guilds, some clergy, and many middle-class citizens. The party newspaper voiced anti-Semitic opinions from time to time, generally opposed the presence of the Jews in the business community, and appealed to the population to buy in "Christian stores." In this way the party represented the competitive nature of the "natives" or rather "religious natives" who opposed those who once had been "complementary" and were now "competitive." There was more to it, however, since prejudices have deeper roots.

The midtown intelligentsia was integrated into one social-cultural class. For all practical purposes, segregation was absent in this section of Cracow. In language, behavior, cultural interest, tastes, and style of life, the intelligentsia formed a subculture. The identification of the Jewish members of this class varied; it was Polish but it was also national-Jewish. Nonetheless, culturally all were of one class. Christians and Jews formed strong friendships. Some division continued in the social life, but the basic trend was toward association.

Public institutions

The government and the bureaucracy followed the general policy of the central government, which traditionally exercised a restraining influence. However, specialized agencies for reducing tensions or encouraging integration and pluralism did not exist. The government limited its effect to regulatory and moderating pronouncements. From 1867, the government had recognized the cultural rights of the various nationalities, and the Austrian bureaucracy followed the official policy of toleration.

The views of members of parliament, some of them of Jewish origin, were officially respected. Since the Democratic, Social-Democratic, and even Conservative parties represented in parliament all opposed anti-Semitism, their influence was reflected in public administration. However, the emphasis of the administration was on the status quo rather than on change. Nevertheless, in spite of the government's casual attitude, Jewish political parties were represented in municipal councils, and Jews were active in municipal government. The vice-president (deputy mayor) of Cracow prior to World War I was of the Jewish faith.

The divisions between classes were not only ethnic or religious but also representative of the ideology of the political parties. Only the Christian-Democrats and the National-Democrats favored certain self-segregation and viewed the Jewish population as antagonists. The identification of the Jew by most of the population varied from that of outsider to friend; a minority viewed the Jewish population as an "anti-group." Among the Jewish population, the Orthodox viewed the Christian as an outsider and a neighbor while the Bundist worker and the middle-class "Independent" considered him a neighbor and friend. The latent prejudice survived, of course, but the diffusion of prejudice was continuously controlled through active political indoctrination by parties that supported religious toleration. Also a restraining effect was exercised by the public institutions in which the Christian and Jewish populations were represented.

The interwar period—increase of anti-Semitism

Conditions changed after World War I. Nationalism increased among both the Christians and Jews. The Conservative Party declined in influence and the Democratic Party practically disappeared. The Independents were displaced by a powerful and well-organized Zionist movement, which had a strong appeal for the younger generation and was supported by the middle class. Among the workers and craftsmen, the Poale-Zion (Socialist Zionists) and the Bund gained ascendancy.[6]

The Polish Socialist Party gained influence. On the extreme right there was a small but vocal National Party, with an accent on "anti-groups," national and ethnic antagonism. The parties of the center declined, and those of the right and the left monopolized the political scene. The political image of the Jewish Street also changed.

At the university the Conservative professors strongly opposed anti-Semitic outbursts, but for the first time mob action against the Jewish students and Jewish stores of Cracow took place. A new antagonistic "focus" appeared—the student body at the university. Only a minority of them were liberal Catholics, populists, Social Democrats, and League of Nations pacifists; the Communists were an insignificantly small group. But those groups, though perhaps more influential in Cracow than in other Polish universities, could seldom counterbalance the aggressive nationalists. Later a Democratic Student Union was formed (ZPMD), which sided with the forces supporting civil rights and toleration.

In the late 1930's, with the growth of fascism in Europe, anti-Semitic tendencies increased and the ambivalent masses were swayed by emotional appeals to prejudice. The ruling military bureaucracy and government also evidenced symptoms of anti-Semitism. The old tradition that the crown or the central government exercises a restraining influence in religious antagonism waned. A Polish prime minister encouraged a boycott of Jewish stores. Even such organizations as B'nai B'rith were closed by the government as dangerous "foreign agencies." [7]

However, the influence of the Polish Socialist Party increased. Harassed by the government, it continued to struggle for the restoration of democracy. It was allied in this struggle with the Peasant Party and the Christian Democrats, now rapidly moving toward a liberal orientation. The Polish Socialists cooperated with the Bund and the Poale Zionists. Together with a small democratic party, a handful of Conservative and Liberal university professors, an influential student pacifist association (the Friends of the League of Nations), and a number of smaller student organizations they resolutely opposed the anti-Semitic actions of the right-wing student associations and of the government party. In opposing anti-Semitism they also rejected dictatorship and totalitarianism in every form.

The political movement of the center and democratic left formed the focus of a policy of understanding, tolerance, and pluralism. The influence of the extremist right-wing nationalist parties increased. The nationalists were more active and vituperous in their "anti-actions." Together with their allies they maintained tension and antagonism.

In the middle 1930's, anti-Jewish pressure increased. The "integrated" intelligentsia and midtown groups began to change. Boycotts of Jewish businesses were organized from time to time, and a steady flow of propaganda was maintained, tacitly supported by the government agencies. The integrated group of intelligentsia and the educated classes grew continuously smaller but remained sincere and dedicated. They now opposed anti-Semitism openly; exposing themselves to insult, physical mistreatment, and beatings. Some conservatives also manifested opposition to bigotry, and retained personal friendship with their Jewish colleagues. This group was small and it is difficult to evaluate its strength, but it was by no means silent.

Thus, the historical pattern continued in a modified and weaker form: neutral self-segregated communities and antagonistic groups coexisted in Cracow next to friendly out-groups and integrated sections of society. Political centers of ethnic and religious antagonism were counterbalanced by left-wing and centrist political parties defending a policy of respect for differences in religion. But tension increased, showing itself in anti-Semitic papers and periodicals, violent speeches, and proposals to limit the number of Jews in legal and medical professions. Still, the two communities were never completely separated. The voices opposing intolerance were never silenced.

Some inferences

We learn from the examples of Cracow and Silesia of the close interaction of political movements on intergroup relations. Political movements and parties represent organized social forces that can spread ethnic antagonism or foster cooperation and integration. In them lie powerful creative and destructive forces.

Secondly, the function of public institutions in this area varies as policies and interests vary. Two institutional structures may represent two different policies. Such a diarchy can shape interethnic or interreligious relations into a multivalent pattern as, in certain historical periods, the crown and the church did in Poland.

Third, the example of Cracow indicates that several types of ethnic patterns—some complementary, some contradictory—may coexist in the same area: antagonistic, pluralistic, or integrationist. As the social-political situation changes the emphasis of certain patterns and their influence may increase or decline. However, they can be extended, strengthened, or weakened by consistent and well-planned social-political action, or by education.

Fourth, the historical development of interethnic relations shows, although in very general terms, the social and political development of an ethnic pattern. The variety of interethnic and interreligious patterns in Cracow was the result of a long historical process extending almost one thousand years back.

The essence of such a pattern survives in one form or another, even in times of crisis. While the social situation changes, certain elements of the historical pattern grow in significance or strength, others weaken, thus reflecting a continuous adjustment to new social conditions.

Similarly, the origin of an ethnic prejudice often can be traced many centuries back. Anti-Jewish prejudice has its roots in medieval conditions and superstitions. It was born of the same imagination which produced witches, love potions, and magic. Some of those beliefs have vanished; others continue, reinforced by new ideologies, by social conditions, or by institutions. But the *reinforcement* of a value, of a social image, or an attitude and its *transmission* are two different aspects of a social process. The transmission of an attitude, a belief, or a stereotype is the result of learning.

We know today that the process of learning begins in the child's formative years. The parents, the peer-groups, and the primary groups transmit and continue values and attitudes. Because they are induced at a very early age, they are strongly anchored. Later they are reinforced by various institutions, among which the school and the church play paramount roles. Thus, prejudice may be perpetuated for centuries in a process which we may call "social inheritance."

A condescending attitude toward a religious or ethnic group is transmitted in proverbs and adages, regarded by many, especially in folk cultures, as a treasure of popular wisdom. Proverbs are transmitted for generations and repeated. In folk cultures, in peasant societies, they form a "social compass"; they regulate or set the direction of behavior. Language, the paramount device of human communication and social intercourse, thus becomes a mechanism that transmits prejudice, and provides and reinforces ready directions for hostility. Language, therefore, requires a careful study, from the viewpoint of prejudice formation and transmission.

Last but not least, the story of this city teaches us about the impact of international tensions on community relations, at least in certain historical periods and under certain social conditions. The political climate of Europe in the late 1930s was charged with hostilities. International tensions were manipulated in Germany and in fascist states into campaigns of national hatred. At this time, radio began to play an important if not a crucial role as means of mass communication, and reading of periodicals penetrated to all social strata. A general political insecurity was felt daily; it arrived with the daily papers. This increase of international antagonism, rationalized by a "political formula" of an extreme nationalism, was not without influence and contributed to the increase of intergroup tensions in a Central European city.

The German occupation of Cracow and Poland marked the beginning of a policy of total biological destruction of the Polish Jews. Those who survived were aided by Christians, who daily risked their life and liberty.

The problem of policy is also a matter of emphasis. Historical traditions of antagonism and cooperation are the warp and woof of ethnic policies; and emphasis on mutual aid in history and tradition can also result in cooperation and mutual aid.

12.

THE INSTITUTIONAL NETWORK
AND THE REDUCTION OF TENSIONS

A Policy of Integration in New York

Public institutions and the control of tensions

The intergroup relations in New York City are not free of tensions. Neither are many New Yorkers free of prejudices. But a powerful apparatus of public institutions, supported by private agencies, proclaims a policy of integration and ethnic pluralism, controls tensions, and restrains hostilities. For many years in this urban area of many minorities the pattern has been efficient and effective.

The public institutions are guided by their own values and ideologies, but they are also under the constant power-pressures of social-political movements. Policies from above and action from below produce a continuous process of change. The pattern indicates that policies of public institutions, and especially government agencies endowed with political power, are sometimes of basic importance in controlling, reducing, or escalating ethnic tensions. The New York area is an example of interethnic tensions skillfully reduced by consistent internal policies. Here, interethnic tensions and relations are combined with intrapolitical intervention and pressures.

A multiethnic urban area

New York City is a community of minorities. Ethnic, racial, and religious groups which differ in language, culture, diet, and personal manners inhabit its five boroughs. With all its difficulties, New York is an unusual city, a dynamic center which in the past was able to control and subdue the potential tensions and even create a limited sense of unity. Its diversity of languages and culture patterns creates problems of its own, especially in education. Also, the diversity of values requires constant adjustment. The nature of this diversity may be illustrated by the variety of ethnic origins in one classroom.

From twenty-four teachers in a seminar on ethnic and race relations in Brooklyn College in 1955, who were questioned as to the ethnic background of the students in their classes, there emerged twenty-two roughly defined ethnic and "religious" groups, as follows (in order of numerical predominance):

Ethnic groups

1. American Negro (17)	7. "American-American" (4)	11. Greek (2)	17. Israeli (1)
2. Puerto Rican (16)	8. Chinese (4)	12. Danish (1)	18. Italian-Irish (1)
3. Italian (14)	9. Norwegian (3)	13. English (1)	19. Moroccan (1)
4. Jewish (14)	10. Polish (3)	14. Filipino (1)	20. Russian (1)
5. Irish (8)		15. German (1)	21. Syrian (1)
6. Swedish (5)		16. Irish-Puerto Rican (1)	22. Ukrainian (1)

These teachers were also asked to state the general problem areas existing within specific groups and in intergroup relations. They were as follows:

Problem areas

1. Belonging and identification;
2. Language and communication;
3. Differences in values;
4. Attitudes toward other ethnic groups;
5. Allegiance toward United States;
6. Economic differences.[1]

In the borough of Brooklyn, the population varies greatly from section to section. One area is inhabited by Scandinavians, another by the Finns; a large section is Italian, with Sicilian-Italians in a separate area. The family structure of the Syrian Jews differs from that of the Polish Jews. The Iroquois Indians who live in Brooklyn and work in the building industry are not very far from the Hassidic Jews from Poland, Lithuania, or Hungary, who are in turn neighbors of Puerto Ricans and Ukrainians. Farther on, the gypsies have a colony; the Poles occupy a large section; and there is a Negro population in a depressed area of the borough. Once, the Hassidic Jews were a self-segregated island between a Negro and an Irish neighborhood. Now, they form "a ghetto within a black ghetto."

Close to the Brooklyn Bridge, a residential section has been preserved in a late nineteenth-century atmosphere. Here, intellectuals, professors, and professionals represent a dominant Anglo-American pattern. This area borders on a section that was at one time a center for "gangs" of rootless young people organized on a "territorial" basis rather than on ethnic lines. The gangs are now on the decline. In Manhattan, on the other side of Brooklyn Bridge, Chinatown adjoins the Italian sector.

According to the 1960 census, the major national groups of New York were born in twenty-three countries. First-generation Italians number over 858,000, making New York one of the largest Italian cities in the world. The Negro population of New York is over 1,000,000. According to Board of Education statistics on the public schools, Puerto Rican pupils comprise over 16% of the school population; Negroes, almost 30%.[2]

The ethnic patterns

New York City is by no means fully integrated or free of tensions. But these tensions are controlled and subdued, or frequently eased by negotiation and mediation. In times of increased tension, the moderating attitude of the municipal and state administration helps to restore balance. The city's ability to maintain unity in diversity, despite difficulties, is unique.

New York has not one, but many, patterns of ethnic and race relations. The processes of integration are encouraged and fostered. At the same time, the processes of de facto segregation and self-segregation continue. Distinct ethnic groups tend to settle in the same neighborhood. This results in self-segregation. On the other hand, patterns of segregation are also the result of discrimination against racial, religious, and ethnic minorities. In certain suburbs, non-Christians are not welcomed. In others, it is difficult for a Negro or Puerto Rican family to find accommodations. Discrimination, self-segregation, and segregation have made the city a mosaic of ethnic and racial settlements, divided largely on class lines. Nonetheless, extensive units of integrated public housing exist, and there are private areas that are partially integrated.

The minorities that form the bulk of the New York population are not free of prejudice against one another. Race prejudice and discrimination among them frequently erupt in hostilities.

Policies of integration

Discrimination in occupations has not completely disappeared either. Nevertheless, in certain social classes and areas of the city integration has made substantial progress. A new generation of Negro professional classes and intelligentsia has arisen since the turn of the century, composed largely of teachers, lawyers, civil servants, and college professors. Negroes and Puerto Ricans are forming an increasingly larger percentage in New York colleges and universities, where they are not only fully accepted but also respected.

American scholars of Negro origin serve on the faculties of the city university. In the trade unions, the influence of ethnic or racial minorities has limited Negro membership until recently. Now, however, Negroes are increasingly occupying leadership posts. Substantial progress has also been made since World War II in the reduction of prejudice and discrimination against the Puerto Rican and Negro in schools and offices, especially in employment by public institutions.

The numerous ethnic and religious minorities enjoy religious and cultural freedom. Newspapers appear in a number of languages, and radio stations broadcast in many tongues. Ethnic minorities have found new economic opportunities, frequently in specialized fields. The municipal administration of New York City has no discriminatory employment policies.

New York public institutions follow a consistent policy of reduction of tensions, integration, and intergroup cooperation. In this respect there is no dualism, diarchy, or inconsistency. The policies are active, vigorous, and under continuous public control. Federal, state, and city laws—the entire legal system—protect the rights of the racial, ethnic, and religious minority. It may be objected that the law represents an "ideal" norm that differs from the "real." This may be true in some cases, but the law in New York is not a dead letter in this respect. It sets a public policy; a policy for the federal, state, and municipal institutions and authorities as much as for the school system.

The educational institutions

The problem of school integration in New York City is serious and difficult. Nevertheless, the Board of Education and the Board of Higher Education have a consistent policy of support for integration and respect for cultural and religious differences. The board by no means follows a paper philosophy. A teacher in the New York City school system who practices discrimination in a classroom cannot maintain his position. In consequence of this philosophy, racial and ethnic democracy is not only fostered, but even indoctrinated in New York schools.

The Board of Education has a special Education Policy Committee on Integration. Local school boards, civic groups, community organizations, and parents' associations are invited to make recommendations. The differences of views on integration, states a board document, "involve primarily not ends, not values of an integrated education, but how best to bring it about; not whether the school system has a positive responsibility with regard to integration, but the extent to which the school system, as one institution of society, can aid those who have been wronged by that society." [3]

The board spends $117 more per pupil per annum in special service schools in the depressed areas than in the higher income sections. It also supplies extensive services to the underprivileged.[4] The educational system cannot answer all the problems. The maladjusted family structure, an absence of preschool educational encouragement and orientation, and the instability of marginal social groups are problems which can be answered only with an adequate effort of individuals, minority groups, and the entire community. The school alone cannot solve basic problems.

State and city institutions

In addition to the general policy of the municipal and state administration, a number of specialized public and private agencies are active in the reduction of ethnic, racial, and religious tensions and in the enforcement of civil rights.

In 1945 New York introduced the first state law against discrimination. Since then it has been amended many times. The law states clearly that "discrimination against any of its inhabitants because of race, creed, color or national origin is a matter of state concern, that such discrimination threatens not only the rights and proper privileges of its inhabitants but menaces the institutions and foundations of a free and democratic state."

A special state agency, first called the State Commission Against Discrimination, and later the State Commission on Human Rights, was created. It investigated discrimination in employment, public housing, places of public accommodation, resort, or amusement. More than 3300 cases of discrimination were brought before the commission between July 1, 1945, and December 31, 1956.[5] New York City also has a special Commission on Human Rights. The activities of the commission are extensive. Some of its officers are sociologists or specialists in ethnic and race relations. According to city laws, discrimination against, or segregation in, housing because of race, color, religion, or national origin is prohibited.[6] The commission enforces the law primarily by conciliation. But should conciliation fail, the commission may initiate an action through the proper courts. It is also a factfinding, consulting, and cooperating agency. Its research unit conducts research on the effects of school desegregation on intergroup relations in changing neighborhoods, and on minority population trends in New York.[7]

Law and enforcement are not identical. But the laws of New York are indicative of public policy. The Commission on Human Rights is a result of social-political action, supported by the city's political power structure. The commission actively exercises its influence. It is a part of the political mechanism and it is also an important part of the institutional apparatus which, in turn, influences interethnic and race relations from above.

Private agencies; workshops

A number of private agencies—public and religious, interfaith and social—are also active in fostering integration, intergroup cooperation, and cultural and ethnic pluralism and racial democracy. They include some general organizations, like the Children's Aid Society, the United Neighborhood Houses, the Community Council, and the Police Athletic League, to mention a few. There are also specialized organizations, e.g., the National Council of Christians and Jews and the Anti-Defamation League.

The Board of Education and the Board of Higher Education have their own extensive programs in this field, as have private academic institutions. Workshops on race and ethnic relations, seminars and institutes, and specialized programs for teachers of Spanish-speaking children, are offered regularly at local colleges and universities. Problems of minority groups are studied and methods are developed, geared to the needs of these groups.

The field of intergroup relations is new, and some of the methods of easing tensions and eliminating discrimination frequently prove ineffective. Nonetheless, there is evidence of continuous and sincere effort. The policies and the attitudes of public agencies as well as of the law are probably much more liberal and progressive than are the attitudes of large sections of the population.

The minorities form powerful groups. The Negro population is well organized. Other ethnic-religious groups constitute powerful electoral blocs. Members of the minorities may and do have individual prejudices against other ethnic racial, or religious groups, but they support political representatives and platforms that protect their civil and political rights. Hence, the democratic mechanism and appeal in a society composed of minorities creates favorable conditions for the development of an institutional apparatus dedicated to the easing of tension and elimination of prejudice. In addition, the traditional, liberal ideological tendencies of New York cannot be underestimated. The old American traditions, rooted in democracy and abolitionism, are alive among the educated classes, in religious organizations, and in universities.

Social-political movements

Public institutions and some agencies are influential groups, oriented toward definite goals. They are centers of decision for the "input" of communications and enforcement. Those institutions exercise a continuous restraining influence, easing tensions, and pressing the enforcement of set policies of integration from above toward ethnic and racial pluralism. Slow as the change may seem, it still occurs.

But pressures are also exercised from below by powerful social-political movements. These movements of the social base affect the political apparatus, the public agencies, and in turn the policies of the noncommitted and the opposed. Between the social base and the apparatus there is continuous interaction in the form of conferences, meetings, mediations, agreements, and decisions.

Certain changes toward integration are effects; the pressure from the social base is the cause. At other times, reduction of tension is an effect of the policy of the apparatus. But the decisions of the apparatus are not merely a reflection of pressures from the social base. The public apparatus, the municipal and state government, and the educational system also follow their own political, social, and economic objectives, rooted in their own tradition, political philosophies, and interests. The government wants to stay in power. The administration seeks re-election. In a democratic system, whatever the oligarchic tendency may be, the opinion of the voter counts.

Powerful social forces act also on the legislative and executive branches of the government through the intermediary of smaller pressure group. These groups represent a variety of social and economic interests. Pressures against certain forms of integration or against integration policies also emanate from opposing groups that exercise their influence.

The "social base" is complex in nature. However, the fact remains that all the major political parties—Democrats, Republicans, Liberals—representing different social-economic interests, advocate integration and ethnic as well as religious pluralism. There is not a single major political party in New York that would support or preach "anti" programs of prejudice or discrimination. They support integration, not only in public statements but in policies.

In addition to the "major" parties (one could call them macro-parties), New York has a small number of "micro-parties" that exercise an indirect influence but do not represent any electoral force. Most of them have only a handful of members, sometimes organized into associations of various types, without any influence on the day-to-day business of government.

In times of crisis and profound social-economic change, the role of some micro-parties may increase, and they could be transformed into "mass" parties, in terms of their electoral force. Such changes have not occurred in New York in the last decades, but they did happen in earlier history. The micro-parties include a small group of right-wing extremists and conservative movements, including the John Birch Society. On the left there are the Socialist Party, the Social-Democratic Federation, and the Socialist Workers Party and on the extreme left—the Communists and, perhaps, a few "survivals," libertarians or the old anarchist groups. The micro-parties sometimes have an indirect influence (for instance, the social-democratic traditions are influential in many unions, as well as in the Liberal Party). Among the micro-parties perhaps few favor white or Negro racist policies, but some may oppose radical integrationist policies directed toward rapid and substantial change. The churches represent a powerful social force in New York. All major denominations support civil rights programs and integration.

In the 1960's, Negro racist extremists have had more political influence and have shown much more evidence of political activity in New York than have the white racists, whose manifestations, at least at the present time, are only an evidence of their comparative weakness. Again, this does not mean that New York is free of prejudice and that race, ethnic, and religious hostilities are absent.

The city's major labor unions support the civil rights program and integration. The AFL-CIO also has specialized committees on human rights. Not all unions, however, favor or practice integration. Some reflect the bias of their members. On the other hand, in certain occupations one or two ethnic or racial groups predominate and are preferred by both the employers and the unions not because of bias or prejudice but for their skills. Historical circumstances and pressures caused certain ethnic or religious groups to specialize in certain trades—for example, Italians, Polish and Russian Jews, and Puerto Rican female workers in the needle trades. However, the needle trades unions strongly support integrationist policies.

Last but not least come the three dynamic and powerful interracial movements "specialized" in race relations: the National Association for the Advancement of Colored People (NAACP), the Urban League, and the Congress of Racial Equality (CORE). All three organizations spearhead the movement toward integration. All are interracial. All have three basic elements of a dynamic social-political movement: (a) a well-developed ideology, (b) an organization (structure), and (c) strategy and tactics. Their tactics are different, but complementary rather than contradictory. In some areas their activities overlap, causing some disagreement among the three, but generally their relations are amicable.

The NAACP was founded in 1909. The Urban League was organized in 1911 to consolidate earlier informal efforts. From the start both organizations included Negroes and whites as members and leaders. They have played a historical role in the movement toward equal rights and racial democracy. The NAACP has a wide range of activities and goals. Its major objective, however, is centered on integration, on the breaking of discriminatory practices, and on civil rights. The Urban League promotes good human relations and is primarily interested in obtaining adequate housing, health and cultural opportunities, and better living standards for the Negro population.

CORE is the youngest of the three movements. It was born after World War II, out of the postwar trend toward equal opportunities and civil rights. It grew out of attempts of American pacifists and liberals to apply passive resistance to the struggle for civil rights. CORE's goal is a fully integrated society. It has a wide scale of activities: educational, conciliatory, and direct. It is the direct action of CORE that has made it the most visible movement in the struggle for civil rights. Its tactics include picketing and various types of nonviolent struggle such as "sit-ins" in segregated public facilities.

In a sense, CORE is culturally "American" in its nonviolent tactics, which received their earliest expression in Thoreau and Penn. CORE's ideology and tactics exercise a strong appeal for American youth, especially students, many of whom are members. At a time of decline in ideological concepts, CORE offers a new vision and definite goals to the socially conscious student.

The tactics of NAACP are primarily legal (court and legislative action); of the Urban League—social policy; of CORE—direct action. Their combined effort exercises a continuous pressure, a continuous movement toward the vision of racial equality in education, public institutions, political parties, and unions. They are "the prodding groups" of the powerful social forces.

Action that is drastic and visible rouses the sympathy of many people in New York. However, when pressure is exercised to a point of violence or the city and its people are hampered in their daily activities, the reaction may strengthen the forces which oppose integration. Repressed prejudice and hostility may then be overtly expressed.

At this point racial and ethnic groups "polarize." In terms of social proximity and distance, the large mass of hesitant and multivalent moves toward sharp divisions, into pro- and anti-groups, while the intermediary ranks weaken. Interracial efforts toward integration and racial and ethnic democracy are threatened. Antagonism sharpens, and physical aggression displaces passive resistance, efforts toward rational cooperation, mutual aid, and the search for workable solutions. Polarization, an extreme form of hostile separation, contains the threat of violence. The only remedy lies in interracial action by both groups.

Pressures from above and below

As I have already stated, New York is not free of prejudice; of ethnic, racial, and religious hostilities. Large sections of the population are probably "non-committed," although they vote for parties that support the civil rights program, and favor some policy of integration. They belong to churches and congregations that support civil rights. However, the policy of those religious organizations may be at variance with that of some members, since the clergy probably represent more liberal views in those matters. The pressure of public institutions, of declarations of public policy is strong, up to a point, so that those who might otherwise support discriminatory practices prefer to remain silent in public. After all, racial, ethnic, or religious bigotry is not a virtue, a fact that is repeated daily in the mass media. Most of the undecided or prejudiced are not organized.

New York supplies an example of strong pressures toward integration from above—by the institutional network, by the public and private agencies—and from below, by organized movements. But this is by no means a static equilibrium, such as one could observe in Chanak. Here, continuous tensions and the process of their reduction supplies a mechanism for intergroup cooperation and social change. It is this action, this change, which permits the easing of tensions. It is the pressure of public institutions which regulates this process, and simultaneously restrains and controls expressions of ethnic, racial, and religious hostility and antagonism through the enforcement apparatus.

New York is an example of both interethnic and interracial joint actions and of internal or intrapolitical action. The federal, state and city governments are by no means indifferent. All are active. They intervene in problems of race and ethnic relations with a definite policy of easing tensions and fostering cooperation and understanding. None of the public agencies has, in modern times, used the pentup ethnic, religious, or race prejudices to win or to maintain power. The full significance of such policies appears only in a comparison with the actions of other states, other nations, and other historical periods.

This case is indicative of the primacy of the political factor in the reduction of tensions. The pressure of the institutional network, of public institutions which have an enforcement apparatus, plays a paramount role in New York ethnic and race relations. New York is the only example in our case histories that has an extensive network of domestic (not international) agencies active in the reduction of tensions.

An efficient network of this type is effective to a degree. It can control and restrain the tensions as long as a part of the "social base," a substantial and active minority, supports its policies, as long as the antagonistic ethnic or racist tendencies are not expressed in dynamic, well-organized, and aggressive social-political "anti" movements. But even then there are ways of controlling the tensions, though not without difficulties and struggles. There are, however, limits to control of such tensions. Beyond a certain point the effectiveness of agencies and public institutions breaks down and ethnic or racial tensions explode into violent actions, sometimes beginning violent social change.

New York teaches us the significance of an institutional apparatus in reducing or escalating tensions. Although New York is not an international case, it offers a device which in the future could be applied in international tension areas.

The application of the New York pattern in Cyprus in 1964 would mean that President Makarios would have to organize local agencies for the reduction of ethnic tensions, composed of Greeks and Turks; all pulpits would participate in a "brotherhood week." Moslem mullas would address Orthodox Christian congregations in churches, while Orthodox priests would appeal to the Turks in their sermons. The local school authorities would send their delegates to Nicosia for a conference on fostering intergroup cooperation and policies of easing tensions in Cyprus. Pressure through international agencies would be exercised on the Turkish minority leaders to cooperate with this program of general easing of tensions.

A very distant prospect indeed.

13.

CASE STUDIES COMPARED:

Inferences, Questions, Hypotheses

Problems of analysis

The six cases indicate a variety of patterns in ethnic relations. How can we analyze these ethnic patterns and tensions? The complexity of variables presents a problem which sociological method may partially overcome by recognizing the complex nature of the situation, and reducing the variety to two major variables, or to such variables as are relevant. A problem-solving approach requires a causal method. Theoretical reservations and arguments in favor of an exclusively "interactional" approach cannot change the exigencies of a practical operational approach. To ease tensions means to control, eliminate, or balance the variables that cause the tensions. Furthermore, an a priori reduction of causal factors to a single one is in practice equivalent to a dogmatic or axiomatic approach. In such an approach, we exclude the possibility of other variables and postulate the certainty of a single cause.

A problem-solving approach would suggest first the listing of possible causal variables in a given case. This can be done, once we know the facts. After the "causal inventory," those variables can be selected that have major revelance to a given case, and the discussion may then be reduced to the major variables. Each case requires a separate inquiry. In two cases, apparently similar on the surface, different causal factors may operate. I have already discussed problems of causation and reduction (see Chapter 6) in general terms, in a "macro-sociological approach" and shall return to this issue (in Chapter 14). But casual analysis on an operational level in a concrete case should be specific, related to the immediate situation.

A global, macro-sociological approach represents a higher level of abstraction than does a micro-sociological analysis of a concrete situation. The latter represents a lower level of abstraction; it is close to facts. One may say that in a case study approach, "conclusions" are derived from directly immediate facts. A hypothesis tested against these data may be revised during the inquiry. The result of this operation is an "inference" or "conclusion." In a global approach, a "generalization" is in turn based on inferences derived from previous "micro-sociological" studies. In a macro-sociological approach, variables are more sharply reduced. The interactional functional approach has a major application here. However, the models of relating causal and interactional facts are complementary.

Social proximity and distance

Not only the ethnic patterns vary. The attitudes of the ethnic groups and the ranking of different ethnic communities are also a complex matter. Man lives within three environments: geographical, technical, and social. The state, primary and secondary groups, institutions, and interrelated social-economic conditions form an interacting social fabric within which man lives, decides, and acts. The technical environment constitutes the artifacts created by man. In time of tensions the social environment is by no means divided simply into pro-groups and anti-groups, or into those with us and those against us. Perhaps with the exception of a violent and open conflict, a reasonable actor, evaluating the situation, sees not only the two striking colors of the "pro" and "anti" groups of friends and enemies, but also a number of halftones. So, acting in an empirical manner, he ranks the proximity and distance. In dangerous times, this is done for practical reasons. The actor has to evaluate how much he can "count on" his neighbor; what to expect from any ethnic group in case of conflict. Family traditions and experiences transmitted from generation to generation, conversations, history, ideologies, and psychological or economic motivation—all contribute to the ranking of social distance or proximity of the perceived ethnic groups in a multinational region.

These differences in ethnic patterns and in distance and proximity ranks have to be considered in a process of tension reduction. Diverse patterns usually require different policies and alternative solutions. The concept of ranking of social distance and proximity between the ethnic groups may offer an approach to moderation in policies. It is difficult to reduce the tension totally and remove prejudice in a short period of time. Prejudices do not disappear overnight. But the overt expression of these prejudices, e.g., discriminatory practices, may be weakened and controlled.

Policies for reducing ethnic tensions attack the problem on two levels: overt discrimination and antagonistic actions and prejudice formation. In the latter, a long-range view should be taken, since this cure requires time. Therefore, the reduction of a tension should first lead to a gradual reduction of ranks of distance. At the initial stage, it is sufficient to move from the distance of archenemy or enemy to a neutral out-group in order to create tolerable conditions of life and neighborhood.

A fundamental method for easing tensions is a policy of integration. Under certain conditions, integration is definitely the most desirable and effective policy, especially in race relations. Why "under certain conditions"?

In certain cases two different ethnic groups (minorities) are unwilling to foster a policy of integration and prefer to practice separation or self-segregation. (The cases of the Arapahos and the Shoshones in Wyoming, and of the Armenians, Jews, Greeks, and Turks in Chanak are studies in separation.) Not every self-segregation or separation necessarily leads to hostility and antagonism. However, a pattern of self-segregation or separation may, in times of crisis, show antagonistic tendencies. The relations between the groups may then move toward sharp antagonism, since the practice of cooperation is limited, and an institutional mechanism for easing of tensions is absent or very limited.

A policy of integration develops its own functional apparatus of institutions. It fosters cooperative patterns, supports education which leads to cooperation and to an understanding of cultural differences. The pattern of self-segregation or separation is by no means a pattern of a dynamic and changing modern society. Nevertheless, in some societies and in certain historical periods, this type of pattern did develop. Perhaps we need further clarification.

Self-segregation or separation, with all its shortcomings, may offer solutions to static-oriented and relatively small communities in interreligious or intercultural relations, but not in race relations. When minorities refuse "to join," it is difficult to "integrate," since integration requires a measure of agreement. A tendency toward religious or ethnic pluralism is the best workable democratic policy in such case.

Pluralism requires a minimum agreement on common principles and values; it is a "bilateral" proposition. However, should an orthodox religious group desire to live a relatively isolated life, a democratic administration would rightly follow a policy of noninterference. Such isolation, in specific cases, may not endanger the entire pattern, and successful pluralism or assimilation may advance among other ethnic and religious groups.

The area of race relations is a different matter. Here policies of segregation, self-segregation, or separation lead eventually to racial antagonism, persecution, and exploitation. In fact, segregation is a symptom of social and political inequalities. It has a tendency toward aggressive forms of hostility. The very fact of segregation or separation indicates an absence of communication and of inter-racial institutions between groups. Self-segregation as a result of religious or cultural difference, faith, and dogma is quite different from a racist segregation due to racial prejudice and hostility.

The dangers of a segregated or self-segregated pattern appear in times of crisis and result in "polarization." Polarization means sharp, antagonistic division between ethnic blocs, with a disappearance of the intermediary ranks of proximity and distance. The community breaks up into definite blocs of "pro" and "anti" groups. The significant intermediary ranks lose their appeal and influence among the noncommitted and multivalent.

In interethnic and interreligious relations, a line must be drawn between pluralism, separation, self-segregation, and segregation. Pluralism (discussed more extensively in Chapter 18 (Part V) combines cooperation with respect for cultural or religious difference. Separation is a de facto situation. Pluralism is part of a broader idea system, requiring a limited cooperation. "Separation" is indicative of restraint and limited but "correct" relations, reinforced by periodical or spon-taneous intergroup meetings, and by specialized institutions. Segregation is a coercive pattern, imposed by force or custom. It results from the subordination of racial or religious groups, usually as a reflection of economic and political domina-tion. Self-segregation and segregation reflect tendencies toward social isolation of cultural groups. They are "unilateral" patterns, the result of actions by one racial, religious, or ethnic group. Integration, pluralism, even "separation" are "bilateral" patterns, requiring the agreement or minimum assent of two groups.

The process of racial or ethnic integration leads to the formation of a unified social community. Such a process involves modification of values and institutions, and the development of a new social-political culture. Substantial cultural differ-ences in values, institutions, and behavioral patterns are obstacles that are often strong enough to slow integration. Differences in color are sometimes surface issues and not the basic cause of self-segregating tendencies. Disparity of values, of culture, or of institutions are strong causative actors. Therefore, a policy of integration depends on changes within the minority group; on action within the community. Integration, like pluralism, is a definite policy; it is one result of a broad social philosophy and ideology. Unlike self-segregation and segregation, this phi-losophy must be shared by both social groups; the effort must be mutual. To forget this is to defeat the entire policy. A limitation of the effort to the majority alone will sooner or later create difficulties.

Integration may break down the prejudices of a part of a social group, class, or community. But it may also increase prejudices of some individuals, especially in the initial stage. Integration is a "two-way" proposition: it requires an adjust-ment from both the majority and the minority and understanding and respect for cultural differences.

Political power and ethnic relations

All of the case studies indicate the close connection and interaction of political, religious, and ethnic relations. Since the state and the public agencies penetrate into the very fabric of society and control substantial power, their role in ethnic relations is significant. The pressures of the institutional apparatus of the state or of the church may intensify or reduce the tensions. Hence, the system of private and public institutions which we have called the "institutional apparatus" is a "strategic locus" in times of escalated ethnic tensions. A society in which sections of the population have strong prejudices may still have an "institutional apparatus" geared toward the elimination of prejudice and the reduction of tensions.

The minorities represent political power. They exercise influence through the electoral system on the executive branch of the government. Their pressures also influence the general orientation of policies. Together with the actions of the liberal majority, their pressures may result in the establishment of specific institutions dedicated to the goal of integration or of easing tensions. However, such a development is possible only when there is substantial support for the program of civil rights and ethnic and racial democracy within "majority groups."

Institutions are not separate blocs or social instruments isolated from and independent of society; they are rooted in society and are part of it. They may, however, in times of tension reflect the policy of an active minority. The success of the different agencies is determined by the response to their policies within the area where they are applied.

Education

Thus the distribution of political power is of primary significance in ethnic and race relations. The political power structure forms an important regulatory mechanism which may have a moderating and restraining influence, and may develop long-range policies affecting attitudes. In the latter, the role of the school system is of great significance. A policy directed toward changing the attitudes and social images of various ethnic groups, for the purpose of reducing ethnic tensions, requires special educational policies. Since prejudice is transmitted to a child in his primary groups and reinforced in his formative years, it may influence his general outlook for the remainder of his life. The development of values and attitudes free of hostility toward other racial and ethnic groups is therefore a problem of early training.

A school system has little influence on the family, and on the learning processes within the primary groups. Therefore, the early elementary school days are of major relevance. At this time there is still a good chance of directing ethnic or racial attitudes in the proper channels. There is also a chance of correcting the total "ethnic outlook."

Internal and external tensions

External tensions may be reduced by the intensification of internal tensions, while internal tensions may be reduced by fostering external tensions. On a nation-wide level, this was done frequently in history when weak governments tried to resolve domestic problems and weather revolutionary changes and demands by intensifying international troubles and initiating a war. On a "micro-sociological" level, such a process can also be observed in tensions areas. In terms of theory, a general hypothesis can be suggested that a reduction of external tensions may increase internal tensions, and vice versa. Individual or group values may foster such conflict. Psychological needs may release aggression within a group. Once the opportunities of outside aggression are reduced, psychological urges and established aggressive behavioral patterns may be directed against members of the in-group.

Multiple patterns

Our case studies teach us that a number of ethnic patterns may exist side by side in the same city, in the same state. A dominant pattern, a dominant policy, can be usually identified. Nonetheless, other ethnic patterns continue in times of struggle for integration, and suggest a policy of pluralism as the best solution.

iv. Ideological and Interpolitical Tensions

14.

SEIZURE OF TENSION AREAS

The three major periods of Western antagonism

The history of great antagonisms in the Western world can be divided into three major periods: (1) religious, (2) national, and (3) ideological. In a sense, all are ideological and at certain stages also have a quality of class antagonism. The first period may be traced from the seventh through the seventeenth century. By the end of the ninth century the earlier dissensions within the Christian Church had developed into a great schism and culminated in the division of Christianity into the Western and Eastern churches. This division into the Roman Catholic, on the one hand, and the Greek Orthodox Church, on the other, was the beginning of agelong antagonisms and tensions that have resulted in religious wars, especially on the Polish, Russian, and Ukrainian borders. Religious wars were in a sense ideological. Both were frequently combined with or reflections of social-economic struggles. Often they were only rationalization of political conflicts, conflicts of wills contending for power.

Not all wars were of such nature. Cases and cases can be cited of nations and rulers belonging to the same church conducting long and devastating wars when dynastic or national political interests were dominant. Nonetheless, the "zone of great antagonisms" was persistent. Religious, national or ideological antagonisms supplied the accent and uncompromising style of the conflicts. Reduction of differences to a single ideology or religion does not guarantee peace. Conflicts are reduced when individuals and nations learn how to respect and cherish differences. What is suggested here is the great symbolic theme, the accent of persistent historical conflicts of the past, conflicts in the Western World or on the outskirts of Europe.

The second zone of tensions, between the Islamic and Christian worlds, lasted more than a thousand years. It began in Spain, perhaps with the conquest of Spain in the eighth century, intensified at the end of the eleventh century with the first Crusades, and ended almost in the twentieth century with the disintegration of the Ottoman Empire. The ethnic antagonisms of the Balkans in the nineteenth century also had religious overtones.

The third area of religious antagonisms was the European struggle between units within the Roman Catholic Church that resulted in the Protestant movement. This schism appeared very early. Arbitrarily we may choose the Albigensian-Waldensian Crusade of the thirteenth century as the beginning, after which the long period of religious revolutions and wars extended almost to the end of the seventeenth.

Ethnic tensions in their intensive form appeared in Europe by the end of the eighteenth century in the form of rising nationalism and the struggle for national independence. However, the roots of these antagonisms can be traced to times of early conquest; e.g., Cossack uprisings in Eastern Europe against the Poles and the Russians were in many respects an expression of social-economic class and ethnic and religious tensions.

Modern nationalism appeared in definite form as ideological and patriotic movements. At first, the religious identity was separated from the national identity. It was not until later that the issue of the establishment of a sovereign state through ethnic, national identity developed into a new concept of legitimacy of power: the will of the people ("general will") who belong to the same nation, who speak the same language, who have the same historical tradition and origin, should determine the legitimacy of power and the establishment of the state. The old dynastic, traditional legitimacy was displaced by the new legitimacy of the general will; the monarchic form of government, by the republican. Ethnic tensions combined with nationalism appeared throughout Europe and continued until the end of World War II. This period of national-ethnic antagonisms extended for more than one hundred and fifty years, and overlapped in the twentieth century with ideological tensions.

Ideological antagonisms as a source of international tensions first appeared during the French Revolution. With the defeat of Napoleon Bonaparte and the Congress of Vienna, they largely subsided as international antagonisms, and reappeared only with the Russian Revolution of 1917. They touched the outer fringes of the three major camps: fascism, Communism, and democracy.

European ideologies have a tendency to split, a fact that appeared early in the religious movement. The splits (deviations) might be explained by social-economic conditions, but this is only a part of the total picture. Ideas by their very nature harbor the germs of future dissensions. Contradictions arise on the issues of means and ends. The problem of authenticity of ideologies and of their interpretation results in further deviation.

Two major tendencies are evident in both the religious and political movements: (a) the dogmatic and authoritarian and (b) the liberal or democratic. They appear in the French Revolution, reappear in the Social Democratic movement, and recur in other political forms with an elaborate philosophy and theory. Ideological schisms foster historical divisions and struggles, and are usually the starting point of basic contradictions and antagonisms. Almost every idea system results eventually in contradictory and inconsistent interpretations. This is perhaps the very nature of the ideas, especially those rooted in dialectical philosophies such as grew in Europe.

The potentialities of international conflict arise when militant ideologies unite with control of the state, which has a monopoly of physical and economic power. When proselytizing and militant religions capture the power of the state; when aggressive nationalistic ideologies transform the state; when again proselytizing universal ideologies establish a monopoly of power—the danger of ideological war and conflict appears. At this moment, the intergroup tensions between ideological groups within the state move into a stage of interpolitical tensions.

In a modern democratic system, with its complex value structure and myriad institutions, the power of the state is not under the permanent control of one ideology and one party. In consequence, the state does not become a submissive tool of a single political orientation, and cannot be sublimated to the role of a means to an end. The state is designed to serve many goal systems (objectives) and many ideologies. Political parties win and lose elections and while they are in power, the state machinery is not reduced to the role of an aggressive party apparatus. From the viewpoint of international relations, this is a major merit of the democratic system.

In reality, religious, ethnic-national, and ideological-political tensions and antagonisms are similar in nature. They are all ideological tensions arising from differences in idea systems. (Religion is an idea system.) Ethnicity and differences in ethnicity are expressed in nationalistic ideologies.

Today ideological differences are expressed in social-economic (class) and political outlooks, and can often be creative in nature. In the continuous contest of ideologies, new tendencies emerge and society moves toward new goals. It is the nature of a creative social process to eliminate institutions, customs, and behavioral patterns that are harmful to large sections of the productive population and have a deleterious effect on changes necessary for the improvement of conditions. The institution of slavery can serve as an example.

In the history of the Western world, ideological differences and conflicts led to violent expressions. The idea systems were reflections of social-economic conditions of their times, and were more often than not rationalizations of interests of certain social classes. This relationship should not be underestimated. Nonetheless, by its very nature the incompatibility of values and ideas led to conflict.

It is sufficient to peruse the history of religious wars and study the issues involved in order to find the significance of ideas and concepts in human behavior. In medieval times, the prophesies and interpretations of sacred books had an impact on religious and social mass movements. Confused, mystical, sometimes unintelligible, they impressed not only the uneducated masses, but also the clergy. Unverified vision resulted in mass movements and collective, emotional phenomena. The mystical interpretation of the testament of Joachim of Fiore (1145–1202), with its prophesies of the coming of Antichrist and his overthrow, had an impact on church and politics. Reinterpreted later by a dissident Dominican, it had a wide appeal.[1] Of course, those movements were a reflection of deep, unknown needs. Nevertheless, they integrated multitudes into opposing camps.

Idea systems are incompatible when the basic tenets cannot be reconciled, especially in extreme cases where they are combined with a belief that survival of one precludes the existence (continuance) of others. There are degrees of incompatibility. Idea systems which are not proselytizing might be incompatible, but may not necessarily result in open conflicts. Here the coexistence of religious groups on the level of indifference is both possible and probable, and has occurred many times in history. Once the normative idea system postulates a monopoly of truth and absolute values, and combines these concepts with the duty or proselytizing "sinners," then incompatibility moves toward a militant stage. The "sin" and the "dogma" might be religious or political. Dogmatic absolute concepts do not tolerate deviations from the basic norms. Such idea systems, when combined with a concept of "mortal sin" for those who disagree, are prone to result in conflict.

The question of absolute values is not easy, and we shall return to it at the end of this book. I do not intend to say here that all values, whatever their differences, are equal in significance and merit. What makes an idea system of strong absolute values a motivating force of aggressive and destructive action is not a belief in the validity of basic tenets, but the absence of respect for difference, for doubt, or for creative criticism and the refusal of a possibility of disagreement, even on minor issues. It was precisely disagreements on minor issues that led to strong schisms and mutual extermination, to mention only one of the many issues that troubled the Christian religion.

History teaches us that incompatibility of religious idea systems led to long wars until the exhausted antagonists found that the problem could not be solved by force of arms. Religious wars ended with mutual accommodation (which we have called in our initial chapter "coordination"). None of the groups submitted wholly to the others. Certain countries became predominantly Catholic, others

Protestant; and societies, influenced by political experience, civilization, and a philosophical spirit, introduced a concept of pluralism.

The incompatibility of ethnic, nationalistic ideologies ended in the holocaust of two world wars. In Western Europe during the twentieth century, nationalism led to extreme forms of conflict and to the temporary but total subordination of the militarily weaker nations to the stronger and more aggressive ones, led by Germany. Not before the defeat of Nazism and fascism was a solution possible. And, both were defeated, not by a revolution, but by an international war. Here, the massive change in idea systems was achieved through interpolitical coercive subordination of the violent forms of nationalism, and by repression of the agressive nature of the proselytizing creed; by "ideological" changes, and a de facto or international agreement on noninterference or limited interference.

The further solution of nationalistic antagonism in Europe required new idea systems, new values, and new institutions that would permit the reintegration of European peoples. New loyalties appeared in the wider form of continental integration.

Germany might be a typical example. Here the regional and local values were strengthened, vis-à-vis loyalty toward Germany as a national entity. Now a German was also a Bavarian and a European. Emphasis on the universal and the regional values brought about the reintegration of the German population in the community of European nations.

The world today has moved into a period of ideological antagonism rooted in social, economic, and political outlooks for which solutions have not as yet been discovered. The past gives us a few lessons, but the future may require new answers. In the past, after a thousand years of struggle, solutions were found in noninterference and separation through a profound change in idea systems. This meant simply the end of the crusades, and in time, of inquisitions and persecutions. "Coordination," representing a consensus, was also achieved by the development of new ideas and institutions combined with the physical defeat of groups representing the most aggressive expression of ideological tendencies.

Modern ideologies' appeal to social-economic, religious, or racial-ethnic identity

Man belongs to many groups, not only to one. Man also has many loyalties. In a modern society the religious loyalty may differ from the national or the social-economic. The same person belongs to a church and is a member of a nation and a trade union. In certain historical periods, the three loyalties were complementary, in others they might be contradictory or at least alien to the dominant policy of the state. An individual's identity, united with his social-economic position in society, is of fundamental significance. A person acts in defense of his livelihood if he sees that political change may deprive him of it.

In order to exist, a man must satisfy his basic biological needs, and his level of needs changes with the development of industrial culture. In a different situation or a different historical period, however, another aspect of man's identity may be emphasized. In medieval times the religious identification was generally regarded as a dominant one. In the eighteenth and nineteenth centuries ethnic identification played a similar role. In the middle of the nineteenth century, labor and peasant movements, the social-economic class identification, carried the dominant accent.

Accentuation of identification has an impact on individual and collective motivation. The individual discovers his "social, ethnic, or religious consciousness," or his group identification, his "reference group." His resultant "class consciousness" signifies that he has achieved group identity.

One function of ideologies is group identification, since they are "collective representations," a concept advanced more than a half-century ago by Émile Durkheim. Ideologies serve as instruments through which group identification is emphasized and accentuated. In consequence, they integrate individuals into social groups. Their appeal is strongest when they respond to urgent needs. Thus, the same individual can be integrated to one group through identification of his ethnicity, or to another, through identification of his class.

Various ideologies have different ranges of appeal. Racial ideologies may appeal to people having certain physical characteristics. Consequently, the range of appeal for them is narrowed to certain personality types within a "racial" group. Not all persons of the same race respond to racism. Subnational ideologies appealed to groups smaller than a nation; e.g., a tribe or a regional group. Supernational party appeals to universal ties, superior to the national and racial identity. (The broad proletarian ideologies: socialism, anarchism, syndicalism, and Communism, are universal in nature.) The supernational ideologies, frequently called international ideologies, represent a wide range of potential appeal.

The appeal of religious ideologies depends on the nature of the religions. The Orthodox Jewish religious movement appeals to a narrow group consisting of those who are Jewish or have an orthodox orientation toward the Jewish religion. However, a Catholic ideological movement appeals to people of different orientations, and because Catholicism is a universal religion, it has a wider range of appeal.

Contemporary ideologies appeal primarily to needs and interests related to social, economic, and political conditions. Such is the nature of the anarchist and social-democratic ideologies, syndicalism, trade unionism, cooperatives, and Communism. In Europe, the nationalist ideologies are now in a period of decline. The supernational ideologies, combined with social-economic ideologies, are dominant. This, of course, might constitute a temporary change. But it seems to me that the nationalistic racial identities are on the decline in the Western world, although they still flourish in lands distant from the germinating centers of philosophical idea systems and the social sciences.

Modern social, economic, and political ideologies, combined with the supernational, appeal to a wide range of groups and individuals. In this respect they are akin to the medieval religions, which accentuated the supernational and universal over the ethnic and the national. Nineteenth-century nationalistic ideologies limited their appeal to the ethnic or racial identification.

The range of appeal of an ideology is relevant for our discussion of tension areas. Social-economic ideologies, in which ethnic identity plays only an ancillary or tactical role, have a worldwide appeal. Proselytizing and aggressive ideological movements carrying such ideologies may control tension areas on a worldwide basis. Supernational ideologies complementary to or detached from ethnic identity have a similar appeal, and they contain potentialities for the reduction of tension on a worldwide scale. Thus the range of political operation of nationalistic movements in a definite tension area is geographically limited, while movements universal in nature or appealing to social-economic identity have a global range and lend themselves to centralized control.

When social-economic tensions appear in a zone as a result of economic conditions or oppression and exploitation, a universal ideology can supply a sense of direction, a social image for the future, and possible solutions. It acts as an integrating element, uniting the discontented classes and groups both internally and with a wider community. Such a universal ideology can offer a worldwide appeal, while an ethnic-racial ideology is limited in this respect.

Many social-economic tensions can be reduced by social-economic changes. Often, however, the firmly entrenched ruling classes refuse to yield their privileged positions and the government lacks the imagination and strength to embark on basic reforms and changes. Therefore, once an ideology appears, an outside state identified with the latter may use the movement in the tension area for its own strategic objectives. Here, the intergroup social tension changes to interpolitical tension. Since two or more states are eventually involved, such ideological political tensions may lead to more general conflict. There are moments in history when revolution is a necessary vehicle of change and a condition of peace.

Strategy of conquest

In our era of worldwide strategies of conquest and control, local ideological tensions change rapidly from intergroup to interpolitical tensions. A local tension may, through the intervention of outside powers or organizations, become an international issue, especially in strategic areas. Social disorganization as an "objective" revolutionary condition is created or escalated by external forces. The area has strategic significance, therefore the tension is escalated to a local war with the purpose of capturing the area, since it forms a stage in the strategy of conquest. Tensions can be "real" or "manipulated." We may call them "real" if the ideological tensions are strongly reflected in local social-economic discontent arising from social-economic relations, class structure, and the situation of the population. The tension is "manipulated" if the ideology is represented by only a small group and is not reflected in the "social base," in the mass of the population, but used and intensified for the purpose of transforming the conflict from local to interpolitical, and of furthering the objective of capturing the area.

There are only a few techniques in the seizure of areas. We shall limit our discussion to some principal models with many variations. A discovery of new tactics creates a new situation, since the state or political party exposed to the new tactical design is usually unable to cope with the new pattern of political attack.

Elements of analysis

The leaders of a political movement oriented toward basic social changes have to consider the social-economic conditions within which the movement operates, its opponents or antagonists, and the strength and organization of the party. Social political movements are not created in a vacuum. They are the result of the conditions in which they operate. However, political movements change the social-economic situation.

I shall call the conditions within which a political movement operates, the social base; later, in my analysis of tension areas, the social-internal base. Organized or unorganized pressures from the discontented multitudes or social classes shall be identified as movements "from below," or of the base. The organized social-political movement which operates within a social base shall be called "the party." The party and the social-economic base form the two elements of an internal political analysis, particularly in times of crisis or of revolutionary changes.

These two concepts appear early in social and political theory. At the beginning of the nineteenth century, they were not formally classified. However, they can be traced in the *Essay on the Revolution in Naples* (1801) of Vincenzo Cuoco, an Italian historian and theoretician of the revolution.[2] The significance of the ideas, organization, and of the masses was also discussed a half a century later by men of action and theoreticians such as Giuseppe Ferrari[3] and Giuseppe Mazzini.

The Russian revolutionary theoreticians analyzed the problem of organization of the party and of social-economic conditions, particularly in the last quarter of the nineteenth century. Joseph Stalin and Lenin formulated these concepts. Stalin, in the lectures on strategy and tactics which he delivered in Svierdlow (and which were later published in *Pravda* in 1926 and reprinted many times later), distinguishes these two elements. He calls the party the subjective element and social-economic conditions the objective element, of a revolution. His theory of strategy and tactics is built on an analysis of those two elements.[4]

The seizure of political power in a tension area requires coordination of the social-economic base with the political movement of the party. Conditions can then be manipulated or created by outside interference. For example, a tactic of individual terror combined with indiscriminate terror may produce a planned disorganization of the society and weaken the institutional structure.

Roughly, three types of seizure of political power can be distinguished: from above, from below, and a combined seizure (an amalgam of the two). The capture of power from above is also called a coup d'état (*colpo di stato, golpo de estado*) or, by many theoreticians, a revolution from above.

A distinction must be made between social and political revolutions. The social revolution is concerned with essential and rapid changes of social-economic conditions, social structure, institutions, and values. A rapid change—peaceful or violent—of these elements reflects a social revolution in many other aspects also. The term "political revolution" is applied to violent transfer of political power, the capture or destruction of the state, or the violent destruction of political institutions, and the establishment of a new power structure or a new social and political organization. The political revolution does not necessarily coincide with a social revolution, or vice versa.

The revolution from above is a simple technique of the capture of basic instruments and symbols of power by a small group of armed men, frequently supported by the military force, the armies. The seizure of weapons is essential in a revolution from above, and the role the army plays in such a coup is frequently decisive.

This type of revolution appeared in Spain, Italy, and Russia in the first quarter of the nineteenth century, and was called a military revolution or uprising. Giuseppe Ferrari, in his book on Italian revolutions, writes that the revolutionary movement of 1820 in Italy was a military revolution (*sollevazione militare*) that collapsed while passing from the military barracks to the public piazza. The masses of the population were passive or indifferent. He wrote later that "the conspirators were the only means, the only force of Italy. On the one hand were the conspirators and on the other, the Inquisition and the brigands."[5]

Vincenzo Cuoco made a distinction between an active and a passive revolution: An active revolution is one that moves from the base; in which the masses participate. A passive revolution is one accomplished without, or in spite of, the people. The passive revolution was for Cuoco one in which a small minority of progressive and enlightened revolutionaries seized power with the support of the invading army.[6] As we shall see, this pattern appears in more elaborate form in the twentieth century, and is sometimes called the external revolution. Cuoco's concern was the establishment of democracy and the victory of enlightenment in Italy. The pattern is, however, "neutral" and can also be used by those who plan authoritarian rule.

The seizure of weapons or other means of violence is typical of the first stage of a revolution from above. The action of the masses is the basic element in the first stage of a revolution from below. In the second stage, arms become paramount. The revolution from below is based on mass movements by ethnic groups or social classes that are dissatisfied with existing social, political or economic systems and revolt against them. The third type, "a combined seizure," is a union of a coup with a revolution from above and from below. The social discontent of the working class, of the peasantry, or of certain ethnic groups becomes an important element of the strategy of a well-organized revolutionary group. This party strikes at the opportune moment, and the seizure of the symbols and instruments of power coincides either with the passive indifference of the masses or with spontaneous revolutionary activities.[7]

The three major revolutionary techniques have an application in the capture and control of tension areas that are basically revolutionary in nature. The political tension in such cases reflects deeper social-economic unrest. The support of an outside government or party, however, modifies the revolutionary pattern. With external political and military pressure, the revolutionary tensions move from an intrapolitical to a complex and international, interpolitical stage, and change in nature. The outside government may now use the local tension and the local party for the capture of the tension area.

With the change of a tension from internal ideological to complex and interpolitical, new elements appear and the nature of the tension changes. Internal tension is reinforced by external pressure. In consequence, two fronts appear: the internal and the external. The external front is formed by the military force and all the other elements of power, such as mass communication, economic support, and the political and diplomatic support of an external government and party. The pressure may be expanded to areas in which the government involved is vulnerable.

All the resources of the outside state form the external base. The latter is well protected, since the internal government is already involved in its own tensions and usually avoids any direct attack against its ideological enemy. First, the domestic tension and unrest concentrate the attention of the home government on its own affairs; secondly, they reduce the government's potential to act effectively and to use its political power in the field of international relations to the full. The explosive ideological and political conflicts in the tension area absorb most of the government's resources.

From the external base the revolutionary party is supplied with money, weapons, propaganda, and trained personnel. This skillful use of the external base as a supply depot and for reinforcement of tension within the social internal base is a key element in the strategy of capture of a tension area.

Thus, we must distinguish between the external strategic base and the internal social base. The first forms a center of operation for the external front; the second, for the internal front. Both, however, are closely connected, since the operations of each are coordinated and reinforced. When the home government acts, exposing the "internal political party," the outside government is still able to reserve its own forces and its own strength for the ultimate coup.

Four "major models" for the capture of tension areas appear in modern history. One is the military internal revolution (coup) combined with external pressure; two, the military external revolution; three, infiltration combined with revolution from above or below and the external front; and four, revolution from below combined with the external front.

Problems of terminology

The distinction between political and social revolution has been already made. At this time, we are primarily concerned with political revolution: the violent transfer of power in a state. In terms of values and ideology, "revolution" is associated with a progressive, enlightened movement that innovates improvements for the underprivileged in an extension of freedom. Such was the concept of revolution in the nineteenth century.

The term "counterrevolution" has been used in the nineteenth and twentieth centuries for the identification of movements that represent a return to the status quo, to conditions favoring the privileged classes. The term "counterrevolution" meant also the introduction of a centralistic versus a liberal and democratic government; a return to the old regime.

Freedom and order are not contradictory concepts. Nonetheless, the forces of counterrevolution stressed the contradiction. Theirs was basically an ideology of "order" versus "freedom," a promise of order and social peace instead of social change combined with democratic and liberal institutions. In such a context the terms "revolution" and "counterrevolution" carry definite values and are also political symbols which appear in proclamations and in theoretical, philosophical discussions. In this normative sense the Nazi revolution was a counterrevolution, as was the victory of Franco in Spain. In a sociological sense, however, the Nazi seizure of power was a revolutionary movement directed toward the violent seizure of a state. Thus, we must distinguish between the sociological and normative (social-philosophical) concepts of revolution, as well as the two concepts of social and political revolution. I shall use the term "revolution" in its empirical, sociological sense, rather than in the normative sense.

In both Latin America and Continental Europe, the term "revolution" has frequently been abused in its normative sense since the nineteenth century, with "democracy" being used for dictatorship and "progress" for changes that moved mankind backward. Nonetheless, the term "revolution" has its attraction, and usage of the term "counterrevolution" results in hostility. In popular parlance, a "counterrevolutionary" is one who is against the people.

As I have said, the interpolitical tensions of our time are largely ideological. Therefore, the choice of symbols is of great significance. Nations that have recent revolutionary traditions are sensitive to the names applied to their actions. Since ideological tensions frequently reflect deeper social or economic unrest, the movements fostering rapid change have an appeal to the people, in contrast to those of the status quo.

The choice of political terminology in times of ideological struggle is not without significance.

Techniques of capture

Various types and techniques of capture reflect relationships of the attacking political party or military group to the internal social base and external strategic base. A small dynamic party or internal front, with external assistance, has succeeded in capturing a strategic area many times in the past when social classes or nonorganized multitudes regarded by them as logical allies were either passive or passively and silently hostile.

Nations in the past have been conquered by foreign armies and also by their own military forces, who consolidated their power for many years. The internal military revolution combined with an external front is a simple technique, representing a coup d'etat, or a revolution from above. A military group, supported by regiments or battalions that blindly obey orders, captures the instruments and symbols of power and displaces the existing government. At the beginning of the nineteenth century, this technique was called a military revolution. In modern times it is frequently supported by an outside power or an external front. The revolutions in the Arab countries of the Near East follow this pattern. That in Iraq, which ended a royal dynasty, was a military revolution, related to a "combined seizure" (there was support from "below") and supported from outside by the might of the United Arab Republic. The external strategic base was in Egypt; the internal social base was in Iraq.

A military revolution is a technique that may serve a variety of objectives. In countries in which the democratic tradition has not yet developed, and where the masses are passive or indifferent under a strong despotic form of government, a military revolution frequently carries through progressive change and reforms. The Turkish Revolution of Kemal Pasha (Ataturk) was primarily a military revolution. The early Russian revolutionaries, the Decembrists, were also military in character, representing progressive ideologies, including the abolition of serf-dom and the introduction of a constitution. A victory of the Decembrists would have marked the beginning of a fundamental social revolution in Russia, but it failed.

In our case, the external military revolution is of greater interest. The technique has been used frequently in modern times, yet its beginning can be traced back at least 150 years. This strategy was applied during and after the French Revolution. During the political revolutions in Italy in 1799, the multitudes, the people of the cities, supported the ruling classes, the aristocracy, the king, and the church. The liberation of Italy from the oppression of feudalism, autocracy, and Inquistion could come only from the outside. Inside Italy, the new ideas of free-dom and enlightenment appealed only to the intellectual elites. (Here is the origin of the passive revolution described by Cuoco.)

The strategy of the passive revolution was a combination of a strong external front—the French army—with a weak internal front, represented by a handful of enlightened Republican intellectuals and Jacobins. Once the French army with-drew, the Lazzaroni and the lower classes took revenge on the unfortunate rebels. There was a real political hunt for Jacobins and Republicans in Tuscany.[8]

In modern times, the idea of an "exported revolution" was advanced by Marshal Tukhachevski, the leading Soviet military theoretician, and perhaps its most gifted military leader. Writing on the Polish-Soviet war of 1920, Tukha-chevski suggested that the Red army, through a strategy of war, could bring the revolution to Western Europe. The defeat of the Bolshevik army at the gates of Warsaw arrested this advance.[9]

Tukhachevski's introduction of parachutist troops as a strategy of war was intended as external support for the internal revolutionary movements. (Accord-ing to Adam Ciolkosz, a German military staff mission first witnessed a para-chutist exercise in Russia, and adapted the tactic for Germany, which used it years later against the Russians.[10])

The tactics of infiltration are usually combined with a revolution from above or below. Two types of infiltration may be distinguished: (1) social-political and (2) geographical. The first type is primarily the tactic of penetrating political parties, the army, the police, and other strategic associations and groups. Geo-graphical infiltration is connected with guerrilla warfare, and its purpose is to ignite a revolution from below. It was applied in Venezuela in 1963 by the fol-lowers of Fidel Castro. A similar tactic is being used by the anti-Castro Cuban revolutionaries who seek to launch a full-scale revolution from below.

The Nazis used political-social infiltration on a large scale to penetrate the state machinery of Austria before that country's capture. Infiltration was used by Stalin between 1945 and 1948, as a stage in a long-range strategy of control over Central and Eastern Europe. It combined an external revolution with social-political infiltration. Stalin exercised military, diplomatic, and economic pressure, and simultaneously infiltrated the military, the police, government apparatus, as well as non-Communist parties. Tension was created, and the area fell under Communist control with simultaneous pressure from outside.

Chinese strategy in Vietnam is an example of geographical infiltration of a territory. The Vietcong infiltrate villages and extend Communist influence through propaganda and terror. Communist China and Viet Minh form the external base from which the Vietcong are supported. The infiltration is intensified; so is the tension through continuous action. A Vietcong victory would mean the indirect extension of Communist Chinese influence over Vietnam. Through such a strategy of war by "proxy," or indirect war, Communist China extends its influence deep into Southeast Asia with relatively small expenditure of its own potential.

Finally, a strong social movement, a real revolution from below, can be assisted in a tension area by an external front. Here, the internal front is really supported by a mass movement, and assisted by external pressure. The combination of external military aid with a revolution from below as an interpolitical conflict is also not new. As early as 1808, Count Neithardt Gneisenau outlined a plan for a national mass uprising in Prussia against the French, with the simultaneous military support of the allies. As a good Prussian, Gneisenau first submitted his plan to the King of Prussia and received royal agreement. In his own way, Gneisenau understood the significance of an ideological appeal. He wrote: "It is cheap and statesmanlike to give the people a fatherland." [11] In other words, the appeal to patriotism is inexpensive.

Of course, the four patterns represent major types only. They also appear in a variety of combinations, which can be used in a strategy of conquest or of revolution. These patterns represent techniques, and as such can be used for a variety of objectives by representatives of various ideologies and orientations.

The choice of technique for the capture of a tension area in a stage of interpolitical tension depends on a number of factors: (1) the nature of the social-economic internal base, the support which the party gets from below, and the attitude of the masses; (2) the size of the party's organization and its dynamism; (3) external support; (4) the time element set for capture of the tension zone. The paramount factors are (a) the relationship between the party and the social-economic base; (b) the relationship between the external and internal base.

The party and the social base

I have already mentioned that social movements should be analyzed in their social-economic context; in other words, the party should be related to the social-economic conditions or social-internal base in which it operates. In itself, however, the party is a complex concept. Four elements are essential in its analysis, especially if it is a revolutionary party: (1) ideology: (2) structure (type of organization); (3) strategy and tactics or pattern of action; and (4) leadership. All are mutually interdependent.

The structure of the party is of paramount significance. A small, very well-organized, and dynamic group may conquer large, but passive and disorganized, multitudes. (The party structure of political movements is discussed at length in Appendix I.) [12]

The pattern of party organization in the tension area depends to a great extent on the nature of the social, economic, and political base. When the movement of the "social base" ("from below") is strong, the party organization usually differs from those where the organized social groups and the multitudes are passive or hostile to the objectives of the party. In such a case, a small, well-organized party must rely on the external front and the external base.

The ideology

Today, ideological political tensions require ideological appeal. The attacking party in a tension area advances its ideas and appeals with symbols and ideas. The defending party must answer these appeals, since ideological attacks require ideological answers. Pragmatic reforms without vision or without symbols will not suffice. A purely military tactical action cannot solve the problems in a tension area. Ideological interpolitical tensions are of a specific nature and require specific action on the social-economic level and in the realm of ideas. Mazzini, in discussing the French Revolution, argued that ideas govern the world and events: "A revolution is a passage of an idea from a theory to practice. The French Revolution," he wrote, "cannot be considered as a program, but as the last formula of the epoch which is concluded. . . . Religion or a philosophy can be found at the base of every revolution." A new revolutionary movement makes new ideas, he argued.[13] Misery and oppression can produce "revolts" (*sommosse*), but a "revolution" needs an idea.

The French anarcho-syndicalist theoretician Georges Sorel, first in his famous book on *Reflections on Violence*,[14] and later in his essay *On the Decomposition of Marxism*,[15] indicated the significance of broad, symbolic visions. Ideas suggest both objectives and answers to vital problems. Not all "political cultures" appeal equally to visions and symbols. In England and America the emotional appeal to distant vision is less effective than in Continental Europe and Latin America, where the mass movements have been motivated by broad visions and symbols.

In ideological interpolitical tension areas, the appeal of ideas is relevant. Of course, the masses are not active in all tension areas. They are often passive and unresponsive. In such cases, the ideological appeal is ineffective, and direct action involving rapid social reform carries more weight.

On certain illusions and on quantity

A few popular illusions have to be dispelled or at least clarified before we can advance our discussion and analysis of strategic-tactical patterns in ideological and interpolitical limited tensions.

When Hernán Cortés left Cuba on Feburary 19, 1519, he had eleven ships, five hundred soldiers and slightly more than one hundred sailors. Of the soldiers, fewer than fifty had muskets or crossbows. They had ten small guns and four culverins.[16] With this small group, Cortés conquered an empire. Francisco Pizarro undertook the conquest of Peru with three brothers, one hundred and eighty-five soldiers, and thirty-seven horses.[17] On November 21, 1873, one hundred and twenty French soldiers took the citadel of Hanoi, marking the conquest of Tonkin.[18]

Small, well-organized groups conquered empires because the conquered were either passive and indifferent or divided and quarrelsome. They prevailed also because of a superiority of weapons. Their rule lasted for centuries, not because of the assent of the governed, but because of the indifference and passivity of the ruled.

In past history, small, oppressive minorities frequently dominated multitudes which hated them. Few governments in the not so distant past ruled by the consent and with the support of the majority, or a substantial minority, of the governed.

There is a persisting illusion to the effect that the aggressing party in a tension area is always on the side of social justice, and always has the massive support of the population. It is often true that discontent, social unrest, and the disorganization of the fabric of society provide favorable conditions for the development of a revolutionary movement, but this is not always so. The 1799 revolution in Naples and the rise and fall of the Parthenopean Republic are examples of social movements in which the mass support of the peasantry and the poorer classes for the cause of social equality and political freedom were lacking. Still, the combination of external and internal fronts resulted in the victory of the republican forces, at least for a time. Vincenzo Cuoco, a contemporary revolutionary author, writes that the "largest part of the nation was indifferent. . . . The immense population of the capital was more stupefied than active." [19]

The political behavioral patterns of the subordinated social classes are not the same in all cultures. The peasantry in Southeast Asia may react differently to political stimuli or exploitation than those in Brazil or Russia. In certain cultures, the peasants are more patient than the working class; in others, they are more responsive to political and social stimuli. The political passivity of the peasant class in Italy, even of the urban classes, in certain historical periods, impressed many Italian sociologists and political theoreticians and served as the basis for their theories of the revolutionary elite. Similar observations had already been recorded by revolutionary leaders of the past century.

A few decades after the defeat of Napoleon Bonaparte, Mazzini noticed the decline of revolutionary dynamism and initiative among the peoples of Europe. At the end of the nineteenth century and the turn of the twentieth, the leading Italian sociologists, Gaetano Mosca, Vilfredo Pareto, and Cesare Lombroso, discussed the passivity and submission of a large section of the population in their writings. Lombroso argued that inertia and resistance to change characterize the broad masses of the population and the general attitude of a society. He called it misoneism. In his view, a revolution was the act of a few that succeeded only in rare moments of history when a number of conditions favored its success.[20] This argument of Lombroso is not convincing, in spite of his maps and statistical data, and is not borne out by such recent experiences as the Russian Revolution of 1917 and the October revolutions in Poland and Hungary in 1956.

Mosca's theory of an elite was the result of observation and experience and, like other Italian sociologists and political scientists, he stressed the passive nature of the large sections of human society.[21] Their experience, however, was based on observation of the Italian scene at times when specific social conditions were present, conditions that differed from those in many other countries. Their generalizations were rooted in those experiences. Actually, there were many periods in Italian history when urban and rural populations and social classes were active or restive. In other periods, large sections of the population were passive.

Countries have been transformed into tension areas through infiltration and guerrilla warfare. Through terror, manipulation, and appeal, minor tensions in a countryside have been escalated to serious conflicts. Terror is cumulative in nature. To the terror of the government, the guerrillas respond with terror, which is, in turn, reciprocated by the terror of the government. Unfortunately, this was frequently the unwise practice of those seeking to defend a tension area. Through fear of terror or oppression, the passive population is compelled to action. An experienced guerrilla leader, Che Guevara of Cuba, argues that it is not necessary to delay a revolution until conditions for such a revolution exist. The revolutionary activity, he argues, may create such conditions.[22]

Another illusion is that the underprivileged represent the progressive element that always reacts to slogans of liberation, freedom, and social justice. In most cases, it is the organized working class and peasantry that react to the appeal of equality and freedom. Nonetheless, certain sections of the working class supported fascism and Nazism, and Juan Peron in Argentina was able to win large support among the underprivileged. Even in the glorious times of the Renaissance, in 1478, the crowds in Florence were aroused against those who attempted to weaken the tyrannical rule of the Medicis in the name of freedom. The appeal "Liberty" was countered successfully with "Viva Lorenzo che ci da la pane" (Long live Lorenzo who gives bread).[23]

It is the combination of an external front with the internal front that forms the crux of operation in a tension area. A small group that is: (1) properly structured; (2) dynamic; (3) well-equipped, with efficient control of substantial means; (4) applies an effective pattern of action; and (5) has the strong support of an outside power—can successfully extend control in a tension area over large but passive or indifferent masses of population.

One hundred years ago Mazzini had already observed that the strength of a party is not in its numbers, but in its cohesion; in its union and composition.

The internal base

While tension areas vary in nature, it is also true that the "classic pattern" prevails in many cases today. By this pattern we understand conditions of social discontent and disorganization that favor dynamic social revolutionary changes. Such conditions appear especially in areas of unequal distribution of property, low working-class salaries, and social, political, or national oppression. In consequence, the parties of rapid social change advocate changes in political institutions, transformation of the class structure, redistribution of land and higher wages, or a new social-economic system that will secure better economic conditions to the workers. Some advocate a dictatorship to administer rapid social-economic change; others propose democratic institutions and the extension of political freedom. When tension arises, social problems present a number of choices and solutions, and there is usually a number of parties offering a variety of answers.

The control of ideological, interpolitical tension areas, their capture or defense, is not purely a matter of military tactical action. The "internal front" is complex, and is primarily a social-political problem. Those sections of the population that demand change are won by new ideas and by rapid social, economic, and political changes, and become a strategic element of defense through efficient political organization and leadership. To consider the tension area solely as a military problem is to overlook its complex nature. As I have said, tension areas vary to a high degree. In one tension area the population may be active; in others, the area is infiltrated and the conflict escalated through guerrilla activities; in yet another, ethnic antagonism dominates; and in still another, the ideological tensions reflect profound social-economic problems. The last-mentioned, the subject of our discussion, requires a broad policy on various levels.

The social base is the subject and the object of the strategic design in an ideological tension area. Action on this level requires imagination and political courage. When the tension is intense, it frequently reflects a serious social and economic unrest. If this is the case, the answers must come fast, and fundamental changes must be made. (We shall use the term "rapid change.") This type of social change is more of a peaceful social revolution than a slow reform movement, since it must be accomplished in a very short time and requires a fundamental change. Tensions of ethnic and political nature call frequently for a revolutionary change. Emancipation, national independence, and self-determination are often necessary stages toward social and political progress. Self-determination and national independence as such offer opportunities for progress but do not by themselves generate a better economy or increase production and the efficiency of a people. In order to give more to its citizens a nation must produce more. National independence is frequently a social myth, a promise of a new millennium. Programs of social change are also empty phrases unless accompanied by skills and capacity for better and more advanced forms of production. The simple fact that in order to improve conditions a nation must produce more and use more progressive techniques is so often forgotten, and foreigners are blamed as the cause of all evil.

A revolution, like any social process, moves in space and in time. In a social revolutionary change, the changes must be telescoped in a very short time span. The dissatisfied segments of the population look for immediate answers. The visible, immediate improvement of conditions has a direct effect and wins the people in the long run. But rapid social-economic reforms alone do not suffice. The strategy in an ideological tension area requires new and imaginative ideas. An ideology incorporating the status quo has little appeal in explosive situations. More than a hundred years ago, Mazzini argued that a revolution is a closing of an epoch rather than a beginning; that what he called the "revolutionary initiative" needed new ideas, in addition to those developed by the revolution.[24]

Perhaps one of the major factors in the success of Tito's partisan movement was his ideological appeal to the various nationalities of Yugoslavia. The partisans waged a three-way struggle: *against* Nazi and fascist occupation of Yugoslavia; *against* the status quo; and *for* a new social and political organization. The opposing Chetniks were identified with the status quo, and primarily with the Serbian nationality.

In a tension area, the ideological appeal of the aggressive party must be answered by the persuasive and efficient appeal of the defending party. The capture of a classic tension area requires well-organized groups, strong ideological appeal, and a program of rapid social, economic, and political changes. In consequence, the defense of the area and the easing of tension require a proper organization and structuring of the parties opposing the attackers. Rapid changes must occur in the tension area or there will be a silent conquest and establishment of a new oppressive regime.

Thus, social and political strategy within an ideological interpolitical tension area has three major components: (1) the party and the ideological appeal; (2) rapid social, economic, and political changes; (3) organization of the population.

The social-political strategy in the Philippines

The recent history of the Philippines may serve as an example of effective social-political strategy in a tension area. The Philippine army took a constructive part in this strategy of relatively rapid social reform. The strategy employed was imaginative and constructive. It was aimed to help the people, to stop the wave of terrorism, and to win over the revolutionary party by a humane policy. The techniques are instructive and point the way to ease certain types of tensions in the future.

Many elements contributed to the rise and development of the powerful revolutionary movement of the Huk (an abbreviation of the Hukbalahap, the local appellation of the movement). However, three major factors can be identified: (1) the early development of a labor movement in the Philippines, as well as later ideological developments and influences prior to the Japanese invasion; (2) the Japanese invasion and the struggle for independence; and (3) social-economic conditions in the Philippines, especially the land-tenure system and exploitation of the peasantry. The third factor comprises the essential element of the internal social-economic base, of which the land tenure is a part.

For the Philippine peasant, the land is not solely the economic base of his subsistence. The yearly, as well as the daily, rhythm of his life is built around agriculture and his land. His rituals and festivities are rooted in agriculture. However, large sections of the peasantry did not own any land at all.

The land-tenure system of the Philippines was inherited from Hispanic times. It involved two different and mostly antagonistic social groups: the peasant and his family; the *Tao* who works on the land; and the caciques, or landowners, and the church, which held claim to vast estates. This system continued under American rule. In certain areas of Central Luzon, only 12 percent of the farms were operated by owners. The remainder was divided between sharecroppers and part-owners.[25] Most of the peasant farms were very small, usually measuring less than 5 hectares (about 12 acres).[26] The haciendas of the church and of the caciques or of private companies ranged from 1,000 to 5,000 acres in size.

The relationship between the landowners and the Tao was highly exploitative. As late as the 1950's, a tenant farmer had to give about 70 percent of his crop to the owner. (The legal limit was 50 percent, but the law was circumvented.) Interest rates were extremely high, reaching 100 percent per year in 1952. The exploited Tao could turn only to the Chinese merchant, who gave him credit at a very high interest and served as his banker and sold his products.[27]

Large groups of the peasantry suffered from this exploitative system for centuries, but they did not always accept it patiently. Revolts against the church and the landowners were recorded as early as 1662.[28]

Socialist and labor ideology has an old tradition in the Philippines. After the Communist revolution and the Bolshevik coup in Russia, the Communist trend appeared in the Philippine labor movement. In the beginning, the Communist Party was legal and held meetings without difficulty. By 1931, the party was declared illegal, and it went underground and infiltrated other movements.

The Japanese invasion of the Philippines changed the political situation. With their coming, a number of underground organizations emerged—among which were the partisans—that harassed and fought the Japanese. The Communists joined forces with other groups in 1942 and formed the organization in Central Luzon known as the Huk.

The social-economic internal base of the tension was rooted in the discontented peasantry of the central Philippines, where the highly exploitative sharecropping practices prevailed. The Huks introduced new ideas and offered a vision of a new world, besides advancing a program of rapid social and economic reforms combined with guerrilla warfare.

The Huks did not disarm after the war. Led by skillful and able leaders, they retained their organization and continued fighting, this time against the Philippine government and the Philippine army. Communist-trained and Communist-led, they transformed the central Philippines into a true ideological tension area, which could have been escalated to the interpolitical level with very little additional effort. The struggle was ruthless and cruel on both sides. Many of the peasants were forced to join the Huks by fear of retaliation against their families. They also joined the Huks because of their fear of government action against the villages occupied by the Huks or as a reaction against the brutal action of the government troops.[29]

Filipino reports admit that the "general situation was bad enough. Even worse, there were . . . instances of officers involved in matters definitely unworthy of one who is by definition an officer and a gentleman by the act of our Congress. Instances, including demanding bribes for the performance or nonperformance of duty, occurred in all ranks. Each, of course was magnified by Huk propagandists and sympathizers. Few of the offenders were punished appropriately and publicly. We had a few big scandals in Central Luzon during this period. In a general statement, we can say that troop behavior was so low that it cultivated an antipathy by the masses for the man in uniform." [30]

Tactics of geographical and social infiltration was widely used by the Philippine government in counteracting the Huks, who numbered 34,000 men.[31] Such infiltration was used by both sides, and resulted in confusion. Terror was also applied on both sides. But it was humanity, not terror, that won back the sympathy of the population. We read in a report on the guerrilla warfare in the Philippines that "Justice and goodwill are keywords to success in any operation." The same report, however, gives a substantial account of tactics of deception.[32]

A fundamental change in social-political strategy was introduced by the secretary of defense, Ramón Magsaysay, later elected president of the republic. At this time, the Huks were well rooted in Central Luzon, and had not only a great deal of military strength but also represented skills in administering the territory. They appointed administrators, controlled schools in the area, and acted as a formal government. Huk units were frequently more powerful and more numerous than the army.

The new defense secretary (Magsaysay) developed an imaginative social-economic strategy and substantially changed the military tactics. He embarked on a process of social-political reforms in the areas affected by peasant misery and exploitation. The army was recruited for this work, and a special section (Edcor) became the instrument of a wide social reform. Magsaysay immediately removed corrupt officers, and advanced those who were efficient. Small farms of six to ten hectares (about 15–25 acres) were distributed among the peasants; cottages and civic centers were built, and new villages and settlements emerged. The Edcor cleared the fields and built houses.

Simultaneously, the defense secretary sought to win the Huks by a policy of social reform and persuasion. Respect for human beings displaced former antagonistic attitudes. By 1954, splits within the Huk party had developed, as the policy of Magsaysay influenced the Huks and their leaders. On May 17, 1954, Luis Taruc, the Huk leader, surrendered and expressed his willingness to work for the government's social reforms. Magsaysay's humane attitude toward the peasant population, his reform movement, and an honest election won large sections of the peasantry to his camp.

Magsaysay was elected president, and under his administration a land reform law was introduced.[33]

The Philippine example was by no means an isolated case. An active policy of social reforms, attempts to win the friendship of the population by constructive action rather than by war, became an important strategy in tension areas. However, this type of action is not equally effective in every place.

The organization of the population

An estimate of the situation in a tension area requires a careful evaluation of the attitude of the population toward the attacking party as well as toward the formal power centers in the territory. During the war in French Indochina, the French were unable to win the support of the population. They operated as in a vacuum, or as in a foreign territory. Without the support of the population, the political action of the formal government was brought to nothing.[34] The support of the population or in many cases its active participation is of primary significance.

The third element of the general pattern is the organization of the population and its structuring into groups. (In this respect, the Viet Minh in French Indochina [now Cambodia, Laos, and Vietnam] may serve as an example.) [35]

A totalitarian system may organize a village population in "parallel hierarchies." On the one hand is the party; on the other, the administrative institutions: the youth and women's organizations, and trade unions that absorb the active element in a system of parallel, mutually interdependent lines of command and organization, dependent on the decision of one central power. Those who are not in the hierarchy have no power whatsoever. Freedom of movement is frequently limited, except by special permission. All other organizations are absorbed or disbanded. Only one central line of command and one powerful structure, built around the party, survives, reducing the other elements of the population to a subordinate position.

The civil organization is of paramount significance in any revolutionary action and in any consolidation of power. However, a democratic libertarian movement cannot apply structures of organization similar to those of authoritarian movements. And, in certain times of crisis, a command structure may act more effectively, since it is under a single command. (See Appendix I, "Command and Consensus Structures.")

The sociology of antagonism and conflict in an ideological tension area is complex, as are the techniques for the reduction of those tensions. In many typical areas, the easing of such tension or even the maintenance of control requires broad action of a sociological-economic, rather than military, nature. An ideological tension has positive results also. It forces change, making man reconsider his present existence and the condition of his neighbors. Violent and dangerous as it is, it challenges both camps continuously and forces them to change.

Again, social causation

An analysis of an ideological tension area revolves around the problems of that area. It is directed toward the understanding and explanation of the reasons for the unrest. The causes explain the nature of the antagonisms. Should we then reduce the causal analysis of a complete social conflict in a tension area to two or three major variables: psychological, ideological, and social-economic, as was once suggested in this volume?

I have already repeatedly indicated that tension areas differ. One tension area may be entirely dissimilar from another in the same country but on a different border. Every single ideological tension area requires a careful consideration and listing of the interacting variables.

What, then, should be the procedure in an analysis of tension areas? A causal analysis requires an inventory of causal factors or variables in order of perception, without attributing any specific weight or priority to them. After the preparation of this inventory, we may proceed to the second table, which we may call the evaluation of causal variables. In this second step, the variables are evaluated according to their relevance, or weight.

Perhaps methods could be devised to assign ranking or weight to various variables, but by the very nature of the process, such arbitrary ranking would serve only for a general orientation. However, after evaluation, the less significant could be reduced. The proper analysis of an ideological tension area implies a pluralistic causal approach.

The antagonistic sequence in ideological-interpolitical tension areas

Ideological tensions may also move through an antagonistic sequence. Such a sequence may start "below," because of social-economic and ideological unrest. From there, it may move to an intrapolitical stage. At this stage, the government, representing the formal power center in the area, intervenes to ease the tension or force the movement into submission. The moment another government intervenes to support one of the parties, the tension changes to the complex and interpolitical. But such a tension can also be manipulated from above, and a government may infiltrate the area from an external base and escalate the tension to an interpolitical status, involving two or more governments or states. Furthermore, as in the case of Berlin, an interpolitical tension can be created by the decision of an outside government.

The type of tension prevailing in Berlin is decided in the capitals of the external powers. The internal base has little significance. The decisions and the policy are determined by the strength of the external base of the decision makers; by their power, strategy, and tactics. Reduction of such tension cannot be accomplished by changes within the social-economic base of the local areas. Easement will not be achieved by improving the social conditions or providing a strong appeal. The tension is purely interpolitical, and its easing requires direct negotiations between the external parties. The psychological devices and techniques of easing tensions developed in interethnic intergroup tensions will be of no use in this case.

An interpolitical ideological tension is settled by negotiation and, in times when the ideologies are incompatible, by an evaluation of the strength of the contending powers and the risks and dangers involved. The reduction of tensions is accomplished by factors outside the tension areas.

The nature of tension areas differs in different cases. The social and political processes are different; the causation is different. In consequence, stalemating or reduction of such tensions requires different means. It is an error indeed to attempt to apply the techniques used in the reduction of an interethnic tension to a purely interpolitical tension of the nature of Berlin. Of course psychological analysis and techniques could be applied in negotiation to create conditions for mediation, but this is a different matter. A purely psychological approach, without the support of the political elements, will not suffice in stalemating or in a reduction.

Tension areas and strategic stages

Certain areas that are affected by ideological or ethnic tensions have as much strategic significance in a policy of expansion and conquest as they have in a policy of maintaining peace. Such areas can be selected by an aggressive government as stages in a strategy of expansion. In that way a government and a state expands through indirect war, or in a war by substitution from one area to the other, from one stage to the next, in a local strategy of expansion. The utilization of geographical areas as stages in an expansionist policy is also "thrifty politics" for the expanding and aggressive state in terms of economic expenditures and human losses. The war is waged by foreign guerrillas and foreign nationals. The damages, misfortunes, and tragedies are suffered in distant lands, while the aggressing nation remains untouched, supplying weapons, money, ideological appeal, and expert personnel.

The ideological tension is initiated in an inconspicuous manner. Infiltration follows, and then the ideological tension is escalated, utilizing the social-economic condition of the area. In consequence, the capture is advanced in a silent war.

A political observer of Communist Chinese strategy and tactics—and Mao Tse-tung is a prominent tactician—may readily notice China's strategy of advance from one area to another. The June 14, 1963, letter of the Central Committee of the Chinese Communist Party to its counterpart in the Soviet Communist Party indicates clearly that peace is not Mao Tse-tung's goal at present. His concept of a protracted war is primarily the idea of a war through stages, in which a variety of means and devices are utilized.[36] The capture of strategic tension areas closely follows Mao Tse-tung's strategy and tactics. Wishful thinking cannot change the hard facts, nor save the peace.

The presence of Communist China in the U.N. may help to break the isolation and modify diplomatic behavior. This may create conditions for negotiations and for at least a "cold peace" at the "point of indifference."

15.

RANKING OF TENSION AREAS

Ranking

A general survey of world tension areas indicates that their significance varies greatly in terms of international politics. Some purely local ethnic tensions have no influence on the grand design of international politics; while other areas are strategic outposts, stages of a general strategy of conquest. How shall we rate their significance? "Significance for whom?" might be another question.

The term "significance" may be related to either a government or the international community. Consequently, it may mean significance from the viewpoint of strategic objectives of a given government, or objectives of a hypothetical international community (maintenance of peace).

Peace can be defined as a condition that permits changes in the existing interpolitical relations without a major use of physical force (violence). From a theoretical viewpoint, we may imagine peaceful international relations as a dynamic equilibrium, with the actions of governments and groups being mutually interdependent; a continuous interactive relationship short of open (violent) conflict. Such equilibrium permits changes and continuous adjustment without violence. Violent action destroys this dynamic equilibrium.

In terms of such a standard, a five-grade ranking of tension areas is suggested: 1] critical; 2] near-critical; 3] consequential; 4] distant; 5] noncritical.

A critical tension area is usually a primary tension area (dependent on the "big power zone") that is interpolitical or complex in nature. It represents a dangerous intensification of conflict that may result in a local (limited) or a general war. Secondary tensions in which open conflict, or local war, occurs belong in this category. (The primary are marked *A,* the secondary *B.*) Primary tensions are those between the so-called "super powers," whereas secondary tensions involve minor powers or states.

The second rank, the near-critical tension areas, can be either reduced or rapidly intensified and "escalated" to the first category. They are usually interpolitical or complex. Secondary tensions which may in the immediate future develop into local war also belong in this category. The tension in East Berlin in 1962 (primary and interpolitical) and the intensification of the antagonism over the administration of Berlin and the access to West Berlin had this quality of a near-critical character.[1] To repeat, tensions may be "moved" up and down; they can be "reduced" (eased) or intensified (escalated).

Both types of tension areas are merely symptoms of a more profound and general development of social, political, and economic processes (since international politics is a social process) and of a general grand strategy. Usually, they are symptoms of tactical or strategic movements; a reflection of the general conduct of international affairs and domestic policies of the initiating party.

Intergroup tensions often serve as a rationalization or a camouflage for expansion. The aggressor uses social-political movements as a political army in the development of an "internal front." As was already mentioned, the internal front is usually built up with a simultaneous military, diplomatic, and propagandistic pressure. Military power is used either as a latent element (threat pressure) or in direct action. This outside pressure forms the "external front."

A general strategy of conquest is usually divided into stages, with a further subdivision into tactical patterns. Strategy is developed in terms of time and space. In a strategy of expansion, stages are plotted as "time tables" and "advanced areas." Tactical movements and patterns are applied at certain times to capture specific areas, or stage-objectives.

In consequential tension areas, aggressive action is initiated, then temporarily discontinued, although problems remain unsettled. In this "interim" period, tensions are "dormant," negotiations are possible, and the situation can perhaps be temporarily eased. Nevertheless, interpolitical relations in this area are tense, and it remains a desirable strategic objective. Tensions may be intensified in the future and thus become more exposed and more explosive: near-critical or critical.

The class of tension that we have called "consequential" has been introduced here as a general category of internationally significant tensions. These are not yet on the critical or near-critical list, but they are neither "distant" nor insignificant.

Distant tension areas are predominantly intergroup domestic, intrapolitical, and the initial stages of international tensions. To this group belong substantially reduced interpolitical tensions, perhaps still significant, but abandoned for the time being. They appear sometimes in strategically sensitive territories and can be developed into near-critical or critical.

Noncritical tension areas are usually secondary, local in nature, or of such a primary nature that they have no wide and immediate significance. The causes of such tensions are frequently social, economic, or ethnic.

Once fixed borders are established, territories of migration (industrial or pastoral-nomadic) may become secondary tension areas. Socio-economic patterns of the inhabitants may conflict with the political actions and interests of the governments in power.[2]

The vagueness of my ranks and types is deliberate, since a system that invited one to classify tensions on the basis of a few known details rather than on all political aspects of a situation would be undesirable.

Ranking of tension areas should be made by a carefully balanced evaluation based on facts and an understanding of social behavior and political patterns. However, such evaluation must reflect general experience, since quantitative methods for such judgment do not exist as yet.

The political behavior of "decision makers" seldom changes. Prominent tacticians develop a few key strategic and tactical patterns and techniques for the resolution of conflict. Their designs are reflected in tension areas. The pattern applied in one of the countries is repeated, with minor changes, in another, thus providing elements of analysis and forecast for the future.

Function and capture of tension areas

Colonel Lacheroy, chief of *Service d'Action Psychologique et d'Information* of the French national defense, outlined a strategy of revolutionary war based in the main on his experience in Southeast Asia. He starts his thesis by stating: "First a problem is created." [3] But this is true not only of a "revolutionary war," but also of other types of conflict. For many decades expansionist actions have begun with the creation of a political problem and a crisis. Ethnic or ideological tensions may serve as an element of tactics. In such a case the government secretly or openly supports aggressive actions of political groups in tension areas that have strategic significance. After "intensification" of tensions, the area becomes an international issue and may be captured by the initiating party, which thus extends its power and strategic-territorial goals.

Ethnic or class unrest usually exists in areas chosen for "created" tensions, and it is utilized and intensified and finally transformed into a critical stage. Social unrest cannot be created by the initiating government but is the result of present social-economic relations and conditions in the area. Intensification or manipulation of such a situation is possible, however, and was frequently done in past history. Secondary tension areas—purely local, interethnic tensions of a noncritical nature—can be intensified and transformed (escalated) into consequential, near-critical, or critical. In that way, an area moves in "danger rating" from the fifth to the first category.

In consequence the analyst asks: "What is the function of a given tension area? What role does it play in the general strategy of the government which intensifies such tension?" And in an analysis of a secondary tension area, another question can be asked: "What function may this tension play in the general strategy of an outside power whose policy is consistently expansionist?" Such a question can best be answered in terms of "alternatives for expansion" open to the latter. This is of course speculation, as any forecasting must be, but analysis permits an anticipation of the dangers.

Tension Inventory and Ranking Table (Tensions Scale): The Purpose

In our time, international politics has ceased to be a local matter. Almost every tension or conflict is capable of assuming global significance. International politics has ceased to be the province of a few diplomats. With the diffusion of a democratic form of government and the growth of international relations in many areas—in economics, health, and sanitation; in cultural exchanges—the interest in and concern with foreign policy has become far more general. However, international relations remain a highly specialized field, and many still look at foreign policy and international politics as a remote professional field.

But, hard facts have resulted in an increase of general interest. These facts are the so-called strategic, unconventional weapons, primarily the nuclear weapons and the missiles. The fortunes of New York, Moscow, or London may depend on tensions in Cuba. The invisible front moves close to Manhattan, Paris, or Calcutta. In consequence proper information on international politics, especially on areas of antagonisms and conflict, are of vital significance in securing effective policies, as well as for the proper conduct of public affairs. An enlightened public opinion is informed about major political issues. An informed public opinion is less prone to panic, and to irresponsible, emotional action, than its uninformed and uneducated predecessor.

A general survey of world tensions and conflict areas seems to be as necessary today as are the weather reports. Such surveys are well reported in the major press of the world. We are concerned here, however, with a general survey and ranking of major tensions at a given period. Such a ranking, arbitrary though it may be, may give general, organized information, coupled with a tentative hierarchy of tension significance. Our ranking, based on a rational evaluation of facts, is simply a general hypothesis, a statement of probability.

Using our five-point scale, I shall apply this tentative ranking to a concrete situation on a global scale. This ranking is a speculative exercise based on the limited information accessible to any interested person.[4]

I shall begin with an "inventory of tensions" and proceed from there to the "ranking table" or "scale of tensions." The inventory of tensions is a register of tensions, containing a general description and evaluation. At this stage, the weight of significance is assigned tentatively. Ranking and ordering belong to the second stage, where they are assigned according to the significance of tension areas in world politics and their threat to international peace in terms of armed conflict. The inventory contains more detailed, though very general, information. It should supply the factual, empirical support for the evaluation and ranking indicated in the Ranking Table of Tensions Scale.

What order should we apply in our general inventory of the tension areas? Theoretically, the inventory is a register; ranks are assigned later. In reality, how-ever, the significance of certain continents or subcontinents at certain times is obvious; the significance of certain tension areas, apparent. Furthermore, tension areas of world significance are not isolated symptoms of conflict. They are tactical and strategic in nature and related to broad strategic plans of conquest or other forms of expansion and control. Thus, in an inventory, as in reality, they appear in "clusters," or groupings, since they are interrelated. Otherwise, one would lose the entire "gestalt," the vision of the general strategic pattern. Single tension areas are merely units of the conflict pattern. An artificial separation of those tensions would create a false picture of isolated tensions.

Tensions which do not have this critical implication for world peace are, in a sense, isolated, but they can be used as strategic stepping-stones. Thus, in an inventory of tensions, I shall start with those continents where major tensions appear, and list tensions according to their over-all evaluation, especially those which appear in groupings. It is probable that such tensions form a part of a general, strategic plan. This involves a working hypothesis, covering the general pattern of action of the initiating party. Within every rank on the scale I shall distinguish two groups: Group *A*—primary tensions; Group *B*—secondary. The primary tensions (*A,* between major powers) have specific significance for gen-eral security.

I shall select—arbitrarily—as our tension period ten days of June, 1964 (the first to the tenth). In a periodical evaluation of tensions, it may be advisable to suggest monthly reports.

Inventory of Tension Areas, June 10, 1964
Asia

The major groupings of tensions comprise areas of pressure and expansion initiated by Communist China: A] Southeast Asia; B] India; C] Soviet-Chinese borderlands; D] dormant reduced tension areas in Korea.

1, 2, AND 3—FRENCH INDOCHINA

Tensions in former French Indochina (the present North and South Vietnam, Laos, and Cambodia, with North Vietnam now a Communist stronghold) are closely interrelated. They are complex in nature, ideological (interideological) and interpolitical (between the states). The expanding, initiating social forces are the Communists and their allies; the resisting are the native political parties or governments of pro-Western orientation in South Vietnam, Laos, and Cambodia. The "external initiating front" is represented primarily by the Mainland Chinese and North Vietnam governments.

The "defensive external front" is formed by the United States; the "internal front," by the local pro-Western governments. In the middle, are those of undecided "neutralist" orientation. Large sections of the population are passive, ideologically uncommitted.

After the liquidation of French colonial rule in this area, its strategic and explosive nature was recognized. Perhaps as a result of cautious strategy and timing, or in a desire for a real truce, attempts were made to neutralize the area. A three-power international control commission was established and a coalition government was formed in Laos based on agreement among fourteen nations. Neither proved workable. In Laos, the Communist Pathet Lao started guerrilla operations against the established government. In South Vietnam, the war between the Communist Vietcong and government forces changed to a protracted war.

There are indications that both the Communist Pathet Lao and the Vietcong are supported by Communist China and North Vietnam. Trained military groups move from North Vietnam to Laos and Cambodia. They have no difficulty crossing the Cambodian frontier, which forms a "secondary base" and a refuge. Raids and counterraids continued in South Vietnam. In Laos, the neutralist forces declined in strength. The United States, while supporting the pro-Western governments, proceeds cautiously to avoid escalating the conflict into a full-fledged war. Meanwhile, the Communist forces continue their attacks. Guerrillas from North Vietnam operate in South Vietnam, establishing supply lines through Cambodia. The Pathet Lao, supported by the North Vietnamese, attack the neutralist forces. We shall briefly survey the situation in this area: [5]

1] LAOS

Laos occupies a strategic position between Western-supported Thailand and South Vietnam, and Communist North Vietnam and China. In addition, it is split politically among the pro-Communist Pathet Lao, pro-Westerners, and Neutralists, with each group headed by a Laotian prince. Since 1962, Laos has been governed by a coalition of the three (neutralist premier and Communist and pro-Western vice-premiers). Recently, however, as the Chinese have displaced the Russians in influence among the Communists, this arrangement has been under increasing Communist pressure for a takeover. International supervision of the new, independent states of Southeast Asia (the old French colonial territories) has already been tried—under the provisions established by the 1954 Geneva Conference—with very limited success. Neutrality of Laos was guaranteed by fourteen nations including the Soviet Union at the 1962 Geneva Conference.

2] CAMBODIA

Cambodia, located between South Vietnam and Thailand, has adopted a neutralist attitude under the leadership of Prince Norodom Sihanouk. In 1963 he rejected United States aid and subsequently broke off diplomatic relations with the United States, accusing it of backing Cambodian opposition to him. The United States and South Vietnam, in turn, accuse Cambodia of aiding the Communist guerrillas of South Vietnam.

3] VIETNAM

Following the Geneva agreement of 1954, this former French colony was split along the 17th parallel north latitude into the Democratic Republic of Vietnam (North) and the National Republic of Vietnam (South). Russian and Chinese influence compete in North Vietnam, while the United States has replaced France as the protecting power in South Vietnam. The Vietcong Communist guerrillas in South Vietnam are backed by North Vietnam and, indirectly, by the Communist protecting powers.

The conflict is primarily interideological and interpolitical in nature. The ideological struggle is between the pro-Communist and pro-Western groups; in particular, between North Vietnam and mainland China on the one hand, and South Vietnam and the United States on the other. This is an undeclared, limited war.

What is the "function" of this area? Its capture by Communist China would be a step toward eventual control over all of Southeast Asia, including Thailand

and, sooner or later, Burma. The Chinese Communist government, controlling the northern borders of India, could exercise a decisive influence over India, a factor that could lead to total control of this subcontinent. This is a struggle for power that cannot be explained solely in terms of materialistic dialectics and economic motivation. It is ideological in its "political formula"; and political in its nature in the sense of struggle between states and governments for or against a position of domination. In their nature, tensions between great powers are primarily complex; both interideological and interpolitical. Escalated tension may result in a long and devastating war on the subcontinent of Southeast Asia. The extension of its influence and control to Southeast Asia would also give the Mainland Chinese government access to raw material—and food-producing areas. In this sense, Chinese expansion in the area is not free of social-economic designs.

4] MALAYSIA

The Federation of Malaysia was established in 1963 from the former British colonies of Malaya, Singapore, Sarawak, and Saba (former British North Borneo). The Indonesian government, which claims Sarawak and Saba, has refused to recognize Malaysia and constantly threatens to invade it. Already, Indonesian guerrillas have infiltrated the disputed territories.

The effort of Indonesian President Sukarno to overthrow Malaysia followed a violent ten-year struggle of the Malayan Chinese Communists to overthrow the Malayan government.

On the surface the tension is secondary—between the Indonesian and Malaysian governments—primarily interpolitical; a struggle for power; an aggression started by Sukarno. Nationalism constitutes Sukarno's political formula. He enjoys strong support from Communist China. This tension is a stage in a grand strategy for control of Southeast Asia, again a stepping-stone toward further expansion.

5] INDIAN-CHINESE BORDER

The frontier between these two countries has never been satisfactorily defined. The present tension, culminating in the Chinese invasion of Indian border territories in 1962, was provoked by the Chinese occupation of Tibet in 1953 and the subsequent Chinese refusal to acknowledge the accepted frontiers of India. As a result of the invasion, India has been reconsidering her neutralist policy.

India received aid from the Western democracies, and, to a certain extent, from the Soviet Union. Domination of India by Communist China would offer a threat to the Soviet Union. A bloc of such magnitude, under aggressive leadership, would be regarded as a dangerous condition by any government of the Russian "heartland."

Chinese aggression ended with a sudden "halt" and a de facto peace. Nevertheless, border problems in this area are not solved.

The tension is primary in nature (between great powers), and also ideological, between two differently oriented governments, and interpolitical (between government-states). By June 1964, the tension was "dormant."

6] KASHMIR

Tension between India and Pakistan arose over the control of the princely state of Jammu and Kashmir, which has a Moslem majority but is ruled by a Hindu Maharajah. The ruler chose to join India, a fact that Pakistan contests. Moslems from Pakistan moved into the area to bolster the claim of their fellow Moslems. Indian troops entered at the request of the ruler. Spasmodic fighting ensued. In 1949 a cease-fire was arranged with United Nations intervention, with Kashmir still primarily under Indian control. At present, Pakistan's bid for a U.N.-sponsored plebiscite is under consideration.

This at present secondary tension is complex, both interpolitical (between the two governments) and intergroup. The differences are interethnic and interreligious. The official policy of the mainland Chinese government supports Pakistan's government on this issue, indicating that it considers this area to be strategically significant. The pressure exercised by Communist China could escalate the tension into a primary one.

7] OUTER MONGOLIA AND SIKIANG BORDERLAND

Although China recognized the independence of the Republic of Outer Mongolia, a Soviet protectorate, in 1924, the Chinese Communists have never quite agreed to its separation from China. Following the Sino-Soviet split, there has been occasional serious tension on the Chinese-Mongolian border. According to Soviet sources, refugees from Sikiang have fled to Soviet territory. However, news from this area is scarce and difficult to verify. Defection because of unrest and dissatisfaction are not normally reported by the Soviet or Chinese press. Information that does arrive may be indicative of more serious tensions than is realized. The tensions are primary (major powers) and interideological. They reflect the ideological split, or the ideological split is a political formula to rationalize other political issues.

8] KOREA

Since the armistice of 1954 ended the Korean conflict, there have been occasional border incidents. So far none of them has caused serious international conflict. The tension, dormant today, is primarily interpolitical (between government-states) and ideological. It is primary in its nature, since both the United States and Communist China are involved, and it can be escalated with ease by the Chinese Communists.

Mainland China's Territorial Plans

("The Chinese territories taken by the Imperialists in the Old Democratic Revolutionary Era, 1840–1919")

The distribution of tension areas in Asia, the "cluster of tensions," may be indicative of a wider strategic plan. Most of these areas are not ethnographically Chinese. Such a hypothesis suggests that certain tension areas mentioned in this chapter are stages of a "strategic pattern." The map, reprinted from a textbook, *A Brief History of Modern China* (published in Peking in 1954), may support such a hypothesis, since maps and books in Peking are not published without official approval.

The legend in the box at bottom left in the map reads: __ __ __Borders at the time of the Opium War, 1840; __ . __ . __Borders at the conclusion of the era of the Old Democratic Revolution, 1919. The map appeared in *Link,* Indian Newsmagazine, New Delhi, issue of November 14, 1962. However, historically the data and facts may be correct.

Near East

The tension in Cyprus is an "isolate," unconnected with other tensions in the Near Eastern area.

Tensions in the Gaza Strip, Yemen, Aden; in the Alexandretta area, even in the Kurdish area of Iraq—belong to the same grouping of Arab expansion, control, and conflict.

9] CYPRUS

Cyprus, a former British colony, became independent in 1960 after the Greek majority conducted an extended guerrilla war against the British. The constitution of Cyprus includes safeguards for the Turkish minority, with international guarantees. In 1963, renewed fighting broke out in Cyprus between Greeks and Turks after President Makarios proclaimed the constitution unworkable. A U.N. force was sent to Cyprus, in 1964, to limit the conflict.

The Cyprus case is highly complex. The tension, thus far, is secondary, among minor powers—Cyprus, Greece, and Turkey—while the United Nations, Great Britain, and the United States intervene in an attempt to moderate and reduce antagonisms. The tension is complex, both interpolitical (among the governments of Greece, Cyprus, and Turkey) and interethnic (between the Greek

PEKING'S DREAM OF EMPIRE

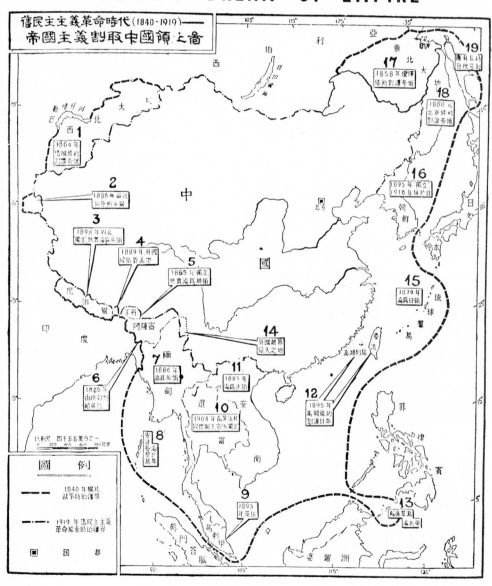

1: **The Great North-West,** according to the Chinese text in the map, "was seized by Imperialist Russia under the Treaty of Chuguchak, 1864." It covers huge segments of the present-day Soviet Republics of Kazakhastan, Kirghizia, and Tajikistan.

2: **The Pamirs** was "secretly divided between Britain and Russia in 1896."

3: **Nepal** went under British rule after "Independence" in 1898.

4: **Che-Meng-Hsiung** (i.e., present-day Sikkim) was "occupied by Britain in 1889."

5: **Pu-tan** (i.e., the whole of Bhutan) "went under British rule after 'Independence' in 1865."

6: **Ah-sa-mi** (i.e., the whole of Assam, NEFA and Nagaland) was "given to Britain by Burma in 1826."

7: **Burma** "became a part of British Empire in 1886."

8: **The Andaman Islands** "went under Britain."

9: **Ma-la-chia** (i.e., the whole of present day Malaya and Singapore) was "occupied by Britain in 1895."

10: **Hsien-Lo** (i.e., the whole of Thailand) was "declared 'Independent' under joint Anglo-French control in 1904."

11: **Annam** (covering the present-day North and South Vietnam, Laos, and Cambodia) was "captured by the French in 1885."

12: **Taiwan and P'enghu Islands** were "relinquished to Japan in accordance with the Treaty of Shimonoseki, 1895."

13: **Su-Lu Island** was "occupied by the British."

14: The Region where the British crossed the border and committed aggression.

15: **Liu-Chiu** (i.e., Ryukyu Island) was "occupied by Japan in 1910."

16: **Ch'ao-Hsien** (i.e., present-day North and South Korea).

17 and 18: **The Great North-East,** covering a huge area of the Soviet Far East, "was given to Russia under the Treaties of Aigun (1858) and Peking (1860)."

19: **K'u-Ye** (i.e., Sakhalin) was "divided between Japan and Russia."

and Turkish populations). The Greek majority is supported by the government of Cyprus. Turkish armed intervention in Cyprus could result in a local war. An international organization (U.N.) and major powers (U.S. and Great Britain) intervene. The conflict has ideological implications (nationalism). Although it is generally secondary and interethnic, it can be modified or escalated.

10] ALEXANDRETTA (HATAY)

The district of Alexandretta has a Turkish majority and is known to the Turks as Hatay. As a part of the French 1939 settlement, it was separated from Syria and returned to Turkey. The Syrian nationalists are not reconciled to their loss. The tension is weak, latent, secondary (between small powers), and complex (interpolitical, and interethnic with ideological overtones).

11] NORTHWESTERN IRAQ—THE AREA OF THE KURDS

The nomadic Kurds occupy the western areas of Iran, Iraq, Turkey, Syria, and parts of the Soviet Union. In 1963 there was a Kurdish uprising in Iraq that the government of Kassem met with ruthless reprisals. The Kurds countered with terroristic action. Tension eased after Kassem was overthrown. This is a secondary, intrapolitical (domestic), and interethnic tension. By February, 1964, through negotiation between the new government and the Kurdish leader, some effort had been made toward a settlement.

12] THE GAZA STRIP

The Gaza strip was formerly a part of Palestine. In 1948, it was placed under Egyptian administration. It shelters Arab refugees from Israel. In the Suez campaign of 1956, the Israeli army occupied the strip, but the great powers intervened and returned it to Egyptian administration. A U.N. force was sent to keep the peace. Tension over the Gaza strip has been accelerated by the Israeli government's program of irrigating for the Negev, using water from the Jordan. This plan is violently protested by the Arab states.

The U.A.R.-Israeli tension is secondary (between minor powers) and dormant, at present. It is interpolitical (between two governments) and, in the border area, interethnic, with nationalistic-ideological appeal. The condition of the refugees forms a serious economic problem which could be solved if the Arab states would negotiate. The political-ideological and ethnic issues predominate in the deepening of tensions by the U.A.R. and other Arab states. These governments do not desire any settlement that would close the issue.

13] ADEN-YEMEN

In 1959, the British formed the South Arabian Federation from the territories of Arab sheikhs under British protection. In 1963, the former British colony of Aden joined the federation. Neighboring Yemen, a republic since 1962, backed by Nasser's Egypt, claims the territory of the federation and supports guerrilla activity.

This is a tension between a great and a small power. It is secondary in nature, interpolitical (governments are involved), interethnic, and ideological (nationalism), though local in character.

14] YEMEN

The military revolt against oppressive and despotic rule in Yemen changed to a domestic war, fought not only by the Yemeni but also by the Egyptians—who support the new republican government—and the royalists, supported by Saudi Arabia.

The tension is secondary (minor powers), interpolitical (between two governments), and interideological (between the royalist conservatives and the nationalists).

As of May 1964, the royalist forces continued to offer a stubborn resistance.[6]

Africa

Tensions in the Congo and Zanzibar belong in one grouping, since they involve the major ideological blocs and reflect Chinese and Soviet influence and penetration. In their general pattern, the Somali-Kenya and Somali-Ethiopia tensions are related. Angola reflects the general anticolonial, native movement. Morocco-Algerian tension is isolated, related in character to the Somali-Ethiopian. (The two latter tensions arose over arbitrary, previously established border lines.) Tension in South Africa—racial and intense—is specific in general character.

15] CONGO

The civil war in the Congo, an outgrowth of its independence, involved major powers and the United Nations. The tension was originally "primary" in nature—between the major powers supporting contradictory propositions and antagonistic groups—and also interideological, between pro-Communist and non-Communist factions. The United Nations and its troops were helpful in restoring a very shaky internal peace, and in supplying an instrumentation for a solution. On June 30, 1964, the last 3,000 members of the U.N. force left the Congo. Nonetheless, serious unrest continues, controlled and supported by a radical-movement National Liberation Committee operating from Brazzaville Congo.[7]

The tension, which is internal and primarily intertribal and interethnic, has ideological and "interpolitical" implications, with major powers (Communist China and the Soviet Union) directly or indirectly involved. It is secondary in character at present, but can be escalated to a primary tension. In terms of our concept of a strategic pattern, the action in the Congo can be related to the development in Zanzibar. Economic interests in the Congo form a major issue.

16] ZANZIBAR

The independence of Zanzibar was ended—almost as soon as it began—following a revolt against the ruling Arab minority, backed by Cuban-trained revolutionary technicians. The tension, reflecting racial, class, and ethnic antagonism, resulted in expropriation, imprisonment, and even death for the Arab population, with no protest raised by any Arab state. A communist-controlled government was established in January 1964, supported materially and politically by Communist China and the Soviet Union.

In April, 1964, Julius K. Nyerere, president of Tanganyika, with President Abeid Karume of Zanzibar, signed articles creating the United Republic of Tanganyika and Zanzibar (Tanzania). With this union, tension was reduced. However, the potentialities for its intensification did not disappear. On the surface, this is a secondary and "intrapolitical" tension; in reality, it is of primary significance.

The nature of this tension is ideological, ethnic-racial, and social-economic. It was a revolt against the ruling Arab minority, extended to include the entire Arab population, with the Communists supplying the ideological flavor. The Soviet Union and China stepped in with assistance, further extending their influence in Africa. However, Zanzibar's potentiality as an "external base" was checked, at least temporarily, by its union with Tanganyika.

17] ETHIOPIA-SOMALILAND

The border tension between Somali and Ethiopia is discussed at length in Appendix III. We will note here only that it is, at present, a secondary interpolitical tension (between minor states), interethnic, and ideological in character (conflict of nationalism), involving the new, "modern elites" and sections of population.

18] SOMALILAND-KENYA

Tension, similar in character to the Somali-Ethiopian tension, is, to some extent, under control.

19] ANGOLA

Operations by nationalist guerrillas have broken the long peaceful development of this Portuguese colony. The first outbreak occurred in 1962, and the Portuguese are still fighting isolated guerrilla groups. There are two Angolan nationalist movements, one backed by Leopoldville Congo; the other by the Casablanca powers.

The tension is secondary, seemingly "intrapolitical," but with interpolitical implications (since other powers are secretly or indirectly involved). The native guerrillas represent an ethnic-racial group, economically subordinated and opposed to Portuguese rule. While ideologically nationalist, the tension is ethnic-racial, and reinforced by social-economic class contradictions. It can be escalated into a major African issue.

20] MOROCCO-ALGERIA

When Algeria gained its independence from France in 1962, its border with Morocco was ill-defined. The following year, Moroccan troops crossed the demarcation line and occupied several strips of disputed territory. Fighting broke out, but the African powers intervened and peace was restored.

The tension was secondary, and generally interpolitical. It reflected two nationalist and ideological movements.

21] REPUBLIC OF SOUTH AFRICA

The interethnic and racial tensions between the ruling white minority and the colored majority have defied all attempts at settlement, because the South African government has refused to modify its *apartheid* policy of racial segregation. In fact, it left the Commonwealth of Nations in 1961 rather than forego its policy, and proclaimed itself an independent republic. The Afro-Asian bloc is seeking to force South Africa to modify its stand by the threat of expulsion from the United Nations. Many African nations also offer shelter to political refugees from South Africa.

The tension is domestic and intrapolitical, but it has wide political international implications. While interracial in character, it is also ideological, as reflected not only in actions but also in a policy and ideology of racism and forced segregation that is opposed by substantial sections of the population.

The Americas

Tensions in Cuba and Venezuela and, in a more complex way, in British Guiana are closely related. All three belong to the same cluster of ideological and political expansion. Tension in Panama is local in nature and isolated.

22] CUBA

This well-known tension in the Caribbean, while latent at present, is primary in character—since the governments of the Soviet Union and the United States are involved. It is complex—both "interideological" and "interpolitical."

Fidel Castro took over the government of Cuba on January 1, 1959, and turned the country into a totalitarian Communist state. The United States consequently broke off diplomatic relations and, in 1961, encouraged an expedition of anti-Castro Cubans that was defeated at the Bay of Pigs. In 1962, the Cuban situation threatened to escalate into international war, following Soviet installation of missiles on the island. After U.S. President John F. Kennedy forced the U.S.S.R. to withdraw its weapons, the international tension relaxed to some extent.

In 1963, Soviet military forces were still in Cuba. Meanwhile, Cuba plays the role of an "external base" for guerrilla operations and ideological action in Latin America.[8]

23] VENEZUELA

This case (discussed at length in Chapter 16) was reduced by June, 1964, but tension between Venezuela and Cuba persists. The establishment of an "internal base" in Venezuela by Cuban-supported Communist guerrillas had wide implications in world politics. At this stage the tension is interideological and interpolitical; officially, at least, between minor powers (secondary). It is a conflict between the Communist movement in Latin America, supported by Cuba and the Soviet Union, and the social-democratic oriented bloc led by Romulo Betancourt, Figueres of Costa Rica, and Haya de la Torre of Peru.

For the sake of brevity we omit a number of other tensions in Latin America that are chiefly the result of social-economic conditions. Colombia has its endemic areas of unrest, which can be traced to the 1948 war between the Conservative and Liberal parties. Peru had its peasant unrest, so had Brazil. All of these tensions can be made use of in a strategy of expansion.

24] BRITISH GUIANA

This British South American colony has a large East-Indian and Negro population. In addition to the tensions between the pro-Communist and democratic and progressive elements, there are ethnic-racial tensions between the East-Indians, now exercising power, and sections of the Negro population. The tension is both ideological and ethnic-racial; domestic and "intrapolitical" in character. Foreign intervention in this area would escalate the tension to a primary stage between the major powers. The British government has postponed the granting of full independence until conditions are less tense. Its attitude is backed by the United States.

25] PANAMA

Early in 1964, anti-American riots broke out in Panama in protest against the American administration of the Panama Canal. According to a treaty signed in 1903 by Panama and the United States, the latter was given full sovereignty over the "Canal Zone,"—a band of territory extending five miles on each side of the canal—in return for a substantial fee that has since been increased. The Panamanians want to abrogate or change the 1903 treaty; the United States stands by it in essence, but is willing to negotiate revisions.

Tension has been greatly reduced. In spite of the fact that one major power is involved, the tension is local in nature and therefore "secondary"; interpolitical rather than a reflection of ideological conflict. The real issues involved are the prize and the symbols: an increase in "rent" for the use of territory and symbols of sovereignty.

Europe

In June 1964, Western Europe was a relatively peaceful area. Prosperous and stable, it moved, with some setbacks, toward greater unity. New loyalties modified the old type of nationalism for most. International tensions were greatly reduced or channelled into an institutional mechanism for arbitration.

Within the Eastern European bloc, ethnic tensions have been officially controlled and reduced, although ethnic antagonisms are still evident in everyday politics. Nonetheless, old tension areas in Eastern Europe, with few exceptions, have ceased to play any significant role. Prior to World War II, Eastern Europe was an area of strong tensions: Silesia, the Danzig Area (the Corridor), Polish-Lithuanian borderland, Macedonia, Dobrudja, Transylvania, and Burgenland, to mention a few.

The basic tension between the United States and the Soviet Union over the East European area was greatly reduced. It remains as a "dormant" issue, but it is not pressed—neither by Moscow, nor Washington, nor London, nor Paris.

Communist Chinese pressure in Asia and the ideological split within the Communist camp affected Soviet policy. It grew ambivalent. On one hand, the Soviet government conducts a policy of penetration and expansion; on the other, signs of rapprochement with the Western bloc appear, while Communist China grows more aggressive.

The Berlin tension, largely reduced, is related to the Oder-Neisse issue. The Albanian tension reflects the broader issue of an ideological split in the Communist camp, with Albania representing the Communist Chinese line. Tension over Alto Adige is an "isolate," and local in nature.

26] BERLIN

The Potsdam Agreement of 1945 put Berlin under four-power jurisdiction; but the three Western sectors were merged into "West Berlin," now an island one hundred and ten miles inside the East German Democratic Republic. West Berlin remains part of the German Federal Republic (West Germany). A series of crises broke over the city, beginning with the Soviet blockade of 1948, caused by the Soviet Union's efforts to deny or limit Western access to West Berlin. Refugees from East Germany moved through West Berlin on their way to West Germany.

The U.S.S.R. advanced plans to change the status of Berlin (including a Soviet plan for a "Demilitarized Free City"). Threats of a separate peace treaty with the East German government were made, freezing the existing division. A wall dividing East and West Berlin was built, intensifying the tension. However, by June 1964, the tension was controlled, with potentialities, however, of almost instant "escalation."

The Berlin situation is perhaps a typical "interpolitical" tension: one between major powers, escalated and reduced; manipulated by the Soviet government, which holds the initiative. True, the revolt of June 1953, in East Berlin was evidence of hidden but powerful social and political discontent; of strong popular opposition to the regime. But the tension—as an international, not a social one—is not ethnic; East and West Berliners are not different. Nor is this a powerful ideological tension between the East and West Berlin peoples; the division is entirely arbitrary. However, as an international tension between the major powers, it has an ideological nature in terms of the different ideological orientation of the powers involved.

The tension is primary—between two major blocs; largely interpolitical; at present controlled and reduced.

27] THE ODER-NEISSE LINE

The Potsdam Agreement of 1945 placed German territories beyond the Oder-Neisse line "under Polish administration." Poles of various political shadings regard this as a permanent settlement and want it to be recognized by the Great Powers. But the government of West Germany, partly under pressure from German refugees, is against such recognition. To avoid antagonizing their West German ally, the Western powers have so far refused to accede to the Polish demand. The issue is controversial. The Polish government argues that the settlement was final; the position of the Atlantic Powers is not definitive. The Soviet and East German governments have recognized the Polish western borders.

The tension cannot be regarded as "locally" interethnic, since the German population in the area has been deported. Since major powers are involved, the tension is above all interpolitical, both secondary and primary. In mid-1964, this tension was "deeply dormant," and de facto controlled or reduced.

28] ALBANIA-YUGOSLAVIA

After World War II, Yugoslavia retained the district of Kosovo-Metohija, inhabited mainly by Albanians, as an autonomous area. (The case is discussed in Chapter 9.) Many Albanians are not reconciled to this condition. Major tension was caused when Tito defied Stalin in 1948 and when Moscow split with Peking, with Yugoslavia backing Moscow. In each case, Albania backed Yugoslavia's enemy.

Albania is today an exponent of Communist Chinese policy in Europe. Its leadership attacks Tito's political orientation and government. The general tension between Albania and Yugoslavia is secondary in nature—between minor powers— but each government has the latent backing of a major power. Antagonism is primarily interideological and interpolitical. Ethnic antagonism may be present, but it is subdued. Tension is continuous but latent, with a tendency at present toward isolation rather than armed conflict.

29] ALTO ADIGE

The largely "intrapolitical" and interethnic tension between the German minority and the Italians in the northern part of Italy has been already discussed. Here, we may add, that nationalist overtones combine the ethnic aspects of tensions with the ideological.

International tensions

RANKING TABLE (SCALE) JUNE 1–10, 1964

Group A: Primary (between major powers)
Group B: Secondary (local; between minor powers)

Critical

A. (B.)   Indochina: South Vietnam, Laos, Cambodia
B.   Cyprus, Yemen

Near-critical

B. (A.)   Malaysia (primary implications)

Consequential

A.   Indian-Chinese border
B.   Kashmir
A.   Korea (stalemate—reduced)
A.   Cuba
A. (B.)   Venezuela
A. (B.)   Congo (intrapolitical and international;
          primary implications)
B. (A.)   Zanzibar (intrapolitical; primary implications)
A.   Berlin (de facto reduced)
A. (B.)   Oder-Neisse (dormant)
B.   Gaza
A. (B.)   Aden-Yemen
B.   Somali-Kenya
B.   Somali-Ethiopia

Distant

A. (B.)   Albania-Yugoslavia
B.   Iraq-Kurds (intrapolitical)
B.   Angola (intrapolitical)
B.   Republic of South Africa (intrapolitical)
B.   British Guiana (intrapolitical)

Noncritical

B.   Morocco-Algeria
B. (A.)   Panama
B.   Alto Adige
B.   Alexandretta

We have listed 28 tension areas in June 1964, some minor, some major; some reduced, others "dormant," or potential. Nonetheless, the number of tension areas indicates the nature of the conflict in international relations that we face, and we have not listed all the tensions. It is perhaps relevant to indicate the differences between various tensions; in significance, in nature, and in the means and policies necessary for their control and reduction.

International tensions scouting post

Informed public opinion is essential for a democratic government in its attempt to eliminate or reduce violence in social, political, or international relations. General information about major tension areas—their mutual relationship, their intensity or danger—should be simplified and made accessible to the same extent as information about the weather. This might help to win support for efforts toward the maintenance of peace or the changing of conditions to make them fit new situations. Such information might also alert us early to a dangerous development as well as restrain our natural propensity for wishful thinking.

At the Disarmament Conference in Geneva in 1964, the British secretary of state, R. A. Butler, suggested the establishment of observation posts covering the territory of the Warsaw Pact and NATO.[9] Such vantage points would give "each side a reassurance about capabilities and designs of the other." Unfortunately, this useful proposition has not been carried through.

Similarly, a tensions scouting post could act as an independent agency, registering and ranking tensions and informing public opinion about them. Such a scouting post could also be formed as an independent agency, possibly connected with a university, with a small staff of experts to evaluate and register tensions. Since government has access to a much wider range of information than a private agency, a public agency could provide an even better informed center.

Monthly reports and ranking tables would keep track of current conflict situations. The two agencies might issue reports reflecting different viewpoints and positions, and contributing to a wider outlook. Other countries might also have tensions posts. A comparison of diverse evaluations could indicate any changes imminent in the international situation.

Even a simple register of tension areas permits us to perceive the connection between various "conflict units" and to understand the broad strategic plans of conquest and expansion. An early realization of the potentialities of a conflict would supply the time element essential for realistic defense or a long-range policy of reduction, or at least a stalemating of the conflict.

Cluster of related tensions

A general inventory of tensions, or a scale of tension areas, does not necessarily provide us with a fuller understanding of the strategic and political functions of certain tension areas. With a tension scale, we are alerted to the intensity of some tensions, but we are told nothing about the possible connections between one tension and another.

The third step in evaluation of tension areas (after the inventory has been made and a rating tentatively established on a tension scale) is the selection of related tension areas from the inventory, where preliminary steps toward grouping of related tension areas have already been initiated.

Through the grouping of related tensions in which similar or complementary tactics appear, a general scheme emerges. We may call it a strategic pattern, since it permits us to discover the strategic objectives or orientations of alternative policies. In such a pattern, a number of tension areas may represent stages in a policy of ideological and territorial expansion.

16.

IDEOLOGICAL AND INTERPOLITICAL TENSIONS IN VENEZUELA

A Case History

Two types of tension areas

Two cases of tension areas have been selected for contrast: Venezuela and Somalia. The former is representative of a pattern that is now apparent in Latin America: ideological and social, with local tensions forming segments or tentative stages of an over-all strategy. The tension is secondary and local (between minor powers) on the surface. In reality, it is part of a great historical drama involving the major powers and blocs.

International-ideological tensions are, to a large extent, results of decisions and definite policies and actions outlined in terms of time and space. Since such policies usually develop in terms of strategy and tactics (even if not so called or intended at first), the proper consideration of an interideological and interpolitical tension area such as Venezuela requires an "action approach," in which the pattern of actions of a political actor is observed and discussed. The strategy of the "initiating" and the "defending" party is the subject of our case study of Venezuela.

The Ethiopian-Somali tension (discussed in full in Appendix III) represents a different type. Here, the tension arises between newly established nation-states with strong tribal traditions. The borders of such states are frequently the result of arbitrary divisions that cross ethnic or tribal frontiers or cut into areas of nomadic migrations. With the creation of new nation-states, these divisions brought tensions between native governments. Thus, the Ethiopian-Somali tensions are interpolitical, as well as interethnic and, sometimes, intertribal.

The emergence of new independent states may also result in an increase of secondary local tensions. The application of the principle of self-determination of nations does not necessarily remove international tensions; it may even result in their increase.

It is very difficult to draw "distinct and clear" ethnic borders that will embrace only one ethnic group, and clearly divide it from others. Less developed ethnic groups, close to tribal organizations, have sometimes "quasi-feudal" relations with other tribes which they protect and exploit. This type of symbiosis results frequently in strong antagonisms. However, long periods of such relations establish a pattern; and their dissolution results in social tensions. Many of the new states also have inexperienced ruling elites, often aggressive and immoderate. They have strong ethnic involvements toward their own in-group as well as against traditional anti-groups. In many cases, local tensions could be reduced. However, once they start in a strategic location, they are apt to be utilized by major expanding powers for their own strategy.

Thus, while the case of Ethiopia and Somalia is an example of an interpolitical tension between an ancient African kingdom and a newly established state, it is also representative of a specific type of intereconomic and interethnic tension, as well as a clash of nationalisms.

The ideological tension area

The tension in Venezuela is primarily ideological. The antagonists speak the same Spanish language, belong to the same race, and similar Hispanic ethnic groups. They also cherish the same general culture, have no ethnic or race prejudices, and share the same religious background. Their personality was formed in social institutions influenced by the same church and Spanish institutions.

Superficially, this is an ideological tension between the Venezuelan Communists and their extremist allies, on one hand, and the Democratic Action Party (AD) and Christian Socialists (COPEI) on the other. In reality, the conflict is an expression of major international tensions and antagonisims.

The Cuban strategy in Venezuela is dependent on the general Communist strategy of the Soviet and Chinese camps. Nonetheless, while the wider Communist support is discreet and indirect, the Cuban-Venezuelan conflict is overt and obvious. The "political formula" of this tension is ideological, reflecting the antagonism between the Communist and non-Communist blocs, under specific Latin American conditions.

Cuba was, and is, an outside base of a grand strategy. The 1962 missile crisis indicated the Soviet Union's substantial military investment in Cuba. Such expenditures were not warranted by local political and military needs. Cuba still remains a Soviet military base, with substantial Soviet military personnel and equipment, although Soviet strength was ostensibly withdrawn after the crisis. The magnitude of this establishment was revealed in the United States Congress.[1]

Venezuela plays a crucial role in Soviet strategy. It is one of the greatest oil suppliers of the world. While the Near Eastern oil resources are within easy reach of the Soviet Union, "Cubanization" of Venezuela would deprive the NATO system of one of its most important oil resources, besides placing Soviet influence in the heart of Latin America. For the Cuban rulers and for ideological Communist expansion, Venezuela has economic significance. This oil and iron rich country could supply the necessary financial resources for Communist expansion in South America. Venezuelan finances could assist the deficient Cuban economy. The Cuban prime minister did not hide the nature of his plans from the Venezuelan president. He stated bluntly that he needed money for a master plan "against the gringoes." [2]

The local ideological tension in Venezuela is maintained and escalated from Cuba. Large caches of Cuban weapons were discovered on Venezuelan soil. Material and political support was given by Cuba to the Venezuelan terrorist and guerrilla groups.[3]

Since the tension in Venezuela became part of a broader strategy, the problem of its reduction is not purely local in nature. It can be effectively stalemated on the local level by the defeat of the local forces. However, complete reduction of the tension involves more than the administration and the people of Venezuela.

First, the Cuban government and political movement are involved in it. Secondly, the Communist bloc is concerned in varying degrees. Thus, reduction on the interpolitical level requires negotiations and agreements between the major powers, although formally this is only a secondary tension area. The Soviet political position is decisive. However, Chinese Communists have gained some influence in certain Latin American Communist parties. Substantial easing of tensions between the Soviet Union and the United States would also involve the withdrawal of Soviet power from the Caribbean. Such a reduction of tensions between the super powers would contribute substantially to the weakening if not the removal of external pressures in Venezuela.

The tension inside Venezuela, however, is by no means solely fomented by external agitation, although it is escalated and supported from an "external base."

After a long dictatorship—in fact, a succession of dictatorships—a successful revolution overthrew the ruling power. The revolution brought the urgent social, economic, and political problems from a potential, latent condition controlled by the police and the army, to manifest demands and expressions. Once the dictatorship was abolished, the need for basic social-economic and political reforms became urgent. The old system was based on corrupt military dictatorship and an exploitative economic oligarchy. The end of dictatorship liberated powerful ideological and political forces of democracy.

The new democratic government faced the problem of a restoration of political and social-economic stability through fundamental changes in both areas. In this respect the new Democratic Action government, headed by President Rómulo Betancourt, has shown initiative, skill, and imagination. A constructive land reform has opened new opportunities to thousands of landless peasants, and proper economic arrangements have secured substantial income from oil resources for the country. The extensive hydroelectric plants, construction, development of iron resources, and attempts toward industrialization have evidenced the skills and pragmatic approach of the new leadership.

The Democratic Action Party also has a definite ideology and appeal. It has support among the peasantry, organized workers, and sections of intellectuals. But it has also a certain inner weakness—a tendency toward splits, personality problems, and difficulties in maintaining cohesion. The strategy of the Betancourt government has been to assure political stability through an improvement of social-economic conditions and through strong support of organized political movements. However, in spite of this sound policy, tensions continue.

It is true that Venezuelan politics are violent and lack the patterns of institutional behavior that permit rapid social or political change without violence. Simón Bolívar once said: "Venezuelans love their country but they do not love its laws." The laws at that time, he argued, were bad, "a melancholy relic" of ancient and modern despotism. But the attitude toward law is also a social one; it does not change rapidly, even if laws change.

The social and political movements of Venezuela as well as its ideologies are subject to continuous divisions that reflect personality and group behavior, values, and patterns. However, a capacity for political action based on a broad consensus between leaders of different parties, or even within the same party, is in its beginning.

The succession of dictatorships in Venezuela reinforced the Spanish colonial institutional pattern. In consequence, the Spanish institutions also shaped the native patterns of political behavior. As a result of this historical experience, a political behavioral pattern developed that does not easily reconcile itself with a democratic system based on stability and change. Open mutiny, disobedience to laws, and irresponsible violence against government are regarded by many as acts of heroism rather than political immaturity. A succession of dictatorships made tyranny a regular form of government, and physical resistance to tyranny became a part of the heroic past. "The government" was an enemy of free men. Thus, with the passage of time, any government—dictatorial or democratic—moved at once into an established symbol, a stereotype of the oppressive past.

A modern industrial and scientific society requires provisions for rapid change and continuity; stability and change are not necessarily contradictory. Contemporary political stability is in fact synonymous with rapid change. Only a system that provides for such change can secure stability. This change occurs in social, economic, political, scientific fields, and it is accomplished without unnecessary destruction and violence. Modern scientific development is cumulative; so is industrial growth. It involves conflicts and antagonism, but it is incompatible with arbitrary destruction and violence, or terror.

The Venezuelan political pattern has its own propensity toward tensions, political splits, irreconcilable differences, and prompt and violent disagreements. An outside power, or a small well-organized group, could take advantage of this instability. It will take time to build a stable democratic system. Under such conditions it is easier to interfere and to intensify tensions than it would be in stable systems. Totalitarian systems resist tensions by extreme forms of coercion and terror; difference and antagonism are a part of a democratic process. Institutional mechanisms as well as the acceptance of common rules, the ability to arrive at a consensus in a democratic order channel the tensions and keep them within limits.

The Venezuelan example suggests an important problem—that of arriving at stability. It is a general premise, almost an axiom, that the solution of social-economic problems will result in political stability. However, social-economic progress and improvement may not provide political stability, because political institutions and behavior are not simple, mechanical consequences of economic changes.

Perhaps, certain types of political institutions favor political stability, which in turn creates conditions of economic stability. We may suggest that they are interdependent. Thus, changes in the social-economic base of Venezuela may not provide the necessary stability and resistance to inner and external pressure, unless, at the same time, the young democratic forces and institutions develop a strength and resilience of their own.

The succession of dictators

Venezuela was not a gold rich country, and this affected its early development. The efforts of the Spanish explorers to find an unlimited source of gold and wealth failed. The future of the country lay in the cultivation of its land. By the end of the sixteenth century Venezuela had a well-developed agriculture, and produced also a number of valuable tropical crops. The Spanish settlers who conquered the native Indian tribes secured for themselves economic and administrative independence from their mother country, at least to a certain degree.[4]

Consequently, three major ruling elites emerged when Venezuela gained her independence: the landed oligarchy, the clergy, and the military elite. Political power was controlled until modern times through successive military dictatorships supported by the oligarchy. The dictatorships maintained the status quo by oppressive and coercive measures.

The first independence movements appeared by the end of the eighteenth century, but collapsed rapidly. They gained in strength after the conquest of Spain by Napoleon Bonaparte and the crowning of his brother Joseph as king of Spain. The provisional junta was formed in 1810, and by 1811 the separation from Spain was proclaimed. The war against the royalists continued for many years, and ended with the establishment of the republic of Gran Columbia. Simón Bolívar's dream did not last, however, and in 1830 Venezuela became a separate state. It played a leading role in South America's struggle for independence from Spain, as did its national patriot, Simón Bolívar.

With independence, the country began a long period of dictatorships. In 1899 Cipriano Castro established a dictatorship. General Juan Gómez, whose provisional presidency ended with his death in 1935, appropriated power in 1909. His generation-long dictatorship belongs among the most cruel regimes in the history of the civilized world. Gómez is little known in Europe, but he was a forerunner of totalitarians in his systematic and ruthless pattern of oppression.[5]

During Venezuela's hundred years of independence a military caste became the most powerful ruling class. However, an event independent of the dictatorship and internal Venezuelan conditions fundamentally changed the country's social-economic base.

In the nineteen twenties, during the administration of Gómez, the discovery of rich oil resources and their subsequent exploitation changed the social structure. A modern industrial working class appeared. The middle classes grew too. The Central University of Caracas became an important center of political action against the dictatorship. Among its students were the leaders of today's democratic and left-wing movements in Venezuela—Rómulo Betancourt, Jovito Villalba, and Gustavo Machado.[6]

After the death of Gómez, the rule of his successor Eleazar Lopez Contreras, was far more liberal. During his administration a left-wing democratic party (Partido National Democrático) was organized, but it soon split. Its platform resembled the programs of European social-democratic parties. This party later became the Democratic Action Party (Acción Democrática), and it gained influence among Venezuelan labor.

A general improvement of political conditions came with the administration of President Isaías Medina Angarita in 1941. However, he opposed a direct, general election for the presidency. Therefore, in 1945, Acción Democrática staged a successful coup with the support of the military and came to power, with Rómulo Betancourt as chief of the new politically liberal and democratic government. In the presidential and congressional elections of 1947, Acción Democrática won two-thirds of the seats in each house of Congress; the Communists won 3 seats. Some months later, the victory of the Democratic Action Party in municipal elections confirmed its decisive influence. Rómulo Gallegas, a candidate of Acción

Democrática, became president of the republic. A number of progressive reforms were carried out, industrialization was encouraged, revenue was spent to diversify the economy, and irrigation was extended.[7] In exploitation of oil, the famous 50:50 formula was established (50 to 50% division of profits between the foreign oil companies and the government).[8]

In 1948 the government of Acción Democrática was overthrown by a military junta. Marcos Pérez Jiménez emerged as a dictator, and ruled for 10 years, until 1958. Venezuela is a classic example of the Latin American coups (*golpo*, "revolutions from above"), which have a certain logic, a repetitive pattern and sequence of stages.

A "model" coup begins with secret meetings between intellectuals, civilians, and professionals; men of politics on the one hand and the military on the other. The former control opinion; the latter, weapons. In the second stage, the military, supported by the intellectuals, stages the coup and removes the existing regime. In the third stage, a junta composed of civilians and military men takes over the government and shares the power. (In those systems where subtle, institutional control of political and military establishments was not yet developed, ultimate power rested with those who controlled the weapons and had skills in the use of violence—the army.) In the fourth stage, contradictions between the military and the civilians increase. The civilians attempt to improve their power position by strengthening the police, building up an independent militia, or winning an important section of the armed forces. Should they fail in their buildup of a counterforce, the military may strike. The second coup forms the fifth stage. Now, a military rule, decisively influenced by the army leaders, is established and power is maintained by coercion. The fifth stage came for Venezuela, this time late in 1948, with Marcos Pérez Jiménez' dictatorship.[9]

The dictatorship was ruthless and oppressive. Political opponents were sent to a concentration camp, and the old oppressive pattern, remembered well from the times of Gómez, was again put into operation. The dictator, courted by the oil companies, amassed a personal fortune and embarked on ambitious economic plans and projects.[10, 11]

The underground activities of Acción Democrática continued. At the same time the Communists divided into "Black" and "Red" groups. "Black" Communists were tolerated by the regime. They maintained regional trade unions and were permitted to travel freely to Communist bloc countries. At that time the Communists were allowed to hold responsible positions in the press, in radio, and in education.[12]

In 1958 the revolutionary action moved into a decisive stage. A "Patriotic Junta" was formed by an underground organization composed of the Democratic Action Party, the Republican Democratic Union, the Christian Socialists, and the Communists.

On January 21, 1958, the junta proclaimed a general strike. The revolution begun to move from below. Street fighting started in the capital and in other cities. On January 22, the revolution moved from above. Rear Admiral Wolfgang Larrazábal and other army officers, supported by a naval revolt, forced the resignation of the dictator. By January 23, the "takeover" stage of the revolution was completed.[13] (Incidentally, one of the prominent leaders of the revolution signed the acts of the military junta "takeover" in 1948.[14]) However, the pattern of Latin American revolutions continued. A military coup was staged on July 23, headed by the defense minister, but was defeated with the help of a movement "from below" —a general strike. This was indicative of the strength of the new government, and of its popular support. However, three years later, President Betancourt listed 20 separate major riots (revolts) and coups d'etat, in addition to a number of attempts to assassinate him.[15]

The Democratic Action Party and the antagonists

The revolution led by Betancourt and his friends had a clear ideology and appeal. It had a progressive and democratic accent, with a wide program of pragmatic reforms of immediate significance.

Betancourt is one of the leading Latin American political theoreticians, with a practical outlook. He has a distant vision of the good society. Nevertheless, his immediate goals of reforms and industrial development are realistic. He would rather see an improvement in the conditions of the peasantry and the working class than impose an ideological, perfectionist system by force and terror. He was and is a meliorist, not a perfectionist. He represents a coalition of democratic parties that prefer to pursue a "better" and workable plan than a theoretically "perfect" but unworkable one. The leadership of those parties prefers to see an increase in oil workers' salaries, general improvement of living standards, and immediate results than the promise of a perfect society after half a century of five-year plans.

Betancourt is an outspoken foe of Latin American dictatorship. His policies invite the antagonism of dictators for many reasons. The revolution which he led set a progressive pattern that posed a treat to dictators, even in such distant places as Santo Domingo. Betancourt and his party actively opposed the Dominican dictatorship of Trujillo. Like Figures in Costa Rica and Haya de la Torre in Peru, Betancourt proposed a democratic way of change, a native "Latin American way." Their ideology is competitive with that of the Communists. Fidel Castro suggested the "Cuban way," of coercion; Betancourt, the "Venezuelan way," based on democracy and consensus. He indicated his position clearly when the government of Venezuela made common cause with the Commission on Human Rights of the Organization of American States in its request to the Cuban government for a cessation of the mass executions that were taking place in Cuba. "We were responding," said Betancourt, "to fundamentally humane considerations. The

firing squad and the death penalty are foreign to the American tradition. . . . Our
political life has been quite turbulent and we have had many civil wars, but the
life of the adversary has always been respected. In our codified public law, as
in the O.A.S. treaties, respect for human life is specifically established." [16] In
addition to his broad philosophy, Betancourt had an understanding of concrete
social and economic problems and supplied answers in terms of action. In international politics, he advanced broad visionary plans of a regional integration of
South America.[17]

A domestic political struggle had to be expected, because a long period of
domestic tensions is the "natural" aftermath of a long dictatorship. Strong personalities with definite views, unwilling to compromise but ready to split a party,
are also a part of the Hispanic cultural pattern, the "national character." All this
was enough to cause powerful post-revolutionary tensions. In addition, there was
an outside factor. The tension almost immediately became international. Attacks
against the new government came from the extreme right and the totalitarian left.
In addition, tension appeared within the ruling party itself. The Dominican dictator Trujillo supported the movements on the right, including attempted assassi-
nations of Betancourt. From Cuba came support for Communist action on a very
wide scale: guerrilla tactics, individual and indiscriminate terror, destruction of
industrial centers, sabotage, fomenting of general disorder. The tension was clearly
international and required more than purely domestic measures for its reduction.

The external and internal front

The tactics employed in a tension area contribute to the development of a
general pattern of tensions. Their real significance emerges by relating the tension
in one area to similar tensions in other areas. Groups of related tensions (clusters
of tension areas) as well as their complementary patterns are indicative of the
general strategic pattern. The tension areas are steps in a strategic advance. Thus,
tensions in Venezuela and Cuba, violence in Peru and British Guiana, activities—
such as guerrilla training—in Brazil form a single group of related tensions. They
are included in a wider strategic plan that follows a normal logic of tensions.
Venezuela is a segment of a general strategy,[18] supported and sometimes guided
from an external base. The combination of the external and internal front supplies
an element of continuity and planning. These tensions have their own impetus
as domestic issues. A result of social discontent and long years of exploitation or
of ethnic-racial rivalries, they call for rapid social change or techniques for an accord between ideologically and racially diverse groups. Such tensions can be used
by an external power for its strategic designs. This, however, does not change
the fact that they do exist independently of the external pressures and call for
rational and democratic solutions.

This strategy moves within alternative courses of action: one, by peaceful penetration and infiltration and by political action; two, by means of limited warfare, escalating tensions, terror, and guerrilla activities. The Communist parties of Latin America are by no means wholly dependent on outside support; they have a sizable membership and strength of their own. The movements also seem to be divided between those oriented toward a "peaceful" way to power and those who choose the violent pattern.

The government must guard itself simultaneously against the right wing and the military coup. In 1958 (July, September) the government defeated two military coups. In 1960 (April), a military rebel group invaded Venezuela from Colombia and seized military barracks in San Cristobal, supported, probably, by Trujillo. This revolt was crushed by the loyal troops. From October 1959 till 1960 terrorist bombs were exploded in Caracas. Betancourt was injured in a dynamite explosion.[19] The attempts of assassination and intervention were identified by the foreign ministers of twenty American states as acts of aggression by the Dominican Republic.[20]

The tactics of the Communists were more elaborate. Under Communist leadership, guerrilla units were trained and organized as Armed Forces of National Liberation (FALN). They met with little success, however, because of the rural population's support of the government and the influence of the Democratic Action Party. The Cuban government supplied the Venezuelan Communists with weapons and equipment to further their general plan for the seizure of Caracas. The plans of capture of the capital city as well as a cache of arms were discovered by the Venezuelan government, and the operation was investigated by a special committee of the O.A.S.[21]

A general calendar covering six months of terrorism against the government and the people of Venezuela gives a general picture of a "tension area." [22]

January 22, 1962. At the opening of the Inter-American Foreign Ministers Conference on Cuba in Punta del Este, the terrorists increased their activities in Caracas: houses were burned; traffic was blocked; the United States embassy was bombed; and snipers shot at police. After four days of bombings and shooting, 39 persons were killed and 280 wounded.

February 13, 1962. A bomb exploded 150 feet from Betancourt as he addressed a meeting.

March 29, 1962. Guerrillas attacked the airbase at Mariscal, with no success.

April 19, 1962. Sporadic guerrilla actions by groups equipped with small arms were reported.

May 4–5, 1962. A revolt erupted in Carupano, the second largest naval base in Venezuela. The rebels seized the radio station and police headquarters, but were defeated by government troops.

May 7, 1962. Disturbances occurred at the University of Caracas and students burned a bus.

May 9, 1962. Student disturbance spread to several cities, resulting in two persons being killed and twenty injured. Students threw rocks and gasoline bombs.

June 2–4, 1962. A battalion of marines revolted at Puerto Caballero, the chief naval base. Government troops recaptured the base; 400 persons were killed, 1,000 wounded.

Terrorism and sabotage spreads to other areas. A bridge was blown up between Caracas and the industrial city of Valencia; 3 bombs exploded in Caracas. Gangs of adolescents in Caracas threw rocks at store windows and burned buses. Sabotage was reported at the Punto Fijo oil refinery. This calendar could be extended to both earlier and later periods than those noted.

Did the Communists and their allies really control the majority? The results of elections indicated that they represented only a small but concentrated minority, principally centered in the capital.

Results of Elections of 1958 *

ELECTION FOR PRESIDENT

	Votes	% of Total
Rómulo Betancourt (Democratic Action Party [AD])	1,284,092	49%
Admiral Larrazabal (Left-wing Republican-Democratic Union [URD] and Communists)	903,479	35%
Caldera (Centrist Christian Socialist Party [COPEI])	423,262	16%

ELECTION FOR CONGRESS

Party	Senate	Chamber of Deputies
Democratic Action (AD)	32	73
Rep.-Dem. Union (URD)	11	33
Christian Socialists (COPEI)	6	20
Communists	2	7

* "Venezuela," *On Record,* p. 9; Chatham House Memoranda, p. 3.

The Communists emerged as the weakest party. Their activities and terror were, however, extensive.

A democratic system can operate only under certain conditions. Certain minimum rules and patterns of institutional behavior must be accepted or the complex political machinery cannot operate. A minority party may, under certain conditions, destroy the system and conquer political power. All three major types of terror—individual, indiscriminate, and mass terror—do not require the support of a vast majority. Some forms of psychological coercion are based on well-armed, active minorities and manipulation of fear. A skillful diffusion of details of an act of terror generates fear and develops attitudes of submission among large sections of the politically timid and passive. Individual terror, a technique used by a variety of political orientations, has the advantage of surprise. It was used by Russian Democratic Populists (Social-Revolutionaries) in their struggle against tyranny. It was also used by German Nazis and other fascist-oriented groups in their struggle against democracy.

Mass terror has been used since ancient times to maintain political power and ideological control. The Inquisition, an extensive institution of religious terror, is indicative of the fact that a machine of mass terror can be maintained for centuries. The institution that grows on mass terror develops a tendency to maintain the terroristic system. In consequence, the ideology of the entire movement, religious or political, is affected and corrupted by it.

Individual and indiscriminate terror is a tactic of weakening the government; a preparation for the violent seizure of power. Individual terror is directed against politically important persons. Sometimes it is used to consolidate power. Indiscriminate terror, directed at the general populace, has at its purpose the generation of general fear among the people by impeding the regular activities of a society or a political system. The organization and tactics of a political party, the use of violence may effectively disorganize an orderly democratic system.[23]

Democratic institutions are used by totalitarian parties to destroy democracy; liberties are invoked by those who intend to abolish political rights and establish a rule of their own, based on unlimited and uncontrolled power.

The strategy of defense

The Democratic Action Party came to power with a philosophy and program of its own. Its policy of reforms was determined by the values the party represented, the ideology it advanced. Reforms were advocated from the party's founding; they were not forced upon it by Communist attack. But, whatever the objectives, the policy of basic reforms defeated the Communist and right-wing objectives, at least for a period of the post-dictatorial era. Certain actions of the Venezuelan government were intended to frustrate Communist actions. Others exercised this function irrespective of their original intention; they were "functional." However, direct, violent, and physical Communist warfare continued. The reform programs had no spectacular effect on the minority that had the definite objective of overthrowing the government and taking over.

The major policies that had an effect on tensions, or were related to tensions, appeared in four areas:

1]

A broad policy of social reforms weakened the Communist appeal, answered some of the problems which contributed to general unrest, and created a stronger social-economic base for the government and the Venezuelan democracy.

2]

Direct police and military action against the terrorists and military conspiracies. The government was supported by sections of the armed forces. In that way, the government strengthened its position, and developed the necessary ties between sections of the armed forces and the civilian government. Official statements of the president indicated support and cooperation between the armed forces and the government. This cooperation between a democratic regime and the army, as long as it can be maintained, secures a certain stability, and represents an important improvement of the traditional, antagonistic relations between armed forces and democratic government in Latin America that usually led to the violent end of democratic rule. How stable and how strong these ties are, how long they will last, is difficult to evaluate. Several military coups indicate, however, that opponents of the government have infiltrated some minor groups.

3]

The Democratic Action Party, combined with the progressive Christian Socialist Party (COPEI), represented an organized political force that had sufficient strength to counter the Communist Party, without resorting to violence.

4]

Diplomatic action, especially in the Organization of American States. The activities of Cuban Communists and their connection with the Venezuelan terrorists were exposed. These, among other factors, led to isolation of Cuba from the Latin American community.

The party

The Democratic Action Party has its weaknesses, but it has also considerable strength, especially when compared with many other political parties in Latin America. Its weakness is by no means characteristic of the Venezuelan party alone.

Many parties which have a well-developed ideology and a program of radical reforms also show a general tendency toward splitting. The Venezuelan party, with its Hispanic cultural background, has a major share of this tendency. A splinter group of the Democratic Action formed a left-wing party, the Independent Revolutionary Movement (MIR). In 1961, a second split occurred, and the right wing seceded.

Political parties that achieve power also have their share of opportunists. The Democratic Action Party has, however, a definite ideology, structure, strategy, and tactics—the important elements of a workable and dynamic modern political organization. It is not solely a party of the political elite. It has influence in rural areas; it gained, together with the Christian Socialists, considerable influence in the unions. Betancourt has well understood that a stable democracy must have a strong social base to oppose a coup and dictatorship effectively. Similarly, a democratic party must have the support of the productive social classes and an appeal to workers and farm laborers to solve their problems. In order to continue in power, in Latin America, a democratic government needs the support of the army, while at the same time educating it in democratic principles. A working democracy needs also the support of militant and strong political parties. Betancourt and the leaders of the Democratic Action Party developed the party along these lines.[24] The alternative is abolition of the army and limitation of law enforcement to the police.

Thus, the Communist Party faced an ideological movement of certain strength and vigor in Venezuela, willing to make alliances with other democratic parties. The party was willing to cooperate with the Communists, within the democratic process. It refused, however, to become a tool of Communists and support unworkable policies and an oppressive dictatorship.

Transformations of the social-economic base

With all its social and economic problems, Venezuela had one major advantage, when compared with other South American republics: great wealth in its oil resources that can be used for financing social-economic changes. The concentration of land, economic resources, and power in the hands of a conservative class of landowners could be counterbalanced through the control of political power and the country's natural resources. The democratic alliance controlling this power used it for substantial changes in two major areas: an increase of productive capacity and a change in the distribution of income and property. To achieve these goals, advances were made in the following fields: a) land reform, b) economic diversification and industrialization, c) the wider distribution of profits from oil, d) development of national resources, especially iron and hydroelectric power, e) housing, f) education, g) social reforms, and above all, h) in the area of salaries and social legislation.

According to the 1937 census, 5% of the farming population owned 79% of cultivable land.[25] In 1960, 1.9% owned 74%.[26] In 1960 the land reform was passed and signed by the president. It is intended to abolish the system of medieval "Latifundistas," and establish properly organized small farms with an adequate credit system. The transformation of the agrarian structure will incorporate the rural population into the general economic, social, and political development of the country. The land reform also guarantees integrity of communal lands to the indigenous population.[27] By 1963, close to $150 million had been spent on agrarian reform; more than 60,000 rural families were settled on 4 million acres; crops were being bought at guaranteed minimum prices; more than 7,000 kms of access roads were constructed; and aid to education was doubled.[28]

The land reform and other social, political, and educational policies won the support of the rural population. In this way, the government strengthened its position. During the mutiny in the army and naval bases at Puerto Cabello and Carupano, the loyal armed forces were supported by peasants armed with home-made shotguns and machetes.

Tax reform was introduced in 1958. Venezuela has also set up a nationalized oil company, and through income tax increases has materially improved its profit share from foreign oil companies to over 60%.[29]

The government began construction of a vast industrial area at the junction of Orinoco and Caroni. This area has excellent iron ore and hydroelectric power potential. In 1962, construction of the *Siderurgica del Orinoco* was completed at a cost of $360 million.[30] A loan of $85 million from the World Bank helped to finance the initial stages of the hydroelectric dam,[31] and Venezuela was able also to secure substantial American economic support.[32]

Illiteracy has been reduced from 60 to 26 percent.[33] Of course a number of problems remain unanswered. In certain industries wages are very high; in others, incomparably lower. Nevertheless, the internal social-economic base of the republic has been transformed in a relatively short time, with reforms moving in the direction of economic democracy.

The external base and internal stability

After overthrowing the dictatorship, the Venezuelan democratic parties undertook substantial and constructive social and economic reforms with vigor and imagination. True, not all problems have been solved, and unemployment in urban areas still remains high,[34] but the change is substantial. What has been called "the internal social-economic base," has been constructively affected by these policies.

In this ideological tension area, Communist-led movements with a program of establishing a dictatorial regime were countered by a powerful social-political movement. Democratic forces were by no means weak or passive. In the 1963 presidential elections, 95% of the people went to the polls in spite of terrorist threats. The Democratic Action Party lost some of its strength. However, the liberal Catholic Social Christian Party (COPEI) increased its influence and both parties, in coalition, control a majority of votes. Venezuela has at least two organized, stable, progressive, and left-of-center political parties.

The ideological offensive in Venezuela was countered; so were the political and the military. But the question remains whether tensions are completely reduced. Of course, they are not. They are, at best, stalemated.

In addition, the tension in Venezuela is by no means solely of internal domestic making. It is singularly international; a combination of two fronts. Therefore a complete reduction of the tension depends on strategic solutions. A general reduction of antagonisms in the Western Hemisphere—by "blocking" of the outside support or by a general agreement—will, to an extent, reduce tension and change the forms of political struggle in Venezuela. "To an extent" of course, since the domestic factors remain. A change of institutions, combined with political educational processes and changes in value structure, and a simultaneous change in the social-economic base, is the right road toward transformation of political and institutional behavior. But it is a long road, and tensions of today require immediate answers even if they invite long-term plans and policies.

Venezuela is the major target of Communist offensive in the Western Hemisphere initiated from Cuba.[35] However, Cuba has its own "internal front" of resistance against Communist rule, while the United States and a number of Central American states form the external base of a powerful front against Castro.

Cuba could well use the money and resources spent on aggression to improve the social and economic conditions of its own people. Instead, the government and the party employ their energies and their finances in a strategy of hemispheric conquest. The Cuban rulers, of course, could not undertake these actions alone.

At the beginning of its subversive activities in 1959, the Cuban government made a number of attempts to win a foothold by direct invasion. This type of action failed, and a new and elaborate tactic was developed.[36] Meanwhile, there has been a shift in orientation among some local Communist groups as a result of the split in basic ideology between the Soviet and Chinese Communist camps. In consequence, the reduction of external pressure depends on changes in world politics. Such transformations may affect the policies and tactics of the Latin American sections. The pressure of Mainland China may force the Soviet government to a more definite rapprochement with the Atlantic Community.

A basic change in strategy may also result in the reduction of local tensions. This may, however, involve major changes in American foreign policy toward Cuba.[37]

Economic and political stability

A modern society—a society of rapid change—requires stability as well as provisions for rapid change. In turn, the constructive change of a modern industrial, or more advanced technological scientific, society needs continuity. The development of science and technology is cumulative, and the process of accumulating knowledge, skills, and resources requires continuity and stability. The process of reducing or channelling tensions is a strategy stage in a system which combines stability with provisions for rapid and nonviolent change.

The politically liberal, progressive school suggests that the strategy of reducing tensions and creating stability should be directed primarily toward the transformation of the social-economic base. Progressive reforms, according to this school, will eliminate the general discontent and result in political stability. This writer agrees with such an approach. The experience of Venezuela indicates, however, that changes in social-economic conditions alone may not produce the necessary political stability in certain situations. Under specific circumstances violent attempts to generate political disorganization may continue. Such actions frustrate efforts toward social-economic changes and, at the end, result in new forms of dictatorships.

In the past, social advance and economic stability were achieved as a consequence of certain types of political stability. Present strategy should be aimed at a wider stability comprising both social-economic and political areas.

Again, past history teaches that after revolutionary changes in the social-economic and class structure of a society, political stability was accomplished often by extreme coercive means—by dictatorships, Caesarist or Bonapartist forms of government—which in turn resulted in long periods of instability. Present democracies face the problem of establishing or reestablishing political stability, with provisions for rapid change by free institutions, consensus-oriented policies, and techniques that do not involve terror, oppressive measures, extreme forms of coercion, or limitations of political rights.[38] Here is an area that needs discussion and a search for new political patterns. The political theory of democratic systems left this area unexplored and unanswered.

v. Reduction of International Tensions

17.

SOME "MEDIUM RANGE" PERSPECTIVES

A general direction

Hostility and aggression are universal collective and individual behavioral patterns. In their most ancient forms—love and hostility—the two polar attitudes are rooted in the biological nature of man. Both behavioral patterns can be observed also among predatory animals. Hostility and aggression against a different species, frequently a more "peaceful" species, is in turn related to hunger, and to ways of satisfying this drive. Anyone who has seen a predator attacking its prey has witnessed, in terms of our values, an outburst of hostility and a display of terror. Yet, the same predator may show attachment and dedication to its own offspring. Defense against hostile groups, attacks against an out-group, appear in many primitive societies in one form or another. Few react with friendliness to a group of strangers marked by difference in dress, behavior, and language. Suspicion and hostility are attitudes transmitted by inveterate processes of learning from generation to generation.

I shall repeat here—despite all our antecedents, we are only in the initial stages of building a society of nations. Violence and aggression are still a part of our nature, although we are attempting to harness and control them. Not all hostility and aggression are merely morbid. Much of it is a part of human behavior, controlled and restrained by society in a conscious effort to build a more rational society. Thus, efforts, and failure, to reduce tensions should be viewed in this perspective. The failures are part of experience and not the end of effort.

The issue is not the total elimination of antagonism, competition, or difference, nor maintenance of the status quo. It is the creation of a dynamic society free of wasteful, unnecessary, and destructive physical aggression; a society able to rechannel differences, antagonisms, and conflicts into avenues of human actions which negate physical destruction or the use of violence.

Such development requires continuous individual and collective self-control and restraint, a sense of responsibility, and, above all, a social conscience rooted in a strong system of values.

In a long-range development, a general sense of direction can be suggested. Utopian plans for peace have been made many times, and they have had historical significance in international relations. However, the dynamic and rapid change of our society suggests a direction or orientation rather than detailed plans, since future changes in technology, social-economic systems, men's tastes and interests, cannot be fully anticipated. But we may see the direction. We may also suggest objectives. A sense of direction and a certain clarity of objectives are essential to the securing of orderly and rapid change; otherwise man may invite failures, disaster, misery, or destruction.

There are many alternatives open to men. One may choose various roads to the same goal or throw before himself a variety of goals, a variety of orientations. And let us add that the same, or closely related, goals can be achieved by a variety of means. Alternative goals are not necessarily contradictory; the choice does not lie solely between good and evil.

The reduction of tensions covers a wide field of effort, and it is beyond the scope of this book to discuss it fully. Extensive literature in this field is indicative of both the interest and significance of the problems. Our discussion will center on the long-range "orientation" and on certain selected problems of short- and perhaps medium-range action, as well as on a general review of certain issues; techniques of reduction mainly of intergroup, racial, and ethnic tensions; on institutional approach, value approach, legitimacy, and the problem of borders and of direct intervention in tension areas.

First, those tensions which are of major significance are the primary ones: those between the so-called great powers. The tension areas are nothing else but tactical steps, perhaps stages, of wider plans and strategies. They are only reflections and forms of the basic antagonisms. These antagonisms are political and ideological. They appear in tension areas as struggles of social movements and political parties and are reinforced by the intervention of outside states. Here are our primary and complex tensions. The usual counteracting policy has been to produce a stalemate. But this does not solve the major, the central antagonism.

The current primary tensions are a result of Soviet and Mainland Chinese pressure and expansion. Soviet policy is ambivalent. On one hand, a certain tendency toward easement can be noticed; on the other, pressures in the Carribbean continue. The Chinese objectives have been stated by Marshal Lin Piao (Chinese Communist Defense Minister and deputy Prime Minister) in an article which appeared in all major Mainland Chinese newspapers and also in the official English-language *Peking Review* (September 3, 1965).

Marshal Piao writes about war against the United States and Western Europe. Once one deletes the official party expressions and language the objectives become clear. There is a kind of praise of war. He writes: "War can temper the people and push history forward. In this sense war is a great school. In diametrical opposition to the Khrushchev revisionists the Marxists-Leninists never take a gloomy view of war." (Incidentally, Marx took a most gloomy view of war indeed.) The article also calls for a crusade against America and Europe: The old colonial empires have disappeared or are in a process of rapid transformation and dissolution. The new expansionists move into areas of weakness.

The resolution of local tensions through stalemating is a Fabian policy with a central strategic element—time. Time is here the great general. Fatigue and frustration, internal political and ideological change, economic problems may perhaps affect the policies of the aggressive nations and channel them into non-violent or less violent expressions. The answer to pressures is firmness and alerted patience. Weakness and hesitation only invite still stronger attacks and further pressures.

The policy of stalemating, however, is only a negative one. The initiative always rests with the aggressors. A long-range strategy requires a constructive vision and a more definite, a clearer orientation. At present, under favorable conditions the antagonistic process may progress to the point of indifference. In a long-range approach, which involves changes in attitudes and values, ideologies, and actual behavior, pluralism suggests a sense of direction.

Reduction of ethnic and racial tensions

The reduction of racial and ethnic tensions is a major field of interest in American sociology, reaching back almost half a century to the time of Robert Ezra Park and his generation. The last twenty years have witnessed increasing interest, especially in the field of sociology, social psychology, and educational psychology. In a sense, science became the ideology of the United States, and the social sciences—especially sociology, psychology, and education—have supplied the necessary philosophy and, above all, the necessary argument for the movement toward civil rights and racial equality of the 1960's.

In addition to a sense of direction and a social philosophy, these disciplines supply practical devices, ways, and suggestions toward the reduction of intergroup tensions. They are clearly problem-oriented, and in spite of the fact that science claims objectivity (the absence of moral judgment is a disputed issue), the social sciences have supplied a social philosophy and moral objectives.

Interethnic or race tensions will not disappear within a few years, or even in a generation. They will remain with American society, and the rest of the world, for many years to come. Within the last two decades, a new profession seems to have developed, that of the social scientist trained in the reduction and control of intergroup tensions. Many American states and cities have commissions on human relations, especially in the North. These institutions require specially trained personnel able to handle tensions and conflicts of an interethnic or racial nature. Moreover, perhaps more important, is the need to prevent racial explosions, to subdue or rechannel antagonisms before they become explosive. Thus, racial democracy requires a well-planned action and extensive educational effort. Broadly speaking, the policies for the easing of intergroup tensions are divisible into the following categories: (a) preventive, (b) constructive-developmental, and (c) intervening.[1]

The first and second categories are closely related. Their aim is to prevent racial or ethnic tensions by fostering cooperation and understanding between different groups, and by developing long-range constructive policies in the realm of education, legislation, housing, and other fields. The third category represents courses of action taken by authorities or institutions at the moment of actual conflict when tension must be immediately reduced, through persuasion, negotiation, or even by the use of force.

The major policies which apply here are the "direct" and "indirect" approaches. In the direct approach, face-to-face contacts are encouraged, such as group participation or school integration. As I have said, personal contact may increase certain prejudices. On the other hand, meetings between tolerant, intelligent, reasonable people usually lead to a more sophisticated perception of differences. The nature of stereotype becomes clearer. Even a temporary association of persons of different race and ethnic background for definite objectives fosters cooperation. Therefore, the development of short- and long-range goals for mutual action is relevant. Short-range goals in such areas as housing, urban renewal, education, neighborhood problems, or even in church and community affairs, extend the time span of casual contact. Thus, the experience of Northern cities teaches us that, in most cases, a well-conceived integrated action leads to the lowering of discriminatory barriers or, at least, to some control of prejudice. The prejudice does not necessarily disappear, but some of the major visible forms of discrimination do, paving the way to mutual contact. This in turn, in most cases, results in better understanding between individuals and groups.

Formal education is perhaps overly stressed. Currently, American experience indicates that support for integration is strong at universities and colleges. Past European experience, however, suggests some less encouraging experiences. The personality of an individual, his general value structure and orientation, and frequently his political identification reflect his overt attitude toward a minority. An educated professor, of an authoritarian personality, may exhibit strong prejudices, while a worker whose education did not go beyond the elementary level but who is humane in his world outlook may actively oppose discrimination.

The United States navy has made an interesting experiment on the destroyer, *The Biddle*. The crew consists of representatives of seven nationalities, among them, Greeks, Italians, Americans, Germans, and British. Direct tasks in situations that require cooperation—and the price at sea might be survival—may result in new effective forms of cooperation. The navy has begun a similar experiment on the *Claude V. Ricketts,* a guided-missile destroyer, with a six-nation crew.

Public and private agencies apply indirect methods of mass-communication and mass education. Movies, television, radio, and newspapers are being used, with varying degrees of effectiveness.

The state and the apparatus

The race or ethnic prejudice of an individual shopkeeper in a small town is of no significance in international relations. Collective prejudices among substantial groups, however, have an impact on internal domestic affairs. Even in a formal democracy, they sometimes produce phenomena of discrimination that take shocking and unusual expressions. When a white citizen refuses to swim with his colored neighbor, then discrimination is a reflection of a prejudice bordering on psychological obsession. But even such strong prejudice as this may have little impact on international politics in terms of aggression and hostility. It may play a role in an actual combat situation, but in the general conduct of international relations, in an interpolitical sense, in relations between states, the fact that some citizens are prejudiced may not increase differences or antagonisms among countries with no tendency toward expansion. The danger begins when those who believe in prejudice and discrimination form a political organization or develop a social-political movement or a political party.

A political party's objective is the capture of the power of the state. Since the state has a monopoly of legitimate physical power, the control of the state also means the control of violence. A combination of political power with ethnic or racial hostilities makes a state a danger point in both internal and international relations. This has been evident in our case histories. Internal domestic-racial or ethnic tensions do not necessarily produce wars or increase international tensions or result in the outbreak of wars. Regrettable as it is, adverse not only to democratic but also to general humanitarian principles, this type of antagonism and tension does not result in wars. However, the tension becomes interpolitical, with international political significance, the moment an outside state intervenes in this type of tension and escalates, intensifies, and transforms it into open conflict. Pressure "from below"—hostilities expressed by the masses—may also influence the government and force its hand.

Again, as the case histories have indicated, the government may manipulate latent prejudices and hostilities "from above," and escalate them into open antagonism and conflict. It is the government that can transform a tension area from a domestic to an international affair; but there are also government agencies that can work toward the reduction of tensions. Everyone is aware that the government cannot always control tensions. Racial and ethnic antagonisms may be so explosive that the structure of public institutions breaks down and the government or the state is too weak to control them. However, the government can play an important role.

The nature of methodological inquiry forces us to separate the psychological or sociological phenomena from the political. Thus the study of sociological and psychological aspects of ethnic and race prejudice is frequently isolated from political realities, and from the political scene. Yet, the political issue is perhaps the decisive one. The distribution of political power decides the way in which minorities are treated. Should the minorities have a share in power distribution through the electoral process in a democracy, then their political rights are more respected and they have a certain influence on the general conduct of public affairs.

When political parties have to rely on the vote of the minorities, then concessions are usually made. In consequence, race and ethnic prejudice in public institutions is either controlled or not tolerated. Special agencies function to ease or reduce tension between ethnic groups. The system of public education also reflects the political tendencies of the community and of the state. Thus, the political influence of the minority is reflected as well in the general philosophy of the educational system.

The general value structure of a democratic system postulates respect for the minority. A democracy is not the rule of the majority only; it embodies a system of protection for the dissident or the different minority. Experience teaches that in properly functioning democracies, the "philosophical minority" within the political majority, within the privileged racial or ethnic groups, supports the demands of the racial minority. This support is relevant when it affects the political structure on one hand, and the private social institutions on the other.

In the United States, public institutions and private agencies are frequently far more outspoken and resolute on civil rights issues than are the individual citizens. The agencies of the city and the state of New York, for example, always take a strong position on the issue of civil rights. They are far more democratic in this respect, far more respectful of the minorities, than the private companies or many of the citizens. It is easier for a member of a minority (ethnic race) to get a responsible position in federal, state, or municipal institutions than in a minor private corporation. The ancient Romans used to say, "Senatori boni viri, sed Senatus mala bestia." (Senators are good, genteel men, but the Senate is a bad animal.) In other words, the individual is better than a public institution. However, this is not true in our contemporary scene, where the public institutions are frequently more respectful of civil rights than the individual citizen.

Within a city, race and ethnic tensions appear in definite geographical areas. These are of domestic, internal significance. However, certain experiences acquired in domestic tension areas may have an application in international tensions. We have learned from our case studies that the role of public and private institutions is of paramount significance in times of tensions. We have called the network of those institutions the apparatus. The public and private apparatus may escalate the tension to open conflict, but it may also reduce or ease the tension.

For the sake of brevity we will limit ourselves to five major patterns:

1]

All the public institutions—the entire apparatus—are directed consistently against definite ethnic and race groups and support a policy of antagonism.

2]

Two major centers—a diarchy—develop in which one protects the minority, and the other supports an antagonistic policy.[2]

3]

The public institutions leave the minorities to themselves and do not interfere, or interfere only in cases of urgency and violent conflict.

4]

The public institutions take a restrained position of limited interference. They act primarily as moderating and regulatory agencies, protecting the minorities against violent forms of aggression.

5]

The network of public and private institutions is consistently applied to the easing and reduction of tensions, and the securing of equal rights for all religious, ethnic, and racial groups.

In international tension areas, specialized institutions for the reduction of ethnic and race tensions could play a constructive role in the future. The cumulative effort of state, municipal, federal, and private institutions and agencies, combined with the effort of religious denominations and political parties, results in a continuous policy for the solving of urgent problems and the building of an integrated community (as in the case of New York City cited in Chapter 12). The pattern in tension areas, as our case histories indicate, was usually different in the past. The network of public institutions was used to escalate the tension rather than reduce it. Only in rare cases did the public institutions play a neutral role, seeking to mitigate the tensions between the majority and the minority.

On a noncoercive censusus level it was tried in many communities of the

United States. Here, both the movement "from above" and "from below" contributed substantially to the effectiveness of public and private institutions in their policies of reducing tensions and educating the public toward racial and ethnic democracy.

On the other hand, in the Communist bloc, ethnic and race tensions have been subdued by coercive measures. However, while open conflict in the old tension areas might be absent, latent antagonism and hostilities, as well as discrimination, may still continue.

There is no ready-made recipe. The policies or methods effective in New York City may not be effective in Uganda. Nevertheless, the basic principles of easing tensions through a network of institutions have a general broad application.

The United Nations is, of course, the logical center for an international human relations agency. But today, it may be premature to expect an effective human rights agency or activity in the international tension areas under United Nations control. But, another more homogeneous regional or intercontinental organization, such as the European Community, or the North Atlantic Treaty Organization, could make a more effective beginning on a smaller scale. A central agency for human rights could support local agencies in tension areas. It could exercise moral pressure on recalcitrant governments, and open new possibilities and new perspectives through mediation and arbitration. Of course, such policies are feasible only if the sovereign government of the territory supports and encourages such activities. Perhaps step by step from the experience of continental organizations we could move further to an effective action by international intergroup agencies or human relations agencies operating on a wider area.

The changing emphasis of values

In a modern industrial society, an individual usually belongs to many diverse groups that differ essentially in their value structure. Men's actions and general behavior are anchored to not one but several systems of values, corresponding to the institutions and groups to which they belong. In consequence, they frequently operate on a number of parallel value systems, using different values in different situations and acting as representatives of different "reference groups." Sometimes their values are complementary; at other times, contradictory.

Identification with a group also involves certain responsibilities toward the group, a certain conformity of behavior. It is expected that each member is willing to assume burdens, responsibilities, and even sacrifice to secure the group's continuity. In consequence, self-identification with the group leads to acceptance of certain obligations, which we call loyalties. Every type of human society imposes a certain amount of conformity; it requires from its members the acceptance of certain behavioral patterns. Because of this conformity, group and individual behavior is predictable to a certain degree.

Thus, values, self-identification, loyalties, and responsibilities are interrelated elements of collective behavior and group formation. A sailor from Barcelona in Spain identifies himself as a Catalan. In a French port, his self-identification may be Spanish. For all the differences between the Catalonians and Castilians, he still may feel an affinity to Spain. In New York or Singapore he may discover a community of values and interests with other European sailors and identify himself as a European. His regional, national and continental identification, values, perhaps loyalties, are in this case complementary. In medieval times, the religious self-identification, the religious reference group, was frequently emphasized, while the national one was deemphasized.

Since the end of World War II, Europe has shown a different side to the picture. The postwar situation created conditions in Germany for the acceptance of European identification. In other parts of Europe, the ferocity of extreme nationalism and racism resulted in political fatigue and the weakening of nationalist appeal, and the European idea penetrated among the new leadership of the conquered nations. New leaders appeared who sympathized with supernational solutions and collective security. They succeeded in developing highly technical European institutions whose significance was probably not realized by the general public. These institutions corresponded to definite needs at the time and, with the pressure from outside during the Stalinist period, rapidly advanced European integration.

The idea of European community gained in appeal and influence. The values and loyalties which had been limited to a small group at the beginning were extended over wider groups and had a wider appeal. European identification became complementary to national identification and, in certain cases, even a symbol of a stronger appeal. General Charles de Gaulle's formula for European integration reflected the competitive nature of the two symbols, the national and the European.

Reduction or rechannelling of tensions in a given area may also be facilitated by de-emphasizing one identity or loyalty and emphasizing broader, universal identifications and loyalties that will permit hostile groups to change their attitudes to at least those of indifference and distance. In the tension areas of the European community, such a policy of emphasizing European solidarity and identification may supply an interesting experiment for the future. With the development of this continental community, more vigorous, European intervention may supply an instrumentality toward reduction of tensions. Intergroup activity, in which human rights action would be fostered by an international institution emphasizing broader solidarity while respecting the national identification, may have a wider acceptance than agencies set up by a sovereign state. We shall return to an analysis of these broader, universal values in our concluding chapter.

Boundaries in tension areas

A political frontier or boundary is also a concept charged with values. The changing of attitudes, or even of the concept of the boundary, in a tension area may liberalize the population movement and foster an improvement in some if not all intergroup relations. Professor George T. Little of the University of Vermont argues convincingly that the concept of boundary is relative. In a series of studies he indicated the difference in defining, and in the general approach to, the concept of frontiers in diverse cultures. Various cultures have different concepts of what constitutes a borderline. Islamic concepts of territorial frontiers differ from those of Western political science usage.[3]

A distinction between the concepts of frontier and boundary has developed in American historical and geographical theory. Interestingly enough, some European languages do not provide for such a differentiation.[4] The term "frontier" has a specific meaning in America—it is the concept of an unsettled, not yet fully civilized borderland area, rather than of a single line separating two political entities— but it is sometimes used as a synonym for the concept of boundary. In Europe, the concept of a historical border is frequently only a social myth manipulated for policies of expansion. Not all so-called historical boundaries are indeed the traditional borders of the settlement periods. Many overlap and are those of two different nations in different historical periods. The concept of borders, boundary, and frontier, calls for revision and a rational evaluation, and adjustment to the need of our century.[5]

Even in primitive societies we may observe that tribes inhabit certain more or less definite areas which we shall call "core territory." Long observation of a tribe, or of the historical records of a nation, may indicate that certain frontiers are permanently established, and that beyond such a frontier a given tribe or a nation-state would not, and did not, move. We may call such frontiers "fixed frontiers." We shall also find certain areas that are visited frequently, whether for pastures or for purposes of exchange and trade, by two or more tribes. Similarly, we shall find border areas to which a number of nationalities migrate and settle. Such areas we may call "periphery."

The periphery is a natural area of economic and cultural exchange; it is a meeting point of many ethnic and culturally different groups. In some parts of the world, it is an area where culturally different groups meet but do not assimilate, and where they have retained their original ethnic characteristics for centuries. The Balkans have an abundance of this type of periphery, as has the rest of Eastern Europe. The imposition of fixed borders, which are strongly guarded and difficult to cross, in a periphery that is a natural area of exchange and trade creates hardship and results in tensions. Therefore, the easing of ethnic antagonisms in tension areas may require a change in the concept of frontiers, and transformation of the area into an open periphery.

The concept of boundaries calls for a reappraisal of the rigid historical or juridical approach, and for a reevaluation in terms of their sociological, economic and political functions. In our contemporary world, the functional types of boundaries differ greatly. The walled boundary constructed in Berlin by the East German government is functionally different from that of the civilized boundary between Canada and the United States. While the first is definitely restrictive and isolating, the second favors an exchange of population and trade within the limits imposed by legal agreements.

We may distinguish between two extreme models of boundaries: free and closed. Free boundaries are administrative lines, permitting free movement of population and trade. The boundaries within the European community are moving toward this "ideal type." The function of closed borders is the isolation of the enclosed nation. Between these two extremes there are a number of gradations. Russian borders since the Czarist regime were "closed" and isolating, and this policy has been reinforced under the Soviet regime.

A specific type of tension within an area may also require a definite policy toward boundaries. Perhaps the introduction of a functional type of boundary would assist in easing tension, if it were combined with a liberal policy toward population movements. Sometimes, however, a closed boundary may be a functional device to isolate foreign military, and, prevent political, infiltration.

Direct intervention

Explosive situations in a tension area require immediate, direct action. When violence appears between ethnic, racial, or political groups, there is no time for long- or medium-range policies involving changing values, institutions, and educational processes.

The use of United Nations forces was an important innovation in the handling of tensions in limited geographical areas. Thus far, the United Nations force has been more restrained in the use of force to restore order than are the national forces of the tension area. The very presence of the force has had an impact on the behavior of the population and of the antagonistic parties. It may contribute to the rechannelling of antagonism into less violent avenues.

Sometimes neutralization and demilitarization of a tension area, combined with intervention of an international police force, is more effective than the use of United Nations forces. In an ideal approach to intervention, neutralization and demilitarization require a number of simultaneous and gradual steps. First, an area has to be declared critical or near-critical by an international authority recognized by both parties. Second, the same authority resolves on demilitarization of an area and requests such a condition from the contending parties. Third, at the same time, a United Nations, or regional international, force is moved in to maintain order. This ideal arrangement suggests only a temporary, immediate action to restore order; but intervention alone does not solve the essential problems.

Application of our model would raise a number of serious questions. First, how to enforce the decision of an international authority. What happens if one of the parties refuses to accept the decision of the international authority? We move here into the vast area of international law and juridical innovations. The definition of aggressor in the Geneva Protocols—according to which a party which refuses to submit to arbitration is declared an aggressor—may be worthy of reconsideration. In such a case, international sanctions could be applied to the aggressors.[6]

Our model is, however, only a stop-gap technique. Certain tensions may require definite and radical changes. Armed action of a subject nation against a historical conqueror may call for self-determination and the establishment of a new sovereign state. Neutralization—easing of the tensions by the use of international military force—will not solve the real issues involved. The presence of international authority, however, guided by broad principles, may reduce the violence and assist in problem-solving.

Social and political emancipation, and the self-determination of nations, are legitimate objectives of ethnic and political groups in tension areas, as long as such demands are not made at the expense of other nationals. Of course the proliferation of small sovereign territories creates new problems, since they are usually unable to support themselves and must rely heavily on foreign aid. Today's economic and industrial development calls for integration and interdependence rather than independence. But here again there are a number of alternatives, and self-determination may lead to the establishment of autonomous self-governing territories integrated into broader communities or federations.

The methods of reduction of tensions in a dynamic changing world can be of course misused as techniques for maintaining the status quo. Such risks cannot be overlooked.

Therefore, the problem of reducing tension cannot be divorced from broad political and social, as well as economic, objectives. The methods of easing tensions are not of a purely scientific scholarly nature. They are anchored in goals, and goals are normative. They contain political values and objectives. In the world community of the future we may hope that agreement may be reached on a minimum set of rules or norms governing international conduct.

Stalemating and reduction of interpolitical tensions

Although tension areas vary, a general pattern for the capture of an area prevails which suggests alternatives for defense and reduction. In such a strategy, two major components should be distinguished: the military and nonmilitary.

The military attack is usually countered by similar action by the attacked. But a nonmilitary internal front works on a different level. It contains three major distinguishing elements: 1] the party and the ideological appeal, 2] the social-economic base, and 3] the organization of the population.

A political-ideological attack cannot be effectively countered by military means. A political party is a social force, and can be opposed only by another strong political party with a powerful appeal for the electorate. In our time, success in the capturing of tension areas has been due to aggressive political parties supported by a military internal arm and an external front. Unless such political force develops in the opposing political party, the defense of an area is difficult and sometimes impossible.

The major components of a party are: 1] ideology, 2] structure (organization), and 3] strategy and tactics. (See Appendix I, "Command and Consensus Structures.") Political parties of attack usually have all three elements well coordinated. Thus far, in contemporary tension areas, the party of defense equals the party of attack in those qualities only in exceptional cases (see the Venezuela case history, Chapter 16).

The second component of a nonmilitary strategy is rapid social action, transformation of the social-economic base; social-economic change.

Thus, in a general policy, we have the following circumstances: a] The defending political party opposes the aggressing party by vigorous action, b] it simultaneously embarks on a policy of social-economic reforms, and c] proceeds to secure workable and acceptable forms of organization and institutions for the population. The defense of an ideological tension area requires ideological, political, and social-economic answers. The reduction of tension is possible, if adequate social force opposes aggression. Conquest is not a reduction of tension, nor is it a modern concept of peace.

If a tension area is only one stage of a broad aggressive strategy, a successful stalemate does not resolve the basic antagonism. The aggressive government will move to another area, where less resistance is expected. A basic strategic conflict cannot be reduced "locally," since the problem is between the governments representing—in primary tensions—the superpowers. The stalemating of strategic plans of world conquest does not yet solve the basic antagonism.

We have moved a long way from eighteenth- and nineteenth-century diplomacy. Foreign policy and international relations today are not purely a matter of diplomacy, and peace is not synonymous with the absence of military actions. Maintenance of peace has become more complex and requires various types of action. The problems of ideologies, class structure, political distribution of power, and social-economic systems are now part of international relations and politics. Peace today involves continuous social, economic, and political action.

18.

LONG RANGE ORIENTATION
IN QUEST OF UNIVERSAL VALUES

Pluralism as general direction

Extreme forces of antagonisms, open violent conflicts on a global scale, cannot be fully answered by methods which might be effective for limited tensions. Mankind remains diverse in culture and political institutions. Therefore, the problem of his peaceful existence is not one of complete and terminal solution by a perfect plan of international organization, but one of general direction; of general orientation toward a reduction of violent tensions both in small areas and on a global scale. In this sense, pluralism offers a general orientation toward an international system that would reduce or eliminate violence from international relations. Differences, contradictions, even antagonism, will remain. In a sense, as long as antagonism does not assume violent forms or lead to subordination and exploitation of the weak, it can supply the element of drive for movements which foster change and progress.

Pluralism is not contradictory to federalism or other functional forms of union. Cultural pluralism, in terms of respect for differences, is complementary to federalism. The right of minorities to maintain their own culture is a condition of both federalism and democracy. Political pluralism is, of course, a weaker proposition than a federal union. It suggests a general direction rather than an institutional form; an effort toward elimination of violence prior to the achievement of greater unity, or a peaceful international arrangement of diverse systems, even in cases when close union is not desired. In a sense, pluralism is a general philosophy, an orientation, which merely suggests a sense of direction.

Federalism, integration, and union (in a general sense) are "bilateral propositions" requiring consensus or agreement of both parties. Both must surrender part of their institutions and interests in order to form a new community oriented toward a new common interest. Integration in a cultural sense means mutual assimilation, the creation of a new culture.

Let us separate the "interpolitical" from "intergroup," intercultural, relations: Federalism in a political sense requires a greater measure of "political assimilation" than initial forms of pluralism. In a cultural sense, pluralism requires certain minor changes, but by no means a basic change, in the entire culture; agreement but not fusion.

Orthodox, dogmatic groups prefer self-segregation rather than integration. They do not want to integrate in a cultural sense. Let us remember that I am discussing cultural or political issues only, not racial problems. Integration, voluntary assimilation, and pluralism require agreement, a consensus of all, or at least large sections of both groups. This is frequently impossible to achieve. Differences are too great. If mankind were reduced to one simple cultural pattern, it would probably lose its creative capacity for continuous innovation. Probably few desire to disappear in a vast standardized cultural pattern. Mankind is too complex to create, without intermediary groups and loyalties, a comfortable and secure "cultural home," a social or political family. The intermediary groups and structures are essential to support the complex cultural architecture of mankind. Here a pluralistic approach that recognizes the value and strength of differences can suggest limited forms of cooperation leading to unity and breaking the isolation, since one condition of pluralism is a minimum set of shared values among the diverse cultures.

International order and universal values

To write that, as a result of the development of communication and transportation, the world has become small, and to continue that the development of nuclear weapons has made total war obsolete—is a statement of the obvious to a point of a platitude. One hesitates to begin any discussion with such a statement. Still, these two propositions are supported by the hard facts of our times and are problems that have to be faced and answered. As obvious as it might be, large parts of our planet have become more crowded and generally much smaller than they were previously.

Somehow we have to learn to live together in this new closeness in spite of the fact that we profess different views, religions, ideologies, and values. It is also true that the devastating power of modern weapons is of such magnitude that total war would mean the destruction of large sections of the population and perhaps threaten the very existence of modern culture. The desire and the need for peace have been expressed for centuries. But in our time the elimination of war and violence in international relations has become for some nations simply a matter of survival.

I do not intend to discuss here this broad problem of the need for peace. My subject is much more limited. Cooperation in human society, especially international cooperation, is possible only under certain conditions. The will to cooperate of a single partner is not enough. Actually, a single party is not yet a partner. The conditions of cooperation require that all the partners who are part of a "plan" must have similar intentions, unless, of course, coercion is used to force one or more of the partners into a forced cooperative pattern. Frequently, as a consequence of war, conditions of this nature are created temporarily. Voluntary cooperation, however, requires in principle a sincere intention of conciliation by those participating in the plan. Not only the intention but the objectives must be shared, at least in part. Frequently economic interests, for instance, can be invoked to provide such a common objective.

The conditions of cooperation between states or governments have been discussed in Part I. One condition is a minimum set of common values, or at least a minimum set of common rules or standards of behavior. The question is: Do such common values, rules, or norms exist among the varieties of cultures and nations which inhabit this world? Can we find among the contradictory ideologies of the present time any values, any interests, which are shared?

In a *rational,* a priori approach, common interests can be clearly indicated: biological survival and economic advancement and at least the minimum satisfaction of the basic needs, such as hunger, thirst, and shelter. Simple as it may sound, these goals may not be shared equally by all. Certain ideological groups might not be interested in the biological survival of the population of other nations.

Economic advancement is not necessarily a goal shared by all cultures or nations. Even the satisfaction of basic biological needs may be questioned by some. Certain religious sects prefer asceticism to comfort. In a rational approach to the world, a sane majority of mankind would probably indicate the issues of biological survival and of hunger, thirst, or misery as those where a common interest could be identified. The development of a community of nations requires, in addition to common interests, a minimum set of shared values; otherwise cooperation is scarcely feasible.

It is true that, in the absence of such a community of values, other solutions are feasible, at least in theory. History gives some examples. Some nations, like Japan, sought protection in total isolation from other nations, especially from Western civilization. By closing its doors to trade and to visitors, as much as to warriors, Japan was able for a long time to maintain its isolation and protect itself against Western intrusion.

Various cultures provide examples of man's ingenuity in the field of inter-tribal relations, which were the early forms of international relations. Many developed special devices to control aggression. Since aggression is a part of human behavior, occurring in most societies and among individuals at certain times, dangerous contacts which may release aggression can be eliminated in some cases by rules of avoidance. For example, the Veddas of Ceylon arranged to trade with the local Tamils and Singhalese without ever coming in personal contact with them. Intertribal avoidances can also be observed among other cultures; the primitive Australians had an elaborate system of intertribal avoidances.[1]

Rules of avoidance also remind us of various projects for the neutralization of large geographical areas between hostile camps; between countries which cannot maintain friendly relations and where hostilities are a continuous danger. Large belts of land have been emptied or high walls have been constructed. However, only certain forms of isolation are tantamount to the principle of avoidance, since the function of the latter is the avoidance of aggression and conflict. It is questionable, however, whether isolation is the best choice for mankind in a time when the exchange of ideas, experiences, and discoveries is of paramount significance; and whether it is at all feasible in a world based on interdependence.

The problem can now be narrowed to the question of whether any set of minimum shared universal values can be identified as common to all mankind. Rules, regulations, and customs are complex phenomena. The problem is whether interests and values can be indicated which would prompt men to live together free from the continual threat of extermination or of war.

The desire for peace has frequently led men to wishful thinking. Theories have been advanced to prove the existence of a desire for peace in antagonistic political philosophies. Well-meaning partisans of peace policies frequently act as if every political leader and every head of a government desired nothing more than peace. To achieve this peace, they argue, one need only make certain concessions and compromises, and even a war lord will agree to terms.

However, not all governments and not all nations really desire peace. This is the problem. History tells us about many leaders whose main goal was war and conquest and who could not be won and had no desire to be won to the side of peace. Even in our time government leaders do not always desire peace. The same is true of many ideologies based on the concept of conquest. Our concern at this point, however, is with the various cultures in an anthropological and sociological sense, since this is not solely a problem of ideologies. The problem is whether national characters (as we once called them) or ethnic values (as we say today) are really so distinct that there are no links common to all of humanity.

Three schools

The problem of universal human values is by no means new. It has been debated since antiquity. The approach has varied in different historical periods and with each school of thought. Those who represented the philosophical or theological outlook usually had a different approach from others who studied values by empirical methods. Roughly, however, three schools of thought can be distinguished. We shall call them, arbitrarily: a) the relativist; b) the absolutist; and c) the universalist.

The extreme relativist can see no universal values common to all humanity in the empirical sense, i.e., values that can be observed here and now. Values are relative, they say, and are linked with the totality of the culture (in the anthropological sense of the word) and of its social conditions. Anthropological observations show that various societies show major differences in their value systems.

In America or Britain today, productivity, profit, and punctuality are values which are considerably appreciated. But among American Plains Indians, such as the Shoshones or the Arapahos, none of these values plays an appreciable role. The Arapaho Indian is not interested in the high efficiency and high productivity or profitability of his work. Time is not money to him, and his punctuality is far from that of an American worker. Again, in the primitive stage of the Eskimo tribes, when starvation threatened, tribal members abandoned their own parents. Darwin also tells in his memoirs how the starving inhabitants of Tierra del Fuego smothered their aged members in the smoke of their fires and used the bodies to still their hunger. Did these people have any values in common with their contemporary, Charles Darwin? In rebuttal, the relativists emphasize that cultural differences and hence value differences are substantial. They say that we must judge the actions of men within the context of the society in which they act and of the social conditions that mold them. Therefore, we cannot judge the people of Tierra del Fuego, or the Eskimos, or the Arapahos by our own values, because our values—and the conditions of our life—differ from theirs.

A distinction must be made, however, between cultural and ethical relativism. On the basis of his observations and the facts at his disposal, a sociologist or an anthropologist may argue that values are relative in a variety of cultures, and that the differences are essential to prove that no common values, with the exception of, perhaps, a common attitude toward incest, can be identified in various cultures. This does not mean that the same sociologist or anthropologist who suggests such findings is professing his own ethical relativism. His personal philosophy may be, and usually is, different, since his findings do not necessarily lead him to a personal ethical relativism. A statement of cultural relativism is based on an evaluation of findings; ethical relativism is an attitude toward life.

Contrary to the relativists, the absolutists begin with the assumption that the dominant values are the same for all mankind and all cultures, and that they exist independent of time and place. They are—in a word—eternal. Thus, justice, charity, love of neighbor, and honesty are values with an identical content; or, rather, they impose an identical sanction on all men at all times. Murder is evil under all geographical latitudes, and the deeds of Nero were as evil as those of Hitler or Himmler. Matricide is evil—on Tierra del Fuego as much as in Europe—for absolutes have an objective, not a subjective, existence. The farthest we can go in such a judgment is to call the actions of primitive men errors.

Absolute values are the foundation of certain religious moral systems. They are clearly marked in Judeo-Christian ethics, and are fundamental in Catholic philosophy. But this view is by no means confined to Catholicism and Judeo-Christian ethics. It was well represented in Greek philosophy.

"Ethical absolutism" is thus both a philosophical and a religious-philosophical premise pointing to the existence of a higher moral order bestowed upon man and, in a sense, independent of him. The eighteenth-century philosophy of natural law underlines in secular form the absolute nature of such values as personal freedom. As Otto Gierke has indicated, the founders of the philosophy of natural law were concerned with the basic problem of the relation of the individual to the community, and of the ruler to the people. Certain rules or values determining this relationship were regarded as immutable. The concept that certain values, or elements of a moral order, are immutable or eternal was expressed in a variety of ways by a variety of authors and writers.

Man is often unconscious of the fact that certain values reflect interests and social position. Nevertheless, he has been willing to surrender his vital interests, even his life, for values that he considered to be of a higher order. The belief in a general moral order which is absolute, immutable, a belief having a strong tradition in ethics and in the development of certain philosophical schools, later became part of an individual or group outlook not necessarily identified with a specific school.

The difference between the absolutist and the relativist viewpoints is one of outlook, method, and values. We may call the outlook a general idea system (*Weltanschauung*); a closely related and integrated pattern of thought. Within this pattern, methods of analysis and values are again closely related. In a sense, the absolutist viewpoint represents a philosophical outlook; the relativist, an empirical and sociological one. The absolutist viewpoint tries to identify what "ought to be" and what "is" in a philosophical, rather than in an inductive, sense. The relativist viewpoint limits its findings to the question of what "is," what can be observed, and what can be inferred and generalized on the basis of observed and verified facts.

However, there are limits of observation. There are limits to the understanding of the value problems solely on the basis of observation and collection of data. The initial outlook therefore determines the choice of method. Thus, a person's choice may be determined by his own values, and by his philosophical, ethical outlook and his position in a given class or social structure, as well as by his personality. What is relevant for us is that two different value structures will result in different interpretations of the same body of facts, and the interpretation selected may further influence or reinforce the outlook and the decision.

Considering Adolf Hitler's actions from a very rough approximation of the two attitudes detailed above, we can see how an interpretation of his deeds might reflect the difference in outlook and also present a different social image. An extreme—I repeat—an extreme relativist might explain that Hitler's deed is contained in his system of values. Therefore, from the point of view of his and his society's values, it is not immoral, any more than cannibalism was immoral for some natives of New Guinea or, until recently, for the Tiv tribe of Nigeria. In the value system of Hitler and the German Nazis, the exploitation of weak nations by the militarily strong is a virtue, and this subjugation, a national duty. These values are the very opposite of our ethics.

For a person who believes in absolute or universal moral values, Hitler's system of values is the equivalent of insane morality. But the relativist, or at least the extreme relativist, may say, "We cannot judge Hitler or the New Guinea cannibals according to our values." The absolutist, on the other hand, will judge the deeds of Hitler and the Nazis as being contrary to morality, i.e., to values whose nature is unchangeable. He may very well use the additional argument that, while the New Guinea cannibal may well be unaware of the evil nature of his deed, Hitler and his adherents were fully aware of the nature of the crimes which they committed, despite all relativist arguments.

Let us now turn to the third school which I have called, arbitrarily, the universalist. Like the absolutists, this school holds that certain values and institutions can be observed in all societies. What, then, is the difference between the two schools?

The school of absolute values is founded on a belief in, or theory of, a higher moral order. It has a religious or philosophical view. The school of universal values, on the other hand, is based on facts alone, i.e., observation. The universalists say, "We can observe the presence of certain values in all human societies," without drawing any conclusions as to the existence of a higher moral order, independent of man, time, and place.

In the sociological sense, neither values nor more complex idea systems can be studied as abstract, detached, independent concepts or blocs. They are connected with certain behavior, and above all with particular institutions. In consequence, the sociological or anthropological study is made in a social context, in relation to the social-economic conditions within which they operate.

Values or institutions correspond to certain needs on which their existence, continuity, and development depend. Such needs are not solely economic; they may correspond to the psychological or even ethical needs of an individual or of a group. Both values and needs are interdependent phenomena. Once values are internalized by individuals they affect his perception. His position within the social, political, and economic structure influences his choice of values. But, however powerful the social-economic position of an individual is in the formation of his judgment, it is not the only variable that influences his outlook.

Individual values frequently differ from group values. The psychological needs of an individual and even his moral sensitivity might differ substantially from the general outlook of the group. The sociologist or anthropologist tries to explore the relationship between the entire fabric of a society and its values as well as its institutions. In an absolute approach, values are norms, ideas. Since they exist per se, they have to be observed in every circumstance. Values set the direction of man's activities and regulate his action, irrespective of time and space.

My terms of relativistic and universalistic approach were chosen arbitrarily. An extreme relativist viewpoint is probably limited to a very small group of students of human society. Anthropologists have observed the great differences between human societies which do indeed exist. Simultaneously, however, they have observed certain similarities or universal traits, indicative of the unity of mankind. While the relativist has emphasized the differences, the universalist has placed his emphasis on those elements of society common to mankind. This search for universals can be found among the early classic sociologists and social theoreticians, and is both speculative and empirical in nature. Early representatives of utilitarian schools sought to explain universal values by biological determinism or, we may say, by biological utility.

Herbert Spencer explained the existence of universal value in a rational manner, with some utilitarian orientation. Altruism forms the center of Spencer's ethical system, but the altruism, or mutual aid, in Spencer's approach is not an idea independent of time and space with an existence of its own. To him, altruism is conduct that is determined by human and social needs.

Self-preservation is essential for every society, and "in each generation has all along depended on the preservation of offspring by preceding generations," wrote Spencer. The growth of the society makes the self-preservation of individuals dependent on the entire society. He argues further that if altruism means action by which others benefit instead of oneself, modern altruism is as essential as egoism and can be traced to the very beginning of human society. Through acts of altruism, offspring were preserved, species were maintained, and the continuity of society was established. Spencer speaks of "automatic altruism" which is not accomplished on a conscious level,[2] and in his view, altruism is a universal phenomenon of ethos.

The search for universal positive (in the ethical sense) conduct appears early in Russian social theory. In the middle of the nineteenth century, nihilist theoreticians such as D. I. Pisarev suggested that cooperation and mutual aid were essential for the very existence of society. The same theme continues in the populist political and social theory of the nineteenth century, and was emphasized by anarchist theoreticians such as Peter Kropotkin.[3] Kropotkin said that mutual aid exists in all societies, even animal societies, and argued against Huxley's interpretation of Darwin's theory: that struggle and conflict are the essential factors of survival. On the contrary, self-preservation in nature is possible through mutual aid rather than through conflict. Kropotkin supports his hypotheses by observations of animal life made during his stay in Siberia, stressing in particular the fact that migratory birds assist their weaker fellows, defending them against both natural hazards and birds of prey. Without this mutual aid, argues Kropotkin, many species might have perished.

Although Spencer, Kropotkin, Marx, and Karl Mannheim may differ substantially in the interpretation of the nature of ideologies or values, they apply a similar approach. They study values, institutions, or human relations within the context of a society in an attempt to answer the questions: "To what needs do they correspond? What functions do they perform?"

Toward the end of his life Kropotkin wrote his *Ethics,* in which he outlined in detail his thesis on the nature of morality and its universal character.[4] In this book he accepts certain of Darwin's theses, chiefly, the evolution of morality from lower to higher forms.[5] He sees a development of ethical values to even higher forms. He also finds the beginnings of morality among animals, observing among them the awakening of a social instinct.

Kropotkin's view becomes more normative than empirical as he continues his analysis of ethics. Furthermore, he follows the evolutionary theory, accepting certain ethical forms as higher; others as lower. In this respect we may find a position similar to Spencer's considerations of ethics. As society develops, Kropotkin argues, the ethical form becomes a "higher form."

A relativist viewpoint avoids an evaluation of social phenomena in terms of higher and lower, better and worse. An evolutionary approach recognizes higher and lower stages of development. A nonevolutionary approach to society, made from a purely analytical empirical view, may recognize the difference. At this point we can only indicate that the study of human norms and conduct, in addition to empirical studies, requires a long-range view that eventually involves an evolutionary outlook. Without this view of development and change of conduct; without historical perspective and comparison, it is scarcely possible to identify universal elements.

In his final work, Kropotkin undoubtedly comes closer to an absolutist view. His editor, Lebedev, notes that Kropotkin did not recognize distinct "bourgeois" or "proletarian" ethics. He had one system of ethics for everybody, because for him mankind was one. In other words, he felt that fundamental values, like mutual aid, are universal. Kropotkin was far from being a utilitarian. He saw the weakness of the Communist revolution in its lack of a fundamental moral direction; in the ethical breakdown of Communism.

The universality of certain institutions and of conduct has always been stressed, especially by modern functional anthropologists, whose findings are a result of field studies and observation. We may mention Bronislaw Malinowski as representative of this school. In his analysis, cooperation is essential to every society. Basing his views on field studies of primitive societies in such varied areas as the South Sea Islands, Africa, and Central America, Malinowski emphasized the significance of cooperation as the very nature of human society.[6] A similar mutuality of relations has been stressed by functionalists as common universal conduct which is observable in human societies.

For a functionalist, mutual aid, cooperation, or the general principle of mutuality performs a definite function within society. Without one or more of them, society cannot exist. Since cooperation is essential for the existence of any society, institutions and values connected with coordinated or cooperative effort perform a definite social function. The functionalist school in anthropology is strongly oriented toward the study of institutions rather than to norms or standards of behavior. In such an approach institutions correspond to definite needs. Nevertheless, values are also rooted in institutions. The study of values as a basic concept and a frame of reference in anthropological research has arisen in recent years. An attempt is now being made to combine a theoretical approach with empirical studies in order to identify basic value orientations.[7]

It was proposed at the beginning of this discussion that cooperation between nations of different cultures requires a minimum set of common values and rules as well as common interests and goals. From such a proposition the relevant issue emerges as the empirical identification of shared or similar values and the pragmatic issue of the development, the "construction and grafting on society" of shared norms which would permit the cooperation of different groups. I shall not discuss at this point the problem of what "ought to be," what type of values mankind should have, or whether the values are absolute or not. This is a philosophical problem and, relevant as it is to our study, it is not at this moment the proposition under discussion.

As a consequence of the original thesis, there are two questions which we cannot yet answer but which should be discussed: first, whether in an empirical way, through observation, we can discover such norms or types of conduct as are universal to all societies. Secondly, whether as a result of social developments, social change, interests, and needs appear which in turn are reflected in those norms which favor wider cooperation. The second question also suggests another proposition: Men may develop norms and minimum sets of values which, related to existing social, economic, and political conditions and needs, may foster the development of limited cooperation directed to the easing or reducing of tensions that involve the use of force or the more general threat of war and destruction. The development of such norms in a long-range effort could form part of a general strategy for the maintenance of international relations in which conflicts and antagonism could be resolved without resort to violence.

Differences of values and universals

Values form part of a culture. They do not comprise a separate block, but are an "interacting" segment of the entire fabric of society. Values are closely related to both actions and institutions.

Spencer defined the purposeful action of man as conduct. By conduct he understood those actions that were related to specific goals. Values are also goals motivating human actions. Man's purposeful actions are directed toward goal achievement. On the other hand, institutions such as the state, the family, or a college are built around specific goals and functions. The goals of the institution are also values, and the institution can function only if certain minimum sets of values are shared and correspond to certain needs or interests, or if certain conduct is forced or imposed by coercion. The college can function best when the value of education is shared by the faculty, the administration, and the students. A corporation functions properly when an efficiency and profit orientation forms the goal orientation of its employees, or at least of those who exercise a crucial influence. Values have to be studied in their social context, not as separate and independent entities.

Mankind represents a multitude of cultures that vary from tribe to tribe. Differences in cultures and institutions, even in thought patterns, are frequently substantial. Some differences are so strong that it is difficult for one group to convey an idea or concept to another speaking a different language. The semanticist is concerned with this aspect of human culture and with the problems inherent in the communication of ideas. Such difficulties are due not only to differences in language sounds or symbols, but also to the fact that in different cultures the same symbol may represent a different concept. In addition, certain concepts actually may not exist in some cultures.

Cultural differences do exist. The question is whether we can identify any universal elements common to mankind. Perhaps in proceeding from problems that are simpler than the complex issue of values, we may find a way to identify needs similar to all mankind; needs which can be found in all the various and different nations that inhabit this globe.

It has long been known that certain needs and cultural elements in mankind are universal. Without this universality, without certain basic similarities, a comparative study of human societies would not be possible. These similarities were established first by historians, later by philosophers, and finally by such modern social sciences as social anthropology and sociology.

On the other hand, man is different and societies are different. This difference in cultures (group differences) as well as in individuals (personality differences) has been generally accepted by the students of man for as long a period as has the theory of basic similarities. In consequence, the general proposition of the universality and diversity of culture and needs is widely accepted today. Some anthropologists stress the differences, others the unity, of mankind. Nevertheless, both can be identified. As we shall see later, such a proposition is not necessarily contradictory to the relativist point of view.

We may start with the basic biological needs and corresponding drives such as hunger, thirst, and the sexual drive. These are common to all mankind and form the biological determinants of man's existence and society. All human individuals are born with these drives, which have to be satisfied one way or another. The satisfaction of human needs, however, depends on the ability of men to associate.

The existence of the group is a condition of man's survival, since such basic needs as the satisfaction of hunger or thirst or the building of shelter require some coordinated effort. The continuation and preservation of the species also depends upon the existence of an organized human group which can shelter, feed, and protect the child for the initial period of its development. The social group, in this case the family, is also the main agency in the process of learning, by educating the child in the pattern of communal living and in ways of coping with the physical environment. Thus, all individuals, wherever they are born, have similar biological drives. Wherever we find man on this globe, we find him living in groups and establishing institutions such as the family or rudimentary organizations such as groups, clans, and tribes.

Biological differences between male and female determine the division of functions and labor. The mother takes care of the infant's nursing and education, and the survival of the child in the initial period depends largely on her. The father provides for the necessities of life. A division of labor appears in other fields as well, and in most early societies it can readily be observed. In a hunting tribe, the man provided the meat and the woman gathered the fruit and vegetables. Such divisions of labor and of function are interdependent and result in patterns of cooperation. Thus, in addition to the universality of drives, institutions, and functions, we may now identify the universality of certain patterns of action and social relations. Here, for example, belongs cooperation, which could be observed in most primitive societies. The universalist school and the functional school in anthropology have gathered strong support of empirical data in this area. In order to cope with his environment, man has to explain its working to his own satisfaction, since the conditions of survival require a certain elementary understanding and explanation of nature. Certain phenomena are explained in an empirical or pragmatic way, even in a primitive society; others are explained by religious idea systems and, later, by science. As a result, in all societies men have some explanation of the universe; some concepts by which they relate facts and explain their sequence. Finally, man in coping with his environment acts in a certain way, and he has to evaluate his conduct as effective or noneffective. He has to evaluate further the actions of his group to determine whether or not they agree with the rules and taboos of his religion or ideologies. In consequence, we shall find in all societies certain norms related to man's institutions, idea systems, and actions.

Thus, the universals, both biological and social, found in all societies, are: (1) drives and the ways of their satisfaction; (2) social groups and institutions; (3) the division of labor; (4) patterns of action, such as cooperation; (5) general idea systems such as religion, science, political ideologies, and others; (6) evaluation of conduct and behavior, i.e., standards and norms; and (7) established patterns of behavior (customs, mores, folkways).

Should we finish our discussion of similarities at this point, the reader might rightly suspect that we have selected only such phenomena as validate an assumption of universal values, while omitting contradictory elements. This, it seems to me, was an error made by some proponents of the theory of cooperation who underestimated the role of the conflict in early societies. (I am referring here to intergroup conflict.)

It is the intergroup conflict which also determines the structure of the institution and contributes to the dichotomy between group norms at an early period: different norms for the out-group and the in-group. The solidarity which is mandatory for behavior within the group may not be binding at all outside the group. The murder of an enemy is regarded as an act of heroism, while the murder of a group member is regarded as a crime. In consequence, the dichotomy of norms is an early phenomenon. In primitive groups, conflict is not solely economic. War and struggle by themselves also represent a certain way of life. However, it is beyond the scope of our study to argue this issue now.[8]

The simple inference could be made that since so many elements are similar to all men, there must be a place for universality of values and interests. However, an empirical approach requires specific data, although we may find later that a purely empirical approach may not yield the answers for which we are looking. But for now, let us pursue the empirical road. We know that even in the satisfaction of biological needs, the means by which men achieve their goal (the satisfaction of thirst or hunger) differ from culture to culture. Taste is a value, yet even in Europe today we can recognize a vast diversity of taste, conditioned to some extent by differences in geographical environments and in standards of living.

In a consideration of the institution we may also find a variety of family structures. Here the facts are as widely recognized as in the previous study of values, and need no further explanation. Kinship structures, family forms, the transmission of inheritance and power, differ in different cultures. Similarly, the form of government varies substantially. While we can observe a consensus organization in one area, based on mutual aid, cooperation, and common values, in another we shall find a "command structure," based on absolute power. Thus, differences in values, as indicated in this discussion, arise from:

1]

Differences in the cultures of various social groups, such as tribes, nations, and political parties (group differences);

2]

Inner contradictions between norms governing attitudes and conduct toward the in- and out-groups;

3]

Differences between individual and group values within the same group.

Society imposes certain norms and goals on the entire group. Such goals might be contradictory to the individual goals or to norms. However, group differences and individual differences exist within every culture. This discrepancy between the individual and the whole appears as early as Greek societies and, as Ernest Barker rightly indicates, forms a theme of Greek political science.[9]

We have listed similarities and differences. No doubt there are profound differences between cultures, and the difference of values (as ends) as well as of means (instrumental and consumatory value) is substantial enough to support relativist views. On the other hand, in all cultures a certain community of goals and of elementary concepts can be identified. Some utilitarians like Spencer argue that the value system (ethics) develops in all cultures as a result of the pain and pleasure mechanism. Furthermore, he indicates that the continuation and preservation of the species imposes an elementary altruism on man, since the child who is helpless must be assisted, protected, and fed. In Spencer's system the goal structure is determined by the group interest, and "good" and "bad" are related to the attainment of group goals; to the efficiency of the system.

Evolution of social values and institutions

The problem of international relations goes beyond in-group cooperation. The question is how to extend, or better, how to translate cooperation and mutual aid, which have developed historically as in-group conduct, into out-group behavior and norms.

Man's search for values—for a common moral language, for common rules which will unite a divided humanity and permit men to settle their differences and live as neighbors in spite of cultural differences—has gone on for a time. But we need go back only as far as the Renaissance for an understanding of its many facets.

Giovanni Pico della Mirandola was an advocate of the synthesis of human values. This is perhaps what makes him a "representative" man and thinker of Renaissance humanism. By December, 1486, he had published no fewer than 900 theses on the subject. He summoned philosophers to a great "disputation" on his theses in January, 1487. It never took place because Pope Innocent VIII prevented it. But ideas cannot be put in chains, and Pico's concepts have remained influential.

The theses are prefaced by an "oration" which contains the essential tenets of humanism. Called an "Oration on Human Dignity," its aim is to find values common to all humanity. Pico opens his oration with quotations from the Arab scholars Abdalah, Averroes, and Avicenna; from the Greek philosophers Pythagoras, Plato, and Aristotle; from the Christian theologians St. Thomas Aquinas and Roger Bacon; and finally, from Jewish religious prophets and thinkers. The purpose of this introduction is a search for harmony between all these thinkers. It emphasizes the views and doctrines that link the great religions and philosophies; the ideas that are essential, not those that divide.[10]

Pico's arguments correspond to the spirit and philosophical climate of his time. They are theological, philosophical, and metaphysical. We will not find facts or conclusions based on observation of contemporary societies in the "Oration." Pico looked for proofs of his theses in the writings of prophets, saints, philosophers, and thinkers. But his purpose is clear: to search for what humanity has in common; for universal human values. He finds them in human dignity and in the unity and universality of truth. It was in the fifteenth century—a century of religious struggles and wars—that this independent thinker put forward a revolutionary thesis: that the basic values of men do not differ; that they are universal. There is in them more harmony than variation. Pico also suggested that, despite the many religious wars, the religions of his world advocated charity and human dignity, i.e., basic and universal values.

Mirandola's lecture is the expression of a trend of far deeper significance, traceable to ancient Greece and Judea, where values and concepts of primary significance slowly developed. Out of the dialogue between the individual and the society; out of the contradictions which emerged between the goals of the individual and the community and between those of the individual and state, emerged the ideal: respect for the dignity and privacy of man. It is beyond our scope now to discuss whether this concept can be identified in other cultures, religions, and/or idea systems. The fact remains that it has developed and is closely related to the development of science and the scientific mentality.

The history of scientific development parallels the history of the struggle for freedom of thought, independence of the human mind, and freedom of ways and methods in the search for truth. Science does not develop in intellectual captivity. The worldwide diffusion of scientific method and of the scientific approach to problems of life was and is accompanied by the diffusion of the ideal goal of the dignity of every man, irrespective of race, religion, or nationality; the ideal of human rights. Whether these values can be found in other cultures is beside the point at the moment. What is relevant for us is the fact that shared values can also be developed and diffused, and that this sharing goes far beyond the point of a mere identification of the existing values in a variety of civilizations.

There is an old debate about whether values of this type are inherent in man or whether they are merely a result of definite social-economic conditions and needs. At present I shall confine the discussion of this matter to a footnote.[11] Some values are discovered in moments of profound crisis, not by everyone, but by certain individuals. It is an inner discovery of introspection that is not a subject of empirical studies and would be difficult to identify by purely inductive means. Nevertheless, such experiences form a link between the concepts of individual dignity and sympathy for the weaker and present experience. Perhaps this type of reaction, at least in part, is a result of the early learning processes.

The persecutions and exterminations of World War II provided deep experiences that divided men into classes which were not social but moral. In such moments of crisis, some men show what is called a "strong" character; others, a "weak" one. Similarly, some nations are forced into submission more easily than others. There are differences between individuals and groups. A psychologist, a sociologist, or an anthropologist may attempt to explain the differences in terms of personality structure, of inborn and environmental factors.

The inborn factor is perhaps the simple physical strength of the nervous system. The environmental factors are, of course, the process of learning; and values, they will argue, are a result of this learning. The family structure and the position of the father may affect the development of attitudes toward authority, they may argue. The values of the peer group and of the family may influence the value judgment of the person who offers resistance. A number of other variables could also be indicated as being relevant in influencing attitudes and judgment in such a situation. While all this may be granted, it would seem that there is still an unknown spontaneous intuitive element that must have been present at the initial developmental stage of broad humanitarian ethics. These ethics do not arise from nothing. They could not come solely out of utilitarian judgments or a subconscious tendency toward group preservation.

The search for universal values may, however, require a more tangible approach. The first hypothesis suggests that some values, such as early forms of mutual aid, cooperation, or altruism—or, to put it better, certain types of conduct connected with mutual aid, cooperation, and altruism—may appear on all levels of human society. As another hypothesis it might be suggested that certain universals in the evaluation of man's conduct, from the point of view of an ideal norm, appear only at a certain level in the development of human society. At this point of development, a person or a group acting against the minimum of universal principles is cognizant of the existence of such norms. (Although Adolf Hitler was not motivated by norms of this type, he was aware of their existence.)

Such a proposition, however, has a normative orientation; it contains a judgment guided by the norms of "right" and "wrong" and not solely by an inductive or scientific approach, either valid or nonvalid. It also presupposes an evolutionary, historical, and comparative approach. Since it is argued that universality appears on a certain level, then societies on what might be called "lower levels of development" may not yet indicate the presence of those universal values. Social scientists have argued since the nineteenth century that society grows from a simpler to a more complex form, from smaller to larger groups. In such an approach the norms that integrate a society, at least those shared at the beginning by smaller groups, are shared by larger groups in higher forms of development. We cannot fail to observe the growth of more complex societies and a general tendency toward larger and more complex social organization in recorded history. Large social organizations based on consensus, on voluntary and spontaneous cooperation and action, have at least a few shared values, customs, or rules which are accepted voluntarily by the group.

Our objective here, however, is more definite. We are seeking to identify the minimum set of conditions necessary for limited cooperation between the nations of the world, or for the establishment of conditions that could eliminate or at least reduce the use of force between nations. For such an objective, not all interests and shared values are relevant. However, certain values, like mutual aid, are.

It would seem that elementary ethical conduct requires that the strong assist the weak. Material aid for the weak and their protection against predatory conduct by stronger units are elementary forms of ethical conduct. In a sense, mutual assistance is also the consequence of a relationship between the weak and the strong. It is not argued that this type of relationship appears in an elaborated form in all societies. However, it is suggested that it may be present in its primary form. As a society evolves from the local group to the tribe, mutual aid might be extended to the members of the tribe and later to the members of nations.

In our time, violent forms of international conflict have appeared, notably, a ruthless struggle against and extermination of the enemy, or what was called the enemy, as exemplified by the Nazi conquest of Europe, in which mass extermination and brutalities marked the progress of German armies. There is a tendency toward an identification of our historical epoch with this reappearance and reinforcement of mass cruelty. But at the same time, we must remember that the victors, after having defeated the oppressive nations, did not exterminate them but instead assisted in their economic and political development. It might be argued that that was done for the self-interest of the victors. This may be true to an extent, but the fact remains that such assistance was given. Furthermore, a policy of helping economically weaker and less developed nations, initiated by the Western democracies, and especially by the United States "Point Four" program, became the generally accepted policy in strong contrast to former policies of subjugation and exploitation which followed the principle of the survival of the fittest; "the way nature works."

Again it may be argued that this was done in the interest of the stronger party, which supported the weaker only to maintain peace or control or block an invasion by a competitive power. Let us assume that it is entirely true. Nevertheless, the fact remains that in our historical period mutual assistance, encompassing the assistance of a weaker state by a stronger one, in its economic as well as its social development, appeared as a general policy. In addition, in times of famine and disease, some nations less affected or untouched by the calamity not only do not refuse assistance to their enemies but materially aid the afflicted. Again such conduct might be determined by economic or political exigencies. Nonetheless the fact remains that in our time the assistance of a weaker nation by a stronger has become a matter of prudent policy.

This type of policy results in the development of certain ideal norms of conduct might be determined by economic or political exigencies. Nonetheless, the one of national interest narrowly conceived. But next to the latter the new norms begin to emerge and appear as ideal propositions. The basic concept of humanity—respect for an individual and his rights—is a late phenomenon in the development of a civilization in which slavery has played such a prominent role.

Not all nations have developed a strong humanistic culture geared to the individual rather than to the collective. The concept of human dignity, however, has been accepted by the United Nations Declaration of Human Rights. Of course this declaration has no immediate practical significance, and power politics still plays the dominant role in the United Nations Assembly. Nonetheless, representatives of most of mankind are required to reaffirm certain principles as ideal norms of the future. We are still far from any universal acceptance of such norms but, in spite of pessimists, it is worth indicating that there is the possibility of at least establishing certain limited or universally accepted norms in international conduct.

The history of mankind is marked by dialectics and contradictions; by wars aimed at conquering and exploiting the weak, subjugating the free, and turning men into slaves. But in the history of civilization appears also the struggle against the rule of the might, against exploitation which, as history went on, took the forms of struggles for the abolition of slavery, of serfdom, of feudal and industrial exploitation, and of war.

Ethics of international relations

The principle of defending the weak against the might of the strong is equivalent to the economic aid of the weak by the strong. This is the essence of mutual aid. Let us now look at this principle in its application to politics. In international politics it means the right of small and militarily or economically weak nations to a free and independent existence. In national politics, it means the right of political or religious dissenters to gather, and also the right of the individual to retain his personal freedom and independence. All this, of course, is based on the condition that these nations, groups, or individuals do not aim at subjugating or limiting the freedom of others.

The ethics of international politics is thus founded on a defense of the rights of small and weak nations against conquest and exploitation by strong nations, and on the defense of the rights of minorities against oppression by majorities. In this way, the principle of aid to the weak is linked with the principles of personal freedom and individual rights as the measure of our values. This principle does not create for a minority a license for freedom of action without limitations and without responsibility.

Small nations, sections of minorities, or even single individuals may use irresponsible violence, instigate to race hatreds and hostility, or attack the innocent and the infirm. The fact that a nation is small and weak does not necessarily make it better or more moral. As we have seen, the conditions of minorities in the weak, newly "emerging nations" are by no means better or safer than in powerful and "older" states.

Change of value systems

Resuming our previous discussion on the problem of change, the development of new values, we may ask: How do values develop? How do they change? Can we perhaps evolve new values which will have more universality than previous ones? Perhaps social, economic and political conditions do move in such a direction that the growth of a minimum set of shared values or rules of behavior in international relations becomes imperative for the very survival of mankind.

Values are linked with the totality of political, economic, and social conditions; ideological heritage and psychological needs. We will call this totality of conditions a "situation." Values are also anchored in institutions and in social groups such as churches and political parties with values of their own.

Changes in situations may produce shifts in value systems. We call such changes "transvaluations" or adaptations to changed situations. Revolutionary changes in economic and political conditions may bring about changes in value systems; on the other hand, changes in value systems may cause changes in economic, political or social conditions. The first Industrial Revolution of the eighteenth and early nineteenth centuries produced changes in value systems. But the development of capitalism, linked with the Industrial Revolution, would not have been possible without the preceding deep changes in values, thought, ways, and institutions. The Industrial Revolution was also preceded by changes in emphasis in scientific thinking.

The development of new attitudes toward the environment; attempts to use scientific methods to understand and cope with this environment; perhaps even the growth of utilitarian philosophy, were some of the changes in idea systems essential to produce the Industrial Revolution. The well-known theses of Weber suggest that transvaluation, changes in the ethos, especially the Protestant ethos, were instrumental in the development of a new capitalistic economy.

Two variables, the situation (S) and the value system (V), are mutually interdependent. Changes in the situation may affect the values; and changes in the value structure may affect the situation. Where the original causes are, what affects the change in value systems or changes in situation are beyond our interest in this discussion.

The relationship between the values and the situation can be represented by the following diagram:

MODEL XVIII
Value—Situation Relationship

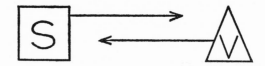

We may call such mutual interdependence a functional relationship. This relationship can be described as interaction. It might be proposed that it can be anticipated, that changes in the situation may affect the value structure or the general idea system in a variety of ways; on the other hand, changes in the value system, in the ideology, may produce a social change and thus change the situation. S acts upon V; in turn, V acts upon S. In a sense this is a causal-reciprocal relationship: in one case, the situation creates the conditions of change; in the other case, values develop such conditions. But the real interaction between the two variables is complex and frequently almost simultaneous, so that it is difficult to isolate the causal variable of the single element producing the change. What we really have is a mutual and simultaneous causal relationship. Without going any further into the question of causality, let us suggest three questions.

Assuming that a situation changes, in what direction do the values change?

When a situation changes, man is forced to respond to a new condition. We may argue that human behavior, norms, and actions will change in the direction imposed by geographic, economic, political, or social changes. However, man may respond to the same change, to the same condition, in a variety of ways. A given change may result in a variety of reflections and suggest a number of choices or alternatives as solutions.

The change in international conditions, in world economy, technology, and the development of weapons, results also in different types of reflections, different proposals for solution, and a different evaluation of the same situation. After all, the perception of two observers of the same international situation may differ, since social position, values, and ideology influence perception. The same international situation may also offer more than one alternative solution.

It has already been indicated that changes in the social, economic, and—we may add—psychological base may affect values in a variety of ways. On the other hand, the values may be so strong that they will not yield, they will not change, in spite of changes in economic conditions. There have been instances in man's history when he preferred death to survival. His values, other than those of survival, were stronger than his desire to live. There were cases when man refused to adjust his way of life to new political, economic, or social conditions; to new ideologies or new religions. After all, Buddhists, Christians, Jews, have sacrificed their lives rather than accept a different religion or a system of government that would threaten their way of life.

Are we certain that a change in technology, in general conditions in a world situation, will reinforce universal values? In the 1930's, various nations and social and ideological groups responded to the tense international situation in a variety of ways. The Nazis responded in an anti-universalistic outbreak, while partisans of democratic ideologies—certain Protestant and Catholic groups, and social-democrats with a stronger tendency toward the easing of international tensions—supported the League of Nations and collective security.

In a given nation, various individuals, groups, and political orientations, and even whole classes, respond in different ways to the same situation, because their values and idea systems are affected in different ways. Therefore, can we identitfy at least a general tendency toward the development of certain values?

Universal values, like mutual aid and the defense of weaker members of the society or family, are subject to continuous transvaluation through adaptation to a changed situation. But their essence, their basic nature, remains. As society develops, there is a tendency to extend universal values to broader groups. With the coming of universalist religions, these values are extended to all of mankind, or even to all forms of life.

Such tendencies are social and ideological. Their appearance does not necessarily mean that the values they hold are put into practice. For, simultaneously, other and opposite tendencies appear—toward domination, conquest, and exploitation. But the consciousness that higher values exist and *can* be put into practice is important. It acts as a social compass—Georges Sorel would have said "social myth"—that gives a sense of direction to certain social movements.

In today's great market of ideas, what kind of values or idea systems will have the stronger chance: narrow nationalistic particular ideas or broader ones? Historical experience teaches us, Adolf Berle argues, that universalist ideas, those appealing to social classes and nations with a humane and universal appeal, usually win over more narrow idea systems where the appeal is limited to a privileged few or to a particular nation or a selected group. In this theory of the selection of political forces, Berle argues that the universalist tendency and the universalist ideology in the long run have a tendency to win over the less humane and less universalist.[12]

Berle's thesis is optimistic. History teaches, however, that there is usually more than one universalistic tendency, and that frequently competition among them produces sanguinary wars. The religious wars, the Crusades, the Protestant revolutions, are indicative of the fact that universalistic tendencies and ideas, being close to each other in content, may result in strongly antagonistic social movements. Small ideological deviation, disagreement in the interpretation of principles or dogmas, often leads to violent opposition. An idea system, even one that is universalist, has elements of contradiction that may result in extreme forms of conflict. Here, of course, Berle may argue that there is a point in history where universalist and humane elements will probably succeed.

We may now move to the next proposition: to the question of whether the present changes in social, economic, and political conditions favor or discourage universal values or a minimum set of common rules acceptable to diverse societies or states.

The development of modern technology and means of transportation has greatly reduced the significance of geographical distance. Nations and countries which only a half century ago were little known, completely unknown, or entirely "exotic," are now relatively near, and their representatives meet with distant neighbors in the United Nations. Mass communication has resulted in fast dissemination of information; the world has become a unity in terms of news diffusion. In spite of the diversity of cultures, there are unifying factors between nations.

Science is an even more powerful vehicle of universality. Instrumental as science is, it has a certain universe of concepts or norms—in a sense, its own morals of intellectual honesty and dedication to the pursuit of truth. Scientific thinking is based on certain thought ways and values. Without such norms as the search for truth, without the concept of probability, without certain attitudes toward the environment which surrounds us, scientific thinking is not possible. In consequence, the modernization of society also requires changes in our thought patterns—in the "modernization" of our thinking.

Science is an idea system, diffused practically all over the world today. Most if not all of the nations represented at the United Nations have representatives trained in institutions that were guided by the scholarly spirit and by scientific methods.

Technological development has made our world heavily dependent on technological information and skills. Self-sufficiency is either impossible or economic nonsense in today's world. Countries must develop a way of life based on industrialization and modern scientific discoveries.

Political and economic independence was once a leading ideal. Today, the interdependence of nations is a condition of further economic and scientific advancement. Changes in social, economic, and political situations, changes in means of production, strongly favor a limited supernational tendency. We stress the adjective "limited," because in spite of the unifying elements in economics, and above all in science, cultures are different, and national values and institutions do not disappear. Nor is there any reason for wholesale regimentation. The tendency is one of reconciliation between native cultures, on the one hand, with the universalistic imperatives of the new world, on the other.

The development of nuclear weapons has created a new situation—new not only politically or internationally, but also psychologically; one practicaly unknown to mankind since medieval times. In the Middle Ages, a universal fear, embracing all of the contemporary Christian world, appeared with the expectation of the end of the world. With the development of the scientific outlook, in the eighteenth century, the prospects of mankind improved, and a number of "utopias" were written outlining the coming era of general happiness and welfare. These utopias were symptoms of an optimistic world outlook. With the advent of the modern totalitarian creed, with the experience of world wars and mass exterminations, the optimistic outlook changed to the pessimism of George Orwell's *1984*.

Then came the nuclear breakthrough. It was a great discovery that did not result in universal joy, or even pride. The pessimistic outlook has spread and the fear of total destruction, of the extermination of mankind, has become general. Perhaps for the first time since medieval times we can witness a universal feeling of anxiety, an expectation of a holocaust, a mood of a catastrophic age, although it is carefully controlled by individuals and by nations, and is subdued by the general leisure afforded by prosperity in the industrialized, advanced countries. But the anxiety is here, and a universal interest and corresponding goals have appeared.

The new value is the simple matter of survival. And this time it is no longer a survival of the fittest. In a nuclear holocaust both the fit and the unfit will disappear; they will share the same fate.

The introduction of the test ban is an evidence of the creative powers of anxiety and reason. Thus, the change in situation has led to the development of a common interest—of biological and economic survival—and to common norms, since survival as such is also a value, a norm.

It should be repeated, however, that this is not the only choice open to mankind. Mass destruction of large segments of the population may be combined with the miserable and tragic survival of a minority. Such a choice can be made by a nuclear power; a choice in which a state, or to put it more clearly, a government ruled by a ruthless dictator, may choose nuclear war in the hope of victory and survival. Although we know that in nuclear war there won't be any victory, those who have power may decide against logic. However, there are hopeful indications that reason will prevail. In spite of adverse tendencies, the strength of an appeal to a limited universal interest such as survival can be clearly noticed, and this appeal finds support in large sections of the world.

Now we may discuss the third proposition: can we develop or "graft" norms that will set the direction of our international development and influence our political and social conditions? In other words, can our ideas, norms, and values influence social, economic, and political conditions or are they only a result of the latter? Perhaps grafting is a somewhat drastic term for a process of rapid and vigorous education by a variety of media. We may repeat, "education," *not* indoctrination. Education is a process which suggests choice of ideas.

The impact of values on social and political situation has already been discussed. Our idea systems, norms and rules, like the law, are not only products of society. They are also factors that contribute to the development of society and set a sense of direction for change. Lucien Levy-Bruhl, an early sociologist of values and of morals, proposed a new modern approach to morals, in opposition to a highly traditional society. Such an approach would require continuous exploration of social reality and a study of the relationship between norms, values, and the social reality of which they are a part.[13]

Levy-Bruhl's suggestion is rationalistic and reflects its time. But it contains constructive elements. The Greeks in their philosophical discussions, as Levy-Bruhl rightly points out, continuously explored the norms. By influencing the norms through their philosophical reflections, they influenced also the development of society and also the direction of the development of the entire Western world.

The Greek discussion of the norms was broad and undogmatic. Early Christian thinkers and later philosophers challenged the area of human judgment, and norms were considerably changed with the development of Christian philosophy. The present historical stage, however, is marked by radical empiricism. Social sciences are focussed on problems that can be observed. The emphasis is on the study of "what is" and not on "in what direction should we move"; "what type of society do we desire."

International politics has changed substantially. Rules and devices developed in the nineteenth century are no longer workable in the modern world of dynamic, rapidly changing technology and nuclear weapons. Yet Levy-Bruhl's forgotten proposition might have been written for our times. The changing social, economic, and political situation needs new norms and new institutions. It is only man himself who can destroy mankind. Finally, the decision as to whether or not to use nuclear weapons will depend on the situation and the norms by which man will choose to be guided.

Our international relations are in need of an advanced system of norms and practical rules of conduct. The new norms and rules can set the proper direction for the emerging forces and tendencies in international politics. The exploration of the new norms requires a free and undogmatic approach, similar to that of the Greeks. The development of nation-states was in part the result of a conscious effort to model diverse tribes into one institution. In the history of the Western world, the development of nation-states and federations is closely related to, and interdependent with, the growth of new ideologies, values, and institutions. The growth of institutions molded the people into a national community, while the coercive nature of the state shaped a unified system of political behavior. In a pluralistic system, however, the emphasis is on consensus, and diversity is essential.[14] The effort to develop such a community of limited interest is not without historical antecedents.

Alternatives and stages

The quest for a perfect solution has been the weakness of peace plans since their very inception. From the fourteenth century on, if not earlier, we can trace a series of perfect plans designed by wise men and by men of good-will. They were significant milestones in our thinking, since they set a direction for development. Nonetheless, their innate weakness lay in a quest for perfection, for the ultimate solution. Man is not yet ready for the perfect brotherhood of all men. The ethical ideal by itself, the goal, has its timeless significance; it gives us a vision and a sense of direction; it indicates the road. But it is not necessary to love one another in order to live and work as neighbors without war and without resort to physical violence.

For 2,000 years we have experimented with love between nations, and the results are not encouraging; for love is a strong feeling that appears chiefly in small, primary groups. Surely it is not necessary to love one another in order not to kill; not to deny one another access to water, sun, or food. It is enough to live as good neighbors. After all, people can be good friends or colleagues without feeling a deep mutual love.

We obviously have degrees and gradations of social proximity and distance. Good neighbors respect one another; they respect differences even if they do not understand or agree with them. But one condition must be met: the differences must not be of the kind that would permit the neighbors to exploit the weak. Good neighborliness does not require love; it requires reason, moderation, and kindness. And the concept of pluralism requires no more than these.

The United Nations is a machinery, a structure. Its workability depends on the will and the intentions of its members; on the skills that operate this international institution; and on some minimum set of mutually respected rules or values. The creation of an international institution by no means assures its workability. In order to achieve workability within the existing frame of an international organization like the United Nations, a certain strategy is needed.

Strategy is like a road toward an objective; it is a direction in which man or society moves in order to arrive at a certain objective. Such an objective cannot be achieved at a single stroke or by a simple brief effort. The elimination of violence from international relations is a clear objective but not a very simple one to attain. Strategy stages are essential in a long term. We move toward an objective by stages, like milestones on a long road. The initial achievements might be modest, but they are revolutionary if they build a foundation, an element of strength, for the next effort. Every stage is closely related to the preceding one and to the strategic goal. The question "where" is one of strategy, of direction; the question "how" is one of stages, and of tactical movements within those stages. The very sense of direction, the vision, reinforces our will to act.

Any question of the direction of a movement requires a clarification of objectives or goals. Their definition is essential for any vigorous or even consistent policy. In our case the clarification of goals requires the following:

1]

The definition of the ends that a given policy seeks to attain; the evaluation of means and of the power at the disposal of a decision maker.

2]

The alternative policies that are open. This implies an inventory of: (a) existing or possible patterns and methods of cooperation and (b) levels of cooperation or patterns of cooperation desired at a given moment and realistic at a given historical period.

3]

The probable sequence of strategic stages.

Let us begin with what we have called the sociological nature of the relationship, in our case, cooperation. We have already discussed the variety of forms of cooperation and their sociological and juridical nature. The very existence of a juridical structure, of a juridical form of a cooperative system in international relations, does not necessarily imply the successful operation of such a system, or its workability.

The members of the Arab League have recently conducted a cruel war in Yemen (1963). All three enemies, the United Arab Republic (Egypt), Yemen, and Saudi Arabia are members of the league, where declarations about the brotherhood of Arab nations are frequently made. The formal structure, however, assures neither adequate cooperation between the Arab countries nor peace in the Near East. The same by-law can be utilized in a number of ways.

The constitution of an international institution can be utilized in a variety of ways and with a variety of "speeds" and intensities. A complex international organization with an elaborate system of agencies may exist for a time without being used by member states; or being used only to a very limited degree. This was the case with the League of Nations after the outbreak of World War II. At that time the international cooperation of the Allies shifted from the league to their own particular systems.

On the other hand, a very rudimentary form of organization may be used successfully with great intensity and may be an expression of a strong cooperative pattern.

The problem lies in the content given to an institution: how the institution is used, what philosophy of international politics is put into operation in everyday life. The juridical form represents the "formal" structure, an abstract proposition; sometimes an "ideal type" of mechanism. But the "informal" pattern, the actual, political behavior, is frequently quite different. The nature of the philosophy that guides the member governments and motivates the international machinery is relevant in this case.

The philosophy of the Organization of American States follows, generally speaking, that of a pluralistic system in which every state preserves its own culture, its own form of government, its own economy. Cooperation is limited, almost by definition, to "good neighborhood" between the states, to mutual aid and cooperation with no intention of complete integration—what has previously been called amalgamation—into one unitary system. The British Commonwealth offers a pragmatic and important example of evolution toward pluralism.

In this sense, the existence of the United Nations does not necessarily generate international cooperation. It is, however, an important instrument which, properly used, assists the world builders in their construction of peace; integrates and gives the necessary permanence and apparatus to the maintaining of peaceful operations. The United Nations instrumentality works for peace and cooperation when it is used skillfully for such a purpose. The question is for what purpose, for what objectives, will the United Nations be used by the member states.

A proper social instrumentality, an organized apparatus, is essential in a world strategy for the elimination of violence from international politics. On a global scale, an adjustment of differences between nations is not feasible without such an instrumentality.

Societies are built through systems of institutions. However, a blind faith in an international institution, without concern for the way in which it is used or how it works, does not contribute to the elimination of danger. A critical outlook is a part of "political realism" in its pragmatic, empirical meaning (not in a sense of power politics); it is a part of a constructive effort.

One of the problems of international cooperation, as viewed from the vantage point of the United Nations, is that of the type of international relationship toward which we aim. A realistic objective of the United Nations is a limited pluralistic relationship. In fact, it was with such an objective in mind that the United Nations was conceived in San Francisco. Whether or not this objective has been achieved is a different matter. Nonetheless, the United Nations has helped to maintain the unstable peace and to move in the direction of limited pluralism. This brings us to the second point: to the problem of alternatives open, and to the variety of classes of cooperation available, at a given historical moment.

The term "cooperation" is a general one. It embraces a variety of patterns in international relations, beginning with very loose exchanges of views and ending with an amalgamation of states. The classification of various patterns of cooperation has already been discussed in the first part of this volume, and we may refer the reader to this section. Nonetheless, at this time we may draw certain inferences.

Policy making is a careful evaluation of a situation and an equally careful choice of alternatives that best fit the situation. The evaluation must be realistic. One may desire an arrangement which will secure a permanent peace; a perfect solution for international relations. But the situation does not permit such a solution. Wishful thinking leads to plans for perfect harmony between prospective aggressors and naive victims.

The unpleasant truth is that not all governments and not all leaders of nations or armies desire peace. Many of them throughout history planned wars from the moment they captured power. Nor is it true that all nations by their very value structure are peaceful. History teaches us that many are, and were, warlike, and that war and robbery have sometimes been part of their trade. Even if two governments or two leaders argue that their final goal is peace, their definitions of peace might be entirely disparate, and the discrepancy of means might be of such magnitude that the desire for peace meant war in reality.

World peace suggested by Ghandi or by Aristides Briand, and world peace suggested by the "Axis"—Mussolini, Hitler—were two different things. Peace based on racist principles, in which one nation or one race rules and all others are subservient, is another concept held by some parties. But this type of solution is incompatible with any international arrangement in which the rights of the weaker nations and of the individuals are recognized. Similarly, peace based on the dictatorship of one party is scarcely acceptable to those who believe in a pluralistic system. In a situation of a discrepancy of goals, one still has to look for a solution in which total war can be avoided, and in such a situation a realistic approach is essential. In consequence, out of the variety of forms and patterns of relations between nations, states, or governments, a number of choices can be made and different alternatives can be selected vis-à-vis different states or nations; this has happened many times in history.

After 1945, the European states and governments made no attempt to expand into the territories of the Soviet Union, nor had the United States any such intention. However, plans for international peace were challenged by the Soviet policy of rapid territorial expansion. The Western plan was a policy of stalemating Stalin's advance, and it led to integration and cooperation between those who had a common interest in this aim. The cooperation of the European states led to economic functionalism, to a real integration of economies, and has paved the way for unification. Cooperation between the United States and the European community was largely forced by external pressures. Nonetheless, it has evolved from a purely military cooperation to more creative forms of cultural and economic cooperation. Again, the relationship between the United States and the South American republics is of a different nature than the former.

The problem, however, is not of European union or Atlantic unity, but how to establish nonantagonistic relations with those powers with which common interests or shared values are of a very limited nature. Here, of course, it would be utopian to suggest an immediate perfect world federation.

This brings us to the problem of stages and of strategy. In a pragmatic approach to the strategy of peace, in the search for some kind of commonwealth in which war would be eliminated, the concept of stages is essential. In a "stage-approach" to the present situation the alternative chosen is not considered a final solution of international relations, but simply a stage in the direction of the long-range goal. At each stage, policies toward advancement to the next stage should be carefully considered. The stages should be complementary; each should advance us toward the general strategic goal.

Foreign policy is a pattern of action, and rational actions are related to goals. The goals are an essential element in the clarification of any foreign policy. If we imagine foreign policy as a process, as a movement, then the goals represent a signpost. Clear goals affect our motivation.

For the sake of simplicity we can divide goals into immediate, intermediate, and distant. In our sense, the distant goals represent the very distant strategic vision we are trying to achieve—the "distant strategic goal." Before we reach this goal it is necessary to move through immediate and intermediate stages. These stages are attainable. The distant goals remain as guideposts that may alter with changes in social, economic, and political conditions, and of outlook. What remains as a real element of policy is the "road," the means, the actual policy. There is no "terminal end" for politics. Democratic politics is a continuous change, anchored to stability.

The strategy of stages and tactics of alternatives suggests a rational choice of policies and a method of policy planning. The concept of stages as a method, how-ever, has a much wider application and significance in foreign policy formulation and development. A peaceful foreign policy has frequently meant the maintenance of the existing international political conditions without change. In consequence, such a policy was also one of a social and political status quo. The revolutionaries of the nineteenth century saw in war a liberating and revolutionary element, because peace in the time of the Holy Alliance meant the maintenance of the status quo and reinforcement of autocratic or monarchical-aristocratic govern-ments.

A long-range policy oriented toward the elimination of war as an instrument of international relations and conceived as a dynamic process moving through a number of stages is by no means a concept of the maintenance of the status quo. On the contrary, such a policy requires substantial changes in international rela-tions and in the social and political fabric of human society. Such a concept is a dynamic one, suggesting continuous social change. We move step by step from one stage to another, with every stage representing a social, political change; a step forward.

Foreign policy is only one part of general public policy, closely related to domestic policies. Both are interdependent. In consequence, a policy directed toward substantial international solutions also requires substantial changes in social, economic and political conditions in many parts of the world. Universal forms of international cooperation require the acceptance of common rules and a substantial sharing of common values. Every stage, every level of closer coopera-tion, requires new values, new customs, perhaps new rules of international cooper-ation.

Pluralism

The general orientation, the general strategic objective and the alternative suggested, is evolution toward a pluralistic world community in terms of social-economic and political systems and cultural patterns. Within such a community, groups of nations may represent a more intensive form of association, such as the European Union or the Atlantic Community. Pluralism on a world scale is not contradictory to free and voluntary associations of economic or political units.

Pluralism is possible under conditions of effective arms controls. (This issue has not been discussed here.) Arms control may be achieved by revolutionary changes of the international system of politics, or by gradual, stage-wise advances. The latter policy seems to be feasible at this time. The limitation of thermonuclear weapons to two superblocs has so far facilitated negotiations, détente, and control. Proliferation of nuclear weapons will only delay and upset development of arms control. However, arms control between antagonistic superblocs does not supply any formula for the general conduct of international politics between the blocs. Nor does it supply any answer of symbiosis with other nations which have chosen their own way of evolution, without threatening others with expansion.

Pluralism is a matter of content, not of form. It is an answer to mankind's quest for unity, which is both similar and different. Since societies are similar and dissimilar, pluralism suggests a general direction toward unity without conformity; toward an ideal type, free of the rule of the powerful over the weak. Pluralism may secure independence for the nations of Africa or Asia while letting them prosper economically.

Pluralism is the theory and practice of good neighborliness between societies and nations which differ in their values, culture, social and political institutions; ethnic, racial or religious origin; and in the variety of their interests. This neighborliness is based on those interests and values that are shared, and on respect for differences in values and in culture. Pluralism, however, excludes uniformity and regimentation. It excludes religious and ideological crusades. It is a theory of limited cooperation that implies privacy in certain areas and, in consequence, a world of different cultural, economic, and political patterns.

A plural religious system operates successfully in the United States. Here is an area in which the United States sets a pattern of a peaceful but limited cooperation for churches that were for centuries in continuous conflict. The minimum values and premises on which this pluralism is based are freedom of conscience, freedom of church organization, and separation of church and state. These values are recognized (sometimes with reluctance) by all religious groups. In addition, there is a minimum set of universal values which all the churches recognize.

The members of various religious denominations do not necessarily love each other. There is intergroup tension and dissent. But all those disagreements are resolved by a subtle social mechanism. Somehow, differences that may lead to conflicts are eased or resolved. Mutual respect, understanding, even intellectual distance contribute to the workability of religious pluralism. It is a combination of limited cooperation and rules of avoidance.

One may argue that a permanent peace requires the imposition of a single unitary political or ideological system on the whole world. Are we morally entitled to bring about the unity of mankind in this way? Partisans of ideological regimentation have never achieved complete victory. Throughout history there have been clashes between the tendencies toward differentiation and uniformity. The experience of history teaches that any attempt to impose a single ideology or a single religion on all of humanity has led to long and disastrous wars. It was the ability to recognize the right of another to be different that secured peaceful neighborliness.

Now we may return to the problem of strategy. How can we attain, within the existing or within the transformed international organization, a system of limited cooperation, of international pluralism? How can we proceed? It has already been indicated that in a strategy for peace based on limited objectives, stages and timing have to be considered. In the first stage, a modest goal could be set which we may call "the rules of the game." In this first stage the objective is limited to those rules that would permit countries to continue their policies free from the use of physical force. Perhaps the test ban is a step in this direction.

The "rules of the game" would permit us to live without continuously shooting at each other. Our problem is not one of written rules or treaties. We have such an arrangement in the United Nations. The problem is one of practice, of real enforcement of these rules, or of respect for them. No treaty will guarantee peace unless there is the will to live by the rule of the norm.

The question can be asked: what if the nations will not agree on a minimum set of rules? The proper strategy then is to proceed with only those nations that agree to accept the rules. They could form an element of strength, powerful enough to discourage aggression. One may argue that this would transform a pluralistic group into a defensive alliance. Perhaps. In a sense this has already happened in world politics. This was a logical answer to a long-range policy and a necessary stage in a movement toward constructive international solutions. Weakness in international relations is not a virtue; firmness against aggression is. The long-range policy toward a community of nations would only be defeated by weakness and submission to threats and aggression.

The proposition of pluralism is flexible and undogmatic. It is an open suggestion to those willing to accept certain rules of international behavior, minimum rules which eliminate war. What is the basic value or norm of this minimum stage of pluralism? It is simply a matter of survival. This value of self-preservation underlies today's arrangements and today's shaky peace. It is the chief norm that led to the test-ban agreement. But this stage in the development of pluralism does not eliminate limited functional, local, or new forms of international conflict or tensions. A more developed form of pluralism, in a long-range strategy, would have to be based on a minimum set of universal values, such as the protection and defense of the weaker individual, group, nation or state, against aggression and physical violence; respect for individual freedom and human dignity within all member states; freedom for the search for truth; freedom of beliefs; and freedom of expression. This demand has already been declared in the United Nations, but from the declaration to reality is a long way.

Pluralism on a world scale is obviously not an easy proposition, especially today. But it is the concept of the future—the concept of free development of individuals, groups, and nations based on the recognition of the fact that cultural and political differences are substantial. Pluralism unites the two basic tendencies of differentiation and integration. It leads to unity only where unity and collaboration are of high necessity and leaves a wide field for the growth of nations, for the maintenance of creative differences, and for the development of individuals and groups. Pluralism is thus a concept that counteracts regimentation. It leaves to different social and cultural systems freedom of development.

However, cultural differences have obvious limits. If they are transgressed, the essence of pluralism is vitiated. The limits imply that a world of pluralism and good neighborliness may require shared values which are not yet acceptable, which have not yet been seriously discussed. And here we come again to the issue that was raised by Levy-Bruhl: that norms can be developed, can be constructed. Further, it leads to an evolutionary concept of norms, one suggesting that, in historical development, certain common values extend from a smaller to a larger group.

Acceptance or development of such values is not a matter of historical determinism alone. But man in his effort to survive and to live together on this planet has to explore their future possibility. Both the universal and the relative approaches to values supply elements for such discussion. Relativism represents an element of respect for difference, of understanding difference in culture, while universalism identifies elements which are common, which are shared. Without an understanding and respect of others, without a certain limited amount of relativism, pluralism is not feasible.

Between cultural and ethical relativism is an inner contradiction that cannot be answered by a simple statement or qualification. This contradiction is a part of the concept of relativism, indicating the basic differences of cultures and values in the context of a given culture; not as "absolutes," irrespective of social setting. In cultural relativism, norms are described by an *observer;* in ethical relativism, choices and decisions are made by an actor, while he regards norms as relative. But even cultural relativism may lead to paradoxes.

In a relativistic approach, values and cultures are recognized as different, without any further evaluation of their quality. A recent publication suggests that a better knowledge of other cultures breeds appreciation and respect. In many, very many cases, yes; in others, no. On the contrary, one may become afraid. A "better knowledge" of the Spanish system of government under Franco, or the practices of the Inquisition, the ideology of Nazi Germany, and the forced labor camps of Stalin will by no means increase our respect. It may contribute to the viewpoint— "I do not wish this type of unity. Let us keep a healthy distance."

The relativistic viewpoint destroys the scale of significance, the hierarchy of importance, and in this sense paralyses the judgment. On the other hand, evaluation and constant stress on such evaluation, on "superior" and "inferior" cultures, sooner or later leads to arrogance, and to ideologies that claim the right to rule and exploit others. Without a certain "quantity" of relativism, tolerance and respect are not possible. In a simple judgment, tolerance means, "I stop here."

An absolute approach has its inner contradictions too. An extreme acceptance of absolute values led in the past to terror and regimentation. The obsession with ultimate and only truth is a dangerous proposition, leading to social paranoia. Robespierre's acceptance of such "absolutes" of equality generated terror, as did Stalin's Communist absolutes. In past history, the extreme expressions of "absolute" and "ultimate" truth are associated with mass terror. Still, without a hierarchy of values, without some concept of continuity in time and space of certain values, continuity of a great and free civilization is not possible, nor is a sense of continuity and unity of mankind.

Each approach makes its contribution, and each contains dangers. In a pluralistic approach, based primarily on universal values, the problem of contradictions has to be recognized. In a long-range strategy, differences—in certain areas— have to be reduced to foster unity. To achieve this, respect and various degrees of distance and proximity may be helpful.

We have emphasized the norms, the rules and regulations, but this is not enough in the formation of a pluralistic world. Ideas, important as they are, are not detached or abstract from real social, economic, and political conditions. Instead of the greater independence of states, a greater interdependence of nations is necessary to create conditions of unity.

Today the norm of biological survival is easily "identifiable"; it is universal, and corresponds to the vital interest of mankind. An understanding of conditions of survival is by no means identical with a philosophy of surrender, as advanced by some. Nor is the price of survival a loss of political freedom. In fact, the de facto nuclear peace is based on strength, not on weakness. The interlude of Cuba indicates that a firm decision, supported by strength and readiness, is today a basic policy in the maintenance of world peace. The norm of biological survival, which forms the base of nuclear peace and which is based on the strength of the Western democracies, does not mean submission, nor surrender of international policies, including nonviolent pressures. Elimination of nuclear wars, or war in general, is not an end to internal basic changes and developments. Domestic moves toward more freedom may actually strengthen the chances of pluralistic solutions.

Contrary to a monistic viewpoint, the changes in the means and modes of production are not the only elements that determine the future social, economic, and political order. Mankind has choices within a single situation, and a proper choice of alternatives may decide future historical trends. More advanced forms of pluralism—further limitations of antagonisms within the international field— are feasible with the attainment of a limited community of values governing the conduct of man.

vi. Appendices

i.

CONSENSUS AND COMMAND STRUCTURES

A definition of terms

Man exists only as a member of human society. His survival is determined by his ability to act in an organized and coordinated manner with other members of society toward a definite end. From the time man first appeared in history, his life has depended on others. It is this mutual interdependence of men that forms the very fabric of society.

The satisfaction of man's basic needs necessitates group action. The gathering of food, the early stages of agriculture, and the building of shelter require common effort. Work, play, religious rites—all complex forms of action—are social phenomena and appear as coordinated group efforts. Man either works and acts together under threat of coercion and fear of punishment or he "cooperates" in a more or less voluntary manner.

Voluntary cooperation in primitive society is a general phenomenon. It is usually based on folkways or customs and is taken for granted. A common set of values or established rules facilitates the voluntary cooperative pattern. Consequently, social relations requiring group action and institutions can be reduced to two, perhaps three, "ideal types": those based on (1) consensus, (2) command, or (3) a combination of both.[1]

Command and consensus represent an abstract polarity, the extremes on a continuum of "ideal type" institutions. Complete consensus or complete coercion is infrequent. Complete coercion comprises such actions as slave-gang work in the fields or a prison labor under guard. At the other extreme, complete consensus is represented by a cooperative effort of fishermen to secure their boats in the face of an approaching storm. Both types of group action are rare.

Certain limited forms of coercion can be observed even in cooperative efforts. In turn, command actions frequently require a minimum of common rules or common values. It is evident, therefore, that most group actions or institutions have both the element of command and of consensus. Nevertheless, it is the dominant pattern of an institution or of an action that determines its character. The degree of emphasis, of quantity and quality, is the deciding factor. Consensus requires: (1) common values (norms); (2) customs (folkways or mores) or a conscious or customary acceptance of common rules; and (3) a common interest.

The elements of consensus

The universal significance of the consensus mechanism was recognized long ago, by students of human society who focussed their interest on problems of work and cooperation. The command structure was soon recognized as an institution that fosters tyranny and despotic rule. However, philosophers and political theoreticians have sometimes overlooked the fact that any complex social organization requires a degree of coercion and command.

In the middle of the nineteenth century, anarchists recognized the compulsory form of social organization as a source of all evil, and outlined plans for an ideal type of society based on consensus and free from coercion. Plans for a coercion-free society can also be found much earlier, particularly in eighteenth-century French theory. But it was during the first and second parts of the nineteenth century that extensive plans and social visions of consensus society were developed, especially by the anarchist school. It is interesting to note the experiences of Peter Kropotkin, a well-known representative of this school, whose philosophical ideals were shaped, in part, by his direct experience and observation of the mechanism of consensus, which he calls "common understanding."

During his formative years, Kropotkin was raised in a society in which the command habit was general. As a member of an aristocratic family, he was part of a society dominated by a system of orders and submission. As a young Cossack officer, he spent several years in Siberia, where he studied the life of Russian and Chinese village communities. A keen observer, he noticed that the coercion and command that formed the basis of official Russian political philosophy, and of his class, were alien to village community life. Instead, cooperation, mutual aid, and consensus prevailed. The picture Kropotkin presents is possibly idealistic, since values frequently condition observation, and Kropotkin was already a humane young social thinker searching for answers and alternatives to the despotic state. In his memoirs he comments:

Having been brought up in a serf-owner's family, I entered active life, like all young men of my time, with a great deal of confidence in the necessity of commanding, ordering, scolding, punishing, and the like. But when, at an early stage, I had to manage serious enterprises and to deal with men, and when each mistake would lead at once to heavy consequences, I began to appreciate the difference between acting on the principle of command and discipline and acting on the principle of common understanding. The former works admirably in a military parade, but it is worth nothing where real life is concerned, and the aim can be achieved only through the severe effort of many converging wills. Although I did not then formulate my observations in terms borrowed from party struggles, I say now that I lost in Siberia whatever faith in state discipline I had cherished before.[2]

Cooperative labor, based on consensus and rooted in common values and customs, was observed by many social scientists in various parts of the world. They found it to be as common among primitive and folk societies as it is in modern advanced societies.

Malinowski reported on extensive communal labor among the Trobrianders, based on custom. Boat building involved the communal labor (without any division of tasks) of 20 to 30 men, who "side by side do the lashing or caulking of the canoe." Here, the cooperation seems to be spontaneous; free of coercion. Malinowski indicates the sociological significance of this work, which implies "mutual help, exchange of services, and solidarity in work within a wide range"— in consequence, a variety of forms of consensus.[3]

Actions and institutions based on consensus are frequently rooted in customs and mores, and long survived in peasant and folk societies. Even after the revolutionary advance of urbanization finally reached the Slavic nations of Eastern Europe, the customs based on these types of consensus still survived in Russia and Poland. They remained vigorous in these areas during the nineteenth century and were so recorded by ethnographers. Spontaneous cooperation also persisted in the peasant communities of Europe and the fishing communities of Maine, where it can still be observed.[4] As late as 1958, a form of these customs flourished in Central Italy, especially near the community of Fumone in the province of Frosinone. Here, spontaneous cooperation gave impetus to the local economy, especially in the pastoral life. Since sheep shearing and wool processing correspond more or less to the harvest period of the agrarian economy, the community's customs of cooperation were related closely to consensus.[5]

The structure of command

There is a fundamental difference between the group action of a consensus, and a command, structure. The command structure operates by means of a latent system of rewards and punishments (positive and negative sanctions), and any member of the intermediary or obedient subgroups is directly involved in it. In a command structure, a goal imposed by the superordinated (commanding) group may replace the common interest. Such a goal is not a "shared" or "common" goal, based on common values, but a "group goal" imposed by a system of punishments and rewards. Goal achievement is determined by the coercive apparatus; e.g., a road gang of prisoners has a "group goal" which is imposed by the prison authority.

The functioning and communication of command-type institutions are based on commands (or orders) and obedience (submission or subordination). Within a simple command-type structure, the personnel is in a position of either command or obedience.

Human relations can also be divided into transitive or symmetric and intransitive or asymmetric. In an asymmetric relationship, A orders B to act according to A's command, and B is coerced to do so; the decision and action flow from A to B. In a symmetric or transitive relationship, decision and action flow both ways, from A to B and from B to A. In a symmetric relationship, partners are of equal strength and nature; in asymmetric relations, one partner's relationship differs from the other's.[6]

Diagram I

1] Asymmetric relationship

$$A \longrightarrow B$$

A orders B to do an assignment

2] Symmetric relationship

$$A \longleftrightarrow B$$

A suggests that B do an assignment, and B
expects reciprocity

A simple command structure is, as a rule, intransitive (asymmetric), as opposed to "spontaneous" cooperation, which belongs to the transitive type of relationship. A more complex command structure is known as a hierarchy, and has at least three subgroups or links:

1] On top, the command or sovereign subgroup. Its members make decisions and issue commands but do not take any orders.

2] The intermediary subgroup. Members of this group accept and obey orders; they also issue orders to the subordinate group. They make decisions within the limits of the orders issued by the command subgroup. But while the sovereign group can change the decisions of the "intermediaries," the latter cannot alter the orders given from the top.

3] At the bottom, the subordinate, or obedient, subgroup. Its members accept, obey, and execute orders.

The members of the command subgroup have the largest share of power; they are the decision makers. The members of the last group have no share in decision making. They are subjected to continuous repression and are trained through long experience to a submissive pattern of behavior.

A complex hierarchical system probably appeared as a result of conquest and the emergence of large states. Hierarchy was a social invention (probably the result of gradual development) that permitted consolidation of power in large areas.[7] With the establishment of a hierarchy, combined with a system of negative and positive sanctions (punishment and reward), a pattern of symbols, symbolic behavior, and elaborate rituals gradually developed or was instituted. The function of the pattern was to reinforce the command structure through repetitive symbolic behavior, which became a generally accepted norm and, with the passing of time, was regarded as part of a divine or "natural" order. To this pattern belongs such symbolic behavior as genuflecting before a lord or a priest and kissing his hand; greeting the symbols of royalty (coat of arms); or baring the head when speaking to members of the superordinated subgroup; behavior that survived in Europe, in one form or another, long after the end of medieval times.

Colors were and are symbols of rank. Power and status were associated with certain colors (for instance, red or purple), and persons carrying such colors were identified as superordinated; their orders were accepted. Other colors indicated subordination (i.e., yellow for Jews; revived by the Nazis during World War II). Elaborate rituals of submission to royalty were well known in medieval times (homage; German, *Huldigung*). The social function of these symbols and rituals is related to the nature of the institutions.[8]

In countries with a long history of feudalism or aristocratic orders, where the peasants or other subordinate groups have long experienced legally sanctioned servitude, the behavioral patterns of passive and symbolic submission have survived long after the disappearance of the original social system. This could still be observed prior to World War II in Eastern Europe or parts of Italy. Thus, the ideological and symbolic "superstructure" survives, though the "economic base" has changed.

The army may well serve as a general example of a hierarchy. To illustrate the simple three-link hierarchy, let us use the case of an imaginary army of a small principality, of which the ruler is also the captain of the army. He represents the command element and issues orders. The noncommissioned officers form the intermediary, while the military band and the foot soldiers belong to the subordinate or obedient subgroup.

As a rule, a military organization has many more steps, or links, in its hierarchy; there are many intermediary links between the command group and the lowest subordinate one. Dictators in command posts are representative of the "sovereign" subgroup. They make the army's basic decisions. Between them and their respective private soldiers or militiamen is a "chain of command" with various levels of subordination and obedience. However, large and democratically structured armies have a much more complex mechanism of decision making, and include a large share of consensus and common values.

Hierarchical military discipline remains a part of the modern army, although in those countries in which political freedom and civil liberties are respected, the army forms a separate structure. The values and status of the individuals in such an army differ from those in the army of an authoritarian state.

How does an army hierarchy work? To take an example from a pre-World War I imperial, continental army: the private was a member of a hierarchical "command structure." He belonged to the bottom or obedient subgroup. If he refused an order, he was punished. On the other hand, if he executed orders well, he expected to be "out of trouble"—meaning that for him there was no immediate prospect of punishment. And if he showed outstanding loyalty or dedication, he obtained some suitable reward, such as a decoration or promotion.

This basic system of rewards and punishments (negative and positive sanctions) was the underlying element of the nineteenth-century military discipline of the dynastic armies. Loyalty to the dynasty formed a "value support" as well as a rationalization of the discipline and was complementary in nature. The behavioral patterns of the military were closely connected with this system of rewards and punishments through military drill. During years of continuous training, the soldier associated command, on a psychological level, with two elements: 1] an immediate and standardized behavioral response; and 2] a "recall" system which reminded him that a refusal of the proper behavioral response, or even its absence, was associated with pain or other discomfort. Perhaps, after a long period of training, the "recall" system may have disappeared on a conscious level and moved into the subconscious. In such cases we say that orders were executed "mechanically" or "automatically."

In a time of crisis (revolution), when the value structure as well as the institution grows weak and discipline and institutions break down, the "recall" system may revert from the subconscious to the conscious level. In the past, when the crisis, or revolution, affected the military establishment, an increase of punishment (a negative sanction) was applied, often without success, to reinforce the behavioral patterns of submission.[9]

The "modernization" of the Western armies in the eighteenth century introduced mechanical discipline and rigor. From saluting, marching, firing, attacking, parading, all the way down to heel-clicking, the behavioral patterns were standardized in the same manner as the instruments of war. In this way, the organizers of armies and the commanding subgroup of the military hierarchy achieved both maximum enforcement of their orders and predictability. The behavior of the army could be predicted, at least *rebus sic stantibus,* provided other factors of the situation remained the same. A command would be followed by an appropriate response unless outside pressures produced a breakdown in the hierarchical system. To prevent this, the army had to be given stronger firepower and better discipline than the enemy.

The military training of the obedient subgroup was a process of conditioning through the association of punishment and reward with definite types of behavior. Rigorous training of this type produced an efficient, "operational" type of social mechanism that responded to commands instantly and with a predictable and co-ordinated group action.

This type of hierarchical social machine proved effective in aggressive actions. Also, in *certain historical periods,* the command type of social organization was useful for large-scale hydraulic schemes, road building, and the erection of monuments and public buildings. The "colossal" architecture of antiquity was built largely, *though not entirely,* by autocracies or hierarchical social structures based on the command mechanism. The Egyptian pyramids represent this class of architecture, as do the Roman *Thermae* and circuses.

The functioning of consensus groups

For its functioning, a consensus group requires an acceptance of common or shared values, customary rules or folkways, and a common interest. In a long historical perspective, simple, uncomplicated communities have acted efficiently through such a consensus-based system.

Social actions and organizations based on consensus embrace a wide range of patterns. Roughly four types can be distinguished:

1]

A general pattern of mutual aid and cooperation based on folkways and customs (consensus by custom). Such a general pattern does not necessarily include a structured institution or organization. To this type belongs the general pattern of spontaneous mutual-aid activities and cooperation, especially focussed around work.

2]

The second pattern is represented by institutions in which a definite effort is made to organize the group around the concept of voluntary, generally accepted, possibly unanimous, agreement. I shall call them the "principal" or "complete" consensus institutions, since they have definite form and a definite pattern in which a centralized power structure is carefully avoided. (The Society of Friends, known generally as Quakers, is an example of a consensus group.) This type of organization requires a large range of shared values and a commonly accepted idea system.

3]

The third type, "consensus-oriented *A*," includes organizations in which a definite effort is made by members to reach as wide a consensus as possible before a decision is made. However, such organizations have definite executive committees, and decisions are reached by majority vote, then commonly accepted and executed. A brotherhood of farmers and fishermen—the Grange—is representative of this type of organization. While in type 2, formal decision is replaced by "the sentiment of the meeting," in type 3, decisions are made and transformed into resolutions that are later enforced.

4]

The fourth type, "consensus-oriented *B*" or "majority vote," represents a general pattern of voluntary association governed by an elected executive committee with the power to execute the decisions of the majority; its resolutions are also reached by a majority vote.

Ethnography and anthropology supply vast data on spontaneous patterns of mutual aid and cooperation in primitive societies as well as in modern agrarian communities, but especially in peasant communities. Perhaps a distinction should be made between mutual aid, assisting a member of the community, and cooperation—in which a goal is attained by voluntary group effort.

The existence of such cooperative customs or folkways does not necessarily indicate that the entire community is free from conflict or tension. A community like that of Trappeto, a village on the shore of Sicily, has its usual share of tensions and hostilities. The fisherman, who may have a few sheep or a goat, may get into trouble with the farmer who owns the land and pastures. In times of emergency and danger it is not easy to mobilize the entire village, yet there are spontaneous cooperative patterns based on consensus or common values and customs.

The waters of Trappeto are shallow and there is no adequate harbor. The fishermen wade into the water to haul the incoming "barcas" of their neighbors or other fishermen onto the shore. This type of cooperation is part of the general pattern of customs or folkways of this village and is done without questioning. There is no conscious effort to maintain such behavior and the customs can be related only indirectly to village solidarity. They form a specific pattern of work and cooperation in fishing.

Unlike that of the Sicilian fishermen, the consensus pattern of the Quakers is the result of a conscious ideological effort. It is rooted in a religious philosophy and values that can be traced to the seventeenth century and the religious philosophy of George Fox or William Penn.

The Seekers, or Quakers, could not find in religion a basis for any form of church government. In this respect they disagreed with the principles of church government advanced by the Catholic, Anglican, and Calvinist churches. The purpose of this group was, then, to form an entirely free society, unfettered by church government, in which religious feelings could be expressed by inner emotions, an "inner light," or inner inspiration rather than by a set ritual. The Quakers represented an effort at emancipation from religious symbolism and ritualism.

Thus the consensus was not necessarily spontaneous in nature. It was based, not on custom or folkways, but on a definite philosophy. As the history of the Quaker movement indicates, throughout its existence there was a conscious effort to build a religious association free from any form of religious government, coercion, or even enforcement of decision. The voluntaristic consensus principle was a fundamental concept, perhaps the only dogma, in this emancipated society. In consequence, the religious philosophy, the value structure, the idea system, have determined the organization and the ways of reaching agreement in the Society of Friends. It is perhaps closer to the anarchist ideal than the anarchist group itself. However, despite all efforts to avoid any form of government or ritual, the Quakers did establish a pattern of behavior, free of an elaborate symbolism but still having the quality of religious customs and of a religious organization.

The meeting of members of a given community constitutes the government of the Quakers. This type of organization, developed in the seventeenth century, has survived with small modifications until the present. The organization consists roughly of four types of meetings: (1) the particular meeting; (2) the monthly meeting; (3) the quarterly meeting; and (4) the yearly meeting.

The particular meeting is for the purpose of worship. It is held weekly and no business is discussed. The monthly meeting is the organizational cornerstone of the Quaker society. All Friends in a given district belong, and it is both their duty and their right to meet and decide the affairs of the church. The monthly meeting owns the meeting houses and the burial grounds of the district, and keeps the civil records. Historically it was responsible for the collection of money and the distribution of poor relief.

The quarterly meeting embraces a larger area. All the members of the monthly meetings in a given area belong to the quarterly meeting, at which wider issues are discussed. The yearly meeting encompasses a number of quarterly meetings, and sets the general policy. However, it has no authority over the quarterly meeting which, in turn, does not control the monthly meeting. All are independent and none has a higher authority than the other. The members of the society make the decisions, which are later voluntarily accepted and executed without enforcement. The advice of the yearly meeting represents the wider and perhaps better established opinion of the various monthly meetings, but there are no orders or resolutions which can be enforced. Every member of the society is expected to attend at least one of the meetings, and he has the right to express his opinions at any and all of them.

The meetings have no formal chairman. A clerk is elected who keeps the records and acts as a convener or substitute chairman. The conduct of the meeting suggests that the Quakers, despite their dislike of regimen, have developed both customs and formalized behavior; e.g., the period of silence that precedes all meetings.

Any Quaker can take the floor and present his opinion or can initiate action. An elected committee may also present a problem or a case at the meeting. The matter is then discussed but no vote is taken. The clerk keeps a record of the discussion, and if he finds that there is agreement on a certain issue, or general support, he will record this as a decision or "sense of the meeting." The clerk, however, does not count the vote and no formal motion is made. Sometimes the opinions are divided and the clerk cannot find formulas that express the general sentiment. In such a case a committee is elected to draft an agreement. If no consensus of opinion is reached, the discussion is postponed. Heated and partisan discussions are carefully avoided. When discussion becomes too heated, the clerk or a Friend asks for a period of silence, after which the discussion is usually more controlled. If a consensus cannot be reached, no decisions are made. A dissatisfied minority has to use prolonged persuasion before it can effect its will.

The history of the Quakers may supply more controversial moments, but, in general, this is the way they operate. There is no organized and ordained clergy; there is no hierarchy. The conduct of the society, the general policies, the leadership, is vested in the meetings. There are, of course, strong personalities who exercise influence in these meetings, playing the role of leaders or opinion makers. Nonetheless, the meetings and the committees form the essential elements of the institution. Strong, definite power structure is absent.

The efficiency of the institution's organization can be measured by its goal attainment. The Quakers have been amazingly efficient in their relief work and in their attempts to liberate the slave, despite their loose consensus structure. Such efficiency depends mainly on the personalities of the members and on a strong system of shared values which fosters self-discipline and dedication.[10]

The mutual aid or cooperation of the Sicilians is an example of a spontaneous consensus; of custom rather than of organization. As I have said, this custom is connected with a special type of community, but such groups have a number of patterns and customs and not all of them are of the cooperative or consensus nature.[11]

The Grange is a transitional type of institution, located between the consensus institution and the "majority type" of association. It contains elements of both. Unlike the Quakers, the Grange has an elaborate system of symbols and rituals, based on Greek mythology, the Christian religion, the Masonic lodges, and, perhaps, on ancient customs of the English guilds. Marching, singing, and prayers form part of Grange ceremonies, and symbols are numerous and elaborate. A member is gradually admitted to a higher degree, and every advance is associated with more elaborate rituals and ceremonies. In this respect the Grange is not unique. Various degrees or grades of membership were general among the Masons and Carbonari of eighteenth- and nineteenth-century Europe, as well as in political secret societies of the nineteenth century. They are still general in Masonic lodges. The "grades" survived in the Grange, which is to an extent a secret society. Most of its rituals and proceedings are secret.

The Grange unites members of many denominations who may not agree on detail but who find agreement on the general religious principles embodied in its ritual. It also represents the economic interests of the farmers and the fishermen, and exercises an influence in community life, in welfare policies.

Although the Grange has standing committees and a highly developed structure, as well as officers with elaborate titles, its meetings are based on consensus. Its activities function on the basis of voluntary acceptance of duties with no pressure whatsoever. However, in certain cases motions are made and seconded, resolutions are passed and accepted, so that, combined with a very general use of consensus, there is a formal system of motion and resolution.

The members of the "majority rule" institutions, which are still part of the consensus group, reach agreement by the mechanism of voting and by the acceptance of the majority view. Here the emphasis is on motion-resolution-acceptance rather than on consensus, while in the two previous groups, the emphasis is on consensus.

In consensus groups, *spontaneous* cooperation does not require any formal decision; the acceptance of behavior is based on values and customs. However, a *"structured," organized action,* or an action within or of an institution, usually requires a motion-resolution-acceptance process. Frequently a simple "arithmetic" majority does not force its will upon the rest, if the minority resistance is strong. The chairman may sometimes interpret the "sentiment of the meeting," that is, a general attitude favoring acceptance or rejection of a motion.

In consequence, we may classify the consensus groups under the following patterns: (1) "consensus by custom"; (2) "principal" or "complete" consensus institutions; (3) consensus-oriented institutions *A;* and (4) consensus-oriented institutions *B.* The difference between *A* and *B* may be measured by the frequency of use of the consensus device.

It might be difficult to draw a sharp line between the third and fourth types of institutions. Still, there is a difference between such organized groups as the Grange and the faculty council of a university, where consensus is recognized and sought—but if not achieved, the majority rule decides. In a creative faculty, debate, discussion, and difference of opinion are not necessarily avoided. Contrariwise, in the Grange this type of debate would probably be avoided.

A consensus does not necessarily indicate that the members of a given group seek to agree on everything. Consensus in institutions, especially in the consensus-oriented (*A*) or majority rule (*B*) institutions with a limited amount of consensus, means a preference for this type of decision. There are disagreements on issues, there are differences of opinion, but when decisions are made and actions are taken, the membership prefers to have general support rather than a simple majority rule enforced. In consequence, members of a consensus-oriented organization may have sharp differences of opinion, even antagonism, but the establishment and execution of a policy engenders a general acceptance of the membership.

Even the so-called permissive system is never completely permissive, unless the concept is confused with a complete absence of discipline, indicative of disintegration. Training in self-discipline through a process of learning and persuasion is not entirely free of the reward and punishment system.

Many institutions which operate efficiently, however, have a combined or complex structure. They have lines of decision making based on consensus and lines of execution based on a command structure. Public institutions, in particular, have this complex structure.

The state represents an integral institution, composed not of one institution but of many, integrated by an internal system of relationships and power structures. The state has a monopoly of physical power which makes it different from all the other institutions.

Now, perhaps, we can extend our classification and distinguish among (a) simple institutions (representing a single type of structure), (b) complex institutions with two lines of structure, one of command and one of consensus, and (c) integral institutions, such as the state, which represent a combination of integrated command and consensus institutions.

Complementary structures

A complex social organism, an integral institution like a state or even a large business corporation, usually has a complementary system of mutually interdependent command and consensus structures. In fact, any modern state must have its command institutions, for without such a system it is impossible to act in cases of emergency or national disaster. A democratic army also has elements of consensus, but to operate effectively it must also have a chain of command. The absence of discipline in an army or armed police force would put the citizen, in many cases, at the mercy of the soldiers and of those who were armed.

The army is part of a war machine geared for defense or aggression. Tactical movements and combat situations require swift decisions. There is often no time for the mechanism of motion-and-resolution. But a military unit which has common values and is used to team work, may often show resilience and determination.

The command structure and institutions probably expanded with the appearance of a military establishment as a specialized institution and with the development of the state, which monopolizes physical power and the means of violence.[12]

As has already been pointed out, a democratic state possesses, as a rule, both consensus and command types of institutional structures. The problem is to determine their relative proportion and strength, which cannot be measured in a quantitative manner. Still, even if the quantity cannot be measured, the distribution determines the quality of the state.

The proportion, distribution, and intensity of the command structure determine whether a state is authoritarian or democratic. A state based primarily on a command structure which extends this structure to such areas as legislation and judiciary, even to the organization of city blocks, is an authoritarian state. Contrariwise, a state whose structure rigorously limits the area and functions of its command system is democratically oriented.[13]

In a democratic state the command institutions have their share of common values and consensus. Hence, in theory, the quality of its "discipline" or command-submission mechanism is different, and self-discipline and spontaneous cooperation should have a wider application. The intensity of the command system is also different, as are its symbolism and the meaning of its behavior.

In a complex society, an individual usually belongs to both types of institutional structures and takes part in both types of social relations. He is, therefore, subject to both types of influence. He learns early by experience what he is "permitted to do," and to associate the symbolism of both command and consensus with appropriate behavior.

The modern state commands a monopoly of physical power. It also controls a number of other instruments of power and influence or even ideologies through symbolism and mass communication. A democratic state emphasizes the symbolism and ideologies of consensus and choice, and advances a pluralistic system that permits a variety of goals, views, and institutions. Autocratic or authoritarian states, on the other hand, stress the values and symbols connected with command action.

The state, acting as a formal and an informal educational agency through its laws and institutions, influences the personality development of its citizens. It shapes their attitudes, values, and behavior. But the state is not the only active agency. Other institutions and social values are also at work, and at certain historical moments their content may be contradictory or even antagonistic, and their influence more powerful than that of the state. In such moments, when the balance between public institutions and the dynamic forces of other social groups is upset, a fundamental change may occur.

Beginnings of the command structure

The command structure seems to have appeared in its elementary forms at a much earlier period than the state and the military establishment. Man's efficiency, and his ability to cope with the natural environment, increased substantially when he was able to organize larger and more efficient groups.

Man as an individual is practically helpless. His ability to organize group work, to build better shelters, to gain food by organized and more extensive activities, and to cope with inclement weather and nature through a coordinated collective effort has determined the conditions of his economic and social advance. Therefore the development of social groups and coordinated group action was of substantial significance in the development of man's culture.

In the early development of man's society, elementary forms of action based on command and consensus probably existed. The consensus structure is a "natural" one, growing out of the family and community organization.[14] It is closely related to family life. This is true of many cultures and can be observed even today in many primitive societies. But the punishment and reward system was probably discovered quite early. It seems that certain forms of domestication of animals might have been closely related to the latter (domestication of the horse, for instance).

Probably at a certain moment of historical development, man discovered that by using punishment and reward (associated with latent fear) he could control large groups. Later, with the development of the state, this method was used for the control of large territories and complex societies. The entire system is closely related to "naked" power and the use of physical force, "physical sanctions" to enforce commands. However, with the development of culture, magical and religious sanctions might probably have displaced the purely physical. The taking of hostages, as another expression of punishment and reward techniques, also appears in early history.

Throughout historical development, the hierarchy and the command system have been associated with various forms of despotic rule. On the other hand, the consensus pattern was often identified, at least by philosophers, with the concept of democracy. As we have already noted, both forms exist in a modern state.

We have become accustomed to normative evaluations of these two systems and to the dichotomy of autonomy and autocracy, a hierarchical authority and democracy, more than to a cold evaluation of their efficiency. The social effectiveness of these structures can be measured on one hand by goal attainment and on the other, by their ability to maintain the continuity of the institution. An efficient institution might be morally wrong or evil. (The Nazi state was at one time very efficient from the point of view of Nazi values, although it negated the elementary moral values of the European tradition.) This does not necessarily indicate that any institution that is inefficient is morally acceptable. We may have institutions that are both morally acceptable and efficient. The concept of social efficiency is not identical with moral adequacy.

We may, however, compare three related moral orders acceptable to and approved by a number of different groups. All are religious in nature and have large followings. Although they are related, a part of their history is marked by conflicts and wars. One is the Roman Catholic Church, another the many Protestant sects, and the third, the Jewish religious community.

The Roman Catholic Church is a moral and religious order accepted by many cultures and nations for centuries, and it has been for the most part efficiently administered. It is perhaps the oldest organization in the world that can claim uninterrupted continuity and the attainment of certain goals, such as religious power, control, and influence. In this respect it is an efficient organization. Its structure is definitely one of command, established on an elaborate and strongly centralistic hierarchy. The punishment and reward system is based on religious sanctions, but there were periods in which physical sanctions were applied.

The strength of the Roman Catholic Church lies in two areas: its value structure and its institutional structure. There is substantial agreement on basic values. The acceptance of absolute and perhaps universal values is an essential part of the Catholic creed; the official interpretation of these values is binding on its adherents. But this does not fully explain the strength of the organization.

The Roman Catholic Church offers a certain limited choice of idea systems and values within the dominant system of its values and dogma. This is reflected in the organization of the religious orders. The various orders offer different types of appeal to differing personalities, and their orientations vary. But all share the same system of values and beliefs, and within this system—within the Church itself —divergence is permitted.

The Roman Catholic political movements range from those on the left to others related to fascism. This broad system supplies elasticity and has a wide appeal. In one country the Church represents a more universal viewpoint; in another, a more restrictive one.

The same religious system includes a wide arc of views and ideologies. Today the left wing of the Christian Democrats in Italy can cooperate with the Socialists and even with the Communists. On the other hand, the aristocracy and the nobility of the Vatican represent a highly conservative viewpoint.

In addition to the value structure, the Church's institutional structure, the hierarchy, has shown strength and resilience throughout its almost two thousand years of existence. The two millennia have supplied experience and skills in the maintenance of large-scale organizations embracing wide areas of different ethnic groups and cultures.

There have been historical periods in which the value structure weakened or was even subject to disorganization. This occurred in the era of schisms and of the Protestant movements. The discord that brought about the separation of certain groups appeared early in Church history, and it has continued through most of its existence.

In the time of the great Protestant revolutions, Church values were subject to very great strains. A general weakening of loyalties appeared in Bohemia, Germany, England, and even Poland, where the Reformation made substantial inroads in the sixteenth century. In such periods, the Church could maintain its control or its influence and authority by two means: One was through the transformation of values, and even dogmas, associated with its religious policy to the extent that it could embrace or recognize the right of the dissidents to a different view. This also involved—sooner or later—changes of the institutional structure, the organization, of the Church. The other was to apply extremes of the punishment and reward system to maintain the membership and the established institutional structure with little or no change.

The Inquisition embodied the latter system. It was applied in a period when the disintegration of the value structure was threatening the very institutional structure of the Church, its lines of command, influence, and control. In this critical period, a number of alternatives were open, but those in control of Church government protected the institutional framework by an increased pressure of sanctions through a rigid institution. In the twentieth century, the late Pope John XXIII sought to maintain the influence and control of the Church by broadening the values rather than by exercising pressures through the institutional structure and reinforcing the command structure. In all cases, however, the institutional framework of the Roman Catholic Church remained a hierarchy based on a command system reinforced by religious sanctions.

Other religious communities have maintained an equally long continuity based on community organization and a mixed consensus and command system or on a consensus-oriented structure. The Jewish religious communities have had no hierarchy, at least in medieval and modern times. The community is based on shared values which are quite intensive in nature. The value structure is reinforced by continuous study and the development of religious philosophy and, in certain sects, by intensification of the emotional appeal and experience.

Nonetheless, Jewish communities have not been free from the command element of punishment and reward. The excommunication of Spinoza was evidence of a required conformity and of a coercive group system. However, the continuity of Jewish religious communities has been secured primarily by strong values and coercive attitudes, not by an elaborate institutional structure. There is no formally accepted centralistic hierarchy in the Jewish church. For all practical purposes, every religious community is independent, although in some, the power of rabbis, coercive control of behavior, and intolerance of difference in views or ritual has been strong.

Some Protestant sects, particularly the Quakers, represent a consensus-oriented group to a greater degree. Yet, the Quakers with their consensus institutional structure were able to maintain continuity for 300 years and to attain certain goals which they had set.

Under certain conditions both types of structure have supplied continuity. Which is more efficient, which supplies a longer continuity? This question is not simple to answer. First of all, the institution under consideration cannot be analyzed out of context. Its working can be understood only within the frame of existing social, economic, and political conditions. Thus, (a) the institutional structure has to be analyzed within its social, economic, and political context, and (b) the structure of the institution is related to its goals and functions. Most of the consensus-oriented churches were either nonproselytizing, like the Quakers, or their missionary work was limited. The Roman Catholic Church was and is an expansive and militant church. Its centralistic structure is closely related to its goals and patterns of action.

Application to tension areas

Let us now return to the problems of tension areas and international conflict.

The seizure of a given geographic (tension) area, is frequently accomplished by the building up of an internal front composed of social forces. These forces are usually social or political movements, properly organized and supported, which also profit from military pressure from the outside. This type of warfare has been called revolutionary warfare.

The concept of revolution implies, in our language, progressive ideas. This is not necessarily so with the revolutionary technique, as it was employed by Adolf Hitler in his capture of Sudetenland. It was also used in different forms by irredentas, by the fascists, and by the Nazis during the late twenties and thirties. It is simply a technique that can be employed for various ends by various ideologies. The dynamic actions of such groups, their combative spirit and energy, often give the impression that most of the population supports their movement. This may be true at times, but it is not always so.

In certain cases the spearheading movement is supported by an outside state, as was the Nazi movement, which had substantial support in Austria and Sudetenland. In other cases, small well-organized groups operate within an area where the population is passive and the militants represent the single active dynamic political element.

The active group in a territory often forms a definite minority, but the manner in which it is organized and the way it operates give it greater efficiency. And here, perhaps, we are coming to the crux of the issue discussed in this chapter. It is the group's structure of organization, its goal orientation, ideology and mode of operation, strategy and tactics that supply its strength and success.

The three elements—ideology, pattern of action (strategy and tactics), and structure—are essential in any political movement. We shall limit ourselves to one, the structure of political parties, to show that the manner in which these groups are structured in a tension area may secure them success, despite the fact that they do not command the support of the majority of the population, but lean against the strong diplomatic, economic, and military support of a neighboring and powerful state. The easing of political tensions may depend on decisions made outside the given area. The social movements within the area and their leaders may not be able or willing to reduce the tension or to find an answer by themselves. However, such an answer could be found and agreement could be reached outside the area, between the supporting power and other major states, if the tension is of a primary nature.

I would not like to suggest that all the tensions in an area should always be adjusted and completely reduced, or that they can be completely reduced. Suppose that a tension arises in a given area because the economic system allows a small minority to exploit the majority. Let us imagine further, that the minority is of a different ethnic background than the majority. The majority can organize itself into a political party to remove the privileges of the social-economic elite and dissolve a system in which the distribution of income is strikingly uneven and improvement of the economy is not possible. Suppose again, that a privileged minority monopolizes political rights while the majority enjoys no political and civil liberties. Should such problems be eased by compromise, or should final solutions be sought in which the political rights and some kind of social-economic system are constituted that would permit a hard-working citizen to live decently?

The easing or reduction of tensions cannot be a goal in itself. It merely points the way to solve problems. Compromise or "adjustment" at whatever price cannot be elevated to the supreme goal. Compromise, after all, is a matter of procedure, and it might not be the best answer or the best solution to problems in a given area.

But let us return now to the problem of the relationship between the type of structure, the form of an organization, and its efficiency in a conflict situation. It has been suggested that a group's structure may be one of the determining factors in a successful action in a conflict area, and that smaller groups structured for conflict may succeed in establishing control over vast majorities which are passive and unorganized, or organized in such a way that they are unable to resist dynamic and well-organized groups. We may further suggest a tentative hypothesis: that in a time of political and social crisis, small command-organized political parties sustained by outside support may establish control over large groups and associations that are neither oriented toward conflict nor organized into command groups, but which are based on consensus.

We shall discuss and classify the various party types from the viewpoint of their efficiency in conflict situations.

Sociological and political studies of political parties constitute a large body of literature. But most of the interest in the study of political parties centers on the problems of ideology, the relationship between social structure, social class, and voting behavior. The classic field of study of political parties is the relationship between the ideology of the party and the social-economic conditions and class structure. The study of the emergence of the elites and of leadership is the focus of attention of the sociologist. The oligarchical tendency of political parties was another area of discussion at the turn of the century. But in most studies of political parties, the problem of organizational structure is secondary.

Organizational structure of political parties

What are the origins of the modern organizational structures of political parties? They can be traced to five major sources, some consensus- and others command-oriented: 1] the Anglo-American pattern of political parties; 2] the movements of the French Revolution, especially the Jacobins; 3] secret societies, such as the Carbonari; 4] the "circles," loosely organized, independent, political discussion groups (characteristic of early Russian and Polish movements); 5] democratic parties with an efficient bureaucratic apparatus; and 6] assimilation of the military pattern by the mass parties of the interwar period.

It is difficult to give a definite date for the origin of political patterns. They change as the social, economic, and political conditions change, as new ideologies develop. And the forms which appeared in the eighteenth, and later in the nineteenth and twentieth centuries were merely reflections or continuations of earlier developments. However, the *modern* forms of political organization can be traced to the eighteenth-century British parties and to the French Revolution.

The British pattern of political clubs and political parties had a wide influence in the United States and the entire British Empire. These parties and clubs were originally loosely organized groups representing vague, general ideologies with definite economic interests. Even today, political clubs of this type have neither a rigid discipline nor a rigid, centralistic organization.

The local clubs or local sections of the party have a certain responsibility and power. However, this does not necessarily mean that the emergence of leadership in those groups is always democratic. Nonetheless, local groups have influence and power, and members and local clubs are not subject to a rigid discipline. This type of party represents a "federalistic pattern."

Political clubs appeared in France at the beginning of the French Revolution, with ideological issues and philosophical problems playing a greater role than they did in the English clubs. An extensive political symbolism appeared at this time: slogans and verbal and iconic symbols such as pictures and idealizations of the revolution. These symbols had a multiple function. They integrated revolutionary groups and intensified the emotional tensions preliminary to political, dynamic action.

The new political party organization appeared with the Jacobin movement. The Jacobins, especially in their later period, introduced a strong political, ideological discipline, a system of coercion by fear (terror) and threat. Now, the political movement had an elaborate ideology and symbolism and a strong political structure of a command type, controlled by a minority. Substantial deviation from the ideological tenets was punished, and those who differed were called enemies of the people.

Since ideological differences grew, since problems of the maintenance of power were difficult, the institutional structure was reinforced by extreme forms of the punishment-reward system: by terror. The appeal of values and of the ideological system was probably weaker than one would suppose, for the maintenance of an ideology and of values became dependent on the existence of a rigid and strong institutional structure.

The French Revolution had a permanent influence on the development of political parties on the European continent, perhaps even greater than had the English political party system. A party based on strong discipline, organized along command lines, with a mechanism of coercion based on punishment and reward; a party with an elaborate and strong ideology, maintaining and preserving the "purity" of the ideology and eliminating political deviancy, was largely a Jacobin invention. In the later period of the revolution, François Babeuf and his friends and allies, representing the radical wing of the Jacobins, outlined a pattern for a political organization based on centralization and military structure.[15]

Centralism in political organization has been accepted in various degrees on the European continent. Some political parties are more, others less, centrally organized, but on the whole, they have more centralization than the British or the American. Between wars, the central committees of continental political parties generally had more power than the national committees of the British or American parties. The decisions of the central committee were, as a rule, accepted by the local committees not only as general directives but frequently as orders that had to be executed. A social-democratic party, a party of labor, was structured according to the needs and political conditions of the country. Since the parties of the working class were struggling for rapid and basic social changes, some centralization was essential to secure coordination of action and rapid goal attainment.

The third pattern appears in the secret societies of the eighteenth and nineteenth centuries, for example, the Italian Carbonari. Techniques of secret action and organization are major characteristics of these groups, methods essential to future underground revolutionary organizations.

The secret societies of the eighteenth century developed strong ideological ritualism and symbolism. They also developed grades of membership according to the level of secrecy. In certain countries, a direct, traditional connection may be traced from secret societies to the first underground movements. This is the case, for instance, in Russia, where the first underground organization emerged one generation after the unsuccessful Decembrist revolution. The Polish revolutionary movement could probably establish a continuity from secret socities to later underground political organizations and movements. The organizational techniques, the ideology, and the historical tradition were transmitted to later generations. This combination, of a centralistic disciplined form of organization with secrecy, suggests the origin of a centralized underground political party.

Small informal discussion groups called "circles" suggest the fourth pattern of political party structure in Eastern Europe, and especially in such countries as Poland and Russia. Small groups, usually of students, met for discussion of political and philosophical issues. From these circles, political movements grew. This informal type of organization can be traced to the early socialist movement and to the populist movement of the 1860's and 1870's in Russia.

The social-democratic movement in Russia and Poland also grew out of the meetings of small informal groups of students and intellectuals which later developed into secret socialist societies and finally emerged as political parties. They were primarily ideological groups, and here ideological differences played a significant role. There were substantial differences between groups and also between individuals within the same circle. On one hand, the pattern of the circle supplied the federalistic structure for party organization in Poland and Russia; on the other hand, it set an example of small units and created a tradition for the "vanguardist-elite" centralistic parties of professional revolutionaries advanced later by Lenin.

In one form or another, the pattern of "circles" survived, and triggered opposition movements in contemporary Eastern Europe. Here belong the discussion clubs of Warsaw or Budapest, where the anti-Stalinist and humanizing tendencies germinated, even before the revolutions of 1956. The old German Social-Democratic party is a broad, democratic political party with an efficient administrative apparatus and substantial power vested in its Central Committee.

The last element, the assimilation of the military pattern into a political party structure, was, however, of major historical significance. Militarization of political parties, among other things, secured the victory of the fascists in Italy and the Nazis in Germany. This type of political organization is almost unknown in Great Britain or the United States, except for the so-called "lunatic fringe" of the extreme right. Where consensus on the basic form of government and basic values and political customs was widely shared, militarization of political parties did not occur.

The projection of the military structure into a political party appeared in the form of a political militia. This is a private military arm of a party. A "parallel organization," or as one may call it, a "sister organization," is a part of the "party establishment." The political militia or army is uniformed, has special symbols and even bands organized in military fashion, and is headed by commanders responsible to the party authorities. Political militias appeared in Germany, Italy, and Russia after World War I. Militias were organized by parties to overthrow the new republics and democracies, or to defend democratic institutions.

How did the political army begin? We may trace it to a number of sources and organizations, some of which are consensus-oriented and democratic in ideology; others are of the extreme right. The end of World War I, however, forms a dividing line in the history of the political armies of Europe.

The militarization of *mass* parties appeared after World War I. Until that time the political fighting squads, political revolutionary groups organized and trained for direct action, consisted of small units of selected and dedicated individuals, highly disciplined but not regimented. Personal sacrifice, individual struggle, was stressed.

The military pattern developed to a limited extent in revolutionary and terrorist organizations. Here, the organization was individualistic and consisted of a selected few. In the latter part of the nineteenth century in Russia there was little chance to achieve reforms through persuasion and regular political action. This led the Populist movement in Russia, especially in the late 1870's, to terrorist action.

Terrorist action by its very nature requires a different type of organization than that of a regular political party, and since the underground party's activities are focussed around direct and ardent struggle, the movement has to assume forms of organization based on strong command lines.

In Poland, the Socialist Party conducted revolutionary activities and was oriented toward the old insurrectionist pattern of organization. In Italy, the unification and liberation of the country was won by an ideological army led by men like Garibaldi and inspired by thinkers like Mazzini. In the Balkans, the political movements of the Serbs and Bulgarians fought for liberation from Turkish domination. Such a struggle involved partisan warfare and military organization. The partisan groups were small, highly mobile, and the membership was limited.

In consequence, the tradition of certain political parties, as well as their actual operation, was closely related to paramilitary organization. After the liberation of parts of territories, political organizations were closely associated with military action in order to complete the liberation of the entire territory. This was the case of the Bulgarian and Serbian organizations that later led to the formation of centralistic, secret organizations such as the Black Hand in Serbia, and the various Macedonian organizations in Bulgaria. In Poland, the leaders of the fighting squads of the Socialist Party later formed the Polish army. The tradition of the prewar "party militia" was innocent of expansionism beyond legitimate bounds. This was not so in Germany.

The beginnings of the military command structure as a parallel organization of political parties can be traced to very modest beginnings or to minor revolutionary parties.

Before the war, the meetings of the social-democratic parties required some kind of organization, some inner maintenance of order, and even protection against attacks of dissidents and enemies. For this purpose, at every meeting certain party members were assigned the function of maintaining order. Usually they had armbands indicating their function, and they would maintain order and secure the proper organization of the meeting. The storm division of the Nazis (S.A.) originated in the 1920's from the "order-keepers" or "bouncers." [16]

The appearance of large political armies in Europe is, however, related to the revolutionary processes following World War I, which was the decisive period in the development of political mass armies. The prewar revolutionaries who harassed the Czar and his system in Russia and the regime in Poland did not develop into large political armies. The postwar development was different. Mass parties produced political mass militias, large paramilitary organizations, symptomatic of the coming of a totalitarian system.

These mass armies have their own roots—the right-wing parties—in military traditions and in the formal training of their commanders and members. These were the mass armies of political conquest, takeover, and defense. They were legal, recognized political militias, with banners and insignia.

The postwar political mass armies historically originated with 1] the Red Guard of the Russian Revolution of 1917, 2] the fascist movement in Italy, and 3] the development of the political mass militias in Germany. The pattern of a militarized mass party was, however, developed primarily by the fascists and imitated by the Nazis.

The end of World War I brought revolutions and profound social change. The old empires disintegrated. Powerful mass movements emerged, among them large nationalist, social-democratic, democratic, Christian-democratic and Communist movements. In Germany a military form of party organization emerged rapidly, especially on the extreme right. Young officers of the disbanded armies organized political movements, structured in military fashion, and directed against the republic and political reforms. The military arm of the Nationalist Party was represented by *Stalhelm,* who wore Prussian-gray military uniforms. In Austria a similar organization known as *Heimwehr* emerged, connected with the right-wing movement. The Social-Democrats formed another, the *Schutzbund.*

In Germany the republican forces could not rely on the army, which was staffed by old imperial officers. It was faced by conspiracies of right-wing groups; the growing nationalist movements which had their private armies. In consequence, the republican forces organized their own political militia, known as *Reichsganner*. Later the Nazis developed a powerful political mass army composed of S.A. (*Sturmabteilung,* storm troops) and S.S. (*Schutzstaffel,* elite bodyguard). Their barracks could be noticed in Berlin in the 1930's. The S.S. and S.A. were trained for direct physical action against political opponents. The Communists developed their own private army, the *Red Front.* The militaristic pattern of organization of the right-wing parties was integral to the party structure.

Between 1920 and 1930, the peoples of Austria and Germany suffered from deep inner divisions. They had lost what Taine called spontaneous national agreement. There was no unity on basic principles of government and change. Both nations were divided into many hostile camps. Political armies of the right were ready for attack; the parties of center and left prepared for defense. Both strategies were related to the values and structures of the parties, with the parties of aggression having a rigid command structure. In the meantime, a show of force was made through manifestations and parades of private armies. The long and highly emotional reviews of *Stalhelm,* S.S., or S.A. had elements of a modern war dance.

Most revolutionary struggles lead to a centralization of political parties and to the development of political military units, in the form of a militia, partisans, or fighting squads. This was as true of the Mexican revolution of this century as of the Irish movements in Western Europe or the Serbian or Bulgarian revolutionary movements in the Balkans. However, with the end of the revolutionary struggle, such units usually disappear or are transformed into highly respected organizations of political veterans. Nonetheless, revolutionary movements had their elements of command structure and centralism, which in various degrees, in various countries, influenced the party organization. This was, however, a different tradition of different times than those of the political mass army of the militarized political party invented or developed by Mussolini and the fascists.

The various patterns of political structure appeared in our history in various combinations. It would seem that the six sources, in various degrees, have contributed to a variety of contemporary party structures.

Types of political parties

We shall review briefly and classify certain "ideal types" of political parties. The classification is focussed on internal structure, the organizational pattern, and the party discipline, not on ideology, values, or strategy.

All parties have some kind of control over their membership, but certain parties are more geared toward consensus, agreement, and persuasion, and others toward coercion and command structure. The selection of types and the classification of the parties follows these basic patterns. However, the two significant types are the centralistic and federalistic.

1]

We shall start with a loosely organized movement which we shall call *Movimiento*. The Latin American countries perhaps fathered this type of social-political movement. The three essential elements are: a definite leadership or leader; loosely organized groups; and a vast mass of sympathizers. This type of movement usually has a definite goal and a definite target of action. Here belongs, for instance, the Mexican revolutionary movement in the time of Francisco Madero. Its target was clear—the overthrow of the dictatorship of Porfirio Díaz. Its goals and ideology were definite: constitutional changes and democratic principles were to be introduced into the Mexican Republic. Later the revolutionary movement extended its ideological and practical socio-economic goals. The early development of the revolutionary movement in Cuba could also be called a *Movimiento,* although there were already well-established groups at the University of Havana.

2]

The federalistic type of party organization is indicated on Model No. I. For the sake of simplification, I shall call the central committee the supreme and decision-making body of the party, and omit the distinctions among deliberating, legislative, and executive bodies. In a federalistic system we distinguish the central committee and local groups. (I have marked the *locus* of power and decision with a triangle.)

In a federalistic system the power and decision are located in local groups and,

Model No. I—The Federalistic Pattern

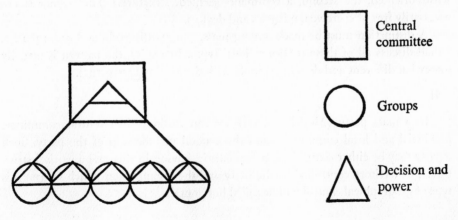

Central committee

Groups

Decision and power

in certain areas, in the central committee. But the central committee's power is relatively weak, and depends on the decisions and on the views of the local committees, whatever may be the internal manipulations and power structure of the latter. (I have used the square to identify the central committee; the circle for local groups.)

3]

In an "ideal type" of centralistic organization (Model No. II), power is vested primarily in the central committee. The local groups have very little decision-making authority and limited or no power. In the Communist Party, for example,

Model No. II—The Centralistic Pattern

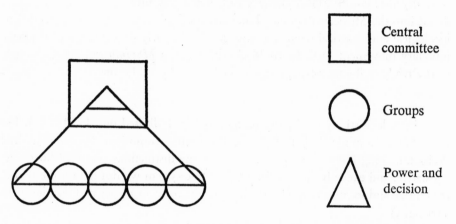

Central
committee

Groups

Power and
decision

the decision-making power lies with the central committee, and not in the local party units. The organization is centralistic. (I have called the first pattern a consensus-oriented, the second, a command-oriented, structure.) The former is not necessarily free of coercive tendencies and devices.

A distinction must be made among mass, vanguardist, cell, and cadre parties. I shall discuss all of these parties as ideal types. In reality, the pattern is actually somewhat different and does not comply with the ideal-type structure.

4]

In a mass party (Model No. III) we can distinguish a central committee, provincial and local committees, and the general membership of the party. Such a party may be either centralistic or federalistic, having in this case a vertical structure. The territory controlled by the party and the organization which secures this type of geographical control will be called horizontal.

Model No. III—The Mass Party

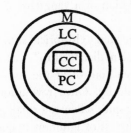

C.C.—Central committee

P.C.—Provincial committees

L.C.—Local committees

M—Membership

5]

The vanguardist party (Model No. IV) consists of a small, all-powerful central committee which makes decisions and a selected number of party members, called "activists," whose profession is politics and party activities. These members are selected carefully. Sympathizers have only a loose connection with the party. Their function is to give the activists and the central committee financial and political support. They have no direct influence on the central committee, nor are they members of the political party.

Model No. IV—The Vanguardist Party

C.C.—Central committee
A.C.—Party members,
         activists

Sympathizers

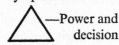—Power and
         decision

This type of party, which was formulated in its classical form by Lenin in his book *What Has To Be Done* (1902), is of much earlier origin. Its beginning can be traced to the end of the eighteenth century, to the Jacobins and to Babeuf, who led "the conspiracy of equals," an attempted revolutionary coup at the end of the French Revolution. In fact, in Babeuf's writings we have indications of a vanguardist type of party.

Later, in the middle of the nineteenth century, the French revolutionary Louis Blanqui, who was a "babeuvian" in his youth, outlined the pattern of vanguardist organization and planned the establishment of a "Parisian dictatorship." In 1875, the theory of a vanguardist organization of professional revolutionaries was advanced by the Russian revolutionary writer Peter Tkachev. In "Nabat," a paper published in London, Tkachev suggested the organization of a vanguardist party that would seize power and establish a dictatorship.

The development of this party structure is closely related to historical situations. Blanqui's suggestion of the establishment of a "Parisian dictatorship" was made because he was convinced that as long as the Church controlled the masses in France, the elections would favor a reactionary majority. Once revolutionaries achieved power, gradual reforms would follow. In Blanqui's scheme, a small group of humane revolutionary altruists would act in the interest of ignorant majorities.

Once the French Republic emerged in the 1870's, Blanqui abandoned his theory as no longer needed, since gradual reforms could be advanced in a democratic way.[16] Similarly, Tkachev witnessed the failure of the Russian Populist Revolutionary movement to win the peasant to the cause of progressive social change and the overthrow of the Czarist system. Also, the ignorant masses gave little hope of following the new, advanced and revolutionary idea of a temporary dictatorship, dedicated to the idea of the abolition of exploitation, and leading to a new political system of freedom and social justice. On the other hand, the fall of the Paris Commune and the suspension of political liberties in Germany disenchanted him with Western democracy as a road of change.

Perhaps Tkachev's writing had some influence on Lenin's theory. It seems, however, that the experience of the Populist movement of the 1870's had greater effect.

After an unsuccessful attempt to win the masses by propaganda for a federalistic type of political organization, the Populists changed their structure to a centralistic one more suited to the new tactics of direct terroristic struggle. Lenin, in his essay *What Has To Be Done*, indicates the need for a small and centrally organized party of professional revolutionaries as more suitable for the objectives of overthrowing the Czarist regime. In some areas, the vanguardist party was effective in attaining the goals outlined by its founders.

6]

The "small units" pattern (Model No. V) consists of two related patterns: the "cell" system and the "fives." Both types are forms of an underground organization; the difference lies in the level of secrecy. The "fives" represent a tighter, more secret organization, in the technical pattern; a "deeper underground."

Cells consist of five to ten or more members who act together, sometimes within another institution, party, or organization. The cell organizes political action and manipulates large organizations, while keeping secret the identity and operations of cell members. Cell members know each other and act together. They are also familiar with the "legal" ("open") structure of their organization and its leadership and may participate in general meetings of the party. The cell system

Model No. V—Small Units

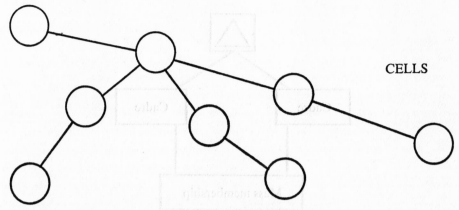

CELLS

was and is also applied as an open (not secret) form of party organization. It is currently used, for instance, by certain Italian political parties.

The cell is frequently the underground structure of a legal party. In essence, it acts as an underground, secret group. Its leader, or liaison, may be known only by a pseudonym. The system permits wide penetration, indirect control, and manipulation of a vast network of a variety of organizations and enterprises, few of which realize that such operations are underway. In that way, a party controls a system of organizations much larger than its limited membership would normally permit.

The "fives" consist, at least in theory, of groups no larger than five. In an "ideal type," no member knows more than five members of the entire political organization, and usually no fewer than two. The leader of the group knows four members of his five and one liaison member of the committee.

The committee may also consist of five members; its "lines of communication" may, however, be different. A nonleader knows one member who brought him (or whom he has won) to the organization, and usually one other member, perhaps the leader. As a rule pseudonyms are used, and a simple inquiry about real names may be regarded as an attempt at treason. Special underground fighting squads (not the "regular" underground army) were probably organized in that way.[18] In case of arrest or treason, the losses are limited, since none of the militants, with the exception of the top leadership, knows more than five, and them only by pseudonym. But theory is different from practical organization and action.[19]

7]

The cadre party (Model No. VI) is a command-oriented party. Cadres comprise carefully selected members of the party who are politically active and dedicated to the party (activists; in French, *militants*). Frequently they derive a number of

Model No. VI—The Cadre Party

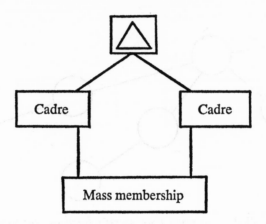

privileges from party membership. This was true, for instance, with the fascist and Nazi parties. In an ideal type of cadre party we may distinguish the central committee, the cadres, and the mass membership, as in Model No. VI. The central committee is usually all-powerful. It controls the cadres, and through the cadres, the mass membership. Cadre parties were specially built and suited for dynamic political action.

8]

We have finally arrived at a combination of a number of patterns, and this combination, containing elements of cadres and private armies, is especially suited for dynamic political action, political attack, and the seizure of political power. This type of party has a command structure. We shall call such parties militarized command parties.

We may now follow Model No. VII. On the top we find the all-powerful central committee; then, what we shall call intermediary committees, provincial or local committees connected with the party cadres. The party cadres and the central committee are closely related, on the one hand, to the mass movement and, on the other, to the cell organization. But this is not all. The central committee also controls, as we see on Model No. VII, private armies or political militias and partisan units.

Let us review for a moment the functioning of various parts of the party. The mass movements supply basic support, membership, and perhaps part of the finances. Usually the main source of the financial support of such a party, which is kept secret, comes from special interest groups, wealthy sympathizers or fellow-travelers, or foreign governments. The running of such an elaborate political enterprise is an expensive proposition.

Model No. VII—Militarized Command Party

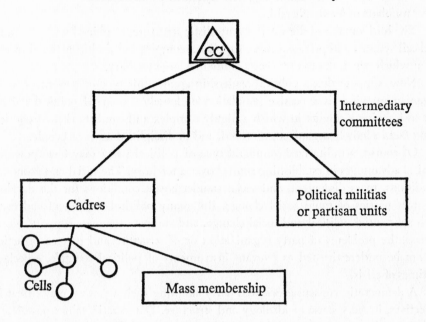

The masses of those parties are rather submissive. They are subject to the decision of the central committee and are directly controlled by the cadres, which obey the former. The central committee, the cadres and the mass movement are "legal" and open. Contrariwise, the cells, the small units, are secret or underground. This supplies unusual strength and maneuverability to the party since it has both a legal, "open," and an underground organization. Furthermore, the private armies or partisan units supply an element of physical force and terror to subdue opponents.

A complex militarized command party is a powerful political instrument of attack. It may force into submission a much larger but differently organized or passive opposition. It is "multi-functional," since the various sections of the party perform different functions and operations. Still, operations are complementary, and permit intensive action and simultaneous attacks.

This complex political machinery, operated on the command principle, was developed and perfected between 1918 and World War II. It was first geared for conquest; later, for the consolidation of power. In the latter stage, the party machinery was integrated with the powerful coercive machinery of the state.

The political strength of the totalitarian state lies, among other factors, in this combination. A similar pattern was applied by the Nazi Party. Emotional tension was built up by propaganda. Then, ritualism and symbolism were used for collective psychological excitement, which in turn was channelled into hostilities and aggression. This combination supplied dynamism and force far superior to the sheer numbers of its membership.

The horizontal and the vertical centralistic structure, combined with the cadre and cell systems and private armies, supplies a complex but multifunctional instrument which penetrates many aspects of life in a large territory.

Now, suppose that a political leadership applies this type of pattern of social organization vis-à-vis a passive population or loosely organized political parties. Let us imagine a conflict in which a highly complex and combat-oriented political party faces a loosely organized, confused, and undisciplined mass of people.

Of course, a militarized-command type of political party may have potential tactical advantages in establishing control over a territory. The social and economic conditions, mass discontent, and social conflict create conditions for the development of parties of rapid social change. But many political movements advocate such substantial political and social change, and compete for mass support. Nonetheless, the problems of party organization or of structure and pattern of action cannot be underestimated as relevant instruments of political struggle, especially in times of crisis.

A democratic, consensus-oriented party adopting such a pattern may defeat its objectives, its very sense of ideology and structure. Democratic values postulate a defense against political attack by a highly coherent and dynamic party without a rigid structure, strongly based on common values and on dedication to principles, not on hatred. The dilemma of a democratic party's successful defense against a powerful, militarized totalitarian party has not been fully answered.

The militarized party

A militarized party is also an instrument for the consolidation of power. Usually, after the capture or penetration of an area, a totalitarian regime breaks any form of organized political life, and sometimes even organizes religious or social life. In that way the population of the area is immobilized and its organizations disrupted and delegalized, while the command party, the conquering party, grows in power and total control. Since this is the party having military units and control of the government, which in turn controls the weapons, the now disorganized population becomes helpless vis-à-vis the growing power system.

In this process of reintegration and consolidation of power, the institutions and values are significant. In the seized territory, even in the case of mass support for the winning party—as was the case in Austria, in the Sudetenland, or in Saarland during Hitler's conquest of the late thirties—opposition still exists and loyalties to old institutions, principles, and values survive. Perhaps certain members of the opposition still form some kind of group, legally or illegally.

The totalitarian ruling party wins power by weakening any forms of organized life outside its control. In consequence, it tries to establish the dominance of loyalty toward the ruling party and ideology. Children in the schools are taught that their first loyalty is to the party and the leader and not to their parents. In that way the essential organized unit, the family, is weakened vis-à-vis the party. Similarly, other forms of organized life are disrupted and a virtual monopoly is established over the social organization.

Control of population movements may further increase the power of the ruling party. Any movement from one town to another, any purchase of a bus or rail ticket, except by members of the ruling political party, may require the permission of the police. In that way the conquering party, even if it is not very strong in numbers, can move its militia, its private army, very rapidly from one place to another by public transportation.

As I have already mentioned, what we are trying to suggest here are not normative issues, but empirical issues of efficiency. The efficiency of an institutional or organizational structure can be measured by goal attainment. Although the winning command party may not necessarily be morally a better party, it is specially built for attack and conquest. It is multifunctional, thus highly differentiated.

What happens to the consensus-oriented political parties when they face this type of situation and a command-structured, aggressive, cadre military organization? It is difficult to give a single answer. More than 60 years ago, George Simmel argued that conflict leads, as a rule, to more centralistic forms of organization.[20]

The fact that conflict strengthens the coherence of a group and contributes to a change in structure, frequently leading to a centralistic form, cannot be denied. The structure of conflict groups no doubt bears many similarities. The organization of the conflict groups of the aggressive party forces the victim to reorganize his groups into a more centralistic pattern. Independently of Simmel, Lenin, in his book *What Has To Be Done,* indicated the need for centrally organized parties in a policy of conflict against a centrally organized autocratic system.

Long before Lenin, the Russian revolutionaries realized the significance of party structure in a conflict situation. The Populists of the latter part of the nineteenth century discussed the problem of party structure. Eventually, after their unsuccessful attempt at mass revolt, the revolutionaries split and the group which embarked on a terroristic action assumed a centralistic form of organization. When, in 1903, the Social-Democratic Party split into the Bolsheviks and Mensheviks, the problem of party structure was again an issue.

In a situation of conflict or defense, institutions usually adjust their structure to the changed circumstances. It would, however, be difficult to establish a single rule for such changes. The democratic organization, the consensus-oriented institution, may change in a variety of ways.

As has been indicated, the change of institutions in a conflict will depend on (1) the nature and the structure of the institutions involved, (2) the value structure of the institutions and the degree in which these values are shared and supported by its members, (3) the pattern of action, the strategy and tactics, that the group controlling the institution decides to use either in defense or in attack, (4) the general conditions: the social, economic, and political situations in which the action is to be developed and in which the group operates, and (5) the very nature of the conflict (whether social, economic, or political patterns of aggression).

The state is an integral institution composed of many diverse institutions, integrated through the government. In a conflict with other states, a democratic state changes in a different way than does an authoritarian state.

The two world wars permitted us to observe the fact that the party organizations within the democratic states did not change substantially during an outside conflict. Perhaps leadership increased its influence and its power. The coherence, the degree of shared values, especially at the first moment of war, might also have increased, but fundamentally the basic structure of the institutions did not change. Within the state as an institution, the government gained in power and here was a centralistic tendency. The role of the military establishment also increased. Charles Beard expressed the fear that, because of wars, the future "military man" and military force will increase in power and significance in the United States to the same extent as in other countries.[21] The power of the executive branch of the government has also increased, and increases continually.

However, changes within certain institutions in a consensus-oriented democracy differ from those in autocratic or command systems. There is not even one type of army, but many types. Even in times of war, when the power of the army increases and discipline is reinforced, the changes in the formal and informal structures of a democratic-oriented army are different from those in the authoritarian one. Nonetheless, the significance of the army and the military not only during but after the war does increase in democratic countries.

During World War I, the civilian government retained control over the army in both Great Britain and France, while in Germany the power shifted to the military and there was a primacy of military over civilian authority. Contrary to George Simmel's thesis that centralization displaces even the most perfect democracy in times of conflict, the world conflict affected nations differently. Democracy in France, Great Britain, and the United States was by no means totally displaced by war. The effects of war were different in Germany than in Austro-Hungary or in Russia. Thus conflict exercised a different influence on different types of institutions and societies.

We may return, however, to our major topic. Suppose we have in a tension area two types of parties: an attacking, militarized, command-structured party and a defending or opposing consensus-oriented party. What effect has such a conflict situation on the consensus-oriented organization? Here too a number of alternatives are open according to the conditions under which the party has to operate. If the command party conquers the territory and establishes very tight control, the opposing democratic parties are frequently driven underground. The history of the underground movement teaches us that the efficient underground parties, democratic or not, assume a centralistic command structure. This, however, is not identical with the displacement of democratic values. Democratic values can be maintained even under conditions of centralistic command party structure, at least for a time. The period of struggle is regarded as one of transition, following which the democratic structure of the party will, in all probability, be reconstructed.

It is also feasible, however, that under specific conditions, the consensus-oriented party with strong shared values may exercise a good deal of influence even without changing its basic concepts and institutional framework. The Indian Congress Party was very efficient in the struggle for independence. The Indians, however, used a strategy and tactics of nonviolence that was effective against the British colonial administration. But this would not work in a conflict with a totalitarian power.

This may lead us to some general inferences. There are varieties of conflicts, but our concern is with changes in institutions in time of international and violent conflict.

No doubt in times of war or violent conflict, the centralistic tendencies of the state increase and the command lines of institutions are reinforced. The conflict has, however, different effects on different structures. The state which prepares for an attack or for aggression displaces its free institutions by an expanse of centralism. A state which is defending its position also changes its structure. In limited tension areas the command structure and highly centralized military parties have shown effectiveness in the initial period of conquest over societies which are consensus-oriented and which have only loosely organized movements. In a contest between command-structured parties which use violence and consensus-oriented parties which do not change their nature, the command, military type of political parties in tension areas, at least in the beginning, usually has tactical advantages.

The democratic organization of a party supplies, however, elements of elasticity, local initiative, and independent action, which the command-structured totalitarian party lacks. Nonetheless, to preserve these qualities, the democratic parties may be forced to regroup the membership, tighten the lines of command, reassign responsibility, and reinforce the consensus structure with additional command lines. Thus, the organization of the aggressor forces changes in the organization of the victim toward centralism and command, and the strategy of political attack determines the strategy of political defense.

ii.

THE STRUCTURE OF HUMAN RELATIONS
IN CENTRAL-EASTERN EUROPE*

The myth of a homogeneous national state: Central-Eastern Europe—an area of minorities

The social myth of "pure races" has an extensive and significant history. It took a long time, indeed, to destroy this fallacy. Still, despite evidence to the contrary, some people believe in it. Another, less harmful social myth that still persists is that of the "homogeneous" nation.

All nation-states in Europe, America, Asia, or Africa have minorities. Adolf Hitler insisted that the Germans were a homogeneous nation and tried to support his theory by mass extermination of non-Aryans. The fact remains, however, that man moves, intermarries, and conquers. Migration and war are sources of minorities, and migration is natural to mankind; it is a part of history.

Nation-states of Central and Eastern Europe are and were, without exception, states with large minorities. Even mass migrations, transfers of population, and deportations, especially after World War II, did not change this characteristic. True, in certain countries there are fewer minorities than there were prior to World War II. Nevertheless, all continue to have minorities.

During and after World War I an effort was made to establish homogeneous national states in this area; mononational states that would correspond to the ethnic identity of their inhabitants. True, after 1918 more nations in this area enjoyed

* This chapter is based upon an article by the author, published in Vol. 9, No. 2 of the *Journal of Human Relations*, with permission of the publisher, Central State College, Wilberforce, Ohio.

their own statehood than at any other time in history except in the ninth and tenth centuries. Nevertheless, not one of the post-1918 Central and Eastern European states was a truly homogeneous nation-state. All without exception were multinational.

With few exceptions, those states with large minorities had strong nationalistic parties, intolerant toward minorities and aggressive in their desire for homogeneity. This was, of course, politically absurd, but politics seldom is logical.

World War II changed this picture in a most tragic way. Many of the descendants of the Jewish exiles who escaped the fires of the Spanish Inquisition in the fifteenth century and found a haven in the Balkans did not escape the fires and gases of the Nazi-German concentration camps. Mass migration of the Nazi-German occupation was followed by postwar population exchanges and expulsions. Despite all those changes, minorities remained and today all the states in this area have their full share.

The tension area of the Western and Eastern Church

Central and Eastern Europe was for centuries a battlefield of nations; an area where Asiatic invasions clashed with European resistance; an area of German, Russian, and French invasions. Germans also migrated peacefully from the West, while Vallachs moved westward in summer with their herds.

In the borderlands the continuous interpenetration of ethnic groups was a part of everyday life.

The dividing line between the great Christian religions—the Western and the Eastern church—runs through Central and Eastern Europe and this division is one of the most significant and culturally important aspects of this area. For centuries this has been a tension area of powerful churches. Sometimes the tension increased, sometimes it lessened. But it left its imprint on the social psychology of the ethnic groups in the area.

One of the oldest historical conflicts is that between the Western church—guided by Rome—and the Eastern church of Byzantine tradition, with its centers in Constantinople, Kiev, and Moscow. Since the great schism of the ninth century, the Western church has sought to extend its influence in the Eastern provinces. The Eastern Orthodox church, in turn, defends its spiritual realm and also tries to extend westward. One need only read Dostoyevski's comment on Catholicism and Rome in his *Journal of the Writer* to realize the intensity of prejudice and conflict. Social wars in this area had religious overtones. In the midst of those strong pressures the Protestants of Bohemia, Poland, and Transylvania could not gain a permanent hold over other national groups. Jewish and Moslem minorities survived the pressures, as did Protestant minorities.

This division is not solely historical or religious. Once a traveller from Cracow in the West to Lvov in the East passed the river San, he would notice that the Gothic towers of the Roman Catholic churches were joined by the onion-shaped domes of the Orthodox cerkievs. Should he visit the villages around, he would notice that some of the inhabitants spoke Ukrainian and wrote in a Cyrillic script—which came from Byzantium—and others in Latin alphabet.

If he changed his itinerary and moved to the Balkans, he would move through areas inhabited by Serbs and Croats. Both speak the same language, but Croats are Roman Catholic while Serbs are Orthodox; the Croat uses a Latin script, the Orthodox Serb, a Cyrillic one.

The dominant tendency—self-segregation

This general background does not embrace the complex social and economic canvas of the nations in this area. It is also necessary to consider the structure of human and social relations, so rich in cultural diversity, so varied in ethnic and religious minorities and subcultures. Above all, it is important to view conditions between the wars, since their effect on ethnic attitudes is still significant.

The tendency of ethnic groups in this area is toward self-segregation. Whether a ruling majority or a ruled minority, the national groups do not indicate any definite tendency toward assimilation. Of course, there were assimilationists; there were groups with a tendency toward cultural integration and the breaking of the rigid border of the in-group, especially among the "intelligentsia." There were situations in which the strong out-group attitude broke down. The dominant tendency was toward self-segregation.

Today, the same pattern prevails. Every nationality has a tendency to adhere rigidly to its traditions, language, cultural patterns, and customs. Since ethnic differences frequently coincide with religious differences, this has only enforced the trend.

The concept of nationality and nation-state in Europe—and more so in Eastern Europe—had and has strong elements of tribalism. A member of a tribe, unless adopted, is one born of tribal ancestry; of "tribal blood." He must prove his long affinity and his ancestry to be fully accepted as a member of a nation. Assimilation, under such conditions, becomes a difficult process. Of course, liberals, socialists, anarchists, or Communists advocated principles of subjective nationality and international tendencies. ("Once you feel you are a Czech, we shall accept you as a Czech" is the principle of subjective nationalism or national consciousness.) This was true also of democrats or Social Democrats. But the revival of anti-Semitic sentiments in the Soviet Union and in Central-Eastern Europe today, as well as antagonistic attitudes toward other ethnic groups, indicates that the behavioral patterns of the "tribal in-group" have not disappeared.

Conditions of integration: Eastern Europe and United States compared

Assimilation as a mass phenomenon, or integration into a pluralistic, co-ordinate, multicultural or multiracial system, appears only under certain, definite conditions. And even while these conditions are present, some tension and a great deal of prejudice remain. The problem of degree is, however, important. Let us glance at some of the determinants:

1]

In the dominant nationality that controls the state, there must be a substantial group which accepts the ethnic or religious minority as equals, even if this should mean a struggle against opposing and powerful forces. Such acceptance must be real.

2]

A latent tendency toward a pluralistic system is paramount. Toleration of different groups is not enough.

3]

A concept of state and the ideology of citizenship must be based primarily on a principle of common values, ideological or philosophical, and not on "common blood," or tribal-national origin.

4]

The process of integration or assimilation must be a two-way passage. The willingness of the majority group to accept the ethnic or religious minority groups does not suffice. An active tendency toward integration on the part of the minority is essential. The ethnic or religious minority must be willing to adjust whichever values, behavior patterns, or customs clash with the accepted way of life, or at least be willing to subdue them. One of those trends is, of course, the tendency toward self-segregation. A religious minority that refuses to associate with "dissidents" cannot be integrated easily.

All of these tendencies were weak among Central and Eastern Europeans as compared with those among Americans, who are a nation of assimilated immigrants.

It is, of course, true that there is assimilation in Central and Eastern European countries, especially among the educated and within the working class, but it is almost absent among the peasantry. This is not accidental. Among the intelligentsia and the workers there was a community of values and interests of an ideological as well as an intellectual nature that played a considerable role. Sizable sections of both groups were willing to accept others as co-nationals or as members of the same social class or political party. Such solidarity on a nonnational level was a bridge toward an effective integration.

Integration—let us call it a "pluralistic integration"—does not necessarily mean total cultural absorption into the ruling nation. The American Jews in New York or Chicago are fully integrated into the American nation, yet they do not have to abandon cherished traditions and values. The cultural integration of an ethnic group merely requires acceptance of certain values and patterns of social and political behavior; that is all. It does not involve total assimilation. However, such a process is one of selective assimilation; it presupposes a set of values rising above any ethnic or national values. In other words, there must be a different level of values that are common to, or accepted by, all nationalities or ethnic groups. This is true of the United States, where the civil rights and basic freedoms comprise a system of rules and values with no ethnic bias. This is perhaps the strongest ideological appeal of the American creed. Of course, this ideological level may often clash with reality—active prejudice does exist. However, the federal government does not incite ethnic antagonism, but makes every effort to lessen prejudices. A racial and ethnic minority can fight for equality by legal means. It has support of the law, of the dominant political philosophy.

Interpersonal and intergroup relations—consistent and inconsistent patterns

We may here suggest a hypothesis. Whenever culturally or racially different groups meet as *groups,* suspicion and even hostility is frequently present. Whenever *individuals* of different racial or cultural backgrounds meet, there is interest and sometimes mutual attraction. When individuals or small groups of different racial and cultural backgrounds meet in primary relations in neighborhoods and communities, friendly relations may develop if time is given and values are present that permit adjustment. This has been the experience in Central and Eastern Europe.

Let us now proceed with this structure of social and personal values:

1]

Interpersonal relations between individuals of various ethnic and religious backgrounds.

2]

Intergroup relations: (a) Primary intergroup relations (peer groups, neighborhoods, communities). (b) Intergroup relations on a secondary level: Here belong the attitudes toward an ethnic or religious out-group as an "abstract collective" (to use Wiese's definition). On this level, the attitude of hostility is strongly expressed among certain sections of the population. These expressions, normally latent, explode in times of extreme crisis.

Perhaps some examples or models will clarify this structure better than a purely abstract presentation.

a)   A Pole, a Catholic, has as his closest friend a Pole of Jewish faith. Our Catholic Pole associates not only with Poles. He does not differentiate on ethnic, racial, or religious lines. He relates on the basis of individual quality. He is a talented writer and has some official status. In his youth he belonged to a political party and organizations that strongly opposed religious and ethnic prejudices. During World War II he hid his Jewish friend in his home although this made him subject to the death penalty. He was and is consistent on his primary and secondary level: *his structure of human relations is consistent.*

A Ukrainian high-school student in a town that was once in Eastern Poland and is now in the Western Ukraine, lives in a community composed of Ukrainians, Orthodox Poles, Catholics, and Jews. His closest friend is a student of Jewish background. He has no prejudice toward his neighbors, and is a member of an organization that advocates good social and human relations between nationalities. We may say that his structure of social relations is consistent, since on the interpersonal and intergroup levels, his behavioral pattern and value system are also consistent. Since they are oriented toward friendship and cooperation, we shall call them a *consistent-positive pattern.*

b)   Another Ukrainian does not fraternize with Poles, advocates a mono-racial state, and shows hostility toward other groups. We shall call his concept of human relations a *consistent-negative* pattern, since it is negative on all levels—interpersonal and intergroup; primary and secondary.

c)   Not infrequently, the pattern is friendly toward individuals, hostile toward the group. A lawyer of Polish and Catholic background is friendly with his colleagues of Jewish faith. He has no intimate, close friends among them, but he has good "colleagues" with whom he chats in court. He is also willing to substitute for them in simple cases, if necessary. In the apartment house in which he lives, he is "correct" with his Jewish neighbors; with some he is friendly. Both in interpersonal relations and primary intergroup relations he shows no open hostility. However, the same man, when at meetings of the Bar Association, favors policies that would limit admission of Jewish lawyers. He supports a party which has anti-Semitic tendencies. In consequence, he is antagonistic on the secondary level of his human relations. We may call his actions an *inconsistent pattern* of human relations or, specifically, *inconsistent-secondary-negative,* since it is negative on the secondary level of intergroup relations. This was a frequent pattern in Central and Eastern Europe.

d) Now, let us take the case of a conservative (not fascist) Hungarian who does not have, nor wishes to have, personal friends among the Serbs; nor does he live with them in one community. However, he opposes their persecution and massacre in Novy Sad during World War II. His behavior pattern and the structure of his human relations is positive on the level of secondary intergroup relations and negative in other areas. We may call it an *inconsistent-secondary-level negative pattern.*

The in- and out-groups—intensive attitudes toward the out-group

The Eastern European area is not a homogeneous cultural area, of course, and there are differences in cultural patterns and value structures of various ethnic and religious groups. Furthermore, social and human relations are not necessarily different from those in other parts of Europe. But there is a certain emphasis on values and behavior to which we have pointed. One of those is the inconsistency in human relations.

The anti-Semitic mayor of Vienna, Luegger, is credited with a famous saying, "I decide who is a Jew," in answer to criticism that he associated with Jews, proving, again, the inconsistent pattern of social relations. But there is also another "emphasis" in human relations in this area.

The strong emphasis on in-group and out-group is also associated with stronger intensity of feelings and attitudes. The enemy is hated more and the best friend is closer to a man in most of the East European national groups than among the Americans. The various types of relationship within the in-group are clearly indicated and identified by verbal symbols.

We shall use as an example of Central and Eastern European relations a "model" of a structure of Polish in-group relations based on student relations, but general to all social classes. This "model" is, in outline, representative also of other ethnic groups. With each out-category, social distance increases strongly, as does rigidity in interpersonal relations.

THE MODEL OF IN-GROUP RELATIONS

1]

The best friend who is the only one, and perhaps closer to a young man than his brother.

2]

A group of friends who are close. Sometimes the change of the "best" friend is accomplished among the five or six friends who meet frequently.

3]

"Kolega" (a colleague)—a man who is much more distant than a friend, but still one who is friendly and who is often called by the first name.

4]

Acquaintance—usually people who are casual friends only, and are not addressed by their first name.

Beyond this fourth category, secondary relationships and out-groups begin. One greets and addresses differently members of those different groups. In this respect, there is a good deal of formality.

On this highway of history which is called Central and Eastern Europe nations have grown among whom hospitality is cordial, friendship intense, but so is antagonism.

Structure of Interpersonal Relationships and Social Distance

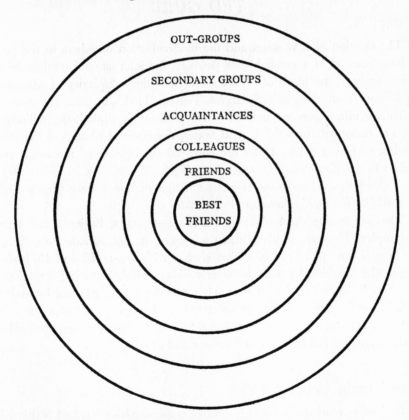

iii.

TENSIONS IN THE HORN OF AFRICA

TED GURR

The creation of new states and the modernization of others in the postwar era have resulted in a much higher potential for international tension. The following study of the Horn of Africa exemplifies the complexity of tensions that can develop among "emerging" nations. Tensions in this instance are secondary—i.e., among minor powers—but the active presence of diplomatic, military, and technical personnel from the United States, the Soviet Union, and the People's Republic of China demonstrates the potential significance of the Horn and its tensions in the East-West arena. Ranking Table *A* (primary and secondary tensions) identifies tensions in the Horn as consequential, secondary (group *B*), with a potentiality for manipulation and escalation.

Tensions among three states of the Horn—Somalia, Ethiopia, and Kenya—are complex. They are fundamentally a consequence of Somali nomadism, and of a Somali concept of the state that clashes with the policies of Ethiopia and Kenya. The resulting tensions are clearly interpolitical, involving state action at several levels, including the military. They are also interethnic and interreligious, for the Somalis have a clear sense of ethnic and religious difference from their neighbors. Intereconomic tensions also are present, since the principal object of Somali migration has been access to water and grazing areas.

Tensions in tropical Africa

In the few years during which most of tropical Africa has had political independence, the tensions among the states have, with the exception of the Congo crisis, been secondary and, in most instances, transitory. Four cases of international tension involving independent tropical African states may be cited: 1] Ghana and Togo, 2] Mali and Senegal, 3] the former French Congo and the former Belgian Congo, and 4] the Somali Republic and its neighbors, Ethiopia, Kenya, and French Somaliland.

In all cases the tensions were of a secondary nature, that is, they did not directly involve the major world powers and were territorially limited. In three of the four—the Mali-Senegal dispute being the exception—the principal source of tension was the division of a major tribal group[1] among two or more countries by arbitrary international boundaries. In all except the Somali case, tensions were limited functionally to economic and diplomatic sanctions or surreptitious intervention in internal politics.

The first two of these tensions appear to have been resolved by accommodation. Tensions between the two Congos appear chronic. The unresolved "Somali question" has been characterized by intensification of tensions on several levels, and was in 1963 the major source of international tension in tropical Africa. The subsidence of open conflict during 1964 and 1965 should not obscure the fact that its sources persist.

These general observations suggest questions on which an analysis of the Somali tension area may cast some light. First is the general question of what relevant factors and sequence of events can lead to international tensions based on tribal irredentism. How important a role can tribalism be expected to play as a source of international tension in Africa? Why has the Somali tension increased in magnitude while comparable tensions in the area have been accommodated? The final question is one of policy: What steps might be taken to alleviate the tensions between the Somali Republic and its neighbors? Since this is merely a case study, clear answers cannot be obtained, but hypotheses may be suggested that will bear testing.

Tribal irredentism and the Somali-speaking peoples

The political boundaries inherited by the independent African states from their colonial rulers bear little relation to traditional tribal areas. Almost all African states have within their boundaries a number of linguistically and culturally distinct peoples and, without exception, every one includes members of tribes that straddle international boundaries. Nonetheless, tribal irredentism has played a relatively small part in relations among them.

Certainly, the disruptive possibilities of tribal separatism are evident to African leaders, notably the attempted secession of the Ashanti tribe from Ghana, of the Buganda kingdom from Uganda,[2] and of a number of tribal groups from the central government of the Congo. Most African leaders have followed policies designed to minimize tribal differences, for any attempt to acquire a tribal irredentia across an international boundary runs the risk of arousing separatist sentiment among the tribe as a whole, and perhaps among other tribal groups as well. In general it may be hypothesized that African leaders of heterogeneous states will tend to avoid policies which encourage tribal irredentism.

Somalia, however, is not a tribally heterogeneous state. It was formed in July 1960, by the union of British Somaliland with former Italian Somaliland. Of its estimated two and a quarter million people, nearly 99 percent are Somalis, the remainder including a few Negroid peoples and about 35,000 Arabs. In addition to a common language and ethnic origin, the Somalis share a common religion—over 99 percent are Sunni Muslims. Most also have a cultural heritage of pastoralism. Even today more than 80 percent are estimated to be nomadic or to combine nomadic husbandry with agriculture; their animals number between 15 and 20 million.[3]

The demographic background to tensions in the Horn of Africa is the fact that a significant portion of the Somali-speaking peoples live outside the political boundaries of the Republic of Somalia, as the accompanying table and map indicate. Kenya's new Northeastern Region, Ethiopia's eastern Harar and Sidamo provinces (including the Haud and Ogaden regions), and the southeastern third of French Somaliland are inhabited by Somalis who number between 1 and 1¼ million. Negroid peoples appear to have inhabited the Horn a thousand years ago, but were displaced by Hamitic Galla tribes during the European Middle Ages. The Somali also are a Hamitic people, who may have migrated from Southern Arabia or may have been a Galla subgroup that was exposed to relatively intensive Arab influence. As early as the tenth century, certainly no later than the fourteenth, an Islamic people calling themselves Somali or Samale began successive waves of migration south and west from the northern Horn. They first crossed the Juba River, in what is now the southern Somali Republic, no more than a hundred years ago, and their expansion into northern Kenya occurred within the last sixty years.[4]

The Somali-Speaking Peoples [5]

Political Unit	Somali-inhab- ited area as percentage of total area	Estimated Somali- speaking population	Estimated total population
Somali Republic	100%	2,450,000	2,450,000
Ethiopia (Haud and Ogaden)	20	1,000,000	22,500,000
Kenya	20	240,000	9,336,000
French Somaliland	40	37,000	70,000

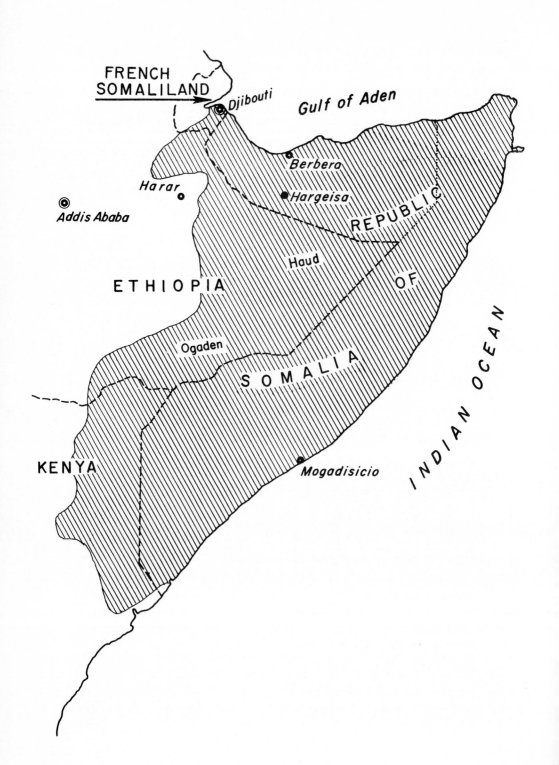

FRENCH
SOMALILAND

Djibouti

Gulf of Aden

Berbera

Harar

Hargeisa

⊚
Addis Ababa

REPUBLIC

Haud

ETHIOPIA

OF

Ogaden

S O M A L I A

KENYA

Mogadisicio

INDIAN OCEAN

THE HORN OF AFRICA, 1965

Broken lines indicate international boundaries, some of them provisional. The dotted line is the former boundary between British and Italian Somaliland.

The shaded area represents the approximate territory inhabited by Somali-speaking peoples.

Sources: Endpaper map in George P. Murdock, *Africa: Its Peoples and Their Culture History* (New York: McGraw-Hill, 1959); Map 4 in J. E. Goldthorpe and F. B. Wilson, *Tribal Maps of East Africa and Zanzibar,* East African Studies No. 13, (Kampala, Uganda: East African Institute of Social Research, 1960); and "Basic Data on the Economy of Somalia (Somali Republic)," *World Trade Information Service Economic Reports,* Part I, No. 61–5 (Washington, D. C.: U. S. Department of Commerce, 1961), map on pp. 8–9.

The immediate, essentially economic, precondition for tensions is the fact that many Somali nomads cross international boundaries each year to find pasture for their flocks. In general, such nomadic movements are neither random nor completely patterned. Three forms have been identified in studies of nomads: *transhumance,* the regular movement among specific pasture areas by season; *migratory drift,* the gradual displacement of old transhumance orbits into new; and *migration* itself, an abrupt shift from old to new transhumance orbits.[6] All three may be observed in Somali nomadism and all three are relevant to the genesis of current tensions and recent violence.

Although nomadic Somalis do not recognize clearly defined territorial units, their clans have "home wells" and customary grazing areas which they inhabit in transhumance orbits during the Horn's rainy and dry seasons. The 25,000 square miles of thorn bush and variable pasture in the Ethiopian Haud have been a traditional part of transhumance orbits for many Somalis who spend other parts of the year in what is now the Somali Republic. As many as 300,000 herdsmen enter the Haud from the republic in the spring or autumn. Some remain for half the year, depending on the rainfall, while others drive their herds beyond the Haud to the Ogaden wells.[7] Competition and conflict over grazing areas is inevitable, but the Somalis' traditional political system, described by Lewis as "pastoral democracy," has provided methods of resolving most such conflicts short of violence.[8]

Though transhumance movements are thus a potential source of internal tension among the Somalis, their relevance for international tension results from conflict between the nomads and non-Somali political authorities, today those of Ethiopia in particular, who have attempted to regulate or halt them.

Migration and migratory drift characterized the persistent southward and westward expansion of the Somalis through the Horn. Their advances brought them into contact with the Christian Abyssinians, with whom they fought a series of holy wars from the fourteenth century through the sixteenth century, and with the Galla, whom they violently displaced or peacefully absorbed in a process that continued until 1934, when the British administration of Kenya demarcated and enforced a limit to Somali grazing areas.[9] The heritage of migration was a cultural tradition, preserved in the oral literature of the Somali, of violent conflict with pagan tribesmen to the south and Christian Ethiopians to the west. This heritage certainly contributes something to modern Somali expectations of conflict with her neighbors. Migratory drift still occurs and may be responsible for some of the sporadic recent clashes between Somali nomads and Ethiopian and Kenyan military forces.

The sources of tension: 1875–1960

There is no inevitable process by which these conditions have generated tensions between Somalia and its neighbors. Although the Somalis have a common language, religion, and ethnic origin, they have had no history of political unity. Their nomadic life was not conducive to the development of centralized political institutions, and there has been and is divisiveness among the Somali clans. The cultural, linguistic, and religious unity of the Somali peoples, their nomadic way of life, and the arbitrary boundaries of the country may be identified as preconditions of Somalia's tensions with her neighbors. However, the development of tensions was the result of a number of specific political conditions and events during the colonial and post-independence periods.

The seeds of Somali self-consciousness were planted in the last half of the nineteenth century, when the Somali Peninsula came under foreign influence. Egypt controlled the Somali coast and the interior as far as Harar from 1875 to 1885, but the Somali peoples ultimately were brought under the rule of four non-Muslim powers—Ethiopia, France, Britain, and Italy—by a series of treaties with local Somali sultans and chiefs, and by conquest. The French and British assumed control of the northern Somali coast, the Italians of the eastern coast, and the Ethiopians of a large portion of the interior. A series of agreements, protocols, and treaties among the foreign powers and other interested parties between the 1880's and 1931, established spheres of influence and set or revised boundaries, most of them arbitrary so far as they affected the Somali. Boundary questions resolved on paper were never entirely resolved on the ground, however, and in 1934 a clash between Ethiopian and Italian-Somali troops over the work of a boundary commission provided the pretext for the Italian invasion of Ethiopia in 1935.

The migration of Somalis across the border between British Somaliland and the Ethiopian Haud was the subject of a series of agreements between Britain and Ethiopia, beginning with the treaty of 1897, which established the southern boundary of British Somaliland and provided for free tribal passage across the frontier. The border cut across customary grazing areas, however, and periodic clashes over grazing areas and wells occurred between British-protected Somali tribes and Ethiopian Somalis.

During World War II, Anglo-Ethiopian agreements placed most of the Somali-inhabited areas of Ethiopia under British military administration to assist "the effective prosecution of the war." The long-range British objective, however, seems to have been the union of all the Somalis under British trusteeship. Failing to gain international support for such a step, the British returned the Ogaden to Ethiopian administration in 1948, and the Haud in 1955. Terms of a 1954 agreement again guaranteed Somali grazing rights and made provisions for regulating the seasonal migration of the British-protected tribes into the Haud, but these provisions proved nearly impossible for British and Ethiopian officials to administer. The agreement lapsed with Somali independence in 1960, and has yet to be renegotiated.

The border between Italian Somaliland and Ethiopia was the subject of various agreements, none of which was effectively implemented. During the decade of the 1950's, when Italy administered Somalia as a United Nations trust territory, repeated attempts to bring about agreement between the two nations failed. Only a provisional administrative line was in effect at the time of independence.[10]

One result of the partition of the Somalis by non-Muslim powers was the awakening of a Somali sense of national identity. A traditional, anti-Christian reaction was the violent "Jihad," or holy war, led by Sayyid Mohammed 'Abdille Hassan, the "Mad Mullah," against the British and Ethiopians from 1900 to 1920. In some respects the Jihad resembled a nationalistic movement, for among its leader's policies were the establishment of his temporal authority over the tribes and attainment of independence from foreign rule. However, most of Mohammed's victims estimated in 1912 as one-third the population of the British protectorate, were Somalis who failed to acknowledge his authority.[11]

In the 1920's and 1930's, Somali antagonism toward alien governments took more modern forms, notably in British Somaliland. There, a small group of Western-educated Somalis formed interest groups and political organizations. During much of the interwar period the Italians and Ethiopians engaged in the pacification of the Somalis in their territories, and few of the Somalis under their rule were assimilated into the ruling culture. In Italian Somaliland, however, a small but rapidly growing number of Somalis were exposed to western life through urbanization and employment, and there is evidence of clandestine urban political organizations among them in the late 1930's.

In 1935 Italy went to war with Ethiopia, and the war proved a major instrument of change among the Somalis. Both Ethiopians and Italians used Somali troops and sought allies among Somali chiefs. Many Somalis were exposed to Western influence and war propaganda through military service, and almost all to varying administrative systems, as parts of the Horn passed to Italian and then to British rule. The British lifted restrictions on political activity imposed by the Italians, and beginning in 1942 economic and political associations sprang into existence in towns throughout the Horn. So rapidly did these modern organizations take root that by 1948 the Somali Youth League, which subsequently became the ruling party of Somalia, had by British estimates 25,000 affiliates in branches throughout the Horn, including Kenya and the Ogaden and Haud.[12]

The intensified contacts among Somalis of various origins during the war and immediately afterward, and British encouragement of Somali political activity in areas under British administration, contributed to the growth of a vigorous Somali nationalism. The Somali Youth League was among the first to advocate a pan-Somali ideology. In 1948 it informed a Four-Power Commission that "the union of Italian Somaliland with the other Somalilands was their primary objective, for which they were prepared to sacrifice any other demand standing in the way of the achievement of Greater Somalia." The 1951 party program of the Somali National League, one of the two major parties of British Somaliland, called for "the unification of the Somali people and territories" and for "the advancement of the Somali by abolishing clan fanaticism and encouraging brotherly relations among Somalis." [13] By the late 1950's, these views were shared by all significant political factions in British Somaliland and Somalia and by the pre-independence government of the trust territory of Somalia. In July 1959 the prime minister of Somalia told the Legislative Assembly that

> all means must be employed—within the framework of legality and the pursuit of peace—in order to obtain the union of all Somali territories, and their reunifications under the same flag. This constitutes for us not only a right, but a duty which one cannot neglect, because it is impossible to want to distinguish between Somali and Somali.[14]

Nationalism among the Somalis of French Somaliland had only occasional political significance in the postwar period. Beginning in 1919, the Somalis of Kenya had been isolated by the British from significant communication with the rest of Kenya, and had taken virtually no part in the country's political and economic development. The Kenya administration proscribed Somali political activity in Kenya in the 1940's and when nationalist activity resumed in the late 1950's, its goal was secession from Kenya rather than participation in African nationalist politics.[15] The Ethiopian Somalis, though persistently at odds with the government, had little opportunity to give formal political expression to nationalism. Their opposition took the form of sporadic violence, motivated by resentment of alien military rule. In 1964, despite four years of pan-Somali propaganda from the Somali Republic, the leader of an estimated 12,000 Somali guerrillas at war with the Ethiopian Army in the Ogaden told a New York *Times* reporter: "My people are under no one's jurisdiction and take orders from no one but me. . . . Our fight with Ethiopia has nothing to do with Somalia. We are indifferent to the government position [of the Somali Republic], though we still expect and hope our movement will be recognized both by Somalia and by the world." [16]

Somalis in all these territories were nevertheless conscious of a Somali identity and shared a resentment of alien rule. The expression of these sentiments was given impetus by the creation of the Republic of Somalia in 1960 and its advocacy of pan-Somalism.

Independence for Somalia and after

The U.N. General Assembly granted Italian Somaliland (or Somalia) independence from its trusteeship status on July 1, 1960. It immediately entered a union with British Somaliland, which had become independent five days earlier.[17] Integration of government operations proceeded slowly and was still in progress in 1964, yet the sense of national unity in the Somali Republic is sufficiently strong to permit vigorous, multiparty political competition, in sharp contrast to other new African states. Union of British Somaliland with Somalia served only to strengthen demands for incorporation of all Somali-speaking peoples into the republic. According to A. A. Castagno:

> If anything, the Somali political parties are more united than they were prior to 1960 on the goal of bringing the Somali populations of the Ethiopian Ogaden, French Somaliland, and the Northern Frontier District of Kenya under one flag. "Greater Somalia" is still defined as the primary objective of the government and of all the political parties.[18]

In the early 1960's Somali leaders made repeated and vehement representations to France, Ethiopia, Great Britain, and the United Nations, asking for the transfer of Somali-inhabited territory, for plebiscites, for any action furthering the goal of Greater Somalia. Responses ranged from sympathy to hostility, but produced no satisfactory results. Instead, migratory patterns have been disrupted, Ethiopian and Kenyan Somalis have risen in revolt, Somalia and Ethiopia have warred openly, and Western and Communist powers have become involved in power manipulations in the Horn. What follows is a chronology of events in the development of post-independence tension between Somalia and her neighbors.

In May 1960, a Somali delegation to Ethiopia found the government unwilling to negotiate any new agreement on grazing rights and unfavorably disposed to a union of Somaliland and Somalia.[19]

In August 1960, a clash occurred between Ethiopians and Somali tribesmen "infiltrating" Ethiopian territory. An Ethiopian source claimed that they had driven off a "gang of bandits" from former British Somaliland who were ostensibly trying to capture an Ethiopian security post. There were reports of Ethiopian military action against other Somalis, and extra Somali forces were detailed to the area.[20]

On September 15, 1960, the prime minister of Somalia, Dr. Abdi Rashid Ali Shermarke, cited Italian and British cession of Somali lands to Ethiopia, and stated that the only boundary acceptable to Somalia was "the one which embraces all the land inhabited by the Somali people. . . . Oppression is being done by those who have our land and refuse to return it to us." [21]

In late December 1960, bloody battles were reported by both Ethiopia and

Somalia in the Ogaden-Damot border area, near Danod, between tribesmen from the Somali Republic and Ethiopian border forces. The Ethiopian government claimed that Somalis from the republic had raided Ethiopian Somalis. Republic spokesmen claimed that the fighting occurred because the soldiers were using the area's reserves of water and food. Other clashes also were reported.[22] A Somali party secretary, speaking in Nairobi, Kenya, suggested that war between the Somali Republic and Ethiopia over the Haud border area might be imminent, and claimed that the Damot incidents were part of a series of hostilities.[23]

Further incidents were reported early in 1961, and the tension level between the two states remained high. An exchange of diplomatic notes took place, in which the Ethiopian government charged the republic with conducting an "unfriendly campaign." [24]

During the latter part of 1961 tension developed between Somalia and Kenya over the fate of the 100,000 Somali-speaking inhabitants of Kenya's Northern Frontier District (NFD). The eastern portion of the NFD, comprising approximately one-fifth of Kenya's territory, is semi-desert country inhabited by Somali nomads. Between 1959 and 1961, several secession-minded parties were established in the district. Kenya's African nationalists were made aware of the depth of Somali sentiment for secession during a constitutional conference in Nairobi in September 1961.[25]

In October 1961, Tom Mboya, a leading Kenya nationalist, announced that his party, the Kenya African National Union, would categorically oppose all attempts at secession by people of the NFD. In November, in response to approaches from the Somali NFD parties, the Somalia National Assembly officially endorsed their efforts to secede, having in mind the imminence of Kenya's eventual independence. Four days later Jomo Kenyatta, the Kenya nationalist leader, stated that "colonialists" were using the Somalis to foster a policy of "divide and rule." [26]

Early in 1962 discussions began between representatives of Britain and Kenya concerning the latter's transition to internal self-government, and the NFD Somalis pressed their case for secession, with assistance from the Somali government. The essence of the Somali demand was that the British government agree to such a secession before granting independence to Kenya. The British position, stated in the official text of the discussions, was that an independent commission would be appointed to determine the opinions of the people of the NFD, and that a decision based on its findings would be made before Kenya received a new constitution. The Somalis, aware of the widespread pro-secession sentiment in the NFD, assumed that secession was therefore imminent.[27]

In mid-1962 Britain appointed a two-man commission to determine the interests of the people of the NFD. It reported in December that Somalis and other Muslims of the NFD almost unanimously favored union with Somalia, though it did not suggest how this might be done without offending the Kenya nationalists. In January 1963, the Somali government criticized the commission report, whereupon the Kenya African government accused the republic of unwarranted interference in its internal affairs.[28]

In February, Somalis rioted in Garissa, a principal town in the NFD. Within a few days massive anti-British, -French, and -Ethiopian demonstrations took place in Mogadishu, the Somali Republic capital. Late in February the British carried out military maneuvers in the NFD, and on March 8 British Colonial Secretary Duncan Sandys announced that the Somali-populated area, as part of the new constitutional arrangements for the territory, would become Kenya's seventh province.[29] Nothing was said of secession for the NFD Somalis or of the previous commitment of the British government to be guided by the commission's findings.

Somali reactions to the British announcement were immediate. On March 11, 1963, in an emergency session of the Somali parliament, the government announced its intention of breaking off diplomatic relations with Britain. (The motion was passed on March 14.) On the 12th, tribesmen gathered outside government offices at Isiolo, capital of the NFD, and tore down the Union Jack. Shortly thereafter, added forces of paramilitary police began patrolling the secessionist areas. Late in the month, 33 Somali chiefs of the NFD resigned in protest. Demonstrations and riots continued at Isiolo during March and April. In May Somalis rioted in an attempt to stop voters going to the polls. The Somalis also boycotted the Kenya elections as a further demonstration of their determination to secede.[30]

The republic's strategy during this period was to maintain that it was Great Britain's responsibility to decide the future status of the NFD, and during 1962 Somalia bent considerable effort to establish good relations with Kenyan nationalists. During the events of late 1962 and early 1963, however, the position of the Kenya nationalists became firmer. In November and December 1962 African ministers of the Kenya government reemphasized their intention to maintain Kenya's territorial integrity, even to the extent of war, though they would allow the Somalis of the NFD to leave Kenya if they wished.[31]

As Kenya prepared for independence on December 12, 1963, it became apparent that the policies of the NFD Somalis and of the republic had failed to gain any significant concessions. Instead they had hardened the position of Kenya's nationalists and initiated an Ethiopian-Kenyan mutual defense pact for cooperative military action against Somali raiders and possible military action by Somalia.[32]

During the same period incidents of violence, instigated by Somalis in the NFD, increased. In the fall of 1963, Somali *shifta* (bandits) raided Kenyan police and army posts in the NFD. On December 31, 1963, shortly after independence, Prime Minister Kenyatta told the Kenya House of Representatives that there had been 33 armed attacks by Somalis on Kenyan police and army posts since November 13. He noted that the Somali raiders were well organized and armed. On December 25, as a result of these continued attacks, a state of emergency was declared in the Northern Frontier Province (the new name for the NFD).[33]

Half the Kenya army was moved to the province in January and February, 1964, and in April the government began "Operation Final Fling," using troops and riot policemen in an effort to suppress secessionist guerrilla activity before the rainy season. The *shifta* numbered about 1,000, and were equipped with weapons which the Kenya government said had been supplied by Somalia. The raiders attacked, usually at night, police posts, military convoys, and Kenyan Somali camps and villages.

The military operation continued into May. On May 24, Prime Minister Shermarke of Somalia asked Prime Minister Kenyatta to have British troops withdrawn from the Northern Frontier Province, claiming that their presence prevented settlement of the border dispute.[34]

Ethiopia: the border war

Overt hostility between Somalia and Ethiopia abated during 1962 and the first half of 1963, in part, one may assume, because the foreign policy efforts of the Somali Republic were directed at the British government. Many Ethiopian Somalis were expelled by the Ethiopian government on suspicion of sympathizing with the republic. Ethiopian aircraft were accused of violating Somali borders, and the Ethiopian government of mounting a propaganda campaign against Somalia.[35]

In the summer of 1963 new Somali allegations against Ethiopia began, and within six months a full-scale border war was in progress. In August the Somali government reported that the Ethiopian Army had carried out massive reprisals against the Ogaden Somalis in an effort to put down a movement called the "Liberation Government." On October 13 Radio Mogadishu reported that Ethiopian troops had occupied a border village, and two days later Somali soldiers (as distinct from tribesmen or *shifta*) launched attacks on Ethiopian border villages.[36]

In mid-January 1964 the Somali government formally protested to the Ethiopian government the destruction of police posts along the Southern Region border. At the beginning of February Ethiopian troops are said to have pursued some Somalis across the border. Somali troops were moved up and heavy fighting broke out on February 6 at the border town of Tug Wajalleh. Two days later the Somali government claimed that Ethiopian jets had attacked a frontier post and bombed three border towns.

Despite air attacks Somali troops apparently were able to advance across the border until forced back by Ethiopian reinforcements. A major action appears to have been fought on the 9th and 10th. Ethiopia reported a major Somali offensive, and said that 307 Somalis had been killed. The Somalis in turn said they had mortared an Ethiopian ammunition dump, killing 350 Ethiopians.[37]

A number of attempts were made to mediate the dispute. African foreign and defense ministers meeting at Dar es Salaam under the auspices of the Organization of African Unity (OAU) appealed for a ceasefire and negotiations. Somalia and Ethiopia formally acquiesced, but sporadic fighting continued.[38] At the end of February the foreign ministers, meeting in Lagos, issued another appeal. Prolonged discussion between Somali and Ethiopian representatives produced no agreements until March 18, when Somalia announced that it would open negotiations with Ethiopia in Khartoum, Sudan.[39] The talks began on March 25 and a joint Somali-Ethiopian announcement on March 30 stated that the two parties had agreed to solve the dispute peacefully, to maintain a ceasefire, and to withdraw military forces to a distance of 10 to 15 kilometers from either side of the border. A joint Ethiopian-Somali commission was to supervise the withdrawal.[40] Hostilities were not yet concluded, however. A battle was reported on March 30. The following day, four Ethiopian aircraft made two daylight raids on an airfield near Hargeisa, the former capital of British Somaliland.[41]

Both Somalia and Ethiopia, however, were apparently sincere in their desire for a peaceful settlement. They ordered cease-fires on April 1. On April 8 the Ethiopian government announced that its troops had withdrawn from the border demilitarized zone. The joint commission announced on April 18 that it had completed supervision of troop withdrawal from both sides of the southern border area,[42] and there were no further reports of military action through July.

An underlying pattern to the violence that contributed to tensions in the Horn may be difficult to discern. One is not justified in assuming that one government or another instigated all incidents. The actions of Somali tribesmen in both Kenya and Ethiopia may have been stimulated by pan-Somali propaganda, but the basic Somali antipathy to non-Somali administration and military forces appears at least equally important. In the Ogaden and Haud, Somali murders of Ethiopian administrators and soldiers led to reprisals by the Ethiopian army against other Somalis, which in turn led to further Somali violence and more reprisals. The result of this ascending spiral of violence was a self-maintaining hostility that needed no external stimulus. The major insurrectional movement among the Ogaden Somali was said by a New York *Times* correspondent to be "a genuine revolutionary movement dedicated to independence from Ethiopian rule. . . . Yet neither Ethiopia nor Somalia has recognized the movement, which is a severe embarrassment to both for different reasons." [43]

Neither the Somali nor the Ethiopian government appears solely responsible for military actions in the Horn. The Somalis are not a peaceful or passive people, and banditry for its own sake is not uncommon. The creation of a Somali state, with policies distinct from those of its neighbors, has simply—or not so simply— given Somali banditry international implications. There presumably has been some flow of modern weapons from the Somali Republic to Somali tribes in Kenya and the Ogaden, but captured weapons have shown no single point of origin.

An explanation of the border war of early 1964 is still needed. It seems unlikely that the republic would have deliberately initiated hostilities, for her armed forces numbered a mere 4,600 compared to Ethiopia's 30,000.[44] If the original initiative was from Ethiopia, objectives were almost certainly limited. Ethiopia could scarcely wish to acquire more Somali-inhabited territory, and the mounting and maintaining of a major military effort in remote, arid country would be difficult for the most modern of armies.[45] There is thus considerable plausibility to the statement of a London *Times* correspondent that limited hostilities were initiated by Ethiopia to force the Somalis to cease supporting the Ogaden Somali rebels.[46] This also was the motive discerned by some Westerners in both Ethiopia and Somalia at the time of the hostilities.

It was thought that Ethiopia had chosen this particular time to initiate hostilities because Somali armed forces were insufficient to mount a major retaliatory military effort. Ethiopia may also have hoped to influence the policies of the Somali political parties in the national elections on March 30. If Ethiopia was in fact responsible for the outbreak of warfare, she may have miscalculated, for if the analysis suggested above is correct, the Ogaden rebellion has become largely autonomous.

To summarize the position of the Somali Republic in 1964, its policy of pan-Somalism had resulted in the aggravation of its relations with Ethiopia and Kenya. The republic had stimulated or contributed to insurrection by the Somalis of Kenya and Ethiopia, but by doing so had forced those countries into rigid positions that decreased the likelihood of achievement of the republic's policies. Perhaps most important, the East-West conflict was injected into the dispute.

Pan-Somalism and the East-West conflict

It seems unlikely that insurrection by isolated nomads, tribal irredentism, and scattered border incidents could offer the Western and Communist nations opportunities for escalating the conflict. The possibilities have nevertheless attracted the attention of both the Soviet Union and Communist China, as well as the United States and her allies.

Major United States military aid to the Ethiopian armed forces, totaling $74 million between 1950 and 1963,[47] has been a source of constant irritation to the

Somali Republic. The December 1960 clash in the Haud was blamed on the United States by Somalia, on grounds that the Ethiopian action was made possible by American training and equipment, and large-scale demonstrations took place at the American embassy in Mogadishu.

During and after the border warfare of early 1964 there were persistent reports in Somalia that the United States was intimately involved. It was said that Americans were flying Ethiopian military aircraft and that American officers were in the field with Ethiopian army forces. As a result, anti-American sentiments ran high.

There is a kernel of truth to the reports. The Ethiopian armed forces are American-trained and -equipped, and there have been substantial numbers of U.S. Military Assistance and Advisory Group (MAAG) personnel in Ethiopia. Private Ethiopian sources suggest that American MAAG crews have flown reconnaissance training missions over the Horn, and that American observers could have accompanied Ethiopian troops in the field. Whatever the extent of American military involvement in the dispute, the conviction of the Somalis that the United States is in part responsible has proved a continuing source of friction between the two nations.

The Soviet Union established an embassy in Mogadishu in December, 1960, and devoted major efforts to establishing good relations with the new government. The fact that the Soviet Union was also providing substantial economic and technical assistance to Ethiopia made it difficult for the Russians to appear solely committed to the Somali point of view, but since they had not provided military assistance, no stigma seems to have attached to them. In May, 1961, Somalia's Prime Minister Shermarke visited Moscow. In the same week the Soviet Union announced a major loan and technical assistance to Somalia. The loan agreement, signed a year later, provided for $55 million to build a deepwater harbor at Berbera and other projects.[48] It was estimated in 1964 that Soviet economic aid to Somalia amounted to $63 million.[49]

In 1963 the republic negotiated substantial aid with the People's Republic of China, giving rise to suggestions that the Soviet Union and China were engaged in an "aid war" in the Horn. The Chinese in fact had been active in the Horn since 1960. Chinese trade and cultural delegations visited Somalia beginning in 1960, Peking established a large embassy in Mohgadishu, and a student exchange agreement was arranged. In May 1963 a trade agreement was concluded. More important was an agreement reached by Premier Shermarke during a visit to Peking in August 1963. A 17-year interest-free loan of $19.6 million was made to the republic, as well as a grant of nearly $3 million to be applied to the Somali budget. Substantial technical assistance also was involved.[50]

Chinese interest in East Africa has been and is strong. It was clearly evident at the Afro-Asian Solidarity Conference in Tanganyika in Spring 1963, where Chinese representatives played a dominant and impressive role. The uses to which such interest can be put are suggested by the widely reported Chinese sponsorship of tribal rebellions in the eastern Congo during 1964. The motives of the Chinese presence in Somalia remain problematic, however.

The United States, more deeply involved in assistance to Ethiopia than the Soviet Union or China, faced certain difficulties in aiding Somalia without affronting Ethiopia. By early 1964, however, the value of American aid to Somalia was estimated at about $31 million. The United States also had a Peace Corps group in Somalia, and participated in a joint Italian-German-American civil aviation project to assist the Somali government in establishing an internal air service.[51]

Military assistance has been the aid issue of greatest concern to the Somalia Republic, however, and is the sphere in which developments most dangerous to the East-West conflict are occurring. Somalia has been profoundly concerned over the weakness of her armed forces in comparison with those of Ethiopia. The British and Italian governments offered Somalia modest amounts of military aid in December, 1961, in what appeared to be an effort to forestall military assistance from the Soviet bloc. Arms also were provided by the United Arab Republic.

During 1963 the Somali army embarked on an accelerated expansion program and, late in the year, rejected a tripartite offer of more than $10 million in military assistance from the United States, West Germany, and Italy because of "quantitative and qualitative inadequacies and above all because of political conditions which accompanied it." Instead the Republic sought and received a Soviet military assistance pact with a value estimated at $28 million.[52]

This extensive Soviet military aid may be a determining factor in future developments in the Horn. In 1964 there were at least 200 and perhaps 400 Somali army officers and noncoms in training in the Soviet Union. The Soviet aid package was also said to include about 30 MIG-15 and MIG-17 jet fighters, while 20 to 35 Somali pilots were in training in the Soviet Union.[53]

Soviet assistance to Somalia has clearly been designed to take advantage of growing Somali hostility toward the West, although the Somali government has persistently stated its neutralism.[54] Before Somali acceptance of the Soviet military aid offer, the United States and her allies appeared to have checked the Soviet Union in any attempt to exert predominant influence in the republic.[55] The balance has now changed. The pan-Somali ideal remains the central theme of Somali political life. It is by no means impossible that a modernized, Soviet-trained Somali army could be used in an attempt to implement that ideal. If so, it would come in direct conflict with the American-trained Ethiopian forces, and the result would be a primary tension area with explosive possibilities.

Policy alternatives

What are the alternative solutions to the Somali question? A Somalia hostile to and isolated from her East African neighbors would be a gain for no one except possibly the Soviet Union or China. The long-proposed Somali solution of voluntary cession of Ethiopian and Kenyan territory is most unlikely, though it is conceivable that France will eventually permit the transfer of the Somali portion of French Somaliland to the republic. Nor is it more likely that adjoining countries will permit internationally-supervised plebiscites or the "principle of self-determination" to be implemented among their Somalis, as suggested by President Aden Abdulla Osman of Somalia in 1963.[56]

The republic also lacks the military capability to achieve her policy objectives by force or threat. As her military capability increases she may attempt to do so, but it is unlikely that either Ethiopia or Kenya would respond with anything but force. Both could be expected to call upon outside assistance, from either the West or other African states, or both, especially if such a course of action was seen as motivated by Soviet or Chinese interests.

A positive solution of a different order was discussed frequently in the early 1960's. In November 1961 Somalia's foreign minister, writing in the *East African Standard,* noted that unification was part of Somalia's national policy, but stated that Somalia would consider favorably any invitation to join an East African federation, the groundwork for which had been laid by African nationalists of Kenya, Tanganyika, and Uganda.[57] In February 1962, at a meeting of the Pan-African Freedom Movement for East and Central Africa, it was suggested that a solution to the Somali question could be found in a federation of Kenya, Uganda, and Tanganyika with Ethiopia and the Somali Republic, and several months later the republic sent observers to a meeting of the East African Central Legislative Assembly, the legislative body of the East African Common Services Organization.[58]

By 1965 the prospects for federation in East Africa—even confined to Kenya, Tanganyika, and Uganda—were much less promising than they were three years earlier. It is also probable that too much blood had been shed and too many accusations exchanged to permit the establishment of any effective and viable federation between Somalia and her neighbors, at least in the near future.

There was, however, a suggested solution from another direction. Both Ethiopia and Somali were subjected to, and ultimately responded to, intense pressures from other African states to resolve their differences at a conference of African states. It may be that neither state was eager for continued hostilities, and welcomed face-saving diplomatic mediation. Nonetheless, a precedent was established, and in working through the agreements and in supervising the border withdrawals, Somalis and Ethiopians had what may have been their first significant occasion for cooperative endeavor.

The same pressures are certain to be generated in any recurrence of violence among the states of the Horn. As the loose apparatus of African unity is strengthened, the African states may be better able to exercise both moral and physical influence on the outcome of violence. There are also other possibilities for long-range solutions that remain to be explored. Some form of joint administration of Kenya's Somalis by Kenya and the republic appears feasible, and a comparable arrangement between Ethiopia and Somalia is not out of the question. Ethiopia might well consider joint administration as a welcome solution to the problems of controlling chronic insurrection. However reluctant the states of the Horn may be to make such compromises, their leaders may certainly expect to face increasing pressures to do so. But it is far from certain that these pressures will prevail in the face of Somali determination to unite as one state. Drysdale cites an appropriate Somali proverb: "Real men prefer to suffer the anguish of hell, than to endure the pangs of unavenged anger." [59] Somali self-determination is not only the dominant objective of the Republic's foreign policy but highly valued by the Somali people. If the demand is not satisfied or compensated for, the possibility that the Horn will be plunged into the "anguish of hell" is all too real a possibility.

Conclusions

As I. M. Lewis aptly points out, "The special predicament of the Somali . . . remains that whereas other independent African States seek to make themselves into nations, they seek to build a State on the basis of their nationhood." [60] The pre-European history of Somali expansion was one of conflict with and assimilation of adjacent tribes. This intertribal conflict gave way to interreligious and interethnic tensions between the Somali and their non-Muslim conquerors. As a consequence, Somali leaders came to see the Somali peoples as a distinct, integral group. Once political independence was achieved by a portion of the Somalis, they continued to view the Somali state in cultural and ethnic terms, and their political goal of unification of all Somali peoples directly reflects this perception.

African nationalists in culturally heterogeneous territories tend to perceive the state—or prospective state—in terms of arbitrary, European-imposed boundaries. The Kenyan nationalists and Ethiopia's rulers conceived of it in strictly political terms. The tensions in the Horn of Africa are the result of what is, fundamentally, a conflict between these alternative views. Arbitrary boundaries, the history of colonial withdrawal, the nomadic life of the Somalis, and competing foreign interests in the Horn have given shape to the conflict.

With specific reference to Africa, the Somali case suggests that interethnic tensions are most likely to result in interpolitical tensions among states one of which has a dominant ethnic or cultural group, significant numbers of whom are outside its boundaries. Few African states meet these preconditions, which leads to the hypothesis that interpolitical tension areas of the Somali type will be uncommon in future African politics. It is quite possible, however, that as Africa's culturally diversified states become secure in their national identity, their leaders may feel sufficiently safe to follow irredentist policies, especially vis-à-vis neighbors that lag in the development of national unity.

The existence of a nomadic people raises the question of the relevance of fixed international boundaries. In the Horn of Africa the creation of such boundaries was a major contributing factor to present tensions. Technically, one can hypothesize that any culturally homogeneous nomadic people whose transhumance patterns intersect international boundaries are likely to be a source of international tension.

Three eventualities may contribute to such tension: the nomads' migratory drift, which is likely to bring them into conflict with sedentary peoples; nomadic resistance to national restrictions; and irredentist policies of nationalist governments. The first has been a characteristic of nomadic movements throughout the history of man. The latter two result from the establishment of nation-states, a process that may be expected to generate future international disputes over nomadic people.

This argument could be extended in a number of directions. Two will be suggested here. One is that even those nomads whose current transhumance patterns lie within the boundaries of a single state are a potential source of international tension, since migratory drift may eventually bring them across international borders. The second is that the hypothesis stated above might be extended from the traditional nomads to the "new nomads" of industrial society, who cross international boundaries in Africa and Western Europe in vast numbers each year. Under circumstances that remain to be specified, they too may be the source of international tensions.

What seems called for, in the Horn of Africa and wherever else such international problems may occur, is a perception of man and the state that permits a greater flexibility in political arrangements. Flexible federations are needed that will allow greater freedom for cultural, ethnic, and economic unities that overlap arbitrary boundaries. Such solutions are being seriously considered by Africa's leaders, who have underway intensive experiments in political cooperation, federation, and union that may greatly influence their own future as well as Western conceptions of what is politically possible.

Notes

Chapter 1

1. Even a weak nuclear potential in the hands of irresponsible rulers or governments of small and weak states may endanger a far more powerful state, hesitant to use the devastating bombs. Authoritarian states have a high proportion of deviants in positions of power and decision. They appeal to the masses through the avenue of emotion, not reason. Emotional tension is increased through mass media; in moments of unreason, control and restraints break down. An aggressive and irresponsible dictator of a small, weak country may force the hand of the sane and self-disciplined government of a great power.

Chapter 2

1. The reduction of variables is an essential methodological device requiring certain flexibility. Since social problems are analyzed on a variety of levels of abstraction, the synthesis of a broad issue requiring broad generalization involves also a reduction of variables. Analytical studies, however, suggest the listing of all perceived variables and an evaluation of their weight. Here, the approach is far less reductive, or, in a certain approach and research stage, not reductive at all. In this work the principle is applied in a variety of ways.

2. Formal classification of social relations was advanced by Georg Simmel more than fifty years ago. However,

classificatory systems do not explain the nature and causes of such processes. (For Simmel's classification, see Kurt Wolff [trans. and ed.], *The Sociology of Georg Simmel,* Glencoe: Free Press, n.d.) Leopold M. W. Wiese followed Simmel's formalistic approach, suggesting a detailed classificatory system of social relations based on various "intensities" of social processes of association and dissociation, cooperation and antagonism. Wiese's system of sociology is based on major concepts of social relations, social groups, and "abstract collectives." (See Leopold M. W. Wiese, *Allgemeine Sociologie als Lehre von Beziehungen und Beziehungsgebilden der Menschen, Munchen, Duncker und Humbolt,* 1924–1929; also, *Sociology,* ed. by Howard Becker; New York: Wiley, Sons, 1932.)

3. For the purpose of our discussion, the terms "institution" and "organization" are used interchangeably in their sociological, not their juridical meaning. Social institutions are tantamount to established and permanent social groups with a certain "charter," indicative of goals, values, interests, and structure for transmitting and making decisions. Institutions have established patterns of behavior and actions, indicative of their functions. (For a definition of social institutions, see Bronislaw Malinowski, *A Scientific Theory of Culture,* University of North Carolina Press, 1945.) "Institutions" in international relations are technically identified with so-called organs: established administrative, legislative, or judiciary structures; while "organizations" are called the all-embracing patterns of social relations tying nations and societies into permanent and integrated systems of societies, nations, groups;

into social, political, and territorial complexes (for instance, regional organizations). Some international treaties (for example, that establishing the European Economic Community) apply the term "institution" to certain judiciary, administrative, legislative, and political structures such as the assembly, the court of justice, or the governing commission. Other treaties call such political structures "organs" (e.g., the statutes of the Balkan Conferences of 1930). Complex or integral institutions such as the state consist, in a sociological approach, of many interrelated institutions. (A dictionary of terms in international relations may be a worthwhile project. The Brookings Institution has already suggested terminology in certain areas.)

4. *The Ottoman Empire and Its Successors* (4th ed., 1936; Cambridge University Press, p. 239).

5. Preface to *The Ancient Regime* (tr. by John Durand; New York: Peter Smith, 1931).

6. Karl W. Deutsch, Sidney A. Burell, Robert A. Kann, *et al., Political Community and the North Atlantic Area* (Princeton University Press, 1957), pp. 5–6. This volume contains a discussion of "background conditions" of integration.

7. For a history of European institutions, their function and development, see Arnold J. Zurcher, *The Struggle to Unite Europe* (New York University Press, 1958); also, Elmer Plischke, ed., *Systems of Integrating the International Community,* with contributions by Francis O. Wilcox, A. J. Zurcher, Carl J. Friedrich, and W. W. Kulski. Various approaches to, and problems of, integration are discussed in the symposium in both a theoretical and pragmatic way. Bibliography in this field is very extensive.

Chapter *3*

1. Conflict has formed one of the central issues and concepts of philosophy and social sciences for more than one hundred years. For a long time more attention was given to the processes of conflict than to processes of cooperation. The study of war goes back to ancient times—not only to the Greeks and Romans but also to Indian and Chinese theoreticians who discussed practical and cynical issues of war and conflict, especially ways of conquering, consolidating, and keeping political power. (For a selection of these writings and a general survey, see: D. Mackenzie Brown, *Indian Political Thought from Manu to Gandhi* [University of California Press, 1959]; and Samuel B. Griffith, ed and tr., *Sun-Tsu, The Art of War* [Oxford University Press, 1963].)

Since the time of Georg Hegel and Charles Darwin, conflict has been the leading theme in philosophy and social sciences. Class-oriented and internationally-minded political philosophers, for example Karl Marx, Friedrich Engels, and Mikhail Bakunin, built their systems or general approaches on a theory of conflict. Racist ideology also made its historical entrance at that time (Count Joseph Gobineau, not to mention his forerunners). Race conflict and superiority are here the leading tenets. The danger of such social myths was anticipated by Alexis de Tocqueville. By the end of the nineteenth and the beginning of the twentieth century, a sociological school of conflict appeared in Austria, led by Polish-born Ludwig Gumplovich (discussed below in Chapter 6), and later, by an Austrian army field marshal, Gustav Ratzenhofer (*Die Sociologische Erkenntnis* [Leipzig: Brockhaus, 1898]; *Wesen und Zweck der Politik* [Leipzig: Brockhaus, 1893]). This sociological school claims scientific objectivity. Nevertheless, most conflict theories have biases, reflecting the values of their authors. (See Ratzenhofer's *Sociologie* [Leipzig: Brockhaus, 1907]).

It is sometimes claimed that conflict is an area neglected in the social sciences. This was not true until recently. In American sociology and theory of education, a tendency toward the reduction of tensions and "adjustments" in various forms has been so notable recently that the study of conflict and violence has been neglected, as J. Bernard and later Joseph Roucek have indicated. This also reflects the general attitude and interests of American educators and intellectuals. Nevertheless, conflict studies are now an important theoretical area of sociology and psychology. The emphasis of these sciences is frequently on the reduction of tensions, e.g., in the extensive studies sponsored by UNESCO. (See *The Nature of Conflict: Studies on the Sociological Aspects of International Tension* by the International Sociological Association in collaboration with Jessie Bernard, T. H. Pear, Raymond Aron, Robert C. Angell [UNESCO, 1951]; see especially, J. Bernard, "The Sociological Study of Conflict" [pp. 33–118], and by the same author, "Where Is the Modern Sociology of Conflict?" *The American Journal of Sociology* [LVI, No. 1, 1950, 11–17]. The UNESCO publication has an extensive and useful bibliography on studies on conflict, prepared by Centre d'Études Sociologiques [pp. 225–310]. See also Joseph S. Roucek, "The Sociology of Violence," *Journal of Human Relations* [Spring, 1957, pp. 9–21; reprint].)

A mathematical and logical school of the theory of conflict, with a frame of reference based on the theory of games, has made headway in the United States. This school also had its forerunners. Some of its approaches are abstract and logical, but distant from realities and pragmatic social processes.

The very limited and incidental definitions and references in this footnote suggest only general current trends and interests, and are not the basis of this chapter, nor are they necessarily reflected in this writer's views. A specialized journal, published by the University of Michigan (*Journal of Conflict and Resolution*), as well as *Sociological Abstracts,* reflect and report the current interest, trends, and research.

For a definition of concepts of conflict and incompatibility, see Jessie Bernard, "Parties and Issues in Conflict," *Conflict and Resolution,* I, No. 2 (University of Michigan, 1957), 111 ff. Bernard suggests a paradigm based on the amount of information available. Perception and evaluation of this information are relevant in interpretation of conflict and policy development. On the basis of information and perception of mutual exclusiveness or incompatability of values, Professor Bernard differentiates among a number of situations.

For a general survey of the patterns, types, and nature of conflict, see Raymond W. Mach and Richard C. Snyder, "The Analysis of Social Conflict—Toward an Overview and Synthesis," *Journal of Conflict and Resolution* (I, No. 2, 213 ff.). For a survey of various theories of conflict, "Approaches to the Study of Social Conflict," (Intro. by the eds.), *ibid.* (I, No. 2, 105 ff.). For the general significance of the study of interna-tional conflict see Quincy Wright, "The Value for Conflict Resolution of a General Discipline of International Relations," *ibid.* (I, No. 1, 1957, 3). On the game theory approach to conflict see Thomas C. Schelling, "The Strategy of Conflict, Prospectus for a Reorientation of Game Theory," *ibid.* (II, No. 3, 1958, 203 ff.). See also Kenneth E. Boulding, *Conflict and Defense* (New York: Harper Brothers, 1962).

2. Georg Simmel, *Conflict and the Web of Group Affiliations,* tr. by Kurt H. Wolff and Reinhard Bendix (Glencoe: Free Press, 1958), pp. 57 ff. For a more extensive discussion of this subject, see Appendix I, "Command and Consensus Structures." p. 273.

3. *The New York Times,* May 7, 1963.

4. Sergei Sazonov, *Fateful Years* (New York: Stokes, 1928), pp. 256–58.

5. Subordination is not synonymous with surrender. Surrender is one form of subordination, combined with a formal act, as the basis of a future *sui generis* legitimacy. Paul Kecskemeti's study, *Strategic Surrender* (Stanford University Press, 1958) indicates basic differences in "handling surrender" by democracies and dictatorships. Subordinations, even surrenders, are not equal; the value structure and personality of victors and the distribution of relative strength at the time of surrender make them different. Lewis A. Coser suggests that definite conflict goals (for instance, annexation of certain territories) facilitate the termination of a conflict. Similarly, assessment of strength, especially of equal strength, may lead to termination of a conflict ("The Termination of Conflict," *Journal of Conflict and Resolution,* [V, No. 4, 1961, 347 ff.]). Experience teaches, however, that assessment of strength, even by a weaker opponent

or aggressor, leads to avoidance of "total conflict," and the process is channelled into a new and sometimes limited form of conflict. Thus, conflict continues as a process.

6. *Conflict and the Web of Group Affiliations* (tr. by Kurt H. Wolff and Reinhard Bendix; Glencoe: Free Press, 1955, pp. 57 ff.).

7. *On Contradictions* (New York: International Publishers, 1953), p. 50.

8. The text of the letter appeared in the *New York Times* on July 5, 1963.

Chapter 4

1. Conflict areas, such as Macedonia and Silesia were at one time, have an extensive literature. The Carnegie Endowment for International Peace is supporting case studies of international conflict in the Saar region, in Trieste, Cyprus, and Morocco. Professor Jacques Freymond, of the Institut des Hautes Études Internationales in Geneva, in his *Saar* (Case Studies of International Conflict, 1960), analyses factors responsible for the Saar conflict.

2. See Appendix I, "Command and Consensus Structures."

3. David D. Lombardo, "Tensions in Alto Adige" (1962), a research paper presented for a New York University seminar in area studies and international relations. See also *The Case of South Tyrol* (Vienna: Osterreichische Staatsdruckerei, n.d.); *Memorandum on Item 68 of the Agenda* (Italian Delegation to the XV Session of the General Assembly of the United Nations, New York, 1960, unpublished); *Alto Adige:* Documents Presented to the Italian Parliament by the Minister for Foreign Affairs, Signor A. Segni, on September 19, 1961 (Italian Republic, Ministry for Foreign Affairs, Rome, 1961, official documents); *German-Speaking Inhabitants of the Alto Adige,* ed. by the Presidency of the Council of Ministers of Italy (Rome: Instituto Poligrafico dello Stato P.V., 1960); *Alto Adige, Acts of Terrorism,* Documents Exchanged between the Italian Government and the Austrian Government 12 July 196– September 1961 (official Italian documents, no date, no publisher); and Heinrich Siegler, *The South Tyrol Question* (Bonn, 1964).

4. The literature on the Czechoslovak-German tensions that led to the Munich agreements is extensive (see John W. Wheeler-Bennet, *Munich: Prologue to Tragedy,* New York, 1948). For historical perspective on the three decades of Czech-German relations, and the transfer (expulsion) of the Sudeten German population, see Radomír Luža, *The Transfer of the Sudeten Germans: A Study of Czech-German Relations, 1933–1962* (New York University Press, 1962).

5. See Appendix I, "Command and Consensus Structures."

6. On social causation see Robert M. MacIver, *Social Causation* (New York: Ginn and Co., 1942). An extensive discussion of social causation in international relations is presented by Oscar Uribe Villegas, in his *Causación Social y Vida Internacional* (Instituto de Investigaciones Sociales de la Universidad de Mexico, 1958). See also Feliks Gross, *Foreign Policy Analysis* (New York Philosophical Library, 1954), Chapter II, "Causation," pp. 22–38.

7. American research and bibliography

in the field of ethnic, religious, and race tensions is extensive. We shall mention only a few here: Gordon W. Allport, *The Nature of Prejudice* (Cambridge, 1954); Milton L. Barron, *American Minorities* (New York, 1957); Otto Klineberg, *Race Differences* (New York, 1935); *Tensions Affecting International Understanding* (New York: Social Science Research Council, 1950); Kurt Lewin, *Resolving Social Conflicts* (New York, 1948); Arnold Rose, *Studies in the Reduction of Prejudice* (American Council on Race Relations, 1947); J. Roucek and F. Brown, *One America* (New York, 1947); Gerhart Saenger, *The Social Psychology of Prejudice* (New York, 1953); J. M. Yinger, "The Sociology of Race and Ethnic Relations," in R. Merton *et al., Sociology Today* (New York, 1953); Robin M. Williams, Jr., *The Reduction of Inter-Group Tensions* (Social Science Research Council, 1947); UNESCO, *De la Nature des Conflits* (Paris, 1955)

contains an extensive bibliography. For applications of social science analysis to tensions in India, see Gardner Murphy, *In the Minds of Men* (New York, 1953).

8. C. A. W. Manning, *International Relations* (Paris: UNESCO, 1954), pp. 46 ff.

9. See Part IV, Chapter 15.

10. Bronislaw Malinowski, "The Deadly Issue," *The Atlantic Monthly,* December, 1936.

11. Bronislaw Malinowski, "An Anthropological Analysis of War," *The American Journal of Sociology,* XLV, No. 4 (January, 1941), 533.

12. *Ibid.,* p. 536. See also Bronislaw Malinowski, *Freedom and Civilization* (New York: Roy, 1944), pp. 252–304.

13. Feliks Gross, "The Sociology of International Relations: Research and Study," *International Social Science Journal* (UNESCO, XII, No. 2 [1960], 269 ff.).

14. See *ibid.,* ftn. 7.

Chapter 5

1. The term "out-group" is used here in a general all-embracing sense, and differs from the more elaborate terminology in Part III, where differentiation and classification of "pro" and "anti" groups is suggested. The classification results from a study of case histories.

2. For the definition and problems of minorities, especially the League of Nations system of minority protection, see C. A. Macartney, *National States and National Minorities* (Oxford University Press, 1934).

In a United Nations memorandum of 1950, presented by the Secretary General to a special Sub-Commission on Prevention of Discrimination and the Protection of Minorities, the minority was defined as follows: "As a provisional orientation, it will be recalled that in modern times the term 'minority' has been applied to more or less distinct groups, living within a state, which are dominated by other groups."

3. For further discussion of this problem, see Appendix II, "The Structure of Human Relations in Central-Eastern Europe."

Chapter 6

1. Gumplovich's early views on race conflict, *Der Rassenkampf* (Innsbruck: Wagner, 1883); also published in an edition of his collected works, *Ausgewählte Werke* (ed. by F. Oppenheimer, F. Savorgnan, and M. Adler; Innsbruck: Wagner, 1926–1928).

2. C. W. Previte-Orton, *The Shorter Cambridge Medieval History* (Cambridge University Press, 1952), I, 549.

3. O. Halecki, *A History of Poland* (New York: Roy, 1943), p. 32; and Stanislaw Estreicher, *Krakow i Magdeburg* (Cracow, 1911).

4. A Russian historian and ethnographer, Michael Kulischer, advanced a theory of the close interrelation between war and great migration. His sons, Eugen and Alexander Kulischer, in *Kriegs und Wanderzüge, Weltgeschichte als Völkerbewegung* (Berlin-Leipzig: Walter de Gruyter, 1932), formulated a theory of migrations based on three great migratory periods: seventh through tenth centuries, sixteenth through seventeenth centuries, and nineteenth through twentieth centuries.

5. Kazimierz Moszynski, "Badania nad Pochodzeniem i Pierwotna Kultura Slovian," Cracow, *Polska Akademia Umiejetnosci* (Rozprawy LXII, No. 2, 1925) (Research on the Orgin of Slavs and Their Culture, Polish Academy of Sciences). Moszynski, like other archeologists such as Robert Ehrich and T. Sulimirski, indicated that in spite of these large migrations, the native endemic cultural pattern has a tendency to persist. As the evidence indicates, the great migrations were not able to eliminate or to absorb the local tribes or nationalities, since the cultural patterns in this area have shown an unusual persistence since prehistoric times. (See T. Sulimirski, *The Background of Modern Racial Developments in Central Eastern Europe* [London: 1953]; and Robert W. Ehrich, "On the Persistences and Recurrences of Cultural Areas and Culture Boundaries during the Course of European Prehistory, Protohistory and History," *Bericht uber den V. Internationalen Kongress fur Vor und Fruh Geschichte, Hamburg, 1958* [Berlin: Gebr. Mann, 1961], pp. 252–257.)

6. Stephen P. Ladas, *The Exchange of Minorities: Bulgaria, Greece and Turkey* (New York: Macmillan, 1932), pp. 3 ff; and Macartney (*op. cit.*), pp. 430 ff. According to Macartney, formal proposals for the exchange of populations were made for the first time in modern times by the Turkish government in 1913, although the beginnings of such proposals can be traced to a much earlier period. In 1914 again, the Turkish government suggested the exchange of Greeks of Smyrna for Moslems of Macedonia. In fact, after the second Balkan War, the Turkish and Bulgarian governments agreed to exchange populations. Macartney concludes: "Such experience as we possess of the exchange of population as a means of solving the minorities problem is not . . . calculated to encourage a repetition of the experiment" (*op. cit.*, pp. 432 ff.).

7. For details on transfer of population after the war, see Inis L. Claude, Jr., *National Minorities and International Problems* (Cambridge: Harvard University Press, 1955), pp. 91 ff. Regarding the Czechosolovak-Hungarian minority controversy, see pp. 120–123, 130–133, 141–143.

8. Eugene M. Kulischer, *The Displacement of Population in Europe* (Montreal: International Labor Office,

1943). See Table of Displacement and Transfer in Europe p. 164, and facing p. 170. See also, Eugene M. Kulischer, *Europe on the Move* (New York: Columbia University Press, 1948) and Joseph B. Schechtman, *European Population Transfers* (Oxford University Press, 1946), and *Population Transfers in Asia* (New York: Hallsby Press, 1949).

9. Donald R. Taft and Richard Robbins discuss causation and effects of international migrations, as well as processes of acculturation. (See their *International Migrations* [New York: Ronald Press, 1955].) For a discussion of, and data on, world migration, especially to the United States (chiefly what has been called "free migration"), see Maurice R. Davie, *World Immigration* (New York: Macmillan, 1936). For a correlation between economic changes and migrations, see Harry Jerome, *Migration and Business Cycles* (New York: National Bureau of Economic Research, 1926). And, more recently, proceedings of a conference on migrations held by the International Economic Association (Thomas Brinley, ed., *Economics of International Migrations* [London: Macmillian, 1958]).

10. The Jews were an ancient stock in central Eastern Europe. Some of them were of Khazar origin, which can be traced back to the seventh and ninth centuries. The Khazars, probably a Mongol tribe who mixed with the Slavic population, established a strong kingdom in what is today southern Russia. Khazars were converted to the Jewish faith. There were probably Jews who migrated with the Greeks far into Southeastern Europe and settled on the Black Sea with the Greek colonies. The Jews who arrived in Poland in the fourteenth century, however, were German Jews.

11. Just before the outbreak of World War II, Leon Petrazycki's essay on the role of the Jews as a complementary nation in the history of Europe was published in Polish. It was a short essay, and I was unable to locate a copy in order to secure the bibliographical data.

12. For a detailed classification of nomadic migration and a discussion of various migration patterns, see the author's *Koczownictwo* (Warszawa: Kasa Mianowskiego, 1936) (*Nomandism*, with an introduction by Bronislaw Malinowski [Warsaw, 1936]; Introduction and digest in English).

13. For further discussion, see Gordon Allport, *Nature of Prejudice* (Cambridge: Addison Wesley, 1954); and John Dollard *et al.*, *Frustration and Aggression* (Yale University Press, 1961). The theory of frustration-aggression is largely based on Freud's theories. An extensive and recent bibliography on this subject is available in a special issue of the *Journal of Conflict and Resolution* (Vol. III, No. 3, 1959); also relevant is Elton B. McNeil's "Psychology of Aggression," in the same issue.

Chapter 7

1. Thirty years ago E. S. Bogardus introduced a social distance scale that can be applied to the study of ethnic and race relations. (See his "A Social Distance Scale," *Sociology and Social Research*, XVII [January-

February, 1933], 265–267; "Social Distance and Its Practical Implications," *ibid.*, XXII [May–June, 1938], 462–476; and "Scales in Social Research," *Ibid.*, XXIV [September–October 1939], 69–75.) The scale measures attitudes toward ethnic and race groups. For a discussion of scales, see Pauline V. Young and Calvin F. Schmid, *Scientific Social Surveys and Research* (New York: Prentice-Hall, 1958).

2. See Hadley Cantril and Lloyd A. Free, "Hopes and Fears for Self and Country," *The American Behavioral Scientist,* Supplement to Vol. VI (October, 1962), No. 2. See also his inquiry into political psychology, *The Indian Perception of the Sino-Indian Border Clash* (Princeton, Institute of International Research, 1961).

3. Gordon Allport, *The Nature of Prejudice* (Boston: Beacon Press, 1954), Chapter 16, "The Scientific Study of Group Differences," pp. 85–107.

4. A representative case study of ethnic tensions, that on tensions in India, was written by Professor Gardner Murphy. This study is the result of extensive research, with the participation of many scholars, sociologists, psychologists, anthropologists, and educators; a cooperative effort and project of UNESCO. See *In the Minds of Men: The Study of Human Behavior and Tensions in India, at the Request of the Government of India* (New York: Basic Books, 1953). For a further discussion of the role of public and private institutions in reduction and intensification of tensions, see Chapter 17. Pars Ram's study of social tensions in Aligarh also belongs here. Ram advances a risky hypothesis and his application of psychoanalysis is open to criticism; however, his observations (rather than statistics) on intergroup relations between Moslems and Hindus, as differences between the two religions and their impact on social behavior and group tensions are of great interest. We learn how theological interpretations in this case increased rather than eased tensions. We also learn, however, about friendship and mutual aid between members of the two religious groups even in times of acute conflict. Pars Ram, *A Unesco Study of Social Tensions in Aligarh* (1950–1951), ed. with an introduction by Gardner Murphy, New Order Book Co., Ahmedabad, India 1955.

Chapter 8

1. The case study of the relations between the Shoshone and Arapaho Indians of Wyoming is based on the writer's own observations and studies during the summers from 1947 to 1950. The descriptive material is largely based on unpublished field notes. Some results of this research were published in the author's paper, "Nomadism of the Arapaho Indian of Wyoming," in *University of Wyoming Publications* (Vol. 15, No. 3 [1950], pp. 37–55); also *Ethnos* (1949), pp. 2–4 (Statens Etnografisca Museum, Stockholm, Sweden).

2. On the historical origins of the reservation and on Washakie, see Clark Wissler, *Indians of the United States* (New York: Doubleday, 1964), pp. 225 ff.

3. Dr. Roberts, an Episcopalian missionary on this reservation who enjoyed the respect of both the Shoshones and the Arapahos, met Washakie when

he arrived on the reservation in 1883. When I stayed at Ethete, Dr. Roberts was about 96 years of age. He converted Washakie to Christianity and built the first schools on the reservation. Both the recorded sources and the conversation with Dr. Roberts refer to Washakie's statesmanship. Washakie realized the weakness of the Indians vis-à-vis modern American culture and power, and the futility of the Indian wars. He was a renowned soldier who took an active part in the wars against the Sioux, and tales of his bravery were still told on the reservation.

4. This note was in my notebook on August 1, 1947. I do not remember any such proposition until 1952, when I was on the reservation for the last time.

5. James Mooney, in his article "Signals," *Handbook of the American Indians North of Mexico* ([Washington, 1910], Smithsonian Institute—Bureau of American Ethnology Bulletin 30) also indicates the significance of buffalo and enemy in idea-systems and lore of the Plains Indians.

6. The description of ethnic relations in Chanak is based on interviews with Professor M. J. Bernadete, Professor of Modern Languages at Brooklyn College, City University of New York. Professor Bernadete was born at Chanak, and he remembers well the Chanak of 1910. He returned to his native town on several occasions, and my interviews were made both before and after his visit.

Other residents who lived in towns administered by the Turks prior to 1910 were interviewed. Their information agreed with the description of Prof. Bernadete. Conditions in different communities and historical periods varied however.

Chapter 9

1. For further discussion see Carlo Tagliavini, "Le Parlate Albanesi di tipo Ghego-orientale," in *Le Terre Albanesi Redente: Kossovo* (Reale Academia d'Italia, Centro Studi per l'Albania), Vol. 3 (Roma, 1942), pp. 9–25.

2. C. A. Macartney, *National States and National Minorities* (Oxford University Press, 1936), pp. 63 ff. During the earlier golden age of Turkish conquest, writes Macartney, Turks were far less harsh masters than the Christians.

3. William Miller, *The Ottoman Empire and Its Successors* (Cambridge University Press, 1936), p. 17.

4. On the role and influence of the Moslem converts, see *ibid.*, pp. 21–23.

5. William Miller, *The Balkans* (London: Fisher Unwin, 1896).

6. Skendo Lumo in *Albanais et Slaves* (Lausanne: Librairie d. Cent. de Nationalités, 1919) uses Turkish statistics prior to the Balkan Wars. According to these statistics, in the entire vilayet of Kossovo Moslems accounted for 64.14% of the population; Serbs, 18.80%; Bulgarians, 15.76%; Catholic Albanians, 1.50%. The Moslems, however, are presented in one class and are not differentiated into various ethnic groups. Therefore it is difficult to differentiate the various ethnic groups. It is difficult to evaluate the reliability of these statistics. However, we find from other sources that the concen-

tration of Albanians was very high 100 years ago in this area. (See, for instance, J. G. V. Hahn in his *Reise von Belgrad bis Salonika,* published in Vienna more than 100 years ago [in 1861] by the Austrian Academy of Sciences.)

The current available data indicate that the Albanians form a majority in Kosmet. According to the Jugoslav Encyclopedia the entire population of the autonomous territory of Kosmet-Metohiya (*oblast*) in 1953 was 809,234, of which 525,000 were Albanians, the rest Serbs, Montenegrins, and Turks (see *Pomorska Enciklopedija,* Vol. IV, Zagreb, 1958, p. 17).

According to the evaluation of Myers and Campbell of the U. S. Census, based on Jugoslav data in 1948, 71% of Albanians living in Jugoslavia were in Serbia, 26% in Macedonia, 3% in Montenegro. Kosmet is a part of Serbia. The total number of Albanians by 1948 for all Jugoslavia was 750,000. Figure 9. of the survey indicates the percent of population by religious affiliation. The table is not too clear, but it indicates about 70% of population in Kosmet identified as Moslem. Moslems in this area are Albanians and Turks (the latter rather few). See Paul F. Myers and Arthur A. Campbell, *The Population of Jugoslavia* (International Population Statistics Reports, Series P–90, No. 5, Bureau of the Census, U. S. Government Printing Office, Washington, D. C.: 1954, pp. 29, 52, 53, 54).

7. Jovan Tomitch, *Les Albanais en Vieille Serbie* (Paris: Hachette, 1913), pp. 2–6. Tomitch writes that the Moslem Albanians, of all the peoples of Europe, were the ones who gave the Turks the greatest

services. But he admits that the Christian Albanians supported the Christian cause.

8. William Miller, *op. cit.*

9. See, for instance, Vladislav Skaric, "L'attitude des Peuples Balcaniques à l'egard des Turcs," *Revue Internationale des Études Balcaniques,* Anne 1 (1935), p. 242. Again, Skaric stresses the Albanian activities against the Serbs.

10. General Mikhailovic, in a telegram of December 22, 1942, indicated that the Ustachi killed 600,000 Serbs. "We are exterminating Ustachi whenever we find them," ends his telegram (*Yugoslav Communism: A Critical Study,* United States Government Printing Office, 87th Congress, Committee of the Judiciary, United States Senate, October 18, 1961). It is difficult to estimate the precise number of the victims. The Albanians estimate roughly about 50,000 Albanians killed. P. D. Ostovic, in *The Truth About Yugoslavia* (Roy Publishers, 1952) quotes the report of a Chetnik commander in an action in Plevije (Sandjak), in which 22 Chetniks perished but 1200 Moslem Albanian fighters were killed and 8,000 other victims were reported, while the Moslem villages were completely burned down. Again the veracity of this source and the figures may be questioned, but it is beyond doubt that the massacres decimated the population.

11. See Joyce Cary, *Memoirs of the Bobotes* (Austin: University of Texas Press), pp. 33 ff. 41, 100, and 101 ff.

12. Pierre Loti, *La Turquie Agonissante* (Paris: Colman Levy, 1913), pp. 220–223.

13. For a description of the massacres in Kraguyevats, see David Martin,

Ally Betrayed (New York: Prentice-Hall, 1946), pp. 23 ff.

14. Joseph S. Roucek, in his *Balkan Politics* (Stanford University Press, 1948), discusses the political pattern in the Balkan politics and rightly indicates violence as a political element (see Chapter 2, "The Political Pattern," and especially page 17, "Violence As Political Routine"). However, violence was used generally in Mediterranean politics, and it declined with the establishment of parliamentary and democratic rule, especially in the nineteenth century. Of course revolutions formed a specific case. The problem is one of assassination and violence as a pattern, as Roucek points out. Again, however, the Balkan states did not share with Western Europe all the slow phases of the development of political institutions and behavior. Once the Serbs and the other ethnic groups emancipated themselves, they generally accepted Western patterns, although they had to start from an entirely different base than their Western neighbors. Some elements of the Turkish pattern remained for a long time in the administration, government, and political patterns of the Balkans.

15. The Regulation of September 24, 1920, which indicated the types of lands subject to the land reform, appears in G. Kristich, *La Colonization de la Serbie Meridionale* (Sara-

jevo, 1928), which in turn is reprinted in a book by Kokalari (*Kossovo*; Tirana, 1943). Kokalari strongly critized the Yugloslav policy. In this respect he represents the viewpoint of certain Albanian parties at the time of the war.

16. A good and comprehensive discussion of Albanian tribal organization, customary law, and customs has been collected in Ludwig Thalloczy, ed., *Illyrisch-Albanische Forschungen* (Munchen-Leipzig: Dunker-Humboldt, 1916).

17. A recent visitor in Kossovo informs me that the Moslem Albanians have shown a preference for marrying Moslem Bosniak girls.

18. This information is based on interviews. Mr. Gashi, who knows this area well from the interwar period and was an Albanian partisan leader during the war, confirms this information, as does a recent visitor who was there to collect some sociological data and made a special attempt to get the facts. These are impressions rather than a rigorous collection of data.

19. On the earlier pattern of blood feuds, see Ludwig Thalloczy (*op. cit.*). This volume contains a number of reports on customary law of Albanian tribes, including blood vengeance and customs connected with the settlement and reduction of feuds.

20. Information based on interviews.

Chapter 10

1. For a general discussion of the protection of minorities under the League of Nations system see: Jacob Robinson *et al.*, *Were the Minorities Treaties a Failure?* (New York: In-

stitute of Jewish Affairs, 1943) and Inis L. Claude, Jr., *National Minorities* (Cambridge: Harvard University Press, 1955), pp. 16–50.

2. Everett V. Stonequist suggested a theory of a "marginal man": one whose ancestry belonged to two dif-

ferent cultures, two different ethnic or racial groups, and who is not fully accepted by either. In this case, marginality in Silesia was largely absent. Stonequist wrote primarily on Mexican-Americans, Mexicans, and related groups (*The Marginal Man*; New York: Scribner's Sons, 1937). Alfred McClung Lee also advanced a general theory of multivalence in his sociological studies.

3. The memoirs of a Polish deputy foreign minister, published in 1964, reveal details of a political undermining action of Colonel Beck, the Polish foreign minister, and his government against the Czechoslovak Republic. (See Tytus Komarnicki, ed., *Diariusz i Teki Jana Szembena*, Vol. I [Polish Research Center, 1964], pp. 312 and 316.

4. On the political activity of German pro-Hitler groups in Poland and of German nationalist groups in Silesia, see: Polish Ministry of Information,

The German Fifth Column in Poland (London: Hutchinson).

5. *Osteuropa Handbuch Polen* (Werner Markert, ed.; Bohlau Verlag [Koln und Graz], 1959–1960): "Politische und Wirtschaltliche Organizationen," pp. 145 ff., and "Die Entwicklung zur Volksgruppe," pp. 148 ff.

6. We refer the reader here to the first section of "Command and Consensus Structures" (Appendix I).

7. For a survey of international treaties in this area see: *Osteuropa Handbuch, ibid.*, "Verträge und Abkommen," p. 689.

8. For a discussion of plebiscites see: Sarah Wambaugh, *Plebiscites Since the World War*, with a collection of official documents (Washington: Carnegie Endowment, 1933); and by the same author, *A Monograph on Plebiscites*, with a collection of official documents (Oxford University Press, 1920).

Chapter *11*

1. *Responsa of Moses Isserles*, No. 95 (Hebrew edition; Hanau, 1710).
2. For a history of the Jews in Cracow, see Majer Balaban, *A History of the Jews in Cracow and Kazimierz, 1304–1868* (*Historia Zydow w Krakowie i na Kazimierzu, 1304–1868*) (Krakow, 1928), 2 vols.
3. See Simon Dubnow, *Weltgeschichte des Judischen Volkes* (Berlin, 1927), V, 180 ff., also p. 217 ff. On Statutes of Kalish see also Izak Lewin, "An Artist's View of the Statutes of Kalish" in *Late Summer Fruit* (New York: Bloch Publishing, 1962), pp. 99–108. For a survey of documents on the medieval church and the Jews see Jacob R. Marcus, *The Jew in the*

Medieval World, Section II, "The Church and the Jew," pp. 101–184 (New York: Meridian Books, 1960).

4. Michal Bobrzynski, *Dzieje Polski w Zarysie* (Survey of Polish History) (Warsaw, 1887), pp. 288–89, pp. 291 ff.
5. The nationality policy of the Social-Democratic parties was influenced by the theories of Bauer and Renner, especially by their writings: O. Bauer, *Die Nationalitätenfrage und die Social Demokratie* (Vienna, 1907); Karl Renner and R. Springer, *Der Kampf der Osterreichischen Nationen um den Staat* (Vienna, 1902); *Grundlagen und Entwicklungsziele der Osterreichisch-Ungarischen Monarchie* (Vienna, 1906). Karl Renner was the first president of the Aus-

trian Republic after World War II.

6. For details on Jewish political movements see: Feliks Gross and Basil Vlavianos, Eds., *Struggle for Tomorrow: Political Ideologies of the Jewish People* (New York: Arts, 1954).

7. The political picture of Poland at this time is not simple. In 1926 a one-time socialist, Marechal Pilsudski, established his personal rule and a kind of military dictatorship. While democratic institutions were either weakened or suspended, political parties of opposition and even political rights were never fully abolished, although freedoms were strongly limited. Democratic parties continued their struggle for reestablishment of a democratic rule. Their leaders and membership were under continuous pressure of the administration; many of them were imprisoned and mistreated, but their parties were never entirely abolished. This was not a fully totalitarian system in the accepted sense.

Pilsudski himself was free of antisemitism and some of his closest friends and associates were of Jewish origin. As long as he lived the government and the administration looked with disfavor at antisemitism, opposing excesses. After his death, the heirs to his military traditions and interests followed the antagonistic trend popular at this time in the right-wing movements of Europe, and moved farther toward authoritarian forms and policies.

Chapter *12*

1. A questionnaire was distributed in the author's graduate Seminar on Minority Groups in Brooklyn College in 1955. One student who taught in a lower East Side school identified 19 different ethnic, religious, and race groups in a class of 22.

2. For general, statistical figures see: Oscar Handlin, *The Newcomers* (New York: Doubleday & Company, Inc., 1959), pp. 136 ff., tables 8–14; The City of New York, Commission on Intergroup Relations, *Negroes in the City of New York: The Number and Proportion in Relation to the Total Population, 1790–1960* (prepared by Florence M. Cromien); "Estimates of the Components of Population Change by Color for States: 1950–1960," *Current Population Reports, Population Estimates* (April 2, 1962); Series P-25, No. 2–7 (Bureau of the Census, Washington, D.C.); Clarence Senior, *Background Data for Discussion on the Changing City Scene* (Migration Division, Commonwealth of Puerto Rico; n.d.); *New York Public Schools, 1963–1964, Fact and Figures* (Board of Education, The City of New York, February 11, 1964).

3. Board of Education, City of New York, *Better Education Through Integration* (January 29, 1964). The board received recommendations from more than 30 citywide organizations.

4. According to Deputy School Superintendent John B. King, "... per capita cost of pupil education in New York averages $730 per child per year. The Board spends an additional $117 in 310 special service elementary and junior high schools, in special high school programs, and auxiliary areas." (Board of Education of the City of New York, News Bureau, May 25, 1964, N351-63/64

[mimeo]). On special services for minority group children see also "Toward Quality and Equality in Education, Additional Services Provided for Our Pupils in Minority Group Areas," *The Public School of New York City Staff Bulletin,* Vol. II, No. 11. (May 18, 1964). Also: Dan Dodson, "Can Intergroup Quotas Be Benign," in Earl Raab, ed., *American Race Relations Today* (New York: Doubleday, 1962), pp. 138 ff. This does not mean, however, that school plants or conditions are better in the depressed areas of New York than in high income sections.

5. New York State Commission Against Discrimination, *1956, Report of Progress* (State of New York), pp. 7–10. Also, State of New York, State Commission on Human Rights, *Law Against Discrimination* (as amended through April 1962) (New York, 1962).

6. A New York City local law (No. 55 for the year 1955, amended by Local Law 11 of 1962) states clearly the public policy of the city:

In the city of New York, with its great cosmopolitan population consisting of large numbers of people of every race, color, creed, national ori-

gin and ancestry, there is no greater danger in the health, morals, safety and welfare of the city, and its inhabitants than the existence of groups prejudiced against one another and antagonistic to each other because of differences of race, color, creed, national origin, or ancestry. The council hereby finds and declares that prejudice, intolerance, bigotry, and discrimination and disorder occasioned thereby threaten the rights and proper privileges of its inhabitants and menace the institutions and foundations of a free democratic state. A city agency is hereby created through which the city of New York officially may encourage and bring about mutual understanding and respect among all groups in the city, eliminate prejudice, intolerance, bigotry, discrimination and disorder occasioned thereby and give effect to the guarantee of equal rights for all assured by the constitution and the laws of this state and of the United States of America. The commission is appointed by the Mayor.

7. City of New York, Commission on Intergroup Relations, *1961, Annual Report* (mimeographed).

Chapter *14*

1. See Norman Cohn, *The Pursuit of the Millennium* (Fairlawn, N. J.: Essential Books, 1957), pp. 99 ff.

2. Vincenzo Cuoco, *Saggio Storico Sulla Rivoluzione di Napoli* (Milano: Universale Economica, 1st ed. 1801), Vol. 1.

3. Giuseppe Ferrari, *La Rivoluzione e i Rivoluzionari in Italia* (Milano: Universale Economica, n.d., first published in *Revue des Deux Mondes,* 1844–1845; in Italian, 1852).

4. J. V. Stalin, *Collected Works,* Volume V, 1921–1923 (Moscow: Foreign Languages Publishing House, 1953). See also, Feliks Gross, *Seizure of Political Power* (New York, 1958), Chaps. 2 and 3, pp. 65 ff. and pp. 241 ff.

5. *Op. cit.,* p. 22.

6. *Op. cit.,* pp. 9, 12, 18.

7. Gross, *op. cit.,* pp. 27, 39 ff., 47, 52 ff.

8. Ferrari, *op. cit.,* p. 21.

9. Tukhachevski presented his views at the Military Academy of Moscow on February 7–10, 1923. His lecture was

reprinted in Joseph Pilsudski, *L'Année 1920* (Paris, 1920).

10. Adam Ciolkosz, "Tajemnica Tucha-czewskiego" (The Secret of Tukha-chevski), *Polemiki*, I, No. 1 (Fall, 1963, London), 103.

11. "Uber die Idee des Volksaufstan-des," in *Historische Zeitschrift*, Neue Folge, Vol. 50 (Munchen-Liepzig, 1901), pp. 78 ff. Reprinted in: Nei-hart von Gneisenau, *Schriften Uber Gneisenau* (Berlin, 1954), pp. 230 ff.

12. See Appendix I.

13. Giuseppe Mazzini, "Sulla Rivolu-zione Francese del 1789," in *Scritti* (Milano: Casa Editrice Sonzogno; n.d.), II, 138 and 154.

14. Georges Sorel, *Reflexions sur la vio-lence* (Paris: Riviere, 1925 edition).

15. Georges Sorel, "Decomposition of Marxism," in Irving L. Horowitz, *Radicalism and Revolt against Rea-son* (New York: The Humanities Press, 1961).

16. "Hernán Cortés," *Enciclopedia Barsa (Encyclopaedia Britannica)* (Buenos Aires, Chicago, Mexico, 1957), V, 173.

17. "Francisco Pizarro," *Enciclopedia Barsa (op. cit.)*, XII, 150.

18. "Francis Garnier," *Larousse du Vingtième Siècle* (Paris, 1930), III, 719.

19. Cuoco, *op. cit.*, Ch. XVI, "The State of the Nation of Naples," pp. 79 ff. and 82 ff. See also Constance A. Dig-lioli, *Naples in 1799, An Account of the Revolution of 1799* (London: John Murray, 1903).

20. C. Lombroso and R. Laschi, *Il Del-itto Politico e le Rivoluzioni* (Torino: Fratelli Bocca, 1890).

21. Gaetano Mosca, *Elementi di Scienca Politica*, ed. Laterza (Bari, 1953).

22. Che (Ernesto) Guevara, *Guerrilla Warfare* (New York: M. R. Press, 1961).

23. Eugenio Garin, *L'Umanesimo Itali-ano*, Laterza, Bari 1964, p. 94.

24. Mazzini, *op. cit.*, p. 211.

25. Reginald G. Hainworth and Ray-mond T. Moyer, *Agricultural Geog-raphy of the Philippine Islands* (U. S. Department of Agriculture, Office of Foreign Agricultural Rela-tions, Washington, D. C., December, 1945), quoted in: Gerald D. Berre-man, *The Philippines: A Survey of Current Social, Economic and Polit-ical Conditions*, No. 19, Southeast Asia Program, Department of Far Eastern Studies (Cornell University, 1956), p. 27.

26. Robert A. Polson and Agaton P. Pal, *The Status of Rural Life in the Dumaguete City Trade Area* (Philip-pines, 1952; Ithaca: Cornell Univer-sity, 1956; mimeo.), Table 34, P. RAP 56: 103–150 ff.

27. Berreman, *op. cit.*, pp. 27 ff. See also Bernard Seerman and Laurence Sal-isbury, *Cross-Currents in the Philip-pines* (New York-San Francisco: In-stitute of Pacific Relations, Far East-ern Pamphlets, No. 13, 1946).

28. Alvin H. Scaff, *The Philippine An-swer to Communism* (Stanford Uni-versity Press, 1955), p. 6.

29. *Ibid.*, pp. 36 ff., pp. 118–134.

30. Napoleon D. Valeriano, Colonel AFP, "Military Operations," in *An-thology of Related Topics on Coun-terinsurgency* (Fort Bragg, North Carolina, June 15, 1961), pp. 144–150.

31. Valetiano, *op. cit.*, p. 147.

32. Some of the cases and tactics de-scribed indicate the ruthless nature of this struggle, which may alienate and discourage friends and the non-com-mitted and challenge the very princi-ple of democracy. Here appears again the problem of moral imperatives im-posed on a democratic system, while

the others may disregard the principles.

33. Frances Lucille Starner, *Magsaysay and the Philippine Peasantry: The Agricultural Impact on Philippine Politics, 1953–1956* (University of California Press, 1961), University of California Political Science Publications, Vol. X. On the role of the army in social and political reform in the Philippines and the effect of those actions on the reduction of friction, see also "Civic Activities of the Military in Southeast Asia," by Col. E. G. Lansdale. Lansdale gives an interesting and general survey of military civil assistance as a policy of easing tensions. The American, French, and Indonesian armies were helping local populations in Southeast Asia, distributing food, giving assistance in agriculture, public works, medical aid, even legal defense. He gives a general account of aid and civil administration in the Philippines, Vietnam, Cambodia, Burma, Indonesia. The general rehabilitation plan, the Edcor Plan, for the Philippines is included. (Anderson, Southeast Asia Subcommittee of the Draper Committee, *Anthology of Related Topics on Counterinsurgency* (Lackland Air Force Base), III, 282–291.

34. N. E. Geneste, "Danger from Below," in *United States Naval Institute Proceedings* (November, 1960), Vol. 86, pp. 33–46.

35. On group structures and organization of the civil population of the Viet Minh during the war in Indochina, 1949 and 1951, see Geneste, as quoted above, and Colonel Lacheroy, "Guerre Revolutionnaire," in *Marine* (September, 1958), No. 21 (Paris), pp. 41 ff.

36. The full text of the letter was published in the New York *Times* on July 5, 1963.

Chapter *15*

1. For bibliography and basic documents concerning the tension over Berlin, see: *Berlin 1961,* Background (Dept. of State Publication 7257, released August 1961).

2. The Somali-Ethiopian tension discussed in Appendix III, a case study prepared by T. Gurr, presents an area somewhere in the consequential or perhaps distant category.

3. "Guerre Revolutionnaire et Arme Psychologique," *Marine* (Paris), No. 21 (September, 1958), pp. 41–52.

4. Our examples are based on current press and general, available documents. Such periodicals were used as sources as the *World Almanac and Book of Facts (New York World Telegram and Sun), The Annual Register of World Events* (Longmans Green, London), New York *Times, Time,* and others. Dr. I. Langnas assisted in gathering and checking the data. The inventory of tensions in this volume may serve only as a general, rough outline, based on easily available information. A substantial inventory requires more space. Neither the purpose of this chapter nor consideration of space, however, justified a more extensive text. Means were also too limited for preparation of a detailed list.

5. New York *Times,* May 24, 31, June 7.

6. *Time,* May 1, 1964.

7. *Time,* June 12, 1964; New York *Times,* June 7, 1964.
8. Senate Armed Services Committee, Investigation of Preparedness Program (May 9, 1963), *Interim Report.*
9. British Information Services, New York, Official Text. *Disarmament,* text of the speech of the Secretary of State for Foreign Affairs, R. A. Butler, at the Disarmament Conference (Geneva, February 25, 1964).

Chapter *16*

1. According to a summary of Soviet strength in Cuba (Senate Armed Services Committee, *Investigation of Preparedness Program,* May 9, 1963; Interim Report), the armed Soviet military forces were estimated at over 17,500. A substantial number of missile sites is also noted. Cuba remains an important strategic advance base for ideological expansion as well as for possible military use. (See also: U. S. House of Representatives, Committee on Foreign Affairs, *Hearings on Castro Communist Subversion in the Western Hemisphere,* Report No. 195, 88th Congress, 1st sess., April 4, 1963.) Senator Kenneth Keating of New York warned in August 1962 about the Soviet build-up in Cuba (U. S. Congressional Record, 87th Congress, 2d sess., 1962, CVIII, Part 14, 18360–18361).
2. Council of the Organization of American States, Pan-American Union, Washington, D. C. *Report of the Investigating Committee Appointed by the Council of the Organization of American States,* Council Series OEASER G/IV C-i-658 (English; February 18, 1964), p. 41.
3. Report of the Investigating Committee, *op. cit.,* pp. 12–32.
4. "Venezuela: Democracy under Fire," *On Record* (New York: Keynote Publications), Vol. 1., No. 9. Salvador de Madariaga, *The Fall of the Spanish American Empire,* new rev. ed. (New York: Colliers Books, 1963).
5. See José Rafael Pocaterra, *La Tyrannie de Venezuela* (Paris: André Delpeuch, 1928). Jorge Luciani, *La Dittatura Perpetua de Gomez y Sus Adversarios* (New York: De Lasne & Rossboro, 1930), and many others.
6. "Venezuela: Democracy under Fire," *On Record,* p. 5; Robert J. Alexander, *Prophets of the Revolution,* Profiles of Latin American Leaders (New York: Macmillan, 1962), pp. 109 ff.
7. Charles O. Porter, Robert J. Alexander, *The Struggle for Democracy in Latin America* (New York: Macmillan, 1961), pp. 112 ff.; Robert Alexander, *Prophets of the Revolution,* pp. 112 ff.; Chatham House Memoranda, *Venezuela, A Brief Political and Economic Survey,* Royal Institute of Internal Affairs (Oxford University Press, 1959), pp. 3 ff. Alexander explains and justifies the coup. Acción Democrática, argues Alexander, was trying to avoid a Gómez-type of military dictatorship. President Medina Angarita insisted on nomination of the president by congress.
8. Porter and Alexander, *op. cit.,* pp. 113 ff. Chatham House Memoranda; "Venezuela," *On Record,* p. 5.
9. *Documentos Oficiales Relativos Al Movimento Militar de 1948* (Caracas: Oficina Nacional, 1949); also Chatham House Memoranda.
10. Robert J. Alexander, *op. cit.,* pp. 135 ff.

11. Chatham House Memoranda.

12. Porter and Alexander, *op. cit.*, p. 117; Council of the Organization of American States, *Report of the Investigating Committee*, Appendix 3 (*Statement of the President of Venezuela*), pp. 40 ff.

13. For the chronological sequence of events see "Venezuela," *On Record*, pp. 7 ff.

14. See signatures in *Documentos Oficiales*, ftn. 9.

15. *The Annual Message to Congress*, in "Venezuela," *On Record*, p. 31.

16. The Organization of American States, *Report of the Investigating Committee*, p. 43.

17. See, for instance, the collection of his articles and addresses: Rómulo Betancourt, *Pensamiento y Acción* (Mexico, D. F., 1954); *Posición y Dotrina*, Cordillera (Caracas, 1959); p. 46, "Visión general de los problemas economicos y sociales de Venezuela"; p. 73, "El Petroleo en la Economía Venezolana"; p. 121, "La Reforma Agraria." Betancourt's major work, *Venezuela: Politica y Petroleo* (Fondo Economico, Mexico–Buenos Aires, 1956), is more than a voluminous economic study. It is a modern history of Venezuela, discussed in terms of major social, economic, and political problems faced by the continuous struggle between democratic movements and dictatorship (una Republica de generales–Presidentes). Petrol and its social-economic problems is the central theme. For a general survey of Betancourt's theory and politics, see Robert J. Alexander, *op. cit.*, pp. 109 ff.

18. The tensions in various areas of the Western Hemisphere are analyzed by Edwin M. Martin, Assistant Secretary for Inter-American Affairs, in "Communist Subversion in the Western Hemisphere," *Foreign Affairs Outlines* (Dept. of State), No. 2 (March, 1963).

19. For details see "Venezuela," *On Record*, pp. 10–15.

20. As above, p. 16, *Meeting of OAS, August 20, 1960*.

21. Council of the Organization of American States, *Report of the Investigating Committee*.

22. "Venezuela," *On Record*, pp. 19 ff. The Library of Congress, Legislative Reference Service, *Acts of Terrorism Against the Government and People of Venezuela since the Beginning of 1962*.

23. The organization of political parties of attack is discussed in Appendix I.

24. Victor Alba, "Il Castro-Communismo nell'America Latina," *Critica D'Oggi* (Roma: 25–28 Novembre-Febraio 1964), pp. 24–25.

25. Betancourt, *Posición y Dotrina*, p. 128.

26. *Time*, February 8, 1960, quoted in *On Record*, p. 12. Victor Alba, in *op. cit.*, gives somewhat different figures.

27. For details see: *Ley De Reforma Agraria*, Gazeta Oficial No. 610 Extraordinario De Fecha (5 de Marzo de 1960). Publicación de la Sociedad Venezolana De Ingenieres Agronomos.

28. Organization of American States, Report of the Investigating Committee, "Statement of the President of Venezuela," p. 46. *Proposed Mutual Defense and Development Program*, FY 1965 (U. S. Government Printing Office, Washington, 1964, 20402), p. 80.

29. *On Record*, pp. 9 and 23. *Declaration of G. Rodriguez Eraso*, Director of Creole Petroleum Corp.

30. *On Record*, p. 34.

31. *Ibid.*, p. 48.

32. *Foreign Assistance Act of 1964*, Hearings before the Committee on Foreign Affairs, 88th Congress, Second Ses-

sion, pp. 271 ff. on H. R. 10502, April 6–9, 1964 (Washington, 1964), p. 80.

33. *Proposed Mutual Defense and Development Programs,* FY 1965 (Superintendent of Documents, U. S. Government Printing Office, Washington, D. C., 1964, 20402).

34. In March, 1964, unemployment in Venezuela was estimated at 12% of the labor force (*U. S. News and World Report,* March 9, 1964).

35. See the report of Special Consultative Committee on Security of the Organization of American States (OEA/Ser. L./X/11.3) of February 8, 1963, reprinted for the use of the Committee on the Judiciary, United States Senate (Government Printing Office, Washington, 1963, 94909), *Cuba As a Base of Subversion in America.* Also 88th Congress,

Committee on Foreign Affairs, *Castro Communist Subversion in the Western Hemisphere,* H. Res. 55, March 14, 1963 (U. S. Government Printing Office, Washington, D. C., 1963, 95630).

36. The report of the Special Consultative Committee of the Organization of American States of February 8, 1963, lists 9 guerrilla and irredentist training centers in Cuba; one of them, Ciudad Libertad School in Marianao, Havana Province, under Russian instructors.

37. Written in June 1964.

38. Under the term of consensus, we understand agreement on a minimum set of rules of political operation and procedures, not an elimination of differences or ideological or political contradictions and struggles.

Chapter 17

1. Robin M. Williams, *The Reduction of Inter-Group Tensions,* Social Science Research Council Bulletin 57 (New York, 1947). Williams discusses at length the types of techniques for the reduction of intergroup tensions. The application of social science research to international tensions is discussed by Otto Klineberg in *Tensions Affecting International Understanding: A Survey of Research,* Social Science Research Council Bulletin 62 (New York, 1950). The literature in this area is very extensive. A comprehensive bibliography of American, and West and East European writings in this field has been compiled in *The Main Types and Causes of Discrimination,* United Nations Committee on Human Rights, Sub-Committee on the Pre-

vention of Discrimination and Protection of Minorities (New York, 1949). Current literature and bibliographies in this field have been compiled in *Sociological Abstracts.* The Anti-Defamation League of New York also publishes information on research in this area. For application of social psychology to international relations and tension see: Otto Klineberg, *The Human Dimensions of International Relations,* Holt, Rinehart and Winston, New York, 1964.

2. History teaches that minorities frequently paid a special tax for such protection. In many cases this protection was lukewarm; in others, it was sincere and strong. Tolerance for an ethnic minority or religious dissident group did not result solely from pecuniary motivation. In times of enlightened despotism, various shades of religious tolerance were a

matter of policies and principles.

3. *Territorial Frontiers in Islam,* Program of Non-Western Studies, University of Vermont (mimeo., 1960); *India's Boundaries,* Program of Non-Western Studies, University of Vermont (mimeo., 1961); *China's South Sea Boundaries: A Cultural Problem,* Program of Non-Western Studies, University of Vermont (mimeo., 1961).

4. The Polish language has a term corresponding in meaning to the American "frontier" (*kresy*), and an expression for "boundary" (*granica*). The former originally had the same meaning as "frontier" in America. On seventeenth-century maps it is marked *"Dzikie Pola"* (savage [wild] fields). For many centuries the eastern Polish borderland was a frontier in the American sense. It was an area in the eastern Polish provinces where the Poles represented the conquering and ruling classes.

5. It is not within the scope of this book to discuss fully the problems of boundaries or to suggest an extensive bibliography. An article by Julian G. Minghi ("Review Article: Boundary Studies in Political Geography," in the *Annals of the Association of American Geographers*, Vol. 53, No. 3 [Sept. 1963], pp. 407—428) gives a comprehensive though general survey of the extensive research, discussions, and studies of the boundary problems.

6. For a discussion of the Geneva Protocol and a definition of aggression see: David H. Miller, *The Geneva Protocol* (New York: Macmillan, 1925).

Chapter *18*

1. Bronislaw Malinowski, "An Anthropological Analysis of War," *The American Journal of Sociology*, XLVI (No. 4), 1941. Malinowski also quotes C. G. and B. Z. Seligman, *The Veddas* (Cambridge, 1911) and G. C. W. C. Wheeler, *The Tribe and Intertribal Relations in Australia.*

2. Herbert Spencer, *The Data of Ethics* (New York: Hurst & Company; written in 1879; no date of publication).

3. See Appendix I, "Command and Consensus Structures," especially the discussion of Kropotkin, Pisarev, and others.

4. Peter Kropotkin, *Ethics, Origin and Development* (New York: Tudor Publishing Co., 1942).

5. Darwin, in his diary of the voyage of the *Beagle* (1831–1836), expresses views of morality that are far removed from relativism.

6. See, for instance: Bronislaw Malinowski, *Scientific Theory of Culture* (Chapel Hill: University of North Carolina Press, 1945); also *Freedom and Civilization* (New York: Roy Publishers, 1944).

7. Florence Rockwood Kluckhohn and Fred L. Strodtbeck, *Variations in Value Orientations* (Evanston-New York: Harper and Row, 1961).

8. Herbert Spencer, in his strongly utilitarian essay *The Data of Ethics* (written before 1879; New York: Hurst & Co.) discussed the development of the dichotomy of norms in human society. Ethics for Spencer is simply "a definite account of the forms of conduct that are fitted to the associated stage." In Spencer's ethical system social welfare is superior to the individual. Subordina-

tion of personal welfare to society is determined, according to his theory, by the existence of antagonistic societies. As a consequence, within the society the values of cooperation for economic objectives (which he calls industrialism) differ from those for militancy. Similarly, the existence of antagonistic societies determines the structure of the society. Spencer's intention is to create a scientific system of ethics. Nonetheless, it is apparent that while he proceeds with scientific apparatus, the value structure of the latter is determined by his own utilitarian values and by his own outlook, which is also a reflection of the contemporary English industrial society. (Chapter 8, "The Sociological View," pp. 162–182). Lecky, a contemporary of Spencer, argues that it is not possible to develop any moral system solely on a utilitarian basis. Lecky represents an "intuitive approach" which may seem antiquated today but which has not lost its significance and its vigor. Lecky correctly sees the basic division of the moralist schools into "utilitarian" and "intuitive," tracing the schools to the Platonic idea and to the Stoics. See William E. H. Lecky, *History of European Morals* (1869), edition of 1946 (London: Watts Company), Chapter 1, "The Natural History of Morals," pp. 1–67.

9. Sir Ernest Barker, *Greek Political Theory* (London: Methuen; New York: Barnes and Noble, 1960).

10. For an English translation of Mirandola's oration see Giovanni Pico della Mirandola, "Oration on the Dignity of Man," in Ernst Cassirer, Paul O. Kristeller, and John H. Randall, Jr., *The Renaissance Philosophy of Man* (The University of Chicago Press, 1948), pp. 223 ff.

11. Lecky (*op. cit.*) argued that these values are as old as humanity and that they do not change but form a permanent element of morals. He followed the so-called "intuitive" school in the theory of morals. This school, which opposed the utilitarian school about a hundred years ago, can be traced to Greek times and to the Greek divisions. In modern times the names have changed, but the tendencies have remained. In this sense only Carl Jung, the psychologist, represents Lecky's viewpoint, interpreted, however, in the scientific terms of psychology. His theory of archetypes more or less corresponds to these eternal elements. On the other hand, in modern sociological- and anthropological-oriented education, as well as in psychology, the various schools would argue that such phenomena as conscience and values are acquired from society and are transmitted from one generation to another through the process of learning. The question can be raised, however, how these values developed in society before they were passed to the individual. It is relevant to know whether such values can be developed or whether there are certain data which cannot be changed. What has been indicated so far is that values have changed and they can also diffuse. Of course, they diffuse very slowly and their development is also slow. The change of values is a difficult process, but in a crisis stituation there is a tendency toward a more rapid change of value structures.

12. Adolf A. Berle, Jr., *On the Natural Selection of Political Forces* (Lawrence, Kansas: University of Kansas Press, 1950), p. 17. Berle argues that selection favors political forces which tend to approach universality and

which give the individuals a "sense of harmony with the universal pattern." Selection rejects those political forces which "(1) are based on limited conceptions such as exclusions, hatred and the like and (2) which tend to concentrate power without modifying that power" and favors those which modify power by introducing some form of responsibility and grass roots participation.

13. L. Levy-Bruhl (*La Morale et la Science des Moeurs* [Paris, 4th ed., 1910], pp. 290 ff.) argues that human morals develop through definite stages of the evolution of norms. The first stage is characterized by what he calls *particularization* of moral practice. At this stage the norms are highly specialized according to sex or particular groups. There are special norms for women, men, and children. In the second period, a *universalization* of moral principles takes place. The same norms of conduct are imposed on all members of a community. In the third period the *relativism* of the norm is observed. It has been observed by scholars that various ethnic groups and tribes have different norms and value systems. Furthermore, the fourth period, which he anticipated, would be oriented to a *scientific approach* to the problem of the norms. In this period man would explore the values and norms and their rationality. He discards those which persist solely due to tradition or to man's passive acceptance, but which are no longer functional. Instead, exploring the continuous relationship between norms and reality, man is developing new norms which will fit the new conditions (see pp. 280–293).

14. Znaniecki has shown the significance and influence of "national culture societies," national associations and institutions, on the formation of modern nationality and the national state and on the development of what he calls "literary cultures." (Florian Znaniecki, *Modern Nationalities,* a sociological study, The University of Illinois Press, 1952). Much earlier, Bagehot stressed the significance of the state in molding social groups into a unified nation. See Walter Bagehot, *Physics and Politics* (New York, 1884).

Appendix *I*

1. A distinction must be made between an institution's "charter," which represents an ideal type of structure (accepted rules and decision-making mechanism) and actual "institutional behavior." The former indicates how a member of the institution *should behave;* the latter, how he actually *does behave.* The former represents a *plan* of behavior, actions, goals; the latter, the actual, observable *performance.* Under similar conditions, actual political behavior in various cultures may be quite different. Not infrequently in the history of Central America or in other parts of the world, a dictatorial government operated under a democratic constitution. This is, of course, the difference between the "ideal" and the "real," between what "is" and what "ought to be."

2. Peter Kropotkin, *Memoirs of a Revolutionist* (New York: Mifflin, 1930), pp. 216–217.

Many social scientists credit Kropotkin with the theory of cooperation, which forms the basis of his philosophy. He advanced this theory in *Mutual Aid As a Factor of Evolution* (1890–1896) and later in *Ethics* (1922). The theory appears earlier in Russian social philosophy and social science. D. I. Pisarev (1840–1868), the leading nihilist, regarded mutual aid as a basic "natural" human need, while work and cooperation were the bases of society, which must above all satisfy the biological needs of its members. (See his "Essay in History of Labor," in *Selected Philosophical, Social and Political Essays* [Moscow, 1958], pp. 172 ff.) Consensus and cooperation of a Russian village community are the basis for populism (agrarian socialism—*narodnichestvo*) advanced earlier by A. Herzen (1812–1870), and by the early Russian sociologists P. Lavrov (1823–1900) and W. V. Mikhaylovski (1842–1904). The interest in social cooperation in Russian social science deserves more space.

Kropotkin, who in his youth was a "narodnik," was familiar with their theories. His own theory is a continuation of earlier contributions. His own experience had its significance as a contributing factor. The utopian political philosophy of Kropotkin was perhaps responsible for some exaggeration of the phenomenon of cooperation. When he argues that he failed to observe a struggle for means of existence among animals of the same species, he is on dubious ground.

3. B. Malinowski, *Argonauts of the Western Pacific* (London: Routledge and Kegan Paul, 1953 ed.), p. 159.

4. Mutual aid is a general rule in American fundamentalist Protestant farming communities, such as the Amish of Pennsylvania, even today. Here, however, the community or group may act under strong moral pressure or what may be called moral coercion. In fishing communities in northeastern Maine, mutual aid in times of need or disaster and customary forms of cooperation are strong, and reinforced by ideologists of various fraternal lodges, service societies, especially the Grange, also very active in this area today. In other parts of the United States, particularly in farming communities, general forms of mutual aid, and cooperation free of any "customary" moral coercion, can be widely observed.

5. The writer observed the customs described here in 1958 while on field trips in Fumone.

6. See E. A. Schermerhorn, *Society and Power* (New York: Random House, 1961), pp. 2–13.

7. Historically, writes Prof. Gyles, Egypt had a dual administration, separate for Upper and Lower Egypt, while the Pharaoh united both. The diagram of the administrative structure, built along traditional lines, indicates the main links: Pharaoh—Governor General—Nomarch. However, the administrative structure was more detailed and complex and, as Prof. Gyles indicates, it is difficult to visualize how the various offices overlapped in their functions, and even more difficult to clarify "the lines of responsibility and loyalty of one official toward his superior." It seems that the Pharaoh controlled many parallel hierarchies, not one, and could balance various power centers (Mary Francis Gyles, *Pharaonic Policies and Administration, 663 to 323 B. C.* [The University of North Carolina Press, 1959], pp. 75 ff.).

8. Symbolism of rank is not the only social function of colors. In an army, the regimental colors are also symbols contributing to group integration.

Colors have a multiple social function. An army or a regiment also builds a tradition of its own (for instance, memory of heroic exploits), which contributes the "esprit de corps." Such tradition also builds common values; it becomes a symbol and integrates the group.

9. Shared values, identification with a military organization (esprit de corps), are also important elements of discipline. In addition to the punishment and reward mechanism, other factors may contribute to the reinforcement of the discipline. In certain societies (in prewar Prussia) the army uniform, even of a private, gives status. In a totalitarian system, a militarized police may enjoy a number of additional privileges, such as better pay, housing, and clothing. Those advantages, in addition to a shared ideology, may contribute to a willingness to accept an authoritarian system. Last but not least, certain personality types find enjoyment in ritual performances, such as parades, marching with a band, and other types of formalized group actions, which, like athletics, require certain physical skills. In a modern army, the soldiers may also share the values of the institution. A democratic army (in the sense of a model), i.e., the Swiss, is a combination of command and consensus.

10. For general history, religion, values, and organization of the Quakers, see: Frederick B. Tolles and E. Gordon Alderfer, eds., *The Witness of William Penn* (New York: Macmillan Company, 1957); Arnold Lloyd, *Quaker Social History, 1669–1738* (London: Longmans, Green and Company, 1950); John Sykes, *The Quakers* (Philadelphia: Lippincott, 1959); Howard Brinton, *Friends for 300 Years* (New York:

Harper and Brothers, 1952). Miss Sandra Needham, in my seminar on Social Institutions at Brooklyn College, prepared a background paper on "The Institutional Structure of the Society of Friends," which was very helpful.

11. Next to mutual aid, one finds in an Italian village strong tensions and conflicts which are a part of daily life.

12. Spencer stresses the relationship between military rank and property in ancient Greece. He also indicates "that in the development of the military institution, the transition from the state of incoherent clusters, each having its own organization, to the state of a coherent whole, held together by an elaborate organization running throughout it, of course, implies a concomitant progress in a centralization of command" (Herbert Spencer, *Principles of Sociology* [New York: Appleton, 1899], Vol. II, p. 486). Spencer, an early student of the sociology of the army, was in this respect much more penetrating than, for instance, Freud. He also indicates that "the process of militant organization is a process of regimentation, which primarily taking place in the army, secondarily affects the whole community" (Vol. II, para. 553). This type of development later became characteristic of the totalitarian states.

Spencer was among the early forecasters of the extension of regimentation over an entire state-system.

13. Gaetano Mosca classified the states into: feudal, bureaucratic, and city-states (of the Hellenic-Roman type). The feudal system is based on territorial organization of power; the bureaucratic, on functional organization of power; and the city-states on a broad "political class" with a frequent circulation or change of the

ruling groups (elites). The latter have shown a miraculous strength of resistance and survival in times of disasters, in spite of their small size. These types of states are, however, very "delicate" and develop solely under certain conditions, in periods of great economic prosperity and intellectual development (*floritura intelletuale*). The city-state is to a large extent based on a consensus mechanism. It is interesting that Mosca advanced this theory at the time of the fascist rule in Italy. (See: Gaetano Mosca, *Storia delle Dottrine Politiche,* Editori Laterza, Bari [ed. 1962], pp. 298–303. [The book was originally published in 1933.])

14. Tönnies divided human societies into two basic types, *Gemeinschaft* and *Gessellschaft,* the former of a higher degree of proximity and cohesion. The family belongs to the former, of course (see Ferdinand Tönnies, *Soziologische Studien und Kritiken,* Jena, 1925).

15. For the party structure of *Conspiration pour l'égalité,* and organization of the insurrection, see Philippe Buonarotti, *Conspiration pour l'égalité dite de Babeuf* (Paris, Editions Sociales, 1957 [originally published in 1828]), especially Volume II, which contains documents (Pièces Justicatives).

16. Alfred Vogts, "Hitler's Second Army," *Infantry Journal* (Washington, 1943), pp. 11 ff.

17. Max Nomad, *Political Heretics* (University of Michigan Press, 1963), pp. 48–50, where he quotes Alan B. Spitzer, *The Revolutionary Theories of Louis Blanqui* (Columbia University Press, 1957).

18. It seems that the "five" system appeared among revolutionary groups of Russia at the end of the 1870's and the beginning of the 1880's. I was unable to trace its historical origins. It probably originated in France or Italy, perhaps in the time of Blanqui or of secret societies. The pattern survives until modern times in a variety of ways. The Soviet partisans during World War II were instructed to form, in addition to combat units, cell units of three, five, or ten. The group—reads the instruction—must be so organized "that the partisans of one group do not know those of any other units." (Instruction for the North West Front of July 20, 1941, in John A. Armstrong, ed., *Soviet Partisans in World War II* [University of Wisconsin Press, 1964], pp. 655–656, Document 2.)

19. During the Second World War, the system of small units, of "fives," was widely used by the Polish Resistance, especially by the Polish Socialist Party (PPS). Some of the prominent leaders of the party, such as Casimir Puzak, chairman of the Underground Council of National Unity, were participants in the Revolution of 1905 and earlier revolutionary movements directed against the Tsarist regime. Those movements had relied on small units, again "fives." Thus, the pattern was transmitted by those whose activities united two generations of resistance.

20. Simmel, in his study of conflict, stresses the centralistic structures of conflict groups. Conflict requires the pulling together of all forces, and this can be effectively accomplished through a centralistic structure. Centralization displaces, in times of conflict, "even the most perfect democracy" (George Simmel, *Conflict and the Web of Group Affiliation,* trans. Kurt H. Wolff and Bernhard Bendix [Glencoe: Free Press, 1956], pp. 88 ff.). Lewis A. Coser, in his study of conflict, interpreting Simmel,

rightly indicates that an outside conflict really integrates the group, but whether it will lead to centralization will depend largely on the structure of the group and the nature of the conflict. After an extensive discussion of Simmel's viewpoint, Coser indicates, with a number of examples, that a variety of types of groups adjusted in various ways to the conflict situation. The change in group structure, according to Coser, will depend on: (1) the size of the group, (2) the degree of involvement of its members, and (3) the situation and general political and social conditions within which these groups operate. Coser rightly indicates that whether a conflict will result in centralization or not depends on the initial structure of the group and the nature of the conflict (see Lewis A. Coser, *The Functions of Social Conflict* [Glencoe: Free Press, 1956], pp. 92–103).

21. Charles A. Beard, *The Economic Bases of Politics and Related Writings* (New York: Vintage, 1957), pp. 90 ff.

Appendix *III*

1. The concept of "tribe" is arbitrary, and when used by Western scholars usually is based on one or two variables: language and culture. Goldthorpe states that: "Perhaps the most important single criterion is language, and we normally call a tribe a group of people who speak the same language and one which is different from its neighbors" (J. E. Goldthorpe, *Outlines of East African Society* [Kampala, Uganda: Department of Sociology, Makerere University College, 1959, 1962], p. 24). The three tribal groups involved in the tensions cited above—Ewe, Bakongo, and Somali—each have common languages, common cultural characteristics, and, most important for their role in modern African politics, a consciousness of tribal identity.

2. *Cf.* David Apter, *The Gold Coast in Transition* (Princeton, N. J.: Princeton University Press, 1957) and *The Political Kingdom in Buganda* (Princeton: Princeton University Press, 1961).

3. "Basic Data on the Economy of Somalia (Somali Republic)," *World Trade Information Service Economic Reports,* Part 1, No. 61–5 (Washington, D. C.: U. S. Department of Commerce), pp. 2, 5; United Nations, *Progress of the Non Self-Governing Territories Under the Charter: Volume 5, Territorial Surveys* (New York: United Nations, 1960), p. 56.

4. Saadia Touval, *Somali Nationalism: International Politics and the Drive for Unity in the Horn of Africa* (Cambridge, Mass.: Harvard University Press, 1963), pp. 10–13; *The Somaliland Protectorate* (London: Central Office of Information, 1960), p. 3; I. M. Lewis, *The Modern History of Somaliland: From Nation to State* (London: Weidenfeld and Nicolson, 1965), pp. 18–32; and Alexander Melamid, "The Kenya-Somalia Boundary Dispute," *The Geographical Review,* LIV (No. 4, 1964), pp. 586–88.

5. Somali population estimates vary markedly, especially as to the number of Somalis in Ethiopia in Kenya. Total population data given here are based on recent United Nations estimates. Somali-speaking population estimates are the larger of figures

cited in Lewis, *op. cit.*, p. 1; Touval, *op. cit.*, p. 12; and John Drysdale, *The Somali Dispute* (London: Pall Mall Press, 1964), p. 103.

6. These distinctions are developed at length by Derrick J. Stenning in "Transhumance, Migratory Drift, Migration: Patterns of Pastoral Fulani Nomadism," *Journal of the Royal Anthropological Institute*, LXXXVII (1957), 57–73, a study of a major nomadic tribe of the West African savannah.

7. Drysdale, *op. cit.*, pp. 79–80.

8. The way of life of the nomadic northern Somalis is ably described by I. M. Lewis, *A Pastoral Democracy* (London: Oxford University Press, 1961). Some implications of these cultural preconditions for the creation of a viable, modern Somali state are drawn by E. A. Bayne, *Four Ways of Politics: State and Nation in Italy, Somalia, Israel, Iran* (New York: American Universities Field Staff, 1965), pp. 99–166; and Alfred Castagno, Jr., "Somali Republic," *Political Parties and National Integration in Tropical Africa*, ed. James S. Coleman and Carl G. Rosgerg, Jr. (Berkeley: University of California Press, 1964).

9. Lewis, *The Modern History . . .*, *op. cit.*, pp. 18–32.

10. Saadia Touval provides useful summaries of the complex events in the partition of the Horn and the delineation of its boundaries (*op. cit.*, Chapter 4, pp. 30–48, and Chapter 13, pp. 154–63). A more detailed account, closely representative of the Somali viewpoint, is Drysdale, *op. cit.*, pp. 25–99.

11. A chronicle of the political and military events of the Jihad is given by D. Jardine, *The Mad Mullah of Somaliland* (London: Jenkins, 1923). For recent interpretations see Lewis, *The Modern History . . .*, *op. cit.*, pp. 63–91, and Touval, *op. cit.*, pp. 51–60.

12. See Lewis, *The Modern History . . .*, *op. cit.*, pp. 113–22, and Touval, *op. cit.*, pp. 76–78.

13. Cited in I. M. Lewis, "Pan-Africanism and Pan-Somalism," *Journal of Modern African Studies*, I (June, 1963), p. 149.

14. *Rapport du Gouvernement Italien à l'Assemblée Générale des Nations Unies sur l'Administration de Tutelle de la Somalie* (Rome, 1959), p. 167, cited in Touval, *op. cit.*, p. 98.

15. *Cf.* A. A. Castagno, "Ethnicity and International Boundaries in North East Africa," paper read at the Sixth Annual Meeting of the African Studies Association (San Francisco, October 1963).

16. New York *Times*, March 27, 1964.

17. *Ibid.*, June 26, 1960.

18. A. A. Castagno, "The Somali Republic in Transition," *Africa Report*, VII (December, 1962), 8.

19. *Somaliland News*, May 30, 1960; London *Times*, June 25, 1960. References to newspaper accounts other than the New York *Times* are from material quoted or summarized in various issues of the periodical *Africa Digest*.

20. London *Times*, August 20, 1960; *Somaliland News*, August 22, 1960.

21. *Somaliland News*, September 19, 1960.

22. London *Times*, January 3, 1961.

23. London *Times*, January 21, 1961.

24. Lewis, "Pan-Africanism and Pan-Somalism," *op. cit.*, p. 153.

25. Touval, *op. cit.*, pp. 147–53.

26. Lewis, *op. cit.*, p. 155; *Africa Report*, VI (December, 1961), 17.

27. A detailed account is Drysdale, *op. cit.*, pp. 100–112.

28. *Africa Digest*, X (February, 1963), p. 129; London *Times*, January 18, 1963.

29. London *Daily Telegraph*, February 22, 1963; London *Times*, February 25, 1963; London *Observer*, March 10, 1963; Manchester *Guardian*, February 27, 1963.

30. London *Times*, March 12, 13, April 1, 15, 1963; *Somali News*, March 15, April 5, 1963; Manchester *Guardian*, May 25, 1963.

31. *Africa Digest*, X (February, 1963), 130.

32. London *Times*, December 30, 1963.

33. London *Times*, November 22, 29, December 4, 27, 1963; London *Daily Telegraph*, January 1, 1964.

34. Manchester *Guardian*, February 26, 1964; London *Daily Telegraph*, February 26, 1964; New York *Times*, April 19, 26, May 6, 24, 1964.

35. *Somali News*, September 21, 1962.

36. London *Observer*, August 18, 1963; London *Daily Telegraph*, October 14, 1963; London *Times*, October 16, 1963.

37. London *Observer*, February 9, 1964; London *Times*, February 10, 12, 13, 1964; Manchester *Guardian*, February 11, 1964. Also private sources.

38. *Somali Times*, February 10, 1964; Manchester *Guardian*, February 15, 1964.

39. *Africa Report*, IX (May, 1964), 20.

40. London *Times*, March 31, 1964.

41. Manchester *Guardian*, March 31, 1964; New York *Times*, April 1, 1964; London *Times*, April 1, 1964. The claims and counterclaims of the two governments throughout the fighting were almost certainly exaggerated, and there appear to have been few if any Western observers to the border warfare. However, from eyewitness and hearsay accounts, the author has made the following reconstruction of the Hargeisa bombing incident.

The bombing of Hargeisa was neither fiction nor accident. The Ethiopian government appears to have had two objectives in mind. The ceasefire was to go into effect the following day, and although military action had been in progress in the immediate border area for eight weeks, there had been no show of force near a Somali town of any size. Ethiopian military intelligence also seems to have been convinced that the Hargeisa airport was being prepared for use by Soviet-supplied jet fighters that had recently arrived in Somalia (see text, below).

Early on the morning of March 31, a flight of F-86 Sabre jets left a new military airfield near Diredawa (about 25 miles northwest of Harar) for Hargeisa, 150 miles away, with orders to attack the Hargeisa airport. They arrived over Hargeisa at 6:30 a.m. local time, but in error attacked not the airport itself but the nearby camp of the international Desert Locust Control Organization, about two miles from the town. The camp was bombed and strafed for somewhat more than half an hour. (The error was not entirely unlikely, since the camp had formerly been a military base.) The jets returned for a second attack at 10:30 a.m. and again attacked the camp for half an hour. Tanks of insecticide stored at the camp exploded, producing heavy black smoke. The town itself was not damaged, though a few Somali women near the camp suffered shrapnel wounds.

The attack had diplomatic but not military repercussions, as the text indicates, and the ceasefire proceeded as planned. There is unconfirmed evidence from the Somalia side that a further attack was planned on April 1, the day the cease-fire went into effect. Sources quoted in Baynes, *op. cit.*, pp. 139, 149, place the strength of the Somali armed forces, including police, at 8,000 in 1963 and those of Ethiopia at 70,000.

42. New York *Times,* April 2, 18, 1964; Paris *Le Monde,* April 8, 1964.

43. New York *Times,* March 19, 1964.

44. George Weeks, comp., "The Armies of Africa," *Africa Report,* IX (January, 1964), 8, 18.

45. A private source states that the Ethiopian army has encountered major maintenance and logistic problems in the Haud and Ogaden, and has been unable to provide sufficient supplies or even water to some units. The problems have not resulted primarily from the terrain and climate, as might be thought, for a fairly extensive system of good military roads is said to exist in the Haud. The problems appear to be principally technical and organizational.

46. London *Times,* February 10, 1964.

47. *Africa Report,* IX (January, 1964), 32. Total United States military aid to all of Africa in this 14-year period was $138 million.

48. A. A. Castagno, "A Neutral Somalia," *Africa Report,* VI (August, 1961), 3; A. A. Castagno, "The Somali Republic in Transition," *op. cit.,* p. 10.

49. *Financial Times,* February 18, 1964.

50. *Africa Report,* VIII (August, 1963), 27; VIII (October, 1963), 24; London *Sunday Times,* November 4, 1963. Also *cf.* Touval, *op. cit.,* pp. 176–178.

51. *Financial Times,* February 18, 1964; Weeks, *op. cit.,* p. 18.

52. London *Times,* May 15, 1962; Weeks, *op. cit.,* p. 18 and Baynes, *op. cit.,* pp. 140–41.

53. Drysdale, *op. cit.,* p. 165 (the author was until recently an advisor to the Somali government); London *Times,* February 12, 1964; and private sources.

54. When the military assistance pact was signed with the Soviet Union in November 1963, for example, Prime Minister Shermarke said: "I can assure you that the Soviet Union took no initiative in this matter. When we failed to get the aid we felt we needed from the West, we turned to the Soviet Union." Cited in Baynes, *op. cit.,* pp. 140–41.

55. Somalia has received aid from other sources than those cited above, in particular from Italy and the United Arab Republic, and also from West Germany and the United Nations. Of the largest magnitude were a $11.4 million credit from the U.A.R. in 1960 and Italian aid in the form of grants and subsidies of $3 million plus 300 technicians. (*Cf.* Castagno, "The Somali Republic in Transition," *op. cit.,* p. 8.) A historical survey through 1960 of the international interests of foreign countries in the Horn, and their involvement in the politics of Somalia and the Somalis, is given by Touval, *op. cit.,* pp. 164–180.

56. The speech, dealing with the relation of pan-Africanism to Somali unity, was given at the Conference of African Heads in Addis Ababa, May 1963. The text, reprinted in the *Somali News,* May 31, 1963, includes the following statement:

It has been maintained that the aspiration of the Somalis for forming a single entity runs counter to the ideal of African unity. In our view there is no contradiction between sound nationalism and our common desire for closer bonds among African countries. Even if we were to establish an African Federation its component States would retain internal sovereignty and autonomy. The Federation would not be stable if a national group living in some of the States was striving to join another State. Regardless of the form of association which will be agreed at this conference, I am therefore profoundly convinced that the fulfillment of the aspirations of the Somali peoples will greatly strengthen African unity.

57. *Africa Digest,* IX (December, 1961), 83.
58. Lewis, "Pan-Africanism and Pan-Somalism," *op. cit.,* p. 157.
59. Quoted in Drysdale, *op. cit.,* p. 166.
60. Lewis, "Pan-Africanism and Pan-Somalism," *op. cit.,* p. 161.

Index